Bureaucratic Politics

Bureaucratic Politics
Executive Reorganization
During the Truman Administration

William E. Pemberton

University of Missouri Press
Columbia & London, 1979

To my mother and father

Copyright © 1979 by The Curators of the University of Missouri
University of Missouri Press, Columbia, Missouri 65211
Library of Congress Catalog Card Number 78-2990
Printed and bound in the United States of America
All rights reserved

Library of Congress Cataloging in Publication Data

Pemberton, William Erwin, 1940-
  Bureaucratic Politics.

  Bibliography: p.229
  Includes index.
  1. United States—Executive departments.
  2. United States—Politics and government—1945-1953.
  I. Title.
  JK421.P36   353.04   78-2990
  ISBN 0-8262-0244-6

Acknowledgments

I wish to express my gratitude to Prof. Richard S. Kirkendall. He first suggested this topic to me as a dissertation subject, guided my work over the years, and always provided encouragement and support.

I also wish to thank Prof. Stanley R. Rolnick who read this entire manuscript and gave me many helpful suggestions. Also as chairman of the history department at the University of Wisconsin-La Crosse, he invariably assisted me in solving problems that resulted as I tried to research and write while carrying a full teaching load. Virginia G. Rolnick and Prof. James R. Parker read part of the manuscript and gave me useful advice, as did Profs. Martin Zanger and Carol Jenson who read earlier versions. Prof. Barton J. Bernstein of Stanford University made several suggestions that helped me broaden the scope of the study.

Every researcher understands the debt I owe to the staffs of all the libraries and archives that I visited, and that are listed in my bibliography. Especially helpful were the archivists at the Harry S. Truman Library and at the Records Division of the Office of Management and Budget. The Harry S. Truman Library Institute also provided me with a research grant to enable me to carry on my research. I wish to thank the personnel of the Murphy Library at the University of Wisconsin-La Crosse for their assistance and cooperation.

My friends Phil McColgin and Patsy McColgin provided me with food, lodging, and companionship during my long stays while doing research in Washington. Phil particularly aided me by acting as a sounding board as I developed my ideas and by using his experience as a Federal Trade Commission attorney to help me better understand the nature of bureaucracy.

Janice M. Larkin and Martha E. Pemberton helped me meet my deadlines by their rapid, excellent typing.

Above all I wish to thank my wife, Martha, and son Gregory for ungrudgingly bearing all the sacrifices required of them during the writing of this book. My wife also assisted me in my research at several of the archives.

W. E. P.
La Crosse, Wisconsin
January 1978

Contents

1. Introduction, 1
2. History and Politics of Executive Reorganization, 9
3. Background of Truman's Executive Reorganization Program, 21
4. The Reorganization Act of 1945, 32
5. The Reorganization Plans of 1946, 47
6. Reorganization and the Eightieth Congress, 64
7. Truman and the Hoover Commission, 79
8. The Reorganization Act of 1949, 97
9. The Reorganization Plans of 1949, 109
10. The Reorganization Plans of 1950: Phase One, 124
11. The Reorganization Plans of 1950: Phase Two, 140
12. Reorganization, 1951–1952, 157
Conclusion, 174
Notes, 178
Bibliography, 229
Index, 256

Chapter 1

Introduction

On 12 April 1945, after the death of Franklin D. Roosevelt, Harry S. Truman became president of the United States. His quick grasp of the burdens of his office led to a prompt launching of one of the major reforms of his presidency. Truman later wrote:

> High on my list of priorities. . .was organizing the machinery of government to meet the new needs and responsibilities that had arisen. I had realized long before I became President that a reorganization of the executive branch was desirable and, in some respects, necessary.[1]

Within a few weeks the president had his executive reorganization program well underway. On 26 April, he requested Harold D. Smith, director of the Bureau of the Budget, to make preparations to gather scattered labor functions into the Department of Labor. He also directed Smith to survey government housing programs, which Truman viewed as an administrative "mess." The new chief executive then requested a study of conflicts between the Bureau of Reclamation and the Army Corps of Engineers. "I gathered that he wants to tighten up in general on the administration of the Government," Smith wrote.[2] On 4 May, Truman introduced the possibility of creating a department of welfare, asked the budget director to make an organizational study of the Executive Office of the President, and told him to have his proposal on labor activities finished by 16 June.[3] Most important, he directed Smith to prepare his first special message to Congress, a request for authority to submit reorganization plans.[4] By 1 June, Truman had established administrative reform as a significant part of his program. "The whole sub-surface flavor of Washington this week," wrote one reporter, "is one of preparations for deep-cutting government reorganization."[5]

In the following months, Truman continued to press for a drastic reorganization of the executive branch. On 6 September, he sent to Congress his

1

twenty-one point program, the basis of the Fair Deal. Point four of the message included a request for permanent reorganization legislation. "The Congress can depend upon the Executive to push this program with the utmost vigor," Truman promised.[6] By 20 December, he was able to sign legislation giving him authority to submit reorganization plans to Congress.[7]

Realizing that any reorganization plan faced vigorous opposition, Truman told Bureau of the Budget officials that any proposals would be "fought about." He suggested, therefore, that the administration should give Congress "something worth fighting about," affirming that "if I don't do anything else, doing a good job on reorganization will be worth doing!"[8]

Reorganization constituted not only the earliest but also one of Truman's most successful domestic reform programs. During his two terms, he won two grants of reorganization authority, submitted to Congress forty-eight plans (thirty-three of which passed),[9] and worked closely with the Commission on Organization of the Executive Branch of the Government (the First Hoover Commission). He also helped protect the New Deal structure by making it work more effectively and by diverting the Hoover Commission from what turned out to be its planned assault on the New Deal administrative setup. Truman and Congress institutionalized the presidency by creating such units as the Central Intelligence Agency, Council of Economic Advisors, National Security Council, and Joint Chiefs of Staff. During his administration and under his leadership, Congress created the Department of Defense, rebuilt the decimated Department of Labor, and prepared for the establishment of the Departments of Health, Education, and Welfare, Transportation, and Housing and Urban Development. Truman also took a number of less dramatic steps to improve management, such as submitting plans to transfer to department secretaries authority over their bailiwicks.

At the end of his presidency, Truman boasted that he had accomplished more organizational reform than "all the other Presidents put together."[10] He said that when he had assumed office the government was confronted with the question of whether the machinery of democracy could be improved sufficiently to cope with the vast and complicated undertakings of the modern era.[11] He proudly believed that he had met this administrative challenge and had provided a new technical foundation for the nation's evolving democratic institutions. When Dwight D. Eisenhower replaced Truman, the government was probably as "inherently manageable" as it had ever been, despite the fact that it dwarfed in size Roosevelt's prewar domain that had then been so gigantic.[12]

Truman once asserted: "The thing we need more than anything in the world is efficient management."[13] This belief had been central to his concept of public service from the 1920s; *efficiency* had long been one of his favorite words. He had unquestioning faith in what were called the "scientific" principles of administration. According to that doctrine, efficiency was the goal of public administration. Managers would achieve efficiency by separating administration from politics, centralizing authority in those responsible for managing an enterprise, unifying command and establishing clear lines of authority, limiting the span of administrative control of the managers, and by placing authority in the hands of individuals instead of boards. Truman, as well as most scholars and public administrators, thought in terms of a hierarchical framework of authority; he viewed the decisionmaking structure as a pyramid with the president at the top. Judged by these principles, Truman's program was successful: If he did not achieve everything the administrative reformers wanted, he did achieve much and he moved the national administrative structure in the right direction.

His ideas were those that had dominated the thinking of administrative reformers since the turn of the century and that found their most celebrated expression in the 1937 report to Roosevelt of the President's Committee on Administrative Management (the Brownlow Committee). The Brownlow Committee, which worked from a hierarchical model of the federal government, concentrated on developing recommendations to give the president authority and means to manage the executive branch. Members of this committee believed that democracy would be maintained and expanded by a strong president who would represent all the people and who would develop national programs to transcend the narrower parochial interests that dominated Congress.[14]

Most historians and political scientists accepted the concept of the strong presidency. They ranked Roosevelt and Truman as superior presidents because of their strength in pursuing the welfare state and internationalism, assuming governmental responsibility for the management of the economy, and in developing stronger concerns for civil rights and civil liberties than had characterized the national government in the past. They believed in the possibility of progress and reform under the leadership of an activist, liberal presidency. The president represented the national interest, while Congress remained an embarrassing hindrance to progress, a conservative, parochial, and indecisive force in national life.[15]

However, many historians, especially in the 1960s, began to question this model of the strong presidency. They challenged the intellectual foundations upon which Truman's, and all other twentieth-century presidents', reorganization programs rested. They asked whether the liberal, activist presidents had really accomplished much concerning civil rights,[16] whether the welfare-regulatory state benefited those it supposedly had been designed to help, whether U.S. foreign policy pomoted the development of peace in the world, whether American society was really healthier and happier because of the actions of these presidents. Such critics began to attract support as the nation divided over the Vietnam War,[17] support that widened as more people perceived the failure of Lyndon B. Johnson's Great Society programs to slow the deterioration of society, the arrogance of power displayed by him, John F. Kennedy, and Richard M. Nixon, and the seeming near breakdown of democracy as symbolized in the Watergate scandals.

The failures and betrayals of each of these men increased concern about the role of the presidency. Critics questioned the Brownlow Committee's conception of the presidency, the "scientific" principles of administration, and the efficacy of reorganization as a reform tool. Many of the challenges stemmed from conceptions of democracy that differed from those of the members of the Brownlow Committee. After two hundred years, Americans still had not agreed on what democracy was or how it was to be achieved. Perceptive critics did not limit their reexamination to the institution as it existed in the 1960s and 1970s but saw that the roots of these abuses extended at least back to Roosevelt and Truman.[18]

Such disturbing and painful questioning brought near intellectual chaos to several disciples. One scholar concluded:

> We are in the midst of a period of disorientation in which many of us have mixed feelings about Presidents and Presidential power. On the one hand, we want to look up to the President as the political key to the improvement of society. On the other hand, we loathe many of the actions of recent Presidents and fear that something inherent in the office and its powers leads to such abuses. We no longer possess a coherent picture of Presidential power and purpose that can be invoked to justify leadership in the White House. There are discontinuities in our perceptions of reality and in that reality itself.[19]

The uncertainty of such disorientation troubled those trying to devise a coherent conception of the presidency. However, this intellectual groping produced interesting and valuable work on the national government. Many authorities began to find new merit in a conception of democracy that differed from the dominant conception. Some argued that the hierarchical model of the presidency had always been a myth, although perhaps a necessary and useful one. In reality, American society could best be described by a pluralistic model, as a diverse, complex tangle of competing interests; the executive branch provided one of many battlefields in which groups fought for their self-interest. This condition resulted in a fragmented administration linked to a fragmented Congress. Rather than being a pyramid, the executive branch resembled a jumble of stones, with lines of authority running between executive agencies and congressional committees and out to interest groups. The president neither controlled the executive branch nor did he represent the national interest in the sense of representing all the people. He had his own constituency of parochial groups, no more nor less legitimate than the interests represented by congressional committees.[20]

Rather than regarding fragmentation as something to be destroyed and replaced by a strong presidency, many observers developed a "revisionist critique" that held this system to be a positive good. They argued that dispersed authority promoted various viewpoints to aid decisionmakers as they developed policy. It also linked expert knowledge with decisionmaking authority, whereas shifting authority upwards often moved it away from professional competence. They asked for proof, rather than faith, that those at the top ruled more in the public interest than those at the bottom.[21]

Reexamination of the nature of the presidency also forced analysts to review administrative theory generally and reorganization specifically. Some critics had asked disturbing questions about reorganization in the 1920s and 1930s. In 1932, Hoover's Budget Director J. Clawson Roop said that at the president's direction he had diligently but vainly searched for scientific principles on which to group government agencies: "We found, in studying the situation and hearing various groups of interested parties who came in to talk the thing over, that there was no such thing as a logical grouping of major functions. It depends upon your point of view."[22] Several scholars asked for proof of the validity of the scientific principles. One referred to reorganizers as "political medicine men" and charged that the quest for efficiency threatened representative government.[23] Charles Hyneman pointed out that many people placed vision, imagination, and courage in government ahead of the reorganization goals of economy and efficiency. It seemed absurd to him that in the age of Mussolini and other dictators reorganizers ignored warnings about giving the chief executive more power. Reorganizers "appear to proceed blithely on the assumption that God looks after fools, drunkards and the liberties of the people."[24]

Criticism of the reorganization movement became more sophisticated after World War II. Several scholars and public administrators questioned whether the benefits of administrative reform matched the costs in time, energy, and political capital.[25] One scholar found a pattern in such reform programs. At the beginning of their terms in office, chief executives immediately began reorganization studies to help them cope with their new, confusing burdens, but by the time the studies were completed they had adjusted enough to the nature of the office to find that reorganization was not worth the political danger.[26]

Other scholars concluded that if reorganization did work it would be undesirable, even for the president. By eliminating fragmentation, reorganization eroded alternative sources of information. Conflict and competition aided, not hindered, the chief executive in his management burden.[27] Conflict among agencies and imperialistic raids on each others' jurisdictions had the beneficial effect of disturbing "stale and archaic routines."[28] Just as engineers purposely built redundant systems into complex machines, so did duplication in public agencies benefit the public: "If there is no duplication, if there is no overlap, if there is no ambiguity, an organization will neither be able to suppress error nor generate alternate routes of action. In short, it will be most unreliable and least flexible, sluggish, as we now say."[29]

Most postwar scholars considered the customary approach to reorganization as simplistic. The "scientific" principles of administration proved to be contradictory, vague, and subjective.[30] Traditional principles and the time-honored organizational charts gave little sense of the political reality within which individuals and agencies operated.[31] Furthermore, an understanding of this political reality failed to explain the behavior and values of the individuals who worked within the agencies to be reorganized and who determined the success or failure of such changes.[32] Nor was efficiency necessarily desirable: "We know now that efficiency has a built-in tendency to take us rapidly to where we will not want to be when we get there. We know this instictively as we sniff the thickening air, stall in the urban congestion, and count the dead that were killed by systems analysis."[33] Perhaps the main use of reorganization was as a tool for elites to use to symbolize change while maintaining the status quo.[34]

Even if they considered the principles of administration valid and the ends of reorganization desirable, some scholars still continued to question the movement. Most realized that the key element in the politics of reorganization, discussed further in the following chapter, stemmed from a triangular relationship among executive agencies, congressional committees, and interest groups. In the day-to-day work of the federal government, Congress and the president were peripheral to this power structure.[35] Reorganization proposals could seldom change this relationship. Proposals that would affect the triangle of power significantly usually failed of passage. Presidents seldom bothered to submit plans that challenged agencies deeply embedded in the triangle of power. If a president did submit such a plan and if it did pass, it generally did not change the existing system because the affected groups normally were powerful enough to reestablish the previous relationships despite the administrative changes that occurred.

Ultimately, Truman's administrative reform program was irrelevant in its impact on the fundamental structure of the government. The structure of the executive branch and of Congress originated in the nature of American liberal democratic capitalism. Meaningful change in administrative organization could only occur with fundamental change in the economic system. For example, the administrative structures designed to provide supervision over the banking system was fragmented with several agencies sharing overlapping authority. This fragmentation occurred not by accident or because Congress failed to understand the need for a unified administrative structure. It was divided because the bankers wanted it that way. Bankers moderated the impact of the government's regulatory endeavors by inducing conflict between the agencies. If the president tried to merge the banking supervisory agencies, he would be opposed by the bankers and their allies in the executive agencies and in Congress. He probably could not overcome this resistance; he probably would not attempt to do so. In any case, in relation to the fundamental problems of society, such reforms were meaningless, a point often overlooked by both supporters and critics of the strong presidency. The basic problems of society could not be solved by administrative reform. Dennis R. Eckart and John C. Ries made this important argument: "We omit consideration of such proposals because of our conviction that without systematic changes (that is, reducing the privileges of wealth) and unless the presidency itself can be more closely tied to the dispossessed, such reforms are literally meaningless. Reforms that will make the presidency more responsive must change the environment in which the presidency operates. Presidents are not the cause of our maladies nor does the burden of reform rest on that office."[36]

This criticism of Truman's conception of the presidency and administrative reform did not necessarily mean that his reorganization program was a

mistake or failure. Most scholars and policymakers, then, and now, believed that the public good would be achieved by using reorganization to
create a strong presidency based on the traditional, though perhaps somewhat modified, principles of administration. If the strong presidency came
to seem more dangerous than beneficial, that was a failure of the 1960s and
1970s more than a failure of the 1940s and 1950s. Nor have critics of the
strong presidency yet developed a convincing alternative. If the idea that
progress would be achieved through the activist presidency rested on faith
rather than on proof, then the belief that such progress would be achieved
through Congress or the bureaucracy seemed just as fanciful. In consider-
ing administrative reform, most current political leaders and scholars were
less confident than Roosevelt and Truman. Yet, they remained committed
to the same reform pattern that was used in the past rather than choosing a
new one altogether. However, they would move more slowly, carefully,
and fearfully down a path that seemed less clearly marked than in earlier
years.

Chapter 2

History and Politics
of Executive Reorganization

By undertaking reorganization of the executive branch, Harry S. Truman became involved in a long tradition of administrative reform. Sooner or later, wrote a government official, "every President stands at Armageddon and battles with the Congress on the subject of reorganization."[1] Organizational change occurred continually from the earliest years of the Republic but developed into a major reform movement after the Civil War, when Congress created many new executive agencies to deal with the problems of an industrializing society.[2] At first, Congress attempted to establish departments composed of agencies carrying out similar functions and to integrate all agencies into the departmental hierarchy. But with new domestic and foreign problems, the federal government became larger and its structure more complex. New administrative structures evolved to handle regulatory functions and to deal with social problems. The executive branch began to fragment as Congress established independent commissions outside the existing administrative structure and grouped unrelated units into the executive departments.[3] During the late nineteenth century, reformers at all governmental levels adopted reorganization as one of their primary goals. These early reformers sought to incorporate into government the administrative techniques of private business. Through reorganization they hoped to achieve economy, efficiency, and honesty in government.[4]

In the 1880s and 1890s, Congress initiated the first of major reform-motivated investigations of the executive branch. Continued use of past procedures had caused some agencies to fall years behind in performing their tasks. The Senate, reacting to many complaints and criticisms, established two special committees to study administrative methods of the executive branch. The thrust of their reports was "Put business into government." They urged that government matters should be conducted in the same way as businessmen handled their affairs.[5]

In 1905, Theodore Roosevelt initiated the next major administrative study by establishing the Committee on Department Methods (the Keep Committee). With the Keep Committee, the executive branch began to seize the initiative in the movement for administrative reform.[6] However, while many congressmen increasingly recognized the necessity of executive leadership in administrative matters, the majority still resisted any weakening of the legislature's traditional role. Congress accepted few recommendations of the Keep Committee.

All of Roosevelt's successors fought to bring order to the executive establishment. At William Howard Taft's urging, Congress established the President's Commission on Economy and Efficiency. Although the commission concentrated on administrative details, it also prepared monographs on the history, activities, and organization of various governmental services. Congress ignored most of its major proposals, but in later years accepted some of its recommendations for agency transfers.[7]

World War I forced the legislators to accept presidential control of the executive branch. The Overman Act gave Woodrow Wilson authority to consolidate or transfer agencies or functions and to create new agencies.[8] This authority, as well as changes made under it, terminated after the war, but the legislature's acceptance of presidential initiative during an emergency foretold changing legislative-executive relationship during the crisis-ridden twentieth century.

During the 1920s, the administrative reform movement found renewed support. Congress established the Joint Committee on the Reorganization of Government Departments and invited President Warren G. Harding to appoint a representative. Unlike earlier studies, it concentrated on developing administrative principles, such as the need for reducing the number of people reporting to the president.[9]

Though these changes occurred, the chief executive found it as difficult as ever to actually recast the bureaucratic structure. Harding and Calvin Coolidge effected a few organizational changes, but administrative problems mounted. Many people believed, however, that Herbert C. Hoover's election in 1928 signaled a major breakthrough in reorganization. Having accomplished many administrative changes as secretary of commerce, Hoover, in the 1928 campaign, promised a general governmental reorganization. Even so, not until mid-1932 did Congress grant Hoover reorganization authority, and then it rejected all of the plans he submitted under the act.[10]

As lenient with Franklin D. Roosevelt as it had been strict with Hoover,

Congress granted the new president almost unlimited reorganization authority during his first two years in office. However, while innovative in other areas, Roosevelt thought little of administrative reform. During his first term, he fully accepted the business derived economy and efficiency approach to executive reorganization.[11]

During the 1932 campaign, Roosevelt promised drastic reorganization to reduce administrative costs of the government by at least 25 percent,[12] but he scoffed at the idea that the president's main job was administrative: "The Presidency is not merely an administrative office. That's the least of it. It is more than an engineering job, efficient or inefficient. It is preeminently a place of moral leadership."[13]

Nonetheless, during the preceding few decades new ideas about governmental administration and reorganization had developed in local and state governments, and by the end of his first term Roosevelt had decided to apply these ideas at the national level. Reorganization now meant more than just improving economy: "The reason for reorganization is good management."[14] Roosevelt viewed "efficiency as a safeguard of democracy, regardless of cost."[15] He now considered administration to be important; after the 1936 election he told reporters that his opponents had failed to attack the New Deal's weakest point—poor administration.[16]

Roosevelt's overwhelming victory in 1936 led to daring and controversial initiatives in strengthening presidential domination of national government. In his second term, he sought to bend the judicial branch in the direction of his political philosophy, to exercise decisive sway over the legislative branch, and to gain for the president authority equal to his responsibility in his own executive domain.[17] He hoped to accomplish this last goal by obtaining legislative endorsement of the proposals of the President's Committee on Administrative Management, under Louis Brownlow, which he had set up even before his reelection. This advisory group modeled its recommendations for enlarged presidential authority and adequate staff support on similar reforms at the state and local levels that dated back to the turn of the century.[18]

In 1937, Roosevelt submitted a reorganization bill embodying the Brownlow Committee recommendations, but after a bitter struggle Congress emasculated and finally defeated the proposal. However, in 1939 Congress gave Roosevelt authority to submit reorganization plans subject to congressional veto, and he effected several important reorganizations, including the establishment of the Executive Office of the President.[19]

Beyond the reorganizations Roosevelt accomplished under it, the Reorganization Act of 1939 had continuing importance. The act reversed traditional legislative procedure by allowing the president to submit to Congress a reorganization plan that would become effective at the end of sixty days unless vetoed by both houses of Congress prior to that. This procedure, the legislative veto, had three distinctive features. First, it provided for congressional review of legislative proposals submitted by the executive branch. Second, the reorganization plans had to be accepted or rejected in their entirety, without amendment. Third, a vote would take place if a single legislator desired it; the plan, therefore, could neither be locked up in committee nor filibustered on the floor.[20]

The legislative-veto mechanism gave the president many advantages in dealing with Congress. It allowed him to submit a package to Congress that had to be accepted or rejected exactly as presented. It also enabled him to appeal directly to the full congressional membership, bypassing the leadership and the committee chairmen.[21] Ordinarily, supporters of legislation had to raise a majority to have it accepted; under the legislative veto opponents had to mobilize a majority to kill a plan. It also gave the president the initiative and allowed him the first chance to "condition the minds" of the legislators.[22] Moreover, it gave him the advantage of secrecy; he could submit a plan without warning, giving opponents only sixty days in which to mobilize their forces.[23]

Roosevelt's administration provided important impetus for reorganization, but a few major questions remained unanswered: Why did an unusual procedure such as the legislative veto prove necessary? Why did presidents find it so difficult to effect reorganization of their own branch of government? Why did such proposals as moving agencies from one department to another or centralizing authority in department heads create such massive opposition? For example, in 1937 and 1938 it seemed that administrative reform would be one of Roosevelt's greatest failures. Secretary of Interior Harold L. Ickes reported that pressure groups flooded Congress with 333,000 telegrams in opposition to Roosevelt's program, forcing telegraph companies to set aside regular commercial service; Ickes said that he had not seen such hysteria since the battle over the League of Nations.[24] Before the heated debate ended, Roosevelt suffered the humiliation of having to deny publicly that he had any ambitions to be dictator.[25] "It was the Supreme Court fight all over again," wrote historian James MacGregor Burns, "but perhaps even more sharp and passionate."[26]

Difficulties in effecting reorganization frustrated the administrative reformers. Everyone agreed on the need for restructuring the executive branch, yet change came slowly, if it came at all. Truman escaped the bitter controversy Roosevelt had faced but understood the difficulty reorganization proposals faced. "The fight for this [reorganization] measure has been long and futile," Truman wrote Hoover. "As you so wisely observe, the overlapping, waste and conflict of policies between executive agencies have been a scandal for the whole thirty-five years during which six successive Presidents have recommended this reform."[27]

Because of various reasons, the president faced tremendous obstacles in trying to carry out his reorganization program. In the first place, even though the legislative veto aided the president in his unending struggle to master the executive branch, it also created certain problems. By reversing the traditional procedure, it allowed the plans to be attacked on constitutional grounds. Many congressmen sincerely regarded the legislative veto as unconstitutional, but, more important, the constitutional argument provided respectable cover for those who had other, less defensible, reasons for opposing reorganization.[28] Moreover, the legislative veto made a reorganization plan a presidential plan; thus, the chief executive's prestige became more closely linked with it than with regular administration bills. His opponents sometimes fought plans because they did not want to increase his power or because they simply wanted to embarrass him. "Such plans," Truman wrote, "are usually looked on with suspicion and fears which are quickly exploited by administration opponents."[29]

Aside from problems caused by the legislative-veto procedure, many other circumstances inhibited reform. The president did not simply reorganize; he reorganized *something*. For example, Truman attempted to restructure housing, labor, and welfare functions. His plans on housing became entangled in the postwar public-housing controversy; the proposals on labor suffered because of the reaction against unions following the great wave of strikes after World War II; and Congress defeated the welfare department plans after they became enmeshed in the fight over compulsory health insurance.

Another major difficulty stemmed from the realization that structural change often led to policy change. As one scholar stated: "Agency organization is not neutral. . . .It is a tool designed by men to achieve particular results."[30] "Governmental reorganization. . .signifies changing policy, a new approach. . . ," wrote a congressional committee staff aide.[31] Even simple transfers could create important policy shifts. The president sometimes demonstrated his commitment to a policy by creating a new agency or department to administer it.[32] If a president found some activity objectionable, he could transfer it to a hostile or indifferent agency.[33] In the same way, he strengthened a favored activity by transferring it to a receptive unit.[34] However, policy changes usually happened more subtly. Paul H. Appleby, a noted scholar and public administrator, pointed out that a bureau that made agricultural loans would follow one policy if located in the Federal Loan Agency, where the banking-function emphasis dominated, but would pursue a different policy if transferred to an agency responsible for raising farmer income.[35]

Partisan conflict also caused problems for Truman and other presidents. Whatever a plan's administrative merits, its potential political impact always affected its chances of acceptance. "In discussing the difficulty of achieving reorganization," recalled a congressional committee staff aide, "the thing to remember is that reorganization of the executive branch is not just an academic attempt to create efficiency. That is part of it, but politics are always involved."[36] "No matter how sound or desirable a reorganization proposal might be," warned a Bureau of Budget official, "it may be dealt with on a partisan basis, rather than on its merits."[37] Sometimes party differences already existed over the policies involved; in other instances, the administration designed plans to achieve specific political goals.

Partisan politics aside, many Republicans (and some Democrats) simply regarded it as futile to try to improve the functioning of government. Congressman Ralph Gwinn (a Republican from New York) wrote his colleague Clarence Brown (a Republican from Ohio), author of the bill that created the Hoover Commission, that he was happy that Brown was so highly praised for his reorganization activity. Gwinn admonished, however:

> I know a hard-headed farmer politician like you entertains no real illusions about improvements in government that you suggest. Government doesn't improve. It is always more or less evil and the longer it lives the worse it gets. I hate to see good Republicans and especially good farmers from Ohio hold out any hope to the people that this corrupt government at home and incompetent one abroad will be changed by any reorganization or streamlining operations.[38]

This attitude did not develop entirely from the fact that Democrats controlled the government at the time. For example, during House hearings on a bill to give reorganization authority to President Eisenhower, Democratic leaders argued for making the bill even stronger than it had been under Truman, while Republican leaders opposed strengthening the bill and indicated that they would happily dilute it even more.[39]

Another major problem existed because, although the president headed the executive branch, Congress had constitutional authority to determine the activities, policies, organization, and administrative procedure of executive agencies.[40] This division of authority became especially important in reorganization because the president and Congress had different conceptions of administrative organization. According to Burns:

> The executive impetus is to. . .coordinate functions, to exert control from the top. . . .The instinct of the executive is to integrate government for the sake of better control. The legislative instinct is pluralistic. Congress. . .[seeks] to fragmentize the executive by means of individual or committee influence over administrative units, or control of specific budgetary items, or through hobbling the executive's power to reorganize.[41]

Besides having different organizational needs and desires, the president and Congress also disagreed on the goals to be achieved through reorganization. Congressmen expected reorganization to lead to better economy by increasing efficiency and by eliminating duplication and conflict. Many of them used lack of savings as a cover for other objections to the president's plans, but most sincerely believed structural changes should, and could, lead to large reductions in the cost of government.[42] One representative from South Dakota complained because in testifying on reorganization plans government officials did not discuss possible savings: "It is the dollar and cents economy matter in which I am vitally interested," he wrote, "I know that most Americans feel the same way."[43]

Executive officials and congressmen held differing viewpoints on reorganization,[44] though custom and politics often required them to use the old labels of economy and efficiency in defending reorganization plans.[45] "We have got to get over the notion that the purpose of reorganization is economy," Roosevelt declared. "The reason for reorganization," he said, "is good management."[46] Truman viewed efficiency as the goal with economy as a by-product. "The principal objective in reorganization. . .is efficiency," he told a friend, "and naturally efficiency always results in economy."[47] "The results of reorganization," he stated, "will be evident primarily in the increased effectiveness of Government operations."[48]

Reorganization plans almost always faced attacks by opponents who used these constitutional and savings issues. In addition, many congressmen opposed reorganization because they feared increased executive power. These men believed that Congress had delegated too much power to Roosevelt during the depression and war crises, and they resisted further delegation to Truman. They wanted Congress to regain its old dominance over the executive branch.[49] "This is certainly turning a blank check of legislative authority over to the Chief Executive," wrote Congressman Marion T. Bennett, a Democratic representative from Missouri, in reference to the Reorganization Act of 1945.[50] It is time to realize, wrote another Democrat, that Congress "has been 'reorganizing' itself out of powers and responsibilities that the Constitution invests exclusively in Congress."[51]

In attacking reorganization plans, congressmen directed most of their rhetoric to the constitutional and economy issues and to arguments against further delegation of authority to the executive. There were, however, more important sources of opposition to reorganization. The most difficult obstacle stemmed from a triangular relationship among congressional committees, interest groups, and executive agencies. Each unit in this system of power had its own reasons to oppose reorganization plans, and each had reasons to join with the others in opposition to the president. These three intertwined groups composed the core of the American power structure.

This triangular relationship developed because social pluralism, combined with federalism, produced a decentralized party system in the United States. Policy issues were not partisan; the chief partisan concern was to get control of the government. Therefore, a considerable amount of policymaking authority devolved upon interest groups, bureaus, and congressional committees.[52] Dislodging these nearly autonomous centers of power "would necessitate a virtual revolution."[53] Each of Truman's reorganization plans disturbed, or threatened to disturb, one or more of these clusters of power.

Evaluation of each unit of this triangle of power must begin with the executive agencies. Truman's reorganization plans often merged one or more agencies, subordinated them into a hierarchy, grouped similar agencies into one structure, or otherwise changed their organization. Agency officials usually resisted any changes. Mergers created fear that a unit's functions might be downgraded, distorted, or disturbed. These officials often resisted integration (that is, subordination) into the administrative hierarchy for similar reasons. A former bureau chief wrote:

> No operating bureau of its free will ever would be in a department, and each can find some special reason to justify its claims. This desire for independence is an apparently innate characteristic of administrative behavior.[54]

Executive officials found even mild reorganizations upsetting. "Major organizational change or just the threat of change can be a traumatic experience in the career of an agency and in the lives of many of its members," wrote Frederick C. Mosher.[55] Every complex organization included groups and individuals whose ambitions, aspirations, and views of organizational purpose conflicted. Within each organization, latent tensions existed. Reorganization, therefore, threatened to disturb existing power relationships within the agency.[56]

Agency officials also resisted reorganization because of he natural desire for stability: "The spirit of adventure may flame high in many of us," wrote Bureau of the Budget Director Frederick J. Lawton, "but resistance to change is firmly embedded in more of us."[57] In addition, the possibility always existed that reorganization would eliminate jobs or place employees in less desirable positions. Proposed cutbacks in federal employees following the war and during later economy drives kept workers nervous and made Truman's job more difficult.[58] Administrators also knew that reorganization demoralized their personnel, because the simplest changes caused immense mechanical problems, especially in large agencies.[59]

Agency officials also had power to fight the president's program. The failure of parties to build a political consensus for specific policies forced agencies to develop their own sources of political support.[60] "When a jurisdictional fight [among agencies] is to be undertaken, you first look around you for your natural allies," wrote a person who had engaged in such struggles.[61] The executive agency's most powerful natural allies, constituting the second leg of the triangle of power, were the standing committees and appropriation subcommittees that had jurisdiction over the agency.[62] Since agencies depended on committees for necessities such as appropriations, they worked to convert the legislators to their point of view.[63] Career officials often matched legislators in length of service in Washington, and both regarded the administration in power as transient. Since institutional considerations influenced both, congressmen listened sympathetically when career officials explained the long-term effects of the president's reorganizational program.[64]

Close ties often existed between executive officials and members of a congressional committee. The committee had sometimes been responsible for creating the agency; the agency's officials may have been recommended for their positions by members of the committee.[65] Some powerful congressmen even regarded certain agencies, which they had helped create, as monuments to themselves.[66] These lawmakers resisted any attempt to destroy their creations. Also, committee staff members frequently had ties with agencies, sometimes based on prior service in those same units.[67] Committee and staff members would especially resist any plan that would remove an agency from their jurisdiction and place it under the authority of another committee.[68]

Even if a congressman was not inclined to oppose a particular plan, an agency sometimes had power enough to force him into opposition to it. "We have six or seven map-printing establishments right here in Washington, and some through the country," said Roosevelt. "Do you think that Congress can ever be induced to consolidate them? Oh, no, the pressure from those six or seven bureaus would be too strong."[69] Republican Christian Herter, a representative from Massachusetts, regarded bureaucracy as "the most powerful and potentially the most dangerous lobby of all. It fought, bureau by bureau, every Congressional move to curb its innate urge to expand."[70] Most federal employees lived outside the District of Columbia;[71] hundreds of thousands of government employees and their families were voting constituents of congressmen and senators and could exert pressure upon them.

Bureaus could also influence congressmen by manipulating their constituencies. Legislators accepted seats on committees that dealt with matters of most interest to their constituents.[72] For example, members from coastal areas dominated the Committee on Merchant Marine and Fisheries and tended to be responsive to constituent opposition toward a reorganization plan involving the U.S. Maritime Commission. Such an agency could influence these congressmen by helping mobilize opinion among their constituents, urging the constituents to inform their congressmen of their opposition to a plan.[73] Congressmen had to take such power into account when they voted on reorganization plans, since few actions affected agencies more directly than such plans. Congressman Morgan M. Moulder, a Democrat from Missouri, stated:

> A friend and fellow Member of Congress recently advised me that it might be unwise to vote for the approval of a reorganization of a certain Government department because that department might be offended and oppose expenditures of money on projects in my district.[74]

Congressmen, then, judged reorganization by its potential impact on their political careers. They realized that structural change could alter agency policy in ways injurious to their constituents and could cause constituents to lose jobs. Organizational changes could also destroy the congressmen's lines of communications with agencies, hampering their ability to provide effective constituent service. Moreover, congressmen realized that it would be harder to defeat or modify bills backed by the president and a unified bureaucracy. Stronger hierarchal control might prevent the flow of information from agencies that legislators found useful to force compromises with the administration. Attempts to get congressmen to loosen their control over an agency, said Avery Leiserson, "are either meaningless or else imply a degree of self-immolation that subverts the very reason for his being in Washington."[75] Congressmen viewed battles over administrative structure as personal conflicts between bureau and department heads or as struggles between regional or economic interests, not as clashes of ideals relevant to the national interest.[76]

Pressure groups formed the third leg of the triangle. Every reorganization involved a redistribution of interests, potential or actual, between an agency and its constituencies.[77] Public clamor against proposed organizational change usually came from such interest groups. This opposition, combined with agitation by bureaus and support from congressional committees (with the interest group, agency, and committee sharing the same constituency), provided formidable opposition to the president's program. Pressure politics became especially effective because the public usually had little understanding of specific reorganization plans. Without public support, congressmen, who usually lacked detailed knowledge with which to evaluate the administrative merits of particular plans, became susceptible to pressure from interested groups.[78]

Alliances between these interest groups and the agencies to be reorganized made reorganization especially difficult. An agency's survival depended on its ability to demonstrate to some group the value of its services.[79] Congress had usually created agencies because of pressure from one or more groups, although sometimes agencies organized or expanded their own clientele.[80] These groups also provided private employment opportunities for agency employees, and social contacts bred familiarity and friendship.[81] Reorganization plans threatened to break these informal ties.

In addition to such ties, interest groups had their own reasons for opposing reorganization. "You will always find long-time vested interests difficult to improve," said Truman, "because they all want to do their work in the old-fashioned way."[82] But group opposition did not develop simply from innate conservatism. The existing governmental structure had developed from efforts of interest groups to serve their own needs.[83] "Agencies provide channels of 'access' through which segments of the public can advance or protect their interests in the executive branch."[84] Therefore, these segments opposed a unified executive branch, because it would lessen their ability to influence the operations of particular units.[85]

Truman designed many of his plans to give agency heads administrative control of their organizations. Although they seemed noncontroversial on the surface, these plans faced determined opposition. If decisionmaking authority remained dispersed, policy would more likely be determined by pressure from various interest groups than would be true with a centralized hierarchy.

Interest groups, as well as bureaus and congressional committees, opposed centralization of authority within the executive branch with remarkable consistency. Robert L. L. McCormick, one of the leaders of the Citizens Committee for the Hoover Report, found this attitude to be a major threat to reorganization. Members of the American Legion, he wrote, do not *"want anything removed from the Veterans' Administration because it is their private preserve and they are able to exercise leverage when it is separate."*[86] "The bankers," he said, "are kicking up quite a fuss about our [Hoover Commission] recommendations. Having an infinite distrust of the Government, they are anxious to maintain the status quo under the dividere et regere theory."[87] According to McCormick, the American Bankers Association strongly opposed certain administrative changes. He stated: "The essence of their argument in this respect is very simple. The more confused the Federal organizations that supervise them, the better the chances that they will be able to do just what they please."[88] The American Farm Bureau Federation and National Grange, both with great power in Congress, opposed anything that weakened legislative control over the executive branch. "Since they do not control the Executive Branch, their attitude on strengthening the Executive is understandable."[89]

Reorganization, seemingly innocuous, struck at the heart of the American power structure. Structural change provoked tremendous opposition from entrenched interests in the executive branch and in Congress and from the clientele groups of the executive agencies. The plans generated such a response because reorganization often threatened to return to the "large public" power and functions that had been captured by these "small publics."[90]

Chapter 3

Background of Truman's
Executive Reorganization Program

Harry S. Truman, who was in the Senate when President Roosevelt introduced his reorganization program, perceived the difficulties and political hazards of administrative reform. However, undeterred by the great conflict he had witnessed in the late 1930s, he initiated his own program a few weeks after he assumed the presidency. To an extent, he had no choice; conversion from war to peace necessitated certain organizational changes.[1] However, reconversion itself required only a limited amount of such change. Truman's background, his administrative ideas, and the problems he faced in 1945 combined to make reorganization a central part of his program.

Truman's early career helped prepare him for his leadership in administrative reform. "My whole experience in public service," he said, "had been executive and administrative."[2] His executive experience began with his military service.[3] His duties in the army varied from running a regimental canteen to taming and leading a company of "Wild Irishmen" into battle.[4] Thirty-four years old in 1918 and unable to find a satisfying career, Truman, once a "momma's" boy, undoubtedly gained confidence by demonstrating his leadership abilities.[5] His war service also helped shape his administrative ideas, as did the reserve army camps after he returned to civilian life.[6] The military served as a model for many students of public administration during this period,[7] and Truman developed a pronounced admiration for army officers: "He admired them for their staff work, for clear chains of command, for orderliness and for getting things done."[8] His experience during the war further made him confident of his administrative abilities. In 1945, in contrast to whatever doubts he had about his other executive capabilities, Truman believed that he was a better administrator than Roosevelt and that he knew what administrative changes the government needed.

21

Truman's military service was important for another reason: "My whole political career is based on my war service and war associates," he wrote.[9] With the support of Thomas J. Pendergast, whose political machine shortly took control of Kansas City, Truman won the election to the Jackson County court in 1922, and soon after his promotion to presiding judge in 1926, he became leader of the machine in the rural area.[10]

Undoubtedly, Truman's political career owed a great deal to his military service and to Pendergast, but his popularity also stemmed from his own record in office. People soon recognized Truman as much more than a typical local official. He brought honesty and efficiency to a position that had been filled by notoriously corrupt, ineffective officeholders.[11] An administrative rather than a judicial body, the county court had authority to levy taxes and appropriate funds, to transact all county business, to manage all county property, to audit and adjust accounts, and to administer county eleemosynary institutions. Truman was innovative and farsighted in carrying out these tasks, especially in developing a major road program for the county, and his friends recalled that he was an able and efficient administrator.[12] Although Truman seldom theorized about public administration, he always read extensively when he undertook a new task, and he adapted that knowledge to the practical problem at hand. A newsman remembered first meeting Truman at a conference on better state and county government:

> Thirty or forty public officials, university professors, social workers and a number of out-of-state experts on governmental problems held a round-table discussion at Columbia [Mo.]. Every subject of debate tended sooner or later to center in the views of a quiet-spoken man [Truman] who sat across the table from me. He was the only Missouri official in the gathering who could discuss administrative problems on an equality with the visiting experts. When he differed with them, it was on grounds furnished by experience. His desire for good government, and readiness to indorse measures to ensure it, were evident at every stage of the meeting.[13]

Truman was a progressive, emphasizing that strand of reform that wanted to bring efficiency, economy, and planning to local government. *Efficiency* and *planning* were two of the words he used most often, and they provided the theme for most of his speeches during the county-court period. He also acted on these ideas. He organized the Regional Plan Association of Kansas City, presided over the Missouri Planning Association, served on the board of directors of the National Conference of City Planning, belonged to the American Civic Association, and published a book, *Results of County Planning*.[14] In his reform activities, he worked closely with Walter Matscheck, "the epitome of pre-World War I progressives." Matscheck, a student of Richard T. Ely, headed the Civic Research Institute in Kansas City.[15]

With the advice and support of Matscheck and others, Truman promoted various reforms in local government, including tax reform and county, regional, and state planning.[16] But more important, previewing his presidential reorganization program years later, Truman attempted to reorganize Jackson County government. He quickly learned that the county government suffered from serious defects.[17] He found that poor organization hindered the court in carrying out its responsibilities and caused political conflicts.[18] An ambitious man trying to effect a far-reaching program, Truman was hampered by outdated governmental machinery and began to work to change it.

A few months after taking office, he warned that the executive head did not control the business of the county.[19] In October 1929, he said that the county and municipal governments were "not efficient or economical." He proposed combining the assessment and collection of taxes and ending the duplication between the city and county in welfare work. He wanted to reduce the number of elective county offices; the court, he believed, should appoint most officials.[20] One plank in his 1930 election platform called for "a reorganization of the county government to. . .effect enormous economies and give a better administration."[21] In November 1931, Truman urged a drastic reduction in the number of Missouri counties and county-court judges.[22] In February 1932, Truman urged the state to combine the county collector, assessor, and treasury departments and to make them responsible to a controller who, in turn, would be under the county court.[23]

Although Truman never gained enough political support to carry out these plans,[24] this experience did help shape his administrative ideas. As head of the county government, he insisted on the necessity of structural unity and clear lines of responsibility and authority. These administrative principles remained central to his reorganization program after 1945. As county-court judge, Truman developed a clear strategy of how to use reorganization as a tool to achieve his political and administrative goals. He clearly understood the connection between reorganization and regional planning. Oddly, as president he did not formulate a reorganization strategy for the national government.

Truman assumed a burden in addition to those associated with the county court when, in October 1933, he became state director of the U.S.

Employment Service. The newly established Missouri employment service suffered from severe organizational problems and from political squabbles. Truman, busy with county-court problems, failed to unsnarl the organizational muddle.[25] He retained his interest in administrative reform, however. He complained about waste and overlapping within the employment service and urged consolidation of various activities.[26] "I am somewhat of a stickler for efficiency, even in public administration. . . ," he wrote.[27]

Truman's superiors spurned his suggestions for administrative improvement, but once again his early career influenced his later reorganization program. As president, he submitted three plans to reorganize the employment service.

Elected to the Senate in 1934, Truman began to deal with administrative problems at the national level. Several committee assignments during his terms as senator provided him with experiences important to his later reorganization program. Assigned at first to the relatively inconsequential Committee on the District of Columbia, Truman withdrew from it as quickly as possible. However, he was still concerned with the district's problems and in 1952 reorganized its government.[28] During his first term in the Senate, Truman focused his attention on transportation regulation. While serving on the Committee on Interstate Commerce, he helped develop important acts on transportation and worked to integrate the national administrative structure dealing with transportation.[29] After he became president, he submitted several reorganization plans that dealt with transportation agencies. From his work on the Committee on Appropriations, Truman gained detailed knowledge of executive branch organization. "I had to make a special study of the organization of the National Government," he remarked, "in order to vote intelligently on appropriations."[30] This knowledge allowed him in 1945 and afterwards to formulate and evaluate quickly proposals for organizational changes.

The experience that most directly prepared Truman for his work in government reorganization came from his service as chairman of the Special National Defense Investigating Committee (the Truman Committee). Created to investigate domestic defense problems during World War II, the committee revealed the inefficient, wasteful, and dangerous effects of poor organization.

During these investigations, Truman often pointed out the perils of faulty administrative organization.[31] In June 1943, he expressed what he regarded as the fundamental administrative principle:

The task of control and guidance is of utmost importance. Clear leadership in strong hands is required. The influence from above must be always toward unity.[32]

Throughout his public career, he emphasized the importance of centralized administrative authority. The committee followed Truman's leadership and avoided the usual congressional tendency to splinter and weaken the executive branch. It pushed instead for strong executive branch control and for centralized organization.[33]

This stress on centralized leadership was the theme in the Truman Committee reports (as well as in Truman's reorganization program after 1945). The committee found that airplane production had been hurt by a "fumbling approach" to the problem, with too many departments involved and too little planning and coordination.[34] Duplication of activities and petty jealousies among the administrators hindered defense housing.[35] Failures in the rubber program resulted "from a lack of centralized and sole responsibility."[36] Five or six overlapping agencies created confusion and led to a delay in barge production.[37] Production of farm machinery remained low because the agencies involved had too little power and did not use what they had.[38] Duplication of functions and lack of ultimate responsibility hindered the collection of steel scrap.[39] Confusion existed in the production of synthetic rubber, aviation gasoline, and escort vessels. The committee charged: "The present conflict is a result of basic weaknesses in the control of the war effort," and added: "The lines of authority are confusing even on paper."[40] The second annual report warned: "During the coming year attention must continue to be focused on the primary need for clearly defined authority in the administration of our domestic war program."[41]

As committee chairman, Truman added to his experience in governmental oversight and won praise for his administrative abilities.[42] His reputation aided him later when he asked his former colleagues to delegate reorganization authority to him. The committee also investigated such governmental activities as the merchant marine, labor, and housing that Truman attempted to reorganize when he became president. His success here, and the public acclaim he received, may have compensated for his earlier failures to reorganize Jackson County government and USES, thereby making him less wary in undertaking general reorganization in 1945.[43]

In summary, from the very beginning of his public career, Truman made administrative reform one of his basic concerns. His early endeavors provided the experience and knowledge that enabled him to begin his reorganization program at the start of his presidency.

However, conditions that the new president confronted in 1945 also made administrative reform desirable, perhaps necessary. In April 1945, uncertainty and fear swept the country following Roosevelt's death. Truman later recalled his own concern when he heard of the tragic event: "I did not know what reaction the country would have to the death of a man whom they all practically worshipped."[44] Within the first few hours of his presidency, he moved to calm the nation by announcing that the San Francisco conference on the United Nations would be held as scheduled, that Roosevelt's cabinet would stay on, and that he would carry on with the former president's policies.[45] This assurance of continuity heartened the American people, but they also needed evidence that the new president could lead. Administrative reorganization, the first major program that Truman initiated, helped provide that confidence. Many Americans found the promise of reorganization especially reassuring because it promised reform of the most unpopular aspect of Roosevelt's presidency—the administration of New Deal programs.

Truman also needed to reorganize so that he could create an office in which he could fulfill his self-image as president. He lacked confidence in himself when he became president. He had not hungered and fought for the power he received in 1945;[46] he did not regard, as had Roosevelt, the presidency as his birthright. He held an office that he neither wanted nor saw himself fitted for. Richard E. Neustadt pointed out that this self-image shaped Truman's presidency. Truman only felt confidence in himself as president when he was making decisions, when he was taking action.[47]

Truman supplemented this conception of the presidency based on his administrative experience with the "book knowledge" he had gained from years of studying history. "It was obvious to me even. . .[as a school boy]," Truman recalled, "that a clear understanding of administrative problems presupposes a knowledge of similar ones as recorded in history."[48] He enjoyed studying the careers of past administrators. "I know of no surer way to get a solid foundation in political science and public administration," he wrote, "than to study the histories of past administrations of the world's most successful system of government."[49] In evaluating former presidents, Truman often mentioned poor administration in connection with those he considered failures. He ranked highest those he considered strong, but he believed even strong presidents, such as Grover Cleveland, could fail if they were poor administrators.[50]

Truman wanted to be a strong president. He was proud of his ability to make decisions. As Neustadt suggested, decisionmaking allowed Truman to live up to his image of the presidency. Perhaps, also, as journalist Richard Rhodes suggested, Truman's view of himself as a decisionmaker fulfilled a deeper need. A physically weak but mentally superior child,

Truman recalled watching his parents, teachers, and friends to see how he could please them, while at the same time getting his own way. His inability to control openly his environment must have been a frustrating experience for a boy fascinated by the great commanders of history. The importance of Truman's military career, Rhodes wrote, was that it had allowed him to command without subterfuge. Truman, Rhodes believed,

. . .became enamored of the process of making decisions, juvenated by the continual rediscovery that it was possible to make things happen, to move the world, to go from A to B to C and even all the way to Z by so simple and logical a procedure as making a decision. It became most of what he talked about and wrote about, and read about as well. He ranks Presidents by their ability to make important decisions, and he will himself be ranked high because he made some of the most important decisions of the century.[51]

But to fulfill this image of the presidency, as sketched by Neustadt and Rhodes, Truman had to undertake administrative reform. "To be more effective as Chief Executive and administrator," he remarked, "I had to reorganize the executive offices."[52] He wanted, Rhodes suggested, to clear away the decisionmaking process "until only the fact of the decision was left."[53] During his first year in office, Truman harped constantly on the need for (1) delegating authority and (2) getting the facts. Both were essential for his decisionmaking role; both required reorganization.

Truman regarded delegation of authority as an indispensable element for his success. He thought, however, that the executive structure had to be reorganized before he could safely place such authority in his subordinates' hands. For example, in order to center responsibility for labor problems in the office of the secretary of labor, relevant functions scattered in other departments and agencies had to be transferred to the Department of Labor. Executive authority had also been diffused by assigning statutory functions or authority to subordinate officials in the executive hierarchy. Truman wanted to return this authority to the department secretaries. This diffusion of authority endangered Truman's strategy of delegation. He wrote:

I told [Harold] Smith I wanted to establish governmental lines so clearly that I would be able to put my finger on the people directly responsible in every situation. It was my intention to delegate responsibility to the properly designated heads of departments and agencies, but I wished to be in a position to see to it that they carried on along the lines of my policy.[54]

Decisionmaking also demanded that the president receive a flow of information. Truman perceived that accomplishing this goal demanded structural reform. He had to reorganize the executive branch, he said, to get the facts.[55] "You know, the hardest thing in the world to find is a fact," he remarked and added: "When reasonable men have the facts, they have no trouble in agreeing on what the conclusions and the results should be."[56] Years later, he summed up his view of the presidency: "Get all the information you can, make up your mind and go ahead—and tell them to go to Hell."[57] Naive, perhaps, in believing that the "facts" would easily resolve conflict, Truman did understand that securing information comprised one the the chief executive's greatest problems. "A President's performance," he wrote, "depends a great deal on the information he has and the information he is able to get."[58] Roosevelt had tried to solve this problem by deliberately creating jurisdictional conflicts, which had forced subordinates to bring matters to him for decision. Truman rejected that approach. He remarked to a visitor:

> Roosevelt, why he had fellows all over the world, one didn't know the other was there, sending the stuff. I declare it was a mess when I got in here. I put an end to that stuff and now they can't put anything over on me.[59]

Truman, Neustadt suggested, later adopted a more realistic attitude toward administration,[60] but in 1945, at least, he believed that a military-type chain of command, which to achieve required reorganization, was necessary to allow the president to receive an orderly flow of vital information.

This does not mean, however, that Truman always acted on his need for decision. His popular image, and his self-image, was that of a courageous, unhesitating man of action, who should be admired for that quality even if one questioned the actions themselves. Actually, Truman often displayed a timorous quality that made him hesitate to undertake controversial decisions. For example, in 1945 Truman convinced his advisers, executive branch officials, Congress, and the public that he was going to undertake reorganization on a scale never before witnessed in Washington. However, after Congress delegated Truman the necessary authority and he was faced with actually carrying out what he promised, he hesitated month after month because of conflicts within the executive branch and Congress. When he finally acted, he submitted mild, relatively uncontroversial proposals. Even though he often talked of it, he never undertook really controversial proposals, such as reorganizing the Forest Service, Army Corps of Engineers, or the banking system regulatory agencies.[61]

In addition to the president's concept of executive authority, the needs of a new era gave added impetus to reform. Truman viewed reorganization as a way to meet both immediate problems arising from the war and long-term domestic and foreign problems. He recalled:

High on my list of priorities in the reconversion program was organizing the machinery of government to meet the new needs and responsibilities that had arisen. I had realized long before I became President that a reorganization of the executive branch was desirable and, in some respects, necessary.[62]

Truman saw need for change in various programs. On 26 April, he told Budget Director Harold D. Smith:

Frankly, I thought the housing situation was a mess. What government participation there was had not been adequately managed during the war. And housing would play an important role in the planning of our peace economy.[63]

On 27 April, Truman outlined his plans for Department of Labor reorganization, aware that reconversion of the economy from war to peace would create many industrial and labor problems.[64] On 4 May, he asked Smith to investigate the possibilities of establishing a welfare department to handle an expanded social-security program and to administer new public health services.[65] In August 1945, Truman told Smith that he had been trying to convince Secretary of State Byrnes of the necessity of reorganizing his department to meet the nation's expanding world responsibilities.[66] Truman also believed that the military had to undertake changes to meet new needs:

One of the strongest convictions which I brought to the office of the President was that the antiquated defense setup of the United States had to be reorganized quickly as a step toward insuring our future safety and preserving world peace.[67]

In each of these cases, and others, Truman prescribed reorganization as a basic tool in the government's effort to cope with new needs, problems, and responsibilities.

Public hostility toward bureaucracy provided another motive for reorganization. The size and scope of the executive branch had been expanding for many years, but the New Deal and the war had speeded the process tremendously, with governmental activities extending into many new aspects of American life.[68] Confusion in government policies and activities at the end of the war increased public concern over bureaucracy. The public displayed conflicting attitudes toward government. Most people reaffirmed their support for the New Deal reforms, but they also increasingly criticized the size and expenditures of the federal government.[69] A mid-1945 poll indicated that 53 percent of the people viewed bureaucracy as an "unmitigated evil"; 32 percent saw it as a mixture of good and bad; and only 15 percent associated it with government services that they liked.[70] An analysis of newspaper reaction to the items in Truman's twenty-one point address on 6 September 1945 indicated that his reorganization proposal rated tenth in interest, a rating higher than the full employment bill, the regulation of prices and wages, the control of the atomic bomb, and the housing shortage.[71]

Many Americans had an ill-defined but strong desire for "normalcy," at least in matters relating to bureaucracy. Some still regarded big government as temporary; they expected it to fade away after the depression and war crises ended. Others realized that big government would be a permanent part of modern America but believed that it had to be made more efficient. Truman's reorganization program, then, received initial support from people with varied attitudes toward government, from both liberals and conservatives. Some saw reorganization as a way to destroy "big government," which also meant destroying the New Deal. Truman, however, could also use reorganization to protect the New Deal from conservative assault after the war. He was very conscious of his heritage from FDR, and as Neustadt said, "he felt obliged to guard it and refurbish it and pass it on."[72]

To guard this heritage, which was endangered by the postwar attitude toward bureaucracy, Truman believed he had to undertake administrative reform. Roosevelt himself thought administration was the weakest part of the New Deal,[73] and he had started his own reorganization program to head off criticism of New Deal agencies.[74] Truman wrote:

> I always fully supported the Roosevelt Program. . .but I knew that certain major administrative weaknesses existed. President Roosevelt often said he was no administrator. He was a man of vision and ideas, and he preferred to delegate administration to others.[75]

Reorganization enabled Truman to protect the New Deal by patching up its assumed weaknesses. Making the executive branch function more smoothly, or convincing the public that steps were being taken to make it function more smoothly, helped ease hostility toward big government. Administrative reform, therefore, acted as a safety valve for public and congressional hostility toward the still strange "big government" of modern America.[76]

Truman also initiated his reorganization program to improve presidential relations with Congress.[77] There were three major aspects of his political orientation: He had grown up as a Southerner, had moved into politics through an alliance with an urban machine, and had evolved into a supporter of New Deal reforms. He thus had ties to the three main components of the Democratic party.[78] "He seemed to place a higher value upon developing and maintaining good relations with the members of that party," wrote one historian, "than upon promoting the point of view of one of its factions."[79] Reorganization, then, provided a good initial reform program upon which the Democratic party could unite. It allowed Truman to assert his leadership without alienating any faction of his party. He followed the lead of Roosevelt, who in the 1940s tried to improve his relations with conservative Democrats by moderating his demands for social welfare and stressing instead the need for governmental efficiency.[80]

Truman believed that through reorganization he could also mitigate conflicts between the executive and congressional branches of government and at the same time help to heal the related split between the Northern and Southern wings of the Democratic party. These conflicts had developed during the New Deal years and widened during the war.[81] As senator and vice-president, Truman had been disturbed by this development. He realized that some tension between the two branches existed inevitably but believed that strife had become great enough to weaken or destroy much good legislation.[82]

Truman viewed reorganization as a partial path to eliminating friction because organizational confusion in the executive branch led to disputes in Congress. Overlapping agencies caused confusion in committee jurisdiction[83] and brought on some of the bitterest fights in Washington. Conflicting policies of executive agencies created other conflicts in Congress. For example, one of many such disputes with which Truman was well acquainted involved the proposed Missouri Valley Authority. Conflicting policies of the Bureau of Reclamation and the Army Corps of Engineers divided the politicians from the Missouri Valley and created strife within Congress and in turn between Congress and the executive branch.[84]

Executive reorganization was a controversial, time-consuming, and often unrewarding program, even when successful. But Truman, dazed by his sudden shift from the Senate, to the vice-presidency, to the presidency, turned to it as almost his first response to his new office. He did so because he viewed reorganization as an initial program upon which Congress could unite, as a way to placate Congress and to moderate its hostility toward the New Deal structure, and as a method of reducing disputes within the Democratic party by dampening policy conflicts within the administration. In addition, his psychological needs and the problems he faced when he became president dictated that he would turn to a program that he had been concerned with for two decades.

Chapter 4

The Reorganization Act of 1945

In 1939, Congress passed an act giving Franklin D. Roosevelt limited authority to draw up reorganization plans for administrative changes and to submit them to Congress under the legislative-veto procedure. President Harry S. Truman won similar but stronger legislation in 1945. Truman did not have to cope with the hate groups that had viciously attacked Roosevelt, nor did the 1945 act become involved in a larger struggle, such as when the earlier proposal became entangled with Roosevelt's attempt to pack the Supreme Court. However, even with these favorable conditions, Truman's proposal for presidential control over the bureaucracy provoked such strong resistance that, said one scholar, passage of the Reorganization Act of 1945 "can truly be regarded as a major feat of political strategy."[1]

On 4 May 1945, Bureau of the Budget Director Harold D. Smith suggested to Truman that it was an opportune time to ask for reorganization authority. Realizing the difficulty of the task and recognizing that the "honeymoon" with Congress would not last long, the two men wanted to take advantage of whatever good will existed. Truman told Smith to draw up a "strong" message,[2] and on 24 May the president submitted it to Congress as his first request for legislation. The chief executive, Truman said, must have power to initiate changes because it was a "positive fact" that Congress could not deal with organizational problems. Congress cannot criticize deficiencies in the executive branch, Truman argued, "and at the same time deny the President the means of removing the causes at the root of such criticisms." He asked for legislation similar to the Reorganization Act of 1939; but, unlike the 1939 act, he wanted the new legislation to be permanent, to have no agencies exempted from its authority, and to be broad enough to allow any form of needed organizational adjustment. Most important, he asked Congress to retain the legislative-veto procedure of the 1939 act.[3] This meant that an individual reorganization plan would go into effect sixty days after its submission, unless vetoed by both houses.

32

Congress had to accept or reject the plan as submitted; it could not amend the proposal.

Opposition began at once. On 25 May, the *Washington Daily News* reported that certain executive branch officials were rallying support to have their agencies exempted from Truman's proposal. Officials of these "agencies are already scampering to their pet congressmen for permanent insurance against any changes that could leave them jobless or considerably less important."[4] The *Washington Post* found the situation even more discouraging; Truman's message, it related, "misfired at the Capitol yesterday in an unhappy second-day reaction that threatened the first congressional quarrel of the new President's honeymoon."[5] On 28 May, Democratic congressional leaders warned Truman to expect a number of agency exemptions.[6]

The situation became even more discouraging when congressional leaders referred the reorganization request to the House Committee on Expenditures in the Executive Departments, chaired by Carter Manasco of Alabama, and to the Senate Committee on the Judiciary, chaired by Pat McCarran of Nevada. On 25 May, Manasco and McCarran asked the White House if a bill incorporating the president's suggestions existed. Truman instructed Smith to draw up a bill, and after clearing his version with the president, Smith submitted it to McCarran and Manasco on 7 June.[7] This draft simply incorporated in legal form the ideas contained in Truman's special message. With a few minor changes approved by Truman, Sen. John H. Overton, a Democrat from Louisiana, acting for McCarran, introduced it as S.1120.[8] However, Manasco, one of the most anti-administration men in the House,[9] had refused to wait for the White House's belated attempt to come up with a bill and had introduced his own (H.R. 3325) on 26 May. His bill exempted twenty-one agencies, provided that either house could kill a plan by vetoing it, prohibited the establishment of new departments, and deviated from the intent of the president's message in several other ways.[10]

Manasco's motives here and throughout the fight remained unclear to observers. His actions at first indicated that he wanted a weak bill, but he later made several timely moves that resulted in the strongest bill possible. Manasco defended his introduction of H.R.3325 on the grounds that he was trying to salvage Truman's proposal. He said that since congressmen had started to try the case in the press, he hurriedly drew up his own bill to ward off criticism.[11] According to Manasco, he offered his proposal only as a basis for discussion and intended for his committee to revise it.[12] But he later admitted also that he believed Congress had given up too much legislative authority to the executive branch and that his bill cut down that authority somewhat.[13]

However, bringing the bills up for committee revision proved no easy matter in either house. Congressmen planned to recess after Germany's surrender and did not want to begin consideration of important legislation until they had a long vacation. On 8 June, Manasco asked Smith if the president wanted hearings held prior to adjournment: "The Congressmen were over-worked," Manasco warned, "and tempers were somewhat frayed."[14] Smith also reported to Truman that congressional leaders advised setting the reorganization proposal aside until the fall session. The leaders believed that it would have a better chance after tempers cooled.[15]

Congress delayed through June and July, and the administration did not protest. By August, however, Truman began to change his tactics. As a senator he had watched Congress rebel against its subordinate role under Roosevelt. When he took office, Truman intended to treat the legislative branch as an equal partner in the governmental process, but he soon found that dropping Roosevelt's domineering approach improved surface relations but did not pass legislation. The president then began to use sterner methods and, acting through Democrat Alben Barkley (Kentucky), the Senate majority leader, for the first time put a "must" label on a proposed law.[16] On 1 August, Barkley reminded his colleagues of certain essential tasks, including the passage of the reorganization bill, that they must accomplish as soon as Congress opened its fall session.[17]

Manasco opened hearings on H.R.3325 on 4 September. Prospects for a good bill were dim. Journalist Frank McNaughton predicted that "government reorganization, a 'must' with Truman, will occasion a hell of a fight." The House committee, he warned, would not give Truman a blank check on reorganization.[18] McNaughton's prediction seemed solidly based. Manasco, who had claimed he welcomed revisions when he had introduced the bill, now indicated that he intended to defend it against any changes. He pointed out that at the time of the 1939 act the Democrats had enjoyed a hundred member majority but Congress still had exempted over twenty agencies. He doubted, after talking to a number of important members, that with a majority of fifty-one the present administration could do any better.[19]

However, Lindsay C. Warren, comptroller general of the United States from 1940 to 1954, caused the committee to revolt and to rewrite completely Manasco's bill. Warren's effectiveness stemmed from his understanding of both Congress and reorganization. This astute North Carolina politician had served in the House of Representatives from 1925 until 1940 and had been an author and floor manager of the 1939 act. He and his colleague

John J. Cochran (a Democrat from Missouri) brought together the key elements of the 1939 act.[20] Though he was no longer in Congress, Warren's role in the legislative history of the 1945 act was almost as important as in the 1939 measure. He was inspired to sell Truman's program because the president first sold him:

> Talking with Truman, Warren bluntly asked what the President meant to do about the vast Roosevelt hierarchy, learned that Truman equally bluntly meant to slash its size as soon as Congress gave him the authority. . . .As a result of this understanding, Warren. . .'sold' Truman to a timid majority of legislators who would like to economize if only the onus weren't placed on them.[21]

Warren attacked the bureaucracy in no uncertain terms:

> The present set-up is a hodgepodge and crazy quilt of duplications, overlappings, inefficiencies, and inconsistencies, with their attendant extravagance. It is probably an ideal system for the tax eaters and those who wish to keep themselves perpetually attached to the public teat, but it is bad for those who have to pay the bill.[22]

Congressmen understood this language.[23] The government's bureaucratic structure had seldom been more unpopular than in 1945, and Warren portrayed reorganization as a weapon in the campaign against big government. But to make that weapon more effective Warren urged the House committee to accept McCarran's Senate bill, especially the two-house veto method, and argued that Congress, by retaining final approval, would not be delegating a vital power to the president. He insisted that pressure from agencies made the two-house veto necessary.[24]

The hearing turned into a "love feast" between Warren and committee members.[25] Despite pressures from private interest groups and Manasco's continued resistance,[26] the committee, in response to Warren's urgings, wrote a new bill (H.R. 4129) that generally followed administration lines. It exempted three agencies outright—Interstate Commerce Commission (ICC), Federal Trade Commission (FTC), and Securities and Exchange Commission (SEC)—and provided that four others—Civil Service Commission (CSC), Federal Communications Commission (FCC), Tariff Commission, and Veterans' Administration—could be reorganized only if they were dealt with in separate reorganization plans. The bill also provided that the civil functions of the Army Corps of Engineers could not be transferred from the Department of War. Following Warren's recommendations, H.R.4129 prohibited the establishment of new departments, permitted the abolition of functions, and limited the life of the legislation to about thirty months.[27]

Even with those deviations from the guidelines offered in Truman's message, H.R.4129 soon replaced the Senate bill as the administration's favorite. Now McCarran, rather than Manasco, posed the greatest threat to Truman's program. Little affection existed between the president and the senator. In early May, Truman had told Smith about "some of the bad things that McCarran had done in the Senate. The President indicated a complete lack of respect for McCarran's performance."[28] He became Truman's number-one enemy in the Senate.[29] Although he belonged to the Democratic party, his views were closer to those of the most conservative Republicans.[30]

Pressure from special interest groups also mounted, and confusion and lack of leadership by administration supporters characterized the Senate hearings.[31] Warren testified along the same lines as before. He seemed especially concerned about increasing opposition to the bill. "Already the whispering campaign is on against this bill," Warren said.[32]

Several other administrative officials supported S. 1120 by testimony or letter, but only one private group, the National League of Women Voters, backed the president.[33] A number of agencies worked for exemptions. John L. Rogers, chairman of the Interstate Commerce Commission, stated that the judicial functions of ICC and its historical position as an agent of Congress justified its independence from the political influence of the executive branch.[34] Leland Olds, acting chairman of the Federal Power Commission, asked for exemption of his agency on the same grounds.[35] Various private groups also requested exemptions for such agencies as the U.S. Maritime Commission, National Mediation Board, Railroad Retirement Board, Civil Service Commission, and others.[36] The American Farm Bureau Federation opposed giving the president any reorganization authority,[37] and various other opponents evidently gave testimony or submitted reports to the closed executive sessions.[38]

The final committee bill was as restrictive as Manasco's original proposal. It provided for a one-house veto, prohibited the establishment of new departments, and exempted twelve agencies completely. It also forbade "divesting any quasi-judicial agency of the means, right, or power to exercise independent judgment and discretion." No one seemed to know what that meant—some feared it exempted all quasi-judicial agencies—but it at least encouraged such agencies to resist reorganization. In an attempt to weaken the legislative-veto procedure, the committee bill also allowed either house to send a plan back to the president for revision.[39]

In the first half of November, the struggle moved to the floor of Congress. From the beginning of 1945, the Republicans had been voting as a rather solid unit.[40] Roosevelt's death had not ended this trend, and Truman found himself faced with an "almost solid line of Republicans" after only a few weeks in office.[41] With the Japanese surrender, Truman declared politics "open and free,"[42] and his liberal twenty-one point message on 6 September unified the Republicans further.[43] The committee hearings indicated that the Republicans stood firm against the reorganization proposal,[44] and in late September, the Republican National Committee attacked the reorganization bill.[45]

Since the administration faced united Republican opposition, its problem was to induce Democrats to vote along party lines. For party lines to hold, executive and congressional leaders had to identify themselves with the proposal. The Democrats already knew that Truman considered reorganization a "must" legislation. Other officials underscored the administration's position. Smith and Warren—one powerful by virtue of his office, the other because of his special relationship with Congress—worked hard for the bill. Also, in August Secretary of State James F. Byrnes, former senator from South Carolina and still highly respected in Congress, published an article calling for "sweeping reorganization" of the executive branch.[46] In addition, on 9 November Truman told Smith that he had "sicked the Cabinet on the reorganization bill and had asked them to do everything they could to secure its passage."[47]

Truman continued personally to work for administrative reform. He became involved in the legislative process on this more than he did on most other issues. He was very much aware of political hazards facing his program. Before the Bureau of the Budget sent McCarran and Manasco the administration bill, Truman agreed, for strategic reasons, to exempt the General Accounting Office, an agency Congress regarded as its own. Because he wanted to avoid the complex and controversial issue of unification of the war and navy departments, he did not ask for authority to consolidate departments.[48] He angered his secretary of labor because he refused to transfer the National Labor Relations Board to the Department of Labor (NLRB). Such a transfer, he explained, might turn Democratic Sen. Robert F. Wagner (New York), and the "Wagner people" who helped to create NLRB, against the reorganization bill.[49]

Congressional leaders also identified themselves with the bill. Majority Leader Barkley designated it "emergency legislation."[50] Speaker of the House Sam Rayburn, a strong supporter of Roosevelt's reorganization proposals,[51] "lashed out" at executive officials who were lobbying against the administration bill. He called a press conference to warn those officials that he would make their names public if they did not stay away. The bill would pass, he predicted, "if some departments downtown don't run too much interference."[52]

Southern conservatives posed the greatest threat. Administration officials feared that they would join with the Republicans as they had done against Roosevelt's reorganization program. Truman had to convince these states' rights-oriented men that he wanted not just to rearrange agencies but to reduce the size of the government. Shortly after taking office, he began using his existing authority to reduce the number of government agencies.[53] Some newspaper analysts added to his image as an opponent of big government by interpreting Truman's reorganization message on 24 May as the beginning of an attack on the bureaucracy. One said that this message, together with his other actions, "has made it so clear that personalized government and executive dictatorship of the Roosevelt regime are gone" that some were talking of the "Truman counterrevolution."[54] "An almost Coolidgean economy note," commented the *Washington Post*, "crept into his reorganization message to Congress."[55] Additionally, a widespread impression existed in 1945 that Truman, unlike Roosevelt, was an orthodox administrator, that he was serious about his reorganization program, and that he would use any authority given to him to decrease waste and confusion in the executive branch.[56]

Truman's actions, as well as the conservative image he projected in the first few months of his administration, influenced many Southern representatives. Asked about rumors that Truman wanted to appoint a general manager to work for "economy and efficiency," Congressman Robert Ramspect, a Democrat from Georgia, one of the best-liked men in the House, said "it fits in with his desire for better management policies in Government."[57] William Whittington, a Democrat from Mississippi, one of the leaders of the "conservative coalition," helped manage the bill during the House debate.[58]

Southerners also led the Senate fight for the reorganization bill. Democrat Harry Byrd (Virginia) and Democrat Walter George (Georgia) emerged as Truman's most important Senate supporters on the issue. These powerful men, with Millard Tydings, a Democrat from Maryland, and others, had opposed Roosevelt's reorganization attempts. Therefore, their conversion had an important effect on the entire Southern delegation. McNaughton, *Time* magazine's Washington bureau chief, reported discussions Truman held with Byrd, George, and other unidentified senators. In September, George said that "Truman is driving hard for a chance to do a real whittling job on the government; if given a real reorganization bill he intends to abolish, consolidate right and left."[59] In October, McNaughton wrote:

> Truman has told Senators [George and probably Byrd] in whom he confided his plans that he is going to abolish many bureaus and agencies, group the remainder in his established cabinet departments, and start a general exodus of a couple of hundred thousand at least from the government payrolls immediately. They have described the President as appalled at the conflicting, opposed functions, the waste of energy, money, time. And these Senators report that he is profane in his determination to get something done.[60]

After George talked with Truman, he reported that the president planned "the most thorough and drastic reorganization the government ever had."[61]

Attention first focused on the House. Since the House committee had reported a fairly good reorganization bill, the administration focused on protecting it from further weakening as it came up for final passage. Strategic compromises by Manasco, intervention by Rayburn, and good floor leadership by other representatives accomplished this.

Republican leaders quickly established their party's position on the bill. Joe Martin, a Republican from Massachusetts, House minority leader, acknowledged only two reasons for reorganization: economy and efficiency. Large government meant inefficiency, Martin reasoned, and inefficiency meant no tax reduction. Large government also caused a concentration of power and a "tendency to control all the activities of the people from Washington." The growth of bureaucracy, he added, "is a New Deal practice which the people are beginning to see through." He concluded that reorganization should lead to a reduction in the number of employees.[62] Republican Charles Halleck (Indiana) agreed to go along with the bill only if it promised a reduction in the size of government and if Congress added safeguards to it.[63]

Representatives made numerous attempts to exempt agencies. The greatest danger was that uncontrolled logrolling would begin, with congressmen interested in one agency trading votes with those interested in another. To prevent this, Democratic leaders, especially Southerners, tried to maintain party lines. Eugene Cox of Georgia, a leader of the "conservative coalition," argued that Congress should not tie the president's hands and should not make any exemptions.[64] Cochran felt that too many exemptions had been made already and that the line had to be drawn to foreclose additional ones.[65] Whittington, another strong leader in the Southern delegation,[66] made a long and effective speech. He denied that Congress could reorganize the executive branch; the authority had to be delegated to the president with Congress providing "the method, the standard, and the yardstick." "Come, reason with me," Whittington pleaded. Congress could not reorganize, he argued: "We have never done it. We are human." He favored retaining the exemptions already in the committee bill but opposed any others.[67]

Pressure for exemption continued despite these appeals, but by offering a series of compromises, Manasco prevented the movement from getting out of hand. He offered a committee approved amendment giving partial exemption to the Federal Deposit Insurance Corporation. He found this necessary because "the banks do not want it reorganized. . .nor do Leo Crowley's [chairman of FDIC] many friends in Congress."[68]

But the danger had only begun. Democrat Robert Crosser of Ohio, a very popular spokesman for the powerful railroad brotherhoods,[69] offered an amendment exempting three agencies dealing with railroad labor problems.[70] Seizing on an opportunity for logrolling, Halleck offered a substitute amendment that exempted the railroad agencies and, in addition, gave full exemptions to the Civil Service Commission, FCC, FDIC, FPC, U.S. Maritime Commission, and Tariff Commission (some of which already had partial exemptions). A number of members from both parties immediately rose to support Halleck, some saying they were interested only in Crosser's amendment but now felt compelled to vote for the substitute first.[71]

Recognizing the danger, Manasco moved to check the drive. He agreed to accept Crosser's amendment if Crosser in turn opposed Halleck's motion. The aged, infirm Crosser denounced the Republican proposal, saying it destroyed the purpose of his amendment and should be rejected unanimously.[72] Halleck's amendment lost by 161 votes to 127. However, with the House then voting by a show of hands, Crosser's amendment also failed, 83 votes to 79. But Manasco, paying off his part of the bargain, called for tellers, and the House accepted Crosser's amendment, 170 to 44.[73] Manasco's action stymied the exemption drive, and all other exemption attempts failed.[74]

Ultraconservative Clare Hoffman (a Republican from Michigan) instigated the last major threat by offering an amendment that required a concurrent resolution of approval by both houses before any reorganization plan could go into effect. This was a reversal of the committee bill's procedure and would have made reorganization difficult; either house could kill a plan by withholding approval. Hoffman argued that this was the only constitutional method of dealing with legislation and the only way to retain proper restraints on the president. Reminding the Southerners of his support for their positions on the anti-poll tax amendment and on the Fair Employment Practices Commission issue, he called on them to break party ranks.[75]

After other Republicans also attacked the delegation of reorganization authority, Speaker Rayburn took the floor to oppose Hoffman. Intervening on the floor only when it was "a matter of life or death of a bill that is all important to the administration," Rayburn carried exceptional weight with party members.[76] The speaker reminded the House that it had set out to pass a workable reorganization bill and to accomplish that it had to remove all obstacles from the president's path. Hoffman's amendment, Rayburn argued, would prevent anything from being accomplished.[77] Party lines held and the House rejected the amendment.[78]

All other attempts to weaken the bill failed. Hoffman moved to recommit but lost on a roll-call vote, 192 to 168, with only seven Democrats and two Republicans crossing party lines. The bill then passed 305 to 56 with no Democrats voting against it.[79]

Although the House bill deviated in several ways from the president's original proposal, it fully exempted only three agencies and retained the vital two-house veto procedure, which required both houses to reject a plan to keep it from going into effect.

For the Senate to pass an equally acceptable bill, it had to revolt against the Committee on the Judiciary. That committee's bill exempted twelve agencies by name as well as an unspecified number of quasi-judicial agencies, limited the reorganization authority to eighteen months, and allowed either house to veto a plan.

The Bureau of the Budget had been working to recover lost ground. On 1 November, Smith telephoned Sen. Abe Murdock (a Democrat from Utah) who, with Barkley's help, was handling the bill. Smith indicated that if the Senate eliminated major weaknesses such as the one-house veto, the administration would accept some agency exemptions. Hinting that Truman might veto the bill if it passed in its present form, he told the senator that the budget bureau had some suggested changes to submit to him.[80]

The "Senate in revolt"[81] did revise the vital adoption procedure. McCarran had been able to weaken S.1120 in the committee because the administration forces had been disorganized, but now ineffective leadership hindered the bill's opponents. With McCarran absent, Murdock presented the bill, and aided by Democrat Carl Hatch (New Mexico), managed it on the floor. Even as he explained his committee's bill, Murdock indicated that the Senate should rewrite it, especially to eliminate the one-house veto provision.[82]

Robert Taft (Ohio) and Forrest C. Donnell (Missouri) presented the Republican position. Taft characterized the bill as one of the most important ever before the Senate because it delegated to the president one of Congress's most important functions—control over executive branch organization. He admitted that Congress had been negligent in reorganization, but he did not believe that bureau pressure was strong enough to block needed action.[83]

Taft declared that if a one-house veto was unconstitutional, as Murdock had argued, the two-house veto procedure was similarly defective. The Senate could find a logical compromise, Taft argued, by agreeing to an amendment sponsored by Donnell.[84] Donnell, who "would far rather suffer the law's delays than advance by one jot the course of human happiness,"[85] wanted to follow what he considered the only constitutional method of passing legislation. His amendment required both houses to pass affirmative resolutions before a plan could take effect.

Since Harry Byrd, Walter George, Millard Tydings, and other Democrats had advocated this same procedure in 1939, Donnell had strong precedent for his argument. However, these same three senators undermined the Republican advantage, and repaid Truman for his work with them, by repudiating on this and on other votes their earlier opposition to reorganization. They frankly admitted that they had not trusted Roosevelt but held that Democrats could put their faith in Truman.

Byrd's support was crucial. Truman won an important victory when he converted Byrd, the "uncrowned" leader of Southern Democrats,[86] into an active supporter of the president's reorganization bill. The fact that the conservative Southern leader, who had been one of Roosevelt's strongest enemies in Congress, now willingly advocated an increase in executive authority reassured others. Early in his administration, Truman had established communication between the White House and Byrd,[87] a task made easier because Truman and Byrd had been friends and desk mates in the Senate.[88] By mid-1945, the administration's course had disturbed Byrd and he became increasingly disenchanted with the president.[89] However, Truman held the Virginian in line on reorganization. On 1 November, Byrd talked with the president and later told reporters that he and Truman regarded the present reorganization bills as too weak to be effective.[90]

This personal attention paid off when Byrd offered an amendment to substitute the two-house veto for Donnell's proposal. Byrd told his colleagues:

> I talked to the President about this matter because I wanted to know his attitude; I wanted to know whether he could convince me that he desired

in his heart to effect a reorganization of the Government if he had the power to do so. He did convince me that he desires to do it.

Agencies could join together to defeat a reorganization plan if Congress retained the initiative, Byrd warned. Government agencies had "life and death" control of a member's political future; they could defeat a congressman by refusing to cooperate in getting government funds for his district. Byrd believed, however, that the president's authority to appoint agency officials limited their power over him. "I am here today for the first time, I think," Byrd confessed, "to say that I have changed my opinion; I have changed my position." He did this in the "desperate hope" that something would be done about the bureaucracy, which "imperils the very foundations of our democracy."[91]

The Byrd substitute passed by a vote of 37 to 26.[92] Not a single Republican voted for it, and only two Democrats defected. Democrat Burton Wheeler (Montana) opposed adding to executive power, and W. Lee O'Daniel (Texas) followed his usual practice of voting with the Republicans.[93]

Tydings now seized his chance to help Truman by arguing against allowing any exemptions in the bill:

> We scuttle like a lot of rats and avoid the issue and repudiate practically all we have said. There should not be one exemption in this bill from top to bottom, and every Senator in his heart knows it.

It shocked him to find that some Democrats did not trust "the patriotism, the Americanism, and the business acumen of President Truman." "Crucify me, if you will," he shouted to those who recalled his 1939 position, "I am crucified on the cross of inconsistency, but I am not crucified on the cross of what is right and what is wrong." He admitted that the continuing increase in the size of government and the replacement of Roosevelt with Truman caused him to change his stand.[94]

The next day, Republican H. Alexander Smith (New Jersey) offered an amendment eliminating all agency exemptions but requiring approval of both houses for the passage of a reorganization plan.[95] George then attacked the new amendment. During the Hoover administration, he had introduced a reorganization bill himself but had opposed Roosevelt's bill in 1939 because he had not agreed with the president's theory of reorganization. Now he said he favored giving Truman this authority because Congress could not reorganize. Senator Smith said that argument was the same as saying Congress would not live up to its responsibilities. George replied:

I entertained the same ideas my friend expresses when I came to Congress, but that was twenty-odd years ago, and my experience has taught me that Congress is not going to reorganize the executive branch of the Government. I lay that down as a postulate: Congress is not going to do it.

Wherever Congress touched an agency, he added, "we have the whole brood on us; they descend on the Congress with such force and such vigor that anyone who proposes to reorganize. . .is going to be driven out."[96]

The amendment failed 40 to 25. Only one Democrat and one Republican crossed party lines.[97]

Thus, party lines held on the two most important amendments debated. However, when it came to exempting certain agencies, nothing could hold the Democrats in line. On the first day of debate, John H. "Flood Control" Overton (a Democrat from Louisiana) offered an amendment exempting the civil functions of the Army Corps of Engineers.[98] Overton shared the Army Corps' concern with flood control and was influential in the Senate on such matters.[99] Throughout the Roosevelt and Truman administrations, the Army Corps resisted any attempt to integrate it into the executive branch, supported by leading allies in Congress including John McClellan (Arkansas), Manasco, Whittington, and Overton. Well-organized local interest groups and large national associations aided the corps and gave it great power in Congress. Most important was the National Rivers and Harbors Congress that had worked during the hearings to have the Army Corps exempted. At various times, McClellan served as its president, Whittington as vice-president, and Overton as chairman of the board.[100]

Overton and McClellan led the fight for exemption. Murdock tried to counter them by appealing to party loyalties,[101] but the amendment passed 36 to 18. Key later classed this as one of three roll-call votes on which the conservative coalition formed in 1945.[102] However, since four of the thirteen Democrats opposing the amendment were Southerners (including the powerful Southern conservatives Byrd and Richard Russell of Georgia) the amendment apparently passed simply because the senators voted their state interests rather than because they formed a "coalition" with conservative Republicans to oppose a liberal measure.

The assumption that state interests were predominant in determining votes gains strength from an examination of senatorial reaction to a proposal to exempt the U.S. Maritime Commission. The shipping industry, anticipating the shock of postwar readjustment, did not want anything to disturb its established relationship with the U.S. Maritime Commission. Commission chairman Vice-Admiral Emory Land told the Propeller Club, the main pressure group behind the commission, that there was going to be an attempt to absorb it into another agency (probably the Department of Commerce under Henry Wallace). "If that is what the shipping industry wants," this government official said, "okay. But if it isn't, let the industry become vocal and make its wishes in the matter known. And let the industry see to it that it gets what it wants."[103] The Propeller Club, representing shipping and related industries such as steel, as well as many other interested associations, passed a resolution demanding the commission's exemption.[104]

Democrat George Radcliffe (Maryland), chairman of the subcommittee on the merchant marine of the Committee on Commerce, and James Eastland (a Democrat from Mississippi) cosponsored the maritime amendment. It passed 30 to 25.[105] The Democratic senators who voted to exempt either the Maritime Commission or the Corps of Engineers, or both, came from states that were affected by flood control and by harbor or intercoastal canal activities of the army engineers, and almost without exception they were coastal states with merchant marine interests. If these senators had been motivated simply by conservative ideology, they would have opposed Byrd's amendment because it increased executive power, but each Democratic senator who opposed the administration on these two exemptions voted with it to require the two-house veto that was, from the administration's point of view, the most important aspect of the reorganization bill.

On 19 November, the bills went to a conference committee. McCarran, Hatch, Murdock, Homer Ferguson (a Republican from Michigan), and Chapman Revercomb (a Republican from West Virginia) served from the Senate. Manasco, Cochran, Whittington, and Republican George Bender (Ohio) represented the House. These men faced a complex task: "It's a mixed up mess," McNaughton reported.[106] Cross pressures made it more difficult because private interest groups continued to oppose the bill.[107]

However, the administration could also focus its efforts on influencing this small group of men, making sure that the conferees understood its position. Smith notified Truman that the principal issue was exemption of agencies. The House version fully exempted three and the Senate version fourteen or more. "Suggestions have been furnished to a member of the conference committee," Smith reported.[108]

By 11 December, the committee members had worked out a compromise. The conferees exempted only seven agencies from the bill's authority: ICC, FTC, SEC, Army Corps of Engineers, and three railroad labor agencies. The committee bill required a two-house veto to defeat a plan and, to prevent reorganization from being used as a political weapon in the presidential election, placed the bill's termination date at 1 April 1948.[109] Both houses adopted the bill with little further debate.[110]

Truman, who had already expressed his approval of the conference committee's work,[111] signed the bill on 20 December. At this point, he clarified his theory of reorganization by a statement that if made earlier would have endangered the bill. He stated that major savings in government expenditures could not be achieved through reorganization. "The results of reorganization," he said, "will be evident primarily in the increased effectiveness of Government operations."[112]

Some critics have disparaged Truman's political skill and leadership, especially in legislative matters.[113] However, his success with the Reorganization Act of 1945 indicated that when he became personally interested in a bill he displayed a great deal of political skill, which perhaps verified another argument these same critics sometimes made: That Truman did not really support some other measures he presented to Congress. Various executive and congressional leaders made important contributions, but Truman guided the struggle from its beginning in May to its successful climax in December. He initiated the program, manipulated his image to gain support for it, sold Warren and other important individuals on his plan, and held the Southerners to a party vote. His skill, patience, and interest raised the legislative-veto process in reorganization matters to its highest level. Although the 1945 act contained flaws, no other, before or since, granted the president as much authority as the 1945 law.

Chapter 5

The Reorganization Plans of 1946

In December 1945, Congress passed the Reorganization Act of 1945. The nation expected President Truman to make full use of the authority granted by the legislation. He had deliberately created the impression that he regarded organizational reform as a primary goal of his administration, and he had seemed impatient with the limitations on his existing authority. When Bureau of the Budget Director Harold D. Smith warned him that he faced "nasty" reorganization decisions, Truman replied: "I want to make them, . . .and I want to get reorganization of the Government under way as fast as possible."[1] After Congress passed the reorganization act, Truman rejected his advisers' cautious approach in using that authority. "Anything we propose will be fought about," he asserted, "let's give them something worth fighting about. If I don't do anything else, doing a good job on reorganization will be worth doing!"[2]

Because of Truman's attitude, many public officials expected 1946 to herald a drastic program to restructure executive branch organization. They became restless when several months passed and Truman still had submitted no plans. In April 1946, Congressman Jennings Randolph (a Democrat from West Virginia) urged Truman to act. Despite his vaunted ability to make decisions, Truman now admitted that it had been easier to talk abstractly about reorganization than to act. Displaying increasing awareness of the reality of public administration, he replied:

> You would be surprised how very difficult it is. I knew it was a difficult job when I began it but to talk about it and to do it are two different things.[3]

In mid-May, Truman acted. However, instead of unveiling a deep-cutting program, he submitted three rather moderate proposals to Congress and again was pessimistic about the chances of success of a major reorganization endeavor. Shrugging off praise for his three plans, Truman wrote:

> I think we will get some results [from a reorganization program] over the

47

next two or three years but I doubt very much whether they will be permanent or not. In fact all the "ballyhoo" about the simplification of the military setup is a shining example of what happens when you try to set up an efficient government department.[4]

When advisers warned Truman that Congress would probably reject his plans, he snapped that "he'd be damned if he could help it, they were good plans and it was up to Congress."[5] Smith found the president in a "despondent mood" regarding the 1946 reorganization program,[6] and Truman later referred to his experience with reorganization as "disappointing."[7]

Truman's growing discouragement with administrative reform stemmed from several sources. Restrictions on the authority granted to the president in the 1945 enabling act raised obstacles;[8] complex foreign and domestic problems prevented Truman from devoting adequate time to administrative problems;[9] technical organizational issues made the process of drafting reorganization plans time consuming and intricate;[10] the fight over unification of the armed forces revealed the difficulty of organizational change.[11]

However, Truman's attitude changed for additional, more complex reasons. He started his presidency with unrealistic assumptions about reorganization. He viewed reorganization as central to all of his major goals. He thought that his effectiveness as president depended to a great extent on administrative reform. He wanted to use reorganization to reduce squabbling within the executive branch, to moderate the growing conflict between the executive and legislative branches, and to help heal splits within the Democratic party. However, Truman soon found that reorganization increased friction in all three areas.

One important conflict within the executive branch developed in 1945 and 1946 as Smith tried to wrest control of the reorganization program from other individuals, many of whom were closer to the president than the budget director. Smith served as director of the Bureau of the Budget from 1939 until 1946. He was a private, modest man, not well known outside of Washington. He "was a kind of myth—in the background somewhere, rarely seen, constantly felt."[12] He served as an arm of the president in budget matters and became, said Vice-President Henry A. Wallace, "the most important man in. . .[Roosevelt's] administration."[13] Since its budget function required the bureau to accumulate detailed organizational knowledge of every executive branch agency, Smith became a key figure in Roosevelt's reorganization program.[14]

However, during World War II, the Bureau of the Budget lost control of organizational matters. The most significant blow came in May 1943 when

Roosevelt created the Office of War Mobilization and Reconversion and gave its director great power over all domestic phases of government.[15] Smith viewed OWMR as an "abortion" that duplicated Bureau of the Budget functions, but OWMR Director James Byrnes regarded himself as assistant president with Smith's agency as part of his staff. This created a good deal of strife between the two agencies.[16]

Jurisdictional problems continued after Truman took office.[17] During the early months of the Truman administration, Smith remained too insecure to push for a clear definition of responsibility,[18] and OWMR retained its supervisory role over reorganization matters.[19]

Although the president never fully accepted him, Smith had gained favor with Truman by the end of 1945, and Truman assigned him a larger role in reorganization.[20] In December 1945, Truman instructed Smith to ask the departments to submit recommendations for reorganization and told him to take the lead in preparing plans for the president's approval. Truman stated that Smith would "work with the Director of War Mobilization and Reconversion *insofar as the reorganization proposals relate to the reconversion of the war agencies*" [italics added].[21]

The presidential order seemed to confine the OWMR role to organizational matters involving war agencies, but John W. Snyder, Truman's close friend and new OWMR head, refused to accept that interpretation. After the Bureau of the Budget asked department and agency heads to submit reorganization suggestions,[22] Snyder reminded Smith that the president ordered them to collaborate in preparing plans. Snyder, noting his desire to be kept informed on reorganization matters, asked for copies of all proposals submitted from the executive branch.[23]

On 14 January, Truman cautioned Smith against unnecessarily involving other agencies in the process of developing reorganization proposals. Truman suggested that the Bureau of the Budget alone formulate the program; otherwise, publicity leaks concerning proposed plans would generate immediate opposition.[24] When Smith met with the president a few days later, he seized on Truman's letter as a way to exclude OWMR from the reorganization program. He told Truman that Snyder's request to see all reorganization plans increased the possibility of leaks. Smith said he did not want anyone to see the documents unless he and the president agreed that the subject could be profitably discussed with others.[25] "The President certainly agreed," Smith observed with pleasure and added:

I think he was a little surprised that his off-the-cuff memorandum [of 14 January] struck Snyder down, but I did not remind him that on other occasions such memorandums have struck me down.[26]

However, Smith's victory benefited his successors more than himself. Some confusion over responsibility for the reorganization program continued until Smith's resignation in June 1946.[27] For example, Truman complained to Smith that conflict within the White House caused him to delay submitting the three plans. He specifically mentioned arguing with Snyder about housing reorganization. Although Truman finally presented the three plans to Congress substantially in the form proposed by the Bureau of the Budget, Smith did not participate in the final White House discussions of them.[28]

This confusion hindered the formulation of the president's 1946 program, but other conflicts also disturbed Truman. He hoped to use reorganization to end wrangling within the executive branch, but he soon found that tinkering with organizational arrangements only increased strife. He knew that reorganization itself would cause some disputes; each department would try to retain its own agencies, programs, and employees while trying to strip other departments of their functions. But Truman was confident that a combination of "facts" and loyalty from his subordinates would allow him to get these executive officials to agree on a reorganization program, which, by clarifying jurisdictions and insuring a smooth flow of information, would reduce future conflicts.[29]

By the end of his first year in office, Truman seemed more realistic.[30] He had begun to realize that neither facts nor loyalty moderated conflict over reorganization. When a visitor remarked that some officials were sensitive about their jurisdictions, the president emphatically agreed. He fumed:

> Isn't it the Goddamnedest thing—what happens to people when they come to Washington? Why even some of these new Cabinet members of mine start right out being that way.[31]

Truman began to understand the difficulty of turning the cabinet into a unified body acting as part of the president's team. Cabinet officers found themselves controlled by the bureaus within their departments. To be successful, the departmental secretaries had to have the support of their bureau chiefs who were linked to relevant congressional committee chairmen and interest groups. These centrifugal forces soon pulled department heads away from the president and moved them into the boundaries of the triangle of power.

Extreme public conflict over unification of the military departments naturally acquainted Truman with the realities of the politics of reorganization, but the strife that occurred when he attempted to reorganize welfare and labor functions also helped riddle his naiveté. Two of Truman's major goals were to rebuild the Department of Labor and to prepare the Federal Security Agency (FSA) for departmental status. He found these goals incompat- ible because transferring welfare activities to FSA frequently required stripping the Department of Labor of additional functions. This incon- gruity caused both friction between officials of the two agencies and clashes between Truman and his old friend Secretary of Labor Lewis W. Schwellenbach.[32]

In addition to predicting that reorganization would end executive branch dissension, Truman also had hoped it would moderate conflict between the executive branch and Congress. He had viewed reorganization as a way to reduce congressional conflict by reducing those divisions within the executive branch that affected the legislative arm. He soon learned, how- ever, that reorganization created additional problems because threatened agencies mobilized their legislative allies against the president's program. In addition, Congress resented the president's gaining increased power over executive branch organization, especially through the legislative-veto procedure. Smith found that this congressional attitude disturbed Truman and caused him to delay submitting the 1946 plans.[33]

In trying to improve relations with Congress, Truman especially wanted to destroy the so-called conservative coalition of Southern Democrats and Republicans. He had hoped that his request for reorganization authority in 1945 would be an initial legislative proposal on which all Democrats could unite. Fearing the reaction of Southern conservatives to his request, he had persuaded them to support the 1945 bill by promising to use its authority to reduce the size and cost of the government. However, by the end of 1945 Truman had moved closer to the liberal wing of the party. He subsequently waited until Congress passed the Reorganization Act of 1945 before he publicly clarified his position on reorganization, but then, as he signed the act, he cautioned supporters not to expect great savings.[34] In late January 1946, he bluntly warned Sen. Kenneth McKellar (a Democrat from Tennes- see) of the realities of the condition of postwar United States:

A great many people seem to think that the Government now can be operated on exactly the same basis as it was after World War I. It is a fallacy and the sooner it is forgotten the better it will be for the efficiency of the program. As soon as I can get to it, under the reorganization act, I am going to try to streamline and consolidate as many of these activities as possible, but there isn't any use endeavoring to put the operations of the Government back to twenty years ago for it simply won't go.[35]

Since Truman now regarded his reorganization program as a way to im- prove the existing governmental structure rather than to reduce it, South- erners did not find his program as attractive after 1945 as before.

Thus, by early 1946 Truman had relegated reorganization from being a central goal of his administration to a secondary priority. After this he sometimes pushed hard for a specific organizational change, and pressure and opportunity encouraged him to flood Congress with a number of plans after the Hoover Commission reported its recommendations. But Truman usually seemed only to be going through the motions in reorganization matters. He offered many plans in the next seven years and achieved a number of changes but never again displayed the interest and political skill that he had shown in the fight for the Reorganization Act of 1945.

Nor did Truman develop a reorganization strategy for the national government, a vision of how reorganization could be used to achieve his larger goals. He had developed such a conception as county-court judge in the 1920s, and in 1945 he had a much clearer understanding of administrative reform than Roosevelt had during his first few years in office. However, although Truman submitted many plans in the future, he did not develop a reorganization strategy. Perhaps he thought that the political costs were too high or that general reorganization was impossible.

However, with the Bureau of the Budget assuming more leadership, the administration's 1946 reorganization program slowly got underway. The program evolved from Truman's own suggestions and from those of executive branch officials and others,[36] but the Bureau of the Budget screened such proposals and measured them against its long-range organizational goals. It did not get all of its suggestions accepted but often blocked proposals it deemed improper.[37]

On 16 May, Truman submitted three plans to Congress, each accompanied by a message explaining and defending it. Plan one would make permanent several administrative changes effected under the First War Powers Act (see the footnotes for the detailed provisions of the plan).[38] The most controversial section of the plan would establish permanently the National Housing Agency (NHA). Of the many crises Truman faced during his first administration, few directly affected more people than the housing shortage. It began during the depression when the construction industry failed to keep up with national needs and deepened during the war when residential construction yielded to military requirements.[39] Urban population swelled during the war and failed to recede with peace.[40] The housing shortage soon became an emotion-filled political issue. To many it symbolized the nation's ingratitude toward veterans, and many also feared it threatened family life, the foundation of a healthy society.[41]

Truman became the first president to commit himself fully to the cause of housing reform.[42] In his twenty-one point address, Truman called for housing reform[43] and formulated a two-part program. The first was a short-range plan to construct low-cost housing for veterans. The second, a long-range program, took legislative form as the Wagner-Ellender-Taft bill. The Senate passed the bill on 15 April 1946, but the House Committee on Banking and Currency blocked it.[44]

Because of this legislative deadlock, many administration officials and congressmen urged Truman to take executive action to prevent a return to prewar administrative confusion. Roosevelt had centralized most housing functions within the National Housing Agency, but since he had acted under the First War Powers Act the agency would disintegrate after the war. There no longer would be an agency to develop and direct a unified housing program.

In 1946, distrust of public housing activity provoked opposition to change. The Federal Housing Administrator Raymond M. Foley and OWMR director John W. Snyder urged that FHA and the Federal Home Loan Bank Administration, both lending agencies with close ties to banking, savings and loan, and home builder interest groups, should be removed from the National Housing Agency and placed within the Federal Loan Agency.[45] Snyder's opposition caused Truman to delay submission of the 1946 plans.[46]

However, these opponents lost the first phase of the battle when Truman submitted plan one. In his message, Truman declared that the establishment of a permanent housing agency was an "indispensable step" in dealing with the housing emergency.[47] The plan proposed a new National Housing Agency to replace the temporary agency of the same name. The new NHA would have three constituent units: the Federal Home Loan Bank Administration, the Federal Housing Administration, and the Federal Public Housing Authority. Most important, the head of NHA would have much more authority over the agency's constituent units than in the past, which would reduce the private housing industry's control over those units.

Plan two also grew from a concern Truman had expressed early in his administration. On 4 May 1945, he and Smith discussed the desirability of creating a department of welfare. They then tentatively agreed that the nation needed such a department, especially if Congress extended social welfare programs to new groups or if it developed additional programs. Truman asked Smith to study the matter.[48]

The Reorganization Act of 1945 forbade creation of new departments under its authority, but the administration designed plan two as final preparation of the Federal Security Agency (FSA) for future departmental status. In 1939, Roosevelt had gathered widely scattered programs into FSA. "The time has now come," Truman told Congress, "for further steps to strengthen the machinery of the Federal Government for leadership and service in dealing with the social problems of the country." Plan two, therefore, transferred additional functions to FSA and strengthened top management's control over its internal organization.[49]

Its provisions abolished the Social Security Board and the U.S. Employees' Compensation Commission and transferred their activities to the federal security administrator. One controversial section transferred from the Department of Labor to the federal security administrator all the programs of the Children's Bureau except those relating to the Fair Labor Standards Act. It transferred the latter activities to the secretary of labor. These transfers, said Truman, would strengthen children's programs by bringing them into closer association with similar activities of FSA.[50]

Not until 15 May did Truman decide to submit plan three, and its final preparation took from 5 P.M. on 15 May until 11 A.M. on 16 May.[51] Perhaps because of haste, this plan, supposedly noncontroversial, included some items the Bureau of the Budget later judged "defective technically or definitely undesirable."[52]

Plan three carried out a variety of reorganizations.[53] It consolidated the General Land Office and the Grazing Service, both in the Department of Interior, into a new Bureau of Land Management.[54] Another section reorganized the Bureau of Marine Inspection and Navigation (BMIN). It transferred most BMIN functions to the Coast Guard within the Department of Treasury. This transfer made permanent the wartime reorganization that transferred BMIN from the Department of Commerce to the Coast Guard.[55]

Immediate reaction to Truman's three plans was generally favorable, though not enthusiastic. Interest in organizational matters had reached unusual heights in 1945, but strikes, inflation, and other postwar crises had diverted public attention from administrative problems. Moreover, the proposals themselves were not particularly interesting. In February, Smith warned that most actions immediately possible did not possess "dramatic quality." Across Smith's memo Truman scrawled: "We are trying for efficiency and economy—not dramatics and publicity."[56] Fear of their effects on the 1946 election also caused Truman to eliminate some of the more "dramatic" plans.[57]

The first opposition to the plans appeared from within the bureaucracy itself. Although Truman failed to exert the leadership and political astuteness that he displayed while pushing the Reorganization Act of 1945 through Congress, he did save plan two by taking quick action to end executive branch dissension over transfer of the Children's Bureau. The reasons for moving the Children's Bureau from the Department of Labor to FSA were complex. The bureau was the nation's only agency organized on an age-group basis.[58] It grew from the progressive movement's attempts early in the twentieth century to deal with the "whole child." Meanwhile, new reform philosophies emerged. By the end of the 1930s, programs provided welfare functions for all age groups, and separate child welfare programs became questionable.[59] Perhaps the immediate reason for Truman's decision to place the Children's Bureau under FSA control stemmed from his fear that dissension between the two agencies over administrative details would make it impossible for him to get his advanced and controversial health program through Congress.[60]

The first attack on plan two came from within the Department of Labor. At first department officials seemed reconciled to losing the Children's Bureau, perhaps because they expected to receive other bureaus to make up that loss.[61] However, on 21 May Children's Bureau chief Katharine Lenroot informed Schwellenbach of her fears that the federal security administrator intended to rip the Children's Bureau apart and scatter its programs among FSA constituent units.[62] Plan two's language increased her apprehension because, complying with Truman's firm belief that administrators had to have complete authority to carry out their responsibilities, the plan allowed the federal security administrator to organize the bureau as he wanted.[63]

Vigorous activity by a coalition of social interest groups made it unnecessary for Lenroot to stand alone in protecting the bureau. The Children's Bureau had been able to maintain its autonomy over the years because of support from women's organizations and social work groups.[64] Edith Abbott, sister of Lenroot's predecessor, established an emergency committee to save the agency.[65] The administration quickly received hundreds of protests from this well-organized campaign.[66]

Although Lenroot realized that she would have powerful support if she decided to carry the battle to Congress, she decided to avoid a complete break with Truman and to try to protect her bureau within the framework of the plan. She met with the President on 3 June and asked him to instruct Federal Security Administrator Watson Miller to preserve the bureau's integrity. Truman refused but agreed to write a reassuring letter to try to mollify the groups opposing the plan.[67]

Truman's letter, which the Bureau of the Budget drafted and Miller approved, stated that since he believed in broad administrative discretion, he did not wish to tell the FSA head how to organize his agencies. However, Truman said he had instructed Miller to discuss with him any major reorganizations affecting the Children's Bureau before they were put into effect.[68]

This satisfied the dedicated bureau chief. "The letter does not give Miss Lenroot all she wants but it is acceptable and she seems to be glad to have it," a staff aide reported.[69] No longer worried about dismemberment of the Children's Bureau, Lenroot and her supporters dropped their opposition to the proposal.[70]

Although it successfully dealt with this dissension within the executive branch, the administration did not handle congressional problems as competently. Not yet understanding how deeply it had to involve itself in the legislative process, the Bureau of the Budget tried to rely on Manasco's Committee on Expenditures in the Executive Departments, which conducted House hearings on 23 May and 25 May. "Apparently our original faith in the Democratic majority on the House Committee. . .was unfounded," a Budget Bureau official wrote later.[71] The bureau soon concluded that the committee itself was the main obstacle to further reorganization progress.[72]

During the hearings, opponents stressed that the plans apparently would not result in important reductions in government expenditures. Economy sentiment dominated in Congress in 1946,[73] and many regarded reorganization as meaningless unless definite savings could be demonstrated.[74] The 1945 reorganization act included a clause that said reorganization plans should result in a 25 percent cut in administrative costs in the agencies affected. The administration found it almost always impossible to achieve this goal. Its failure to comply with the savings clause gave reorganization opponents a respectable cover to conceal other less defensible reasons for opposing the plans.

In addition to general statements on all three plans, the committee heard testimony on each separate plan. Major opposition to plan one focused on the housing reorganization proposal. The administration inserted the housing provisions in plan one after the House refused to act on the Wagner-Ellender-Taft bill. "If you will read my reorganization plan No. 1," Truman wrote American Federation of Labor (AFL) President William Green, "you will see that the principal features of the. . .[Wagner-Ellender-Taft bill] have been implemented in the reorganization setup."[75]

Although the Wagner-Ellender-Taft bill went beyond plan one by providing for an expansion of government housing functions, some housing industry organizations actually regarded the plan's method of unifying housing agencies as more hateful than the bill's. Truman's plan, wrote an official of the U.S. Savings and Loan League, "was a stronger and more dangerous one from our point of view than the one in the W. E. T. bill."[76] The National Association of Real Estate Boards, the National Association of House Builders, and the U.S. Savings and Loan League emerged as especially powerful opponents. The National Retail Lumber Dealers' Association played an important "supportive" role to the three major organizations. The Mortgage Bankers' Association, the U.S. Chamber of Commerce, and the Producers' Council acted as more broadly based opponents of the plan.[77] The U.S. Savings and Loan League claimed that these groups agreed upon "a concerted line of action," which led to the plan's defeat.[78] These groups wanted to keep the organizational structure of federal housing activities splintered so that they could more easily control the individual units without threat of interference from above by a strong administrator.

Plan one did not create additional housing activities; it simply made permanent the wartime unification of major federal housing programs. However, opposition became bitter and emotional, with industry spokesmen charging that the plan would lead to socialism or worse. Such unreasonable reactions characterized the housing industry's attitude toward government activities in general. The industry, decentralized and localized, regarded itself as the embodiment and defender of the free enterprise system. The fact, however, that it benefited from many government programs constantly reminded it of its failure to live up to its self-image. In its frustration at its own hypocrisy, it made public housing a "whipping boy."[79] Thus, industry spokesmen, who appeared in full force before Manasco's committee, denounced plan one because it unified public housing programs with "private" functions, most of which were lending programs administered by the federal housing administrator and the Federal Home Loan Bank Board (FHLBB). Some of these men envisioned socialism or dictatorship resulting from the plan.[80]

Various groups also testified against most of the provisions of plan two and three. Organized labor especially fought the section of plan two that abolished the U.S. Employees' Compensation Commission and the section of plan three that transferred BMIN from the Department of Commerce to the Coast Guard.[81]

Following the onslaught of these interest groups, the House committee voted to reject all three plans, reportedly with 10 votes against and 3 for.[82]

The Bureau of the Budget now rallied to try to save the plans as they came before the Senate Committee on the Judiciary.[83] Here the bureau received strong support. McCarran, powerful chairman of the Committee on the Judiciary, had already started to maneuver the plans through the Senate. He introduced resolutions disapproving the three plans in order to get them before his committee so hearings could take place.[84] McCarran was determined to get the plans accepted. He scrawled a note asking Wheeler for his proxy and explained: *"I Am Going Along With The President."*[85] He wrote Sen. Ernest W. McFarland (a Democrat from Arizona) that "SENATOR MURDOCK AND I ARE GOING TO TRY TO PUT ALL THREE PLANS THROUGH FOR THE PRESIDENT."[86] He told a Nevada newspaper publisher that since Congress granted broad authority to the president under the Reorganization Act of 1945, the major question was whether the president validly exercised that authority.[87] Although McCarran had tried to weaken the 1945 act, he now took the broadest possible interpretation of that act—that if plans were legal, Congress should accept them.

After hearing testimony that largely repeated that which took place before the House committee,[88] McCarran's group approved all three plans.[89] The committee report echoed the viewpoint expressed earlier by McCarran. The Reorganization Act of 1945 delegated broad discretionary authority to the president. Congress understood, the report stated, that any plan would arouse opposition from the agency affected and from a "satellite segment of public opinion which could be readily influenced by that agency." Since the president had to cope with this problem, the report concluded, it was reasonable to assume that Congress intended for the president's decisions to be persuasive, if not controlling. Inasmuch as the president was chief administrator, Congress should not lightly reject his administrative proposals simply because opponents challenged their wisdom.[90]

Despite favorable action by the Senate committee, the first test came in the House. When the plans came up for vote on 28 June, Manasco predicted that the lower chamber would reject all three by the end of the day.[91] Appleby warned Truman that although the Bureau of the Budget would give the plans all possible support, the House would probably disapprove them.[92]

Manasco brought up all three plans at the same time, which increased opportunities for logrolling and which allowed opposition to one plan to feed opposition to the others. Some speakers attacked all three plans, most often on the grounds that they did not save money.[93] Others attacked the reorganization procedure itself: "The President has undertaken in some respects to follow the Russian system and ignore our system of government," said one congressman.[94] Criticism of specific plans largely repeated the attacks interest groups made before the House committee.[95] After a very short debate, the House defeated plan one by a vote of 180 to 37; plan two, 166 to 40; and plan three by voice vote.[96]

Since it took both houses to veto a plan, the fate of Truman's reorganization program rested with the upper chamber. The Senate debated plan three on 13 July and plans one and two on 15 July, with McCarran and Barkley managing the floor for the administration. Donnell and others led the opposition against plans two and three, and Taft directed the onslaught against plan one. Unlike the House, the Senate concentrated on policy effects of the plans rather than on legal issues or on their failure to save 25 percent.

McCarran brought each plan up separately. Since he thought that less objection existed to plan three, he and Barkley opened the debate with it. Barkley said Congress had to expect opposition to reorganization. He and others had been confronted by government employees protesting these plans, he said. "They have been employees of a given bureau or agency from time immemorial," Barkley said, "and they wish to continue in that status." He stressed again and again that Congress could not reorganize: "Congress never could do so, and it had never done it, although it had talked about it for years and years."[97]

As the Senate prepared to vote after a very short debate, Donnell criticized reorganization procedure in general terms, especially because it did not give enough time to study the plans.[98] Republican Wayne Morse (Oregon) agreed. The procedure itself, said Morse, "dictates a vote against it." He argued that Congress should not give the president "autocratic power over the passage of substantive legislation."[99]

The Senate passed plan three with 37 votes for and 30 against. Nine Democrats voted against it and thirty with the majority. Republicans voted 21 against and 6 for.[100] The reasons for deviation from the party line are not clear. Only two Democratic senators voted against all three plans: O'Daniel, who normally voted with the Republicans,[101] and Peter G. Gerry (Rhode Island), who was, according to McNaughton, a "reactionary, diehard, multimillionaire."[102] Four of the nine Democratic opponents of plan three were members of the Committee on Commerce. Of the eleven Democratic members of that committee only four voted for the plan—four were against and three absent. The provision that transferred BMIN from the Department of Commerce and, therefore, out of the committee's jurisdiction probably motivated these senators.

Two days later, the Senate began consideration of plan two. Barkley again defended the plans; he said Congress had either to stop complaining about extravagance and lack of economy or to back the president's reorganization efforts.[103] Donnell, as usual, opposed reorganization on constitutional and legal grounds.[104] Taft objected to giving the federal security administrator so much control over the health, education, and welfare programs of government. Taft asserted that when Congress created a welfare department (and this plan was a final step toward creation of such a department), each of these program areas should have a separate head with the secretary having only general supervisory authority.[105]

The Senate passed plan two with 40 votes for and 37 votes against. Forty Democrats supported it and five opposed it. Thirty-one Republicans voted against it and none for it.[106] Of the five Democrats who opposed the plan three had seats on the Committee on the Post Office and Post Roads; post-office employees had worked against the provision to abolish the Employees' Compensation Commission. Republican unity was a reflection of identification of the FSA and its welfare programs with Roosevelt and the New Deal.

When McCarran brought plan one up for debate, Taft again led the opposition. He had sponsored the housing bill that the administration had endorsed and that the Senate had passed. This was the Wagner-Ellender-Taft bill, which Truman believed went hand in hand with plan one. Taft, however, opposed the plan, and his opposition was important because many Republicans looked to him for leadership on housing issues.[107] The role of public housing in the structure created by plan one worried Taft. He admitted that the Wagner-Ellender-Taft bill also proposed consolidation of these housing agencies but claimed that the bill carried out the consolidation in a different manner from plan one. His bill made the three constituent units of NHA "practically autonomous" and gave the national housing administrator only supervisory power over them.[108] In contrast, Truman's plan gave the administrator power of "general superintendence, direction, coordination and control" of the affairs of the National Housing Agency.[109] The plan also affronted Taft and other senators because they believed the administration had agreed to the administrative provisions of W. E. T. The plan seemed to be a betrayal of this earlier agreement.[110]

Plans two and three, which Congress had accepted, effected many reorganizations but plan one was more important in terms of policy, organizational improvement, and politics. Truman's reorganization program faded into relative insignificance when the Senate defeated plan one with 45 votes against and 31 for. Seventeen Democrats voted against it and twenty-seven for it. Three Republicans voted in the affirmative and twenty-eight against the measure.[111]

Democratic opposition centered in the South, with some opponents from the border and rural western states.

In 1945, Truman had known that FDR had faced great opposition when he tried to get his own reorganization program through Congress. Democrats, led by Byrd, Tydings, and George, had especially fought it. Therefore, in 1945 Truman tried to convince the Southern Democrats that if they helped him gain reorganization authority he would use it not to consolidate and increase executive power but to reduce the size of government. He succeeded in this, and Byrd and George led the fight for his program, along with the Southern-oriented Tydings. Nineteen Democrats supported the administration on four or more of the five important roll-call votes on the 1945 act and of these six were Southern (or 32 percent of the nineteen). Seven of these Democrats voted with the administration on all five votes, and of the seven three were Southern (43 percent of the seven).

By 1946, Southerners realized that Truman had misled them, on reorganization as well as other issues.[112] Byrd and Tydings were absent on all three votes; George voted for two of the plans. Unlike 1945, none of these three spoke on the plans. On the three plans, twenty Democrats (36 percent) voted for all three plans; three of the twenty were Southerners (15 percent of the twenty).

Truman had not deliberately misled the Southerners. When he took office, he believed that government was too big and too disorganized and that he could do something about it. He viewed the executive branch from outside, as a moderate border state senator. But as president, he began to switch constituencies from the Senate and Missouri to the executive branch and the nation. Also, he became more sophisticated in his attitude toward government. In 1945, the immensity of the task he inherited shocked and overwhelmed him. He turned to reorganization as a comfortable program he was familiar with and as a tool to help make his burden manageable. By 1946, he became more confident that he could handle the presidency without the politically costly reorganization that he had first envisioned.

The first evaluations of Truman's 1946 plans proved rather critical. The administration itself referred to them as technical proposals,[113] and a columnist who specialized on the federal bureaucracy charged that they were "notoriously weak."[114] A scholar later characterized them as "comparatively minor," partly because of failure of courage on Truman's part.[115] Truman paved the way for these criticisms by raising expectations to high levels in 1945 then submitting plans that he himself admitted lacked dramatic quality.[116] Truman's courage did fail in the sense that he had come to believe that deep-cutting reorganization was often not worth the political costs.[117] Therefore, he eliminated such controversial proposals as reform of the Civil Service Commission.[118]

However, the difficulty with evaluating these plans went deeper than their lack of drama. Part of the problem with appraising such proposals stemmed from the mistaken assumptions many held concerning the process of reorganization. Most people regarded money savings as the most important goal of administrative reform. When a congressman remarked to a budget official that it would be refreshing if an administrator would admit, just once, that a reorganization plan would not save money, the official replied: "It might be refreshing but it might also be disastrous."[119] In contrast to the public concern that reorganization should save money, public administrators believed that attempting to sell reorganization on the basis of savings was "a snare and a delusion."[120] The fact that presidents specified savings in only three of eighty-six plans submitted from 1949 to 1969 indicated that savings stemmed from eliminating services, not from reorganization.[121] A public administrator concluded: "It is extremely difficult to predict how much, if anything, can be saved by a major reorganization, and it is impossible to prove, after the fact, how much, if any, has been saved."[122]

Doubt also developed about the real achievements to be expected. Frank Pace, Jr., who as budget director helped formulate Truman's reorganization program, admitted: "I have often found that reorganizations, generally speaking, involve the same people, and possibly new titles, but don't really change the basic function."[123] Budget official Harold Seidman said that for the "true believer" reorganization can solve everything from curing sick industries to eliminating crime in the streets: "The myth persists that we can resolve deep-seated and intractable issues of substance by reorganization."[124] One scholar claimed that "there is increasing doubt that the so often widely hailed reorganization does all or even most of the things claimed for it."[125]

Government structure reflected the structure of power in our society. Changing organizations usually did not change these power relationships. If an interest group had been strong enough to dominate an agency in one location it would probably dominate it in another. After making a case study of a controversial agency transfer, an investigator concluded that the politics of reorganization were often based on a myth that such a transfer would bring change. Interest groups and legislators who opposed the change underestimated their own power and ability to maintain the status quo regardless of agency location.[126]

It was also difficult to determine criteria to use in evaluating specific reorganizations. Classical public administration doctrine supposedly provided scientific criteria to use in formulation of administrative reform proposals, but actually these principles proved to be subjective, not capable of objective proof.[127] They were of little help in evaluating reorganization plans. One scholar held that the real goals of reorganization constituted the yardstick with which to measure the effectiveness of a reorganization.[128] But in Truman's proposals the real goals were often unstated,[129] and their perception varied from one party to another—the president, Bureau of Budget officials, affected agency heads, legislators who were consulted during the decisionmaking process, clientele groups, and others. "The actual purposes [of a transfer of programs] as well as the effects of transfer are often obscure."[130] Inability to know the real purpose of a reorganization made it difficult to determine its effectiveness.

Many of these generalizations applied to the 1946 program, which was unusually hard to evaluate because the plans provided for technical administrative changes. The reasons for the individual changes were often obscure, even to Budget Bureau officials who drafted them. One official said "it was difficult to see the exact impetus which carried certain proposals into Plans."[131] Another admitted that several items turned out to be defective technically or definitely undesirable because of the difficulty of knowing what the proposal really was and what it would do.[132]

Steps taken by the administration to compromise the plans before they went into effect further complicated matters. Senator McCarran refused to support plan three until a presidential assistant agreed to support a bill to modify certain provisions of the plan.[133] Truman and Watson Miller made concessions to Children's Bureau Director Lenroot that blunted part of the goals that plan two had been designed to achieve.[134]

The impact of the reorganizations also varied from agency to agency. In an unusual move the Grazing Service had committed "suicide" by asking that it be merged into the Bureau of Land Management. The bureau officials did this because they wanted to gain a wider constituency in order to break the hold of western stockmen over the agency.[135] Other agencies found the 1946 changes less happy. As late as 1949, the Children's Bureau still bore the scars of its transfer to FSA and resentment and suspicion still existed.[136] In 1963, a social security official found adverse effects still stemming from the abolition of the Social Security Board.[137] But generally, the 1946 plans were effective in maintaining arrangements that had been found useful during the war. While they did not meet expectations raised by Truman's 1945 statements and actions, they did provide for limited administrative reform.

Chapter 6

Reorganization and
the Eightieth Congress

The Republican-controlled Eightieth Congress occupied a peculiar place in the history of Truman's reorganization program. Although it defeated two of the four plans he submitted to it, it authorized an important housing reorganization plan and established the Commission on Organization of the Executive Branch of Government (the Hoover Commission), which led to some of Truman's most important reorganization achievements.

In his 1947 State of the Union message, Truman appealed for cooperation between the executive and Congress,[1] commencing a period of good relations during the first several months of the session.[2] This harmony soon waned, and by mid-May yielded to bitter conflict.[3] Inevitably this development affected Truman's reorganization program. Republican congressmen were determined to reduce the power of the executive branch.[4] Hostility to bureaucracy, widespread since the late 1930s, increased. Congress investigated many of the executive branch activities, established the Hoover Commission to examine its organization, and tried to minimize Truman's authority over its functions and officers.[5]

If Truman faced more political uncertainty in 1947 and 1948, he at least received more consistent staff support than in the past. The Bureau of the Budget no longer had to compete with OWMR for control of the reorganization program. The president also had an able new budget director in James Webb, who headed the bureau during 1947 and 1948. Smith had assembled the most capable staff in Washington but had not been able to win Truman's complete trust. Webb was dedicated to the task of regaining for the bureau the status it enjoyed during the Roosevelt administration when Smith had been so influential. A man of great drive and energy with a reputation for integrity, he succeeded in winning Truman's confidence.[6]

Determined to avoid the chaos that had surrounded the preparation of the 1946 plans, the Bureau of the Budget began to develop its proposals for the following year in August 1946. Political considerations remained overriding. Early proposals included such controversial ones as creating a transportation agency,[7] but Budget Bureau officials, already anticipating the Republican capture of Congress, realized that "political and general strategy considerations" would exclude such plans.[8] Webb wanted to deal with some of the broad, controversial organizational problems, but he told other budget officials "that the political advisors of the President would probably feel that this was an unwise move at the present time, since they are attempting to play down controversial issues."[9]

With much less confusion and indecision than in 1946, Truman submitted three plans to Congress, plan one and two on 1 May and plan three on 27 May. Plan one, which contained many routine and minor reorganizations, continued certain arrangements made under the First War Powers Act, including several provisions from the defeated plan one of 1946.[10] It aroused little opposition and went into effect after sixty days without debate and a vote.

Truman regarded plan two as especially important. It retained permanently in the Department of Labor the U.S. Employment Service (USES), which Truman had temporarily located in the department under the authority of the First War Powers Act.[11] Beleaguered by hostile forces throughout its history, the department had struggled for survival for years, and by 1933 had managed to accumulate enough activities to justify its existence. However, after 1933 two patterns emerged: Congress established new independent labor agencies (such as the National Labor Relations Board) outside the department and it removed other agencies (such as USES and the Immigration and Naturalization Service) that it had earlier placed within the department.[12] By the end of Secretary Frances Perkins's tenure in 1945, the Department of Labor retained only a few important functions, including the Children's Bureau, the Bureau of Labor Statistics, and the Conciliation Service. It became increasingly important for the department to acquire USES, especially since plan two of 1946 further weakened it by removing the Children's Bureau and since the Eightieth Congress removed the Conciliation Service.

The nature of USES created obstacles for those trying to decide where it belonged. The Wagner-Peyser Act of 1933 provided for a system of public employment offices to be administered by the states with financial assistance from the national government. It also created USES, empowered the new agency to administer the national aspects of the program, and located it within the Department of Labor. However, by 1935 only twenty-five states, in cooperation with USES, had established public employment offices, and only 184 local offices existed.

Then, central to the history of USES, the Social Security Act of 1935 established a federal-state system of unemployment insurance, administered by the Social Security Board, an independent agency. To insure that applicants received compensation only if suitable jobs were unavailable, the Social Security Board ruled that unemployment benefits would be paid only through public employment offices. All the states then set up public employment systems.

The activities carried out by unemployment compensation officials and by employment service officials were intertwined. However, administrative problems developed because the federal government divided the two programs between the Department of Labor and the Social Security Board.[13] In 1939, after several studies had recommended unification of the two functions, Roosevelt transferred USES from the Department of Labor to the Social Security Board and placed both within the new Federal Security Agency.[14]

When the United States entered World War II, Roosevelt requested that the states transfer administration of the employment service to the national government, and in September 1942, he transferred USES to the War Manpower Commission where it remained until September 1945. Under the authority of the First War Powers Act, Truman temporarily moved USES to the Department of Labor, and in November 1946, Congress transferred administration of the state public employment offices back to the states.[15]

This was the situation when the Truman administration began to study the complex problem of USES's permanent location. Some planners wanted to leave both unemployment compensation and the employment service in FSA, a position that Roosevelt had taken in 1939. Others wanted to place USES in the Department of Labor and leave unemployment insurance in FSA; Truman did that temporarily in 1945 and tried to do it permanently with plan two. Some advisers wanted to place both functions within the Department of Labor; Congress finally adopted that solution in 1949.

Executive officials had the problem under study when Truman took office in 1945. In late 1944, Secretary Perkins had urged that all labor functions scattered outside the Department of Labor be returned at the end of the war. She argued that the nation needed a strong USES to handle employment problems during demobilization of the armed forces and to aid in reassigning wage earners from war to peacetime jobs.[16] Other administrators who viewed full employment as a major postwar goal also argued that such an endeavor required a strong Department of Labor that encompassed USES.[17]

The Bureau of the Budget developed a different position on USES. Bureau staff member Raymond C. Atkinson brilliantly analyzed the issues involved. He pointed to the difficulty of drawing a line between functions of the Department of Labor and those of FSA. He regarded it as impractical to place all activities classifiable as labor within the Department of Labor. He recommended, therefore, transforming it into a department of industrial relations and transferring labor relations agencies, such as the National Labor Relations Board, to the redesignated department. Atkinson recommended moving other agencies, such as USES and the Children's Bureau, to FSA, because he believed the nation needed a strong FSA in order to develop further its social welfare functions.[18]

The Atkinson approach gained powerful support when Budget Director Smith declared that USES belonged in FSA.[19] In early June 1945, he told Truman that the problem of where to locate USES in relation to the future department of welfare troubled him,[20] and on 1 July Smith disclosed his position to Secretary of Labor Schwellenbach.[21]

Both Schwellenbach and Smith began to press Truman for a decision.[22] Actually, the determination had largely been made when Truman appointed Schwellenbach as secretary of labor. Insiders believed that the president had given him a free hand over departmental organization.[23] Truman later recalled that he had told the prospective secretary that he wanted to rebuild a "real" Department of Labor by restoring to it functions that had been moved elsewhere.[24] With this mandate from Truman, Schwellenbach moved to achieve what an associate said was the secretary's dream: "A centralized and integrated Department of Labor with all the major labor functions coordinated through the Department."[25] He regarded reorganization, including the capture of USES, as his first and most important task.[26]

In April 1946, Schwellenbach urged a reorganization that would transfer to the Department of Labor a number of functions.[27] But Truman soon disappointed his friend. The secretary, already angry because he had not been able to get control of the National Labor Relations Board during an earlier reorganization,[28] exploded when plan two further stripped his department of activities.[29] Schwellenbach reacted immediately. Poor organization of labor functions, he warned, had been an important political issue in the 1944 campaign. He repeated earlier requests he had made for the transfer of USES and other functions to his jurisdiction and added: "The above recommendations are matters, which, in my judgment, do not require further length of study. The issues are well known and the proposals do not raise complicated technical problems of transfer."[30]

The conflict surfaced again as the administration began preparing its 1947 plans. The FSA administrator and the secretary of labor each requested transfer of USES to his own agency.[31] Truman gave the first indication of his decision in his state of the economy message by warning against subordinating the placement service to unemployment insurance.[32] The Bureau of the Budget still resisted,[33] but it lost the struggle when its new director, James Webb, recommended transfer of USES to the Department of Labor.[34]

In his message to Congress on plan two, Truman said that the Department of Labor should continue to engage in the most basic of all labor activities—assisting workers in getting jobs and employers in obtaining labor. The policies and operations of USES, he said, must be determined in relation to overall labor standards, labor statistics, labor training, and labor law—all requiring specialized knowledge centered in the Department of Labor. Truman's plan left unemployment compensation in FSA.

Republican Clare Hoffman (Michigan), new chairman of the House Committee on Expenditures in the Executive Departments, held hearings on plan two in late May. An "archconservative," Hoffman opposed the legislative veto partly because it broke with long-established precedent: "This is a new (perhaps unconstitutional) method of legislating," he wrote committee members.[35] Delegation of reorganization authority to the president also symbolized to Hoffman an unacceptable shift of power from Congress to the executive branch. In addition, as a strongly partisan Republican, he opposed reorganization plans partly because Truman submitted them.[36]

Republican control of Congress threatened any presidential plan but especially plan two because it benefited labor, a bloc associated with the Democratic party.[37] However, even if the Democrats had retained control of Congress, plan two would have been in trouble. Because of strikes and other economic problems, public opinion had seldom been more hostile to labor.[38] The Senate, for example, debated plan two only a few days after it overrode Truman's veto of the Taft-Hartley Act.

In addition, the Department of Labor's status as a clientele agency endangered any plan that benefited it. Former AFL President Samuel Gomper characterized the department as "Labor's Voice in the Cabinet." Many people believed that this clientele arrangement prevented impartial administration.[39] Business groups feared placing in the Department of Labor activities that involved discretionary authority, especially functions such as unemployment compensation that directly affected business interests.[40]

Even pro-labor legislators did not always support reorganization proposals favorable to the Department of Labor. They regarded positive labor legislation as more important than departmental jurisdiction. They would not endanger a labor bill merely to insure that the department would administer its provisions.[41] Nor could the department count on its own clientele to give it full support on organizational problems. Unions also considered labor legislation more important than bureaucratic jurisdiction. Union spokesmen called for unification of all labor functions in the Department of Labor but seldom made that a major objective.[42] Neither the AFL nor the CIO testified for plan two before the House committee, for example.

During the hearings before Hoffman's committee, opponents quickly attacked the plan's most vulnerable feature. One asked Webb if disagreement existed within the Bureau of the Budget as to whether USES should be in the Department of Labor or the FSA. Webb frankly admitted that disagreement did persist: "This is a close question," he added.[43] Executive branch discord became obvious when several top FSA officials testified that they had recommended unification of the two functions within FSA and still believed in this approach, although they accepted the president's decision.[44] Opponents exploited this disunity among executive officials.

The most active opposition to plan two came from state officials who feared that the Department of Labor wanted to nationalize the state employment services as had occurred during the war. Stanley Rector represented the Interstate Conference of Employment Security Agencies, an organization of top state officials. The conference opposed plan two, he said, because it severed at the federal level two closely related functions. A poll conducted by the conference indicated that the administrators in thirty-three states opposed the plan.[45]

Opposition from state officials was important because when congressmen found it difficult to judge the merits of a proposal they became especially vulnerable to pressure from interested groups.[46] Organizational problems were complex, and plan two, by separating two related functions, was especially hard to justify from an administrative point of view. Therefore, congressmen readily responded to the criticism of officials from their home states who plausibly explained why Congress should defeat the plan.[47]

On 2 June, Hoffman reported that his committee had rejected plan two,[48] and on 10 June the full House debated the proposal. The plan's political weaknesses now became apparent. The politics of reorganization required the administration to avoid providing extraneous issues that legislators could use to destroy a plan; the administration always tried to place opponents in the position of having to vote openly to deny the chief executive control over the organization of the executive branch. Plan two faced special difficulties because it allowed too many oblique ways to oppose it. It was administratively weak because it separated two closely related functions: the employment service and unemployment compensation. Roosevelt, Schwellenbach, and Federal Security Administrator Watson Miller had all advocated unifying the two functions. It delighted Republicans to be able to quote Roosevelt to justify voting against Truman's plan.

However, the plan's merits aside, opponents had no intention of approving a presidential attempt to rebuild the Department of Labor. The highly partisan debate consisted mainly of extraneous comments and unsupported charges, mixed with some slightly relevant discussion of the plan's provisions. Following this brief discussion, the House rejected plan two without a record vote.[49]

Sen. Joseph H. Ball (a Republican from Minnesota), chairman of the labor subcommittee of the Senate Labor and Public Welfare Committee, presided over the Senate hearings on plan two, which took place on 16, 17 July. Webb defended the plan. USES belonged in the Department of Labor, he said, because it would benefit from being with other labor functions and because the proposed reorganization rightly placed strong emphasis on providing jobs rather than on paying unemployment compensation.[50] But Senator Ball quickly cut through to the heart of the problem. Truman had been faced with three alternatives, Ball said. He could have combined both functions either in FSA or in the Department of Labor, or he could have divided them between the two agencies. Ball suggested that Truman had avoided making the tough decision involved in either of the first two alternatives and had taken the easy way out by choosing the third. He implied that Truman had not based his decision on rational administrative grounds but had sought an easy compromise. Webb, "thrashing about somewhat desperately," did not give a very convincing answer to Ball.[51]

As the hearings closed, the Republican majority was "preponderantly" hostile to plan two, but on 20 June the committee reported it favorably. "This unexpected development," one scholar wrote, "can probably be explained only in terms of the individualistic personality of Senator Ball."[52] Ball, who had been openly hostile to the plan, had changed his position. The committee report said that the employment service was clearly a labor function and should be in the Department of Labor. Placing the employment service in the department emphasized finding jobs rather than paying compensation and lessened the possibility of neglecting the employment needs of groups not covered by unemployment compensation.[53]

Plan two was presented to the Senate on 30 June. Hysteria over labor problems and actions had reached its peak. "The boys are driving with a black snake whip at the moment, and only some intelligent voting will change things," wrote a Labor Department official.[54]

During the debate, supporters stressed the need to rebuild the Department of Labor and argued that moving USES to the Department of Labor rightly placed emphasis on finding jobs rather than paying unemployment compensation to the jobless.[55] Opponents argued that the plan was administratively weak because it separated two closely related functions.[56] Powerful Democratic Sen. Harry Byrd strengthened the opposition when he joined in the attack and spoke on reorganization for the first time since he led the fight to give Truman reorganization authority in 1945. "I have carefully examined this reorganization plan," he said, "It would not save a single dollar. It would not result in the dismissal of a single Government employee." Byrd said that Congress granted reorganization authority to Truman "primarily" as a means of effecting economies.[57]

After this short debate, the Senate narrowly rejected plan two, with 42 votes against and 40 for. Six Democrats voted against the plan and thirty-three voted for it. Thirty-six Republicans voted negatively and seven Republicans voted for the plan. Five of the six opposing Democrats represented Southern states. The Republican supporters included such moderates and liberals as Ball, Langer (North Dakota), Morse (Oregon), Aiken (Vermont), and Flanders (Vermont).[58]

Truman submitted his third plan on 27 May. Plan three included the most important features of the defeated 1946 housing scheme. Truman reminded Congress that the task of providing adequate housing would be a major national objective during the next decade. Even though Congress had various measures under consideration, the nation needed immediately a permanent agency to coordinate and supervise the administration of housing programs. Truman also pointed out that with the termination of the First War Powers Act, the functions gathered temporarily into the National Housing Agency would be scattered among thirteen agencies. Plan three would prevent that.[59]

Plan three modified in certain respects the defeated plan one of 1946. By December 1946, the administration, led by Raymond Foley, the new national housing administrator, had begun to move away from the concept embodied in the first plan—that of a unified housing agency headed by a single administrator with real control over government housing activities.[60] Compared to plan one, the new plan sharply limited the authority of the housing administrator. It brought most housing functions into a unified body to be called the Housing and Home Finance Agency (HHFA). HHFA would have three constituent units: the Home Loan Bank Board (to administer the Federal Savings and Loan Insurance Corporation, Home Owner's Loan Corporation, and Federal Home Loan Bank System), the Federal Housing Administration, and the Public Housing Administration (to replace the U.S. Housing Authority). Each unit, Truman said, would retain its individual identity and responsibility for the operation of its programs. The president, with Senate confirmation, would appoint both the head of HHFA and the top officials of the constituent units. This meant that the subordinate officials within HHFA would have authority independent from the administrator. It would also give the relevant interest groups more security in their relationships with the constituent units. The HHFA administrator had responsibility for "general supervision and coordination" of the agency's constituent units. The plan also established an advisory council that included representatives from the constituent units of HHFA and from other agencies that administered housing activities.[61]

On 9 June, the House committee began hearings on plan three. The American Legion and the Chamber of Commerce opposed the proposal, but strongest opposition came from representatives of the National Association of Real Estate Boards, Commercial Industry Association of New York, National Association of Home Builders, and American Institute of Architects. They fought it on the same grounds as the year before. The changes Truman made did not eliminate their fear of a housing czar or of government control over the industry.[62]

However, the administration received support from the National Savings and Loan League, a competitor of the larger U.S. Savings and Loan League. Cognizant that the National Savings and Loan group had opposed plan one in 1946, Truman's advisers consulted it while formulating the revised scheme and accepted its advice to reestablish the Federal Home Loan Bank Board.[63] The U.S. Savings and Loan League moderated its opposition also, at least publicly. The savings and loan groups believed they could dominate the FHLBB under the reorganizational arrangement.

The committee reported plan three unfavorably,[64] and on 18 June Hoffman, with Manasco's agreement, brought it up for vote in the late afternoon with the chamber almost deserted. After limiting debate to five minutes, Hoffman turned the floor over to Manasco who said a few words. The House then immediately rejected the plan without a record vote.[65]

On 18 June, hearings on plan three opened before the Senate Committee on Banking and Currency, chaired by Charles Tobey (a Republican from

New Hampshire). Raymond Foley and other housing officials provided the main supporting testimony. Foley stressed that HHFA constituent units would retain their independence and that in comparison to the existing organization (and to plan one of 1946) the head of HHFA would have little power.[66]

The various housing interest groups again testified against the plan, but on 30 June the Committee on Banking and Currency reported plan three favorably. The committee report praised the plan for balancing the need for central responsibility with the desirability of preserving the individual identity of the operating agencies.[67]

The Eightieth Congress seldom responded favorably to presidential initiative on domestic legislation, but it did approve this plan when the Senate failed to veto it. Truman's willingness to modify the defeated 1946 plan helped gain his victory in 1947.[68] His appointment of a new national housing administrator was also important. In 1946 when Congress defeated the first plan, Wilson Wyatt, a liberal former mayor of Louisville, Kentucky, headed the housing agency.[69] Wyatt based his program on the premise that the housing crisis could be solved only by continuing, and expanding, wartime emergency controls.[70] But under attack from congressmen, interest groups, and executive branch officials, Wyatt lost Truman's support and resigned in December 1946.[71] Truman remainded committed to the vision of providing decent housing for all Americans, but he developed new means for achieving that goal. "Most noticeable in this new program," wrote a historian, "was the favorable attitude taken toward the business community."[72]

In line with this new approach, Truman appointed Foley as the national housing administrator. Historian Richard O. Davies believed that Congress was aware that Foley would head the new agency and thus prevented the defeat of plan three.[73] Many critics regarded Foley as an unimaginative man, but during long service with FHA he had proved to be an able, efficient administrator. He recognized the need for public housing but held that private enterprise remainded the key to a healthy housing industry. "By appointing Foley to head the housing administration," Davies wrote, "Truman gained the confidence of the industry that his Administration would not attempt to do anything to usurp the industry's position."[74]

Foley's approach also helped him win the confidence of Taft, whose attitude toward the plan became crucial as the Senate prepared to vote. "Senator Taft is reported to be in favor of the President's plan," wrote a housing lobbyist, "if he undertakes to back it agressively, defeating it will be very difficult."[75] Taft's support gave the bill crucial bipartisan support, and his conservative reputation helped offset charges that the plan was socialistic. Most important, a bloc of Republicans, mainly from urban states, consistently followed Taft's leadership on this issue.[76]

Taft had long supported public housing. He regarded decent shelter as the key to healthy family life and good citizenship but believed that business lacked resources to fully meet housing needs. However, he also opposed anything that would allow the public endeavor to encroach on private industry.[77] The modifications the administration made in the 1946 plan (which Taft had helped defeat) and Foley's attitude toward private housing gave Taft those assurances.

Despite Taft's support, segments of the housing industry continued its bitter fight against the plan. In late June, Truman attacked the "real estate lobby." "This group," he said, "has sought to achieve financial gains without regard to the damage done to others. It has displayed a ruthless disregard of the public welfare."[78] A North Carolina savings and loan league official urged members to contact their senators and to lobby other groups such as local chambers of commerce and real-estate boards.[79] California savings and loan league officials gave Sen. William F. Knowland (a Republican from California) a list of names of men who had assisted him in his last election and who now opposed plan three.[80] The implication was obvious. Another group sent Sen. Scott Lucas (a Democrat representing Illinois) a list of "substantial people" in Illinois who opposed the plan.[81] A savings and loan official in New Hampshire tried to influence Senator Tobey by enlisting the aid of Tobey's son.[82] A Kansas official reflected the arrogance of the U.S. Savings and Loan League. He bragged that "my two Senators voted according to their instructions from me."[83]

As the vote neared, the Republican attitude became crucial. The Republican National Committee was opposed to the plan,[84] but then Foley learned that "Republican Leaders" had decided to allow it to pass.[85] Three Republicans led the floor fight for the plan: Taft, Flanders, and Tobey. Louisiana Sen. Allen Ellender also offered important support. Most Southern members of the House of Representatives opposed housing legislation, but many Southern senators, who as representatives of urban areas had become increasingly aware of housing problems, supported general housing legislation. Ellender believed housing to be the most important domestic postwar problem.[86]

Taft summarized the main arguments for the plan: that the housing agencies could not be allowed to revert to their previous disorganized state, that private housing advocates did not have to fear public housing activities of HHFA because such activities had to be approved by Congress, and that top administrators of HHFA only had power to supervise and coordinate housing activities.[87]

After a short debate, the Senate upheld Truman's plan with a vote of 47 to 38. Six Democrats, all from the West or South, voted against it; thirty-five for it. Twelve Republicans voted for it and thirty-two against.[88]

Most surprising was the unity among the Democrats. Seventy-seven percent of the Southern Democrats voted for the plan compared to 78 percent of the non-Southern Democrats. One year earlier when the Senate voted on the 1946 housing plan, only 27 percent of the Southern Democrats voted for it compared to 62 percent of the non-Southern Democrats. On that vote, 45 percent of the Southern Democrats voted against the plan compared to 21 percent of the non-Southern Democrats. Republican support for the housing plan showed a less dramatic change: 8 percent voted for the 1946 plan and 21 percent supported the 1947 plan.

Truman's plan made permanent the temporary unification of housing functions achieved during the war. According to Davies:

> The establishment of the Housing and Home Finance Agency on a permanent basis was an important event in the history of housing reform. The decision to create a permanent agency to conduct an active governmental housing policy was the culmination of various forces working at the local, state, and national levels for over a century. The pioneering efforts of such men as Jacob Riis, Lawrence Veiller, and Robert Wagner had eventually led to the establishment of HHFA.[89]

The plan also prepared the way for the creation of the Department of Housing and Urban Development, which took place in 1965. However, Truman's inability to provide for unified administration of the agency reflected the centrifugal forces that later presidents could not overcome. These forces continued to hamper the development of a meaningful program even as housing conditions deteriorated. HUD became the most troubled of all the departments.

In 1948, Truman submitted only one reorganization plan. He turned again to the problem of rebuilding the Department of Labor, which had been left in a dismal state after the defeat of plan two. "What the future holds here in the Department is anyone's guess," wrote Assistant Secretary of Labor John Gibson, and he added: "We certainly have taken a rough ride in the Congress this year."[90] Not only had Congress refused to transfer USES permanently to the Department of Labor but had also removed the Conciliation Service. If the department did not get unemployment compensation from FSA, warned one of Gibson's friends, "you'll have to use the [Labor Department] building for a rooming house."[91]

Although Congress defeated plan two, the president remained committed to transferring USES to the Labor Department.[92] However, Truman still faced the problem of where to place unemployment compensation. The president accepted the administrative sense of the contention by plan two's opponents that compensation and employment responsibilities belonged in the same executive unit. He decided, therefore, to transfer both USES and the Bureau of Employment Security (BES), which administered unemployment compensation, from FSA to the Department of Labor. He submitted plan one of 1948 to Congress on 19 January. "Both the employment service and the unemployment compensation system are concerned with the worker as a member of the labor force," said Truman. Both activities, he believed, would benefit from being in the Department of Labor.[93]

On 20 January 1948, Clare Hoffman introduced a resolution against plan one, and his committee began hearings on 5 February. The hearings and subsequent debates were stormy. Executive-legislative relations rapidly deteriorated during the second session of the Eightieth Congress, with both sides maneuvering for advantage as the 1948 election approached.[94] Plan one had particular political implications because Truman intended to blame destruction of the Department of Labor on the Republicans.[95]

Hoffman found allies among Southern Democrats. Truman's civil-rights message of 2 February 1948 had already inflamed Southern congressmen.[96] They could retaliate directly against the president by rejecting his reorganization proposal. A Department of Labor official pointedly described the direct link between the civil-rights uproar and the plan's fortunes. He wrote:

> The Southern revolt over the President's Civil Rights Program, which was certainly a courageous document, created a real problem for us, since they are charging that we will set up an FEPC by regulation, if the Unemployment Compensation and USES is placed in the Department of Labor under Reorganization Plan No. 1.[97]

During the hearings and floor debate, opponents argued particularly that Truman's plan conflicted with FDR's 1939 proposal. In addition, since the new plan placed unemployment compensation functions under the secretary, the Department of Labor's clientele status became even more of an issue in 1948 than in 1947. Another new, very compelling attack also developed. In 1947, Congress created the Commission on Organization of the Executive Branch of the Government (Hoover Commission). Congress had directed the commission to report after the 1948 election, and many argued that organizational changes should be delayed until then.

Republican Congressman Forest A. Harness (Indiana) brought up a point that others developed into a major attack. He suggested that the Department of Labor, responding to labor union pressure, would use its control over USES to liberalize the definition of job suitability in order to greatly increase the number of people eligible for unemployment compensation. Unemployment compensation applicants, for example, might be allowed to refuse jobs that paid less than union scale. He ignored Webb's answer that the states determined job suitability. Harness said that since the Department of Labor would control the funds it could influence state regulations.[98]

Business groups opposed the plan even more strongly than the year before because they feared having the unemployment compensation program in the Department of Labor.[99] They also feared that the department would change the merit or experience rating system. Merit rating allowed an employer to pay a lower unemployment compensation tax on his payroll if he stabilized employment. Organized labor opposed merit rating, and business feared this meant that the Department of Labor would use its influence to change or destroy the system.[100] Business organizations argued that USES and BES should be in a neutral agency.

A majority of the committee voted to reject the plan,[101] and on 25 February Hoffman brought it to the House floor. Representatives discussed it very briefly and then rejected it without a record vote.[102]

Next, plan one came before Ball's subcommittee on labor of the Labor and Public Welfare Committee. After hearing testimony similar to that before the House,[103] the committee voted to support the plan. The majority report stated that since all witnesses supported unification of the two functions, only one issue existed: in which department should the functions be located? No evidence refuted the president's argument that the two functions closely related to others in the Department of Labor, and no one presented evidence to show they had any relation to FSA programs. The report concluded that opponents had not produced data to sustain even one instance of anti-business bias.[104]

The Senate debate on 16 March rehashed all the issues discussed over the last two years. In addition, in order to frighten Southern Democrats, opponents charged that a vote for the program constituted, in effect, a vote for the fair employment policy that Truman had included in his civil-rights program.[105] Other opponents said that any organizational changes should await the Hoover Commission report, although Republican Sen. George Aiken, a member of the commission, assured the Senate that the entire commission agreed that its work should not delay the president's reorganization program.[106]

Although few senators spoke against the plan, the Senate decisively rejected it, 58 votes against and 25 votes for.[107] Thirty-nine Republicans voted against it and five for. Nineteen Democrats voted against it and twenty for.

The Senate had defeated plan two in 1947, which also proposed transferring USES to the Department of Labor, by only two votes—42 to 40. In 1947, 59 percent of the Southern Democrats voted for the plan, and 23 percent against it, with 18 percent not voting. In 1948, this support slipped to 27 percent for and 68 percent against. The abrupt drop in support for the plan among Southern Democrats can largely be accounted for by the fact that the 1948 vote took place only a few weeks after Truman's civil-rights message. Indeed, five Southern senators who had promised the administration to vote for plan one later reneged.[108]

However, factors other than Southern anger over civil rights were involved. In 1947, 87 percent of non-Southern Democrats supported the plan, compared to 61 percent in 1948. Increased business pressure, with concern over possible Department of Labor bias, was probably crucial here. This concern was more pressing in 1948 than in 1947 because the latter plan attempted to transfer unemployment compensation, as well as USES.

The Republican party's position remained more stable than that of the Democrats. In 1947, 71 percent of the Republican senators voted against the plan compared to 76 percent in 1948. The Republicans, with their Southern Democrat allies, had proved a formidable obstacle to Truman's program.

However, the Republican Congress had given Truman important victories by passing plan one in 1947, which included many technical administrative improvements, and plan three in 1947, which created a unified housing agency and which was a significant step toward a housing department. Ironically, both plans had been struck down by the Democratic Congress in 1946. This Republican Congress also created the Hoover Commission, and the administration soon gained an unexpected new ally, Herbert Hoover, who it would try to use to offset Republican opposition.

Chapter 7

Truman and the Hoover Commission

Following World War II, the administrative structure previously developed to carry out New Deal reform measures proved vulnerable to attack. Although segments of the population supported individual programs, they had yet to reconcile themselves to the permanent existence of big government. They believed that government had expanded only temporarily in response to the depression and war crises. As an expression of this attitude, the Republican Eightieth Congress created the Commission on Organization of the Executive Branch (the Hoover Commission) to prepare for the Republican housecleaning that it anticipated would follow the 1948 election. Republican leaders intended to use the commission to spearhead a concerted attack on New Deal reform programs. However, the Truman administration thwarted this strategy by molding the commission into an instrument for ratifying, rather than destroying, New Deal innovations. Instead of trying to end the surge of government activities, the commission, led by Herbert C. Hoover, concentrated on making the existing structure work better.

On 10 January 1947, Republican Congressman Clarence Brown (Ohio) introduced a bill to create a commission to study the administrative structure of the executive branch, and three days later Sen. Henry Cabot Lodge (a Republican from Massachusetts) proposed a duplicate measure. Throughout 1946, Brown had studied the reorganization problem.[1] He believed that previous efforts to effect administrative reform demonstrated that giving the president authority to reorganize the executive branch yielded few results. He, therefore, decided that the most promising approach was to create a blue-ribbon commission charged with two tasks: to make a study of the present government organization and, equally important, to generate public support for the recommendations coming from that study. Strong public backing for the commission's proposals might then enable the president to use his reorganization authority with more significant results.[2]

Brown wanted to create a body capable of attracting the broadest possible support, both inside and outside the government. His bill required the president, the speaker of the house, and the president pro tempore of the Senate each to appoint four members to the commission. Each group of four had to include two Democrats and two Republicans, with a balanced mixture of two from public life and two from private life. To further reduce chances of partisanship, Brown provided that the commission would not report until after the 1948 election.[3]

In addition to establishing this procedure, the bill included a declaration of policy that gave the commission almost unlimited authority to examine and make recommendations concerning virtually every aspect of government service, including abolishing activities "not necessary to the efficient conduct of government" and "defining and limiting executive functions, services, and activities."[4]

The Senate Committee on Expenditures in the Executive Departments held hearings on 13 March. Administration figures at first opposed the bill but later reluctantly supported it.[5] Some officials believed that there was no need for the commission because organizational theory and immediate organizational goals were already well established.[6] Others feared that the bill had some "partisan objective."[7] Moreover, some advisers believed that the president's ability to rule was already tenuous because of the Republican control of Congress. They feared creating a powerful group that, backed by Congress, might start undercutting the president's authority.[8]

Budget Director Webb, whose agency had primary responsibility for organizational matters, expressed this ambivalent executive branch attitude. In a letter to the committee chairman, he explained the Bureau of the Budget view of reorganization as a continuous process rather than a one-shot affair and argued that the best hope for organizational reform lay in improving and extending the Reorganization Act of 1945, which gave the president authority to effect structural change subject to congressional veto. However, Webb, who had consulted with Truman, promised that if the bill passed the administration would cooperate fully.[9]

The House hearings, held on 25 June by the Committee on Expenditures in the Executive Departments, drew testimony that indicated the Truman administration had good reason to be apprehensive about the proposed study. John W. Hanes and T. Jefferson Coolidge, both former undersecretaries of the treasury, supported the bill. Hanes said the task was to "shrink big Government" and to insist on an end to "easy, lush spending." Coolidge stressed that the American system was based on private initiative and local governments rather than "Central Government control."[10]

Several other witnesses reflected a distinctly business-oriented, conservative philosophy. Walter D. Fuller, president of the Curtis Publishing Company, said he assumed that commission members would conduct a cost analysis of each unit of government and use the results to determine whether the unit would be abolished or maintained. Lewis H. Brown, chairman of the board of Johns-Mansville Corporation, stated that it was time to cut government growth by one-half. James A. Adams, president of Standard Brands, asserted that a 25 percent reduction in government personnel would lead to a 50 percent increase in efficiency.[11]

In late June, both committees reported. The House committee briefly described the bill and unanimously recommended its passage.[12] The Senate committee, responding to the developing Cold War, linked international considerations with the need for reorganization:

The committee cannot ignore the prevailing misery and economic chaos in the world today. It cannot ignore the suggestions of new and horrible wars. It cannot ignore old nations going under and new ones arising. It cannot shut its eyes to the saturation of population, coupled with the exhaustion of national resources. The conclusion is inescapable that the only force left in the world today which is able to counteract these deadly trends is the United States, acting through its Government. The effectiveness of our Federal Government involves the issue of life and death for ourselves and for the world. The committee, in recommending the enactment of this bill, recognizes that any steps which are taken to increase the operational efficiency of our Government is not only a step toward economy, but is also a step toward peace.[13]

Congress debated the Lodge-Brown bill in late June, and, with almost no discussion, it passed unanimously in both the houses.[14]

The "tripartite monstrosity," as a commission member later called it,[15] began to take shape on 7 July 1947 when Republican Arthur Vandenberg (Michigan), president pro tempore of the Senate, announced his appointments. The background of the twelve commissioners reveals the opportunities and hazards that the Truman administration confronted as the commission began its work.

Vandenberg appointed Sens. George Aiken (a Republican from Vermont) and John L. McClellan (a Democrat from Arkansas), chairman and ranking minority members of the Committee on Expenditures in the Executive Departments, which had jurisdiction over reorganization proposals. Born in 1892, Aiken spent his early life as a farmer and later commercially cultivated wild flowers. Agriculture remained Aiken's main interest in Congress and on the Hoover Commission. Nominally a Republican, he was known for his political independence. McNaughton once wrote: "A common remark is that Aiken ought to be over on the Democratic side of the aisle, where he would be in his own element and less embarrassing to the GOP."[16]

In later years, McClellan's hostile attitude toward reorganization proposals indicated that his service on the Hoover Commission had influenced him very little. His attitude toward the commission basically was one of boredom.[17] An intelligent but unreflective man, he did not like to read long documents, or to sit still for long periods. He started his political career as an energetic stump speaker and retained his love of action and his desire for the spotlight.[18] The Hoover Commission, which worked in comparative obscurity until near the end of its existence and which required long, arduous days of theoretical discussions based on thousands of pages of documents, offered little to attract McClellan's interest.

McClellan's own tendency to cross party lines matched Aiken's political independence. He took pride, at least until the ballots were counted, in being the first prominent Democrat to predict publicly that Truman would lose the 1948 election.[19] A conservative who earnestly talked about states' rights and worried about the growth and centralization of governmental powers, McClellan rejected the "new economics" and feared the trend toward increasingly large government expenditures.[20]

Vandenberg's two appointees from the private sector included one of the commission's outstanding members, James K. Pollock, and its most ineffective, Joseph P. Kennedy. Pollock, born in 1898, received a Ph.D. from Harvard in 1925. That same year, he began teaching political science at the University of Michigan and was chairman of the department when Vandenberg appointed him to the commission. Pollock had a distinguished academic and public career. He wrote extensively on American politics and played an important role in the reform movement that led to the creation of the Michigan Civil Service Commission.[21]

Unlike his colleagues on the commission, Pollock, a liberal Republican,[22] had neither a political power base nor a national reputation outside academe, but he possessed qualities that made him more than a match for the others in the various conflicts that developed. In addition to being exceedingly well informed on organizational matters, Pollock could not be intimidated by his colleagues. He was a complex man who exhibited a self-confidence—which struck many as vanity and arrogance—that enabled him to fight for his beliefs. Pollock's personality traits, along with his knowledge and intelligence, made him one of the commission's most valuable members, from the administration's point of view.[23]

Joseph P. Kennedy, a Boston business executive born in 1888, had served in FDR's administration in several capacities. Although his earlier public career had been distinguished, he proved ineffective as a member of the Hoover Commission and attended only 10 percent of its sessions.[24] From the administration's perspective, Kennedy's absences proved fortunate. Despite the important positions he held during the New Deal, he was much closer to Hoover than to Roosevelt. One of his business associates said that Kennedy worshipped Hoover, and Joseph's wife, Rose Kennedy, said: "I heard my husband say once that Hoover was one of the few people in the world who really enlightened him."[25] When Hoover asked if he could have Kennedy's proxy to cast in votes on commission matters, Kennedy replied: ". . .[Since] I know how your mind works on all of these propositions through my various discussions with you, I am very happy to go along with you unqualifiedly on all matters."[26] Hoover used this proxy to vote Kennedy regularly against the liberal bloc.[27]

On 16 July, Republican Speaker of the House Joe Martin (Massachusetts) announced his appointments to the commission. He named Congressmen Brown and Manasco, senior members of the Committee on Expenditures in the Executive Departments. Born in 1893, Brown held a law degree from Wilmington College, purchased his first newspaper in 1917, and became lieutenant governor of Ohio in 1919. He acquired a number of farms and a chain of Ohio newspapers and then was elected to Congress in 1938.[28] Although highly respected by both parties, Brown earned a reputation as a tough political "infighter" and as one of the most forceful Republican floor debaters.[29] He was, wrote a journalist, "a massively honest and massively unchangeable ultra-Conservative, totally tolerant of all Liberals as men and totally intolerant of any and all of their designs."[30]

Manasco, born in 1902 as the son of a tenant farmer, overcame great hardships during his early life. He worked in coal mines for seven years in order to pay for his education. He became a lawyer and later, in 1940, was elected to Congress.[31] "I am one of those unfortunates who has labor and capital against me," Manasco once remarked.[32] The combination turned out to be too much for this conservative Southerner; Manasco lost in his 1948 reelection attempt but remained on the commission.

Martin named Hoover and Rowe as his appointees from private life. During the New Deal and World War II, many Americans had forgotten Hoover, but conservative Republicans such as Brown had continued to look to him for leadership. In late January 1947, Brown conferred with Hoover about the Lodge-Brown bill and found the former president pessimistic about the prospect of accomplishing much with such a commission.[33] Hoover later explained to Lodge that he had appointed a similar commission himself but "when the government employees got ahold of it, it seemed to have lost all of its friends!"[34]

However, after the bill passed, Speaker Martin interrupted one of Hoover's fishing trips to ask him to serve on the commission. "This can be the biggest thing that has happened in a generation if it works out the way I think it will. . .," Martin told the reluctant ex-president.[35] On 18 July, Hoover agreed to accept membership, with the condition that he be named chairman, a demand the other commissioners readily accepted.[36]

Rowe, the youngest member of the commission, was born in 1909 in Butte, Montana. After graduating from the Harvard Law School in 1934, he served as secretary to retired Associate Justice Oliver Wendell Holmes in 1934-1935 and then began a brilliant career, moving rapidly through a succession of government positions. Then from 1939 to 1941, Rowe worked as administrative assistant to President Roosevelt who made him an assistant attorney general for the next two years. After distinguished service in the Navy, Rowe held the post of technical adviser at the Nuremberg trials in 1945 and 1946.[37] Undecided about his future career upon returning to the States, Rowe looked upon the Hoover Commission as an interesting temporary diversion.[38]

Rowe demonstrated considerable knowledge of organizational reform. He had lobbied for FDR's 1937 reorganization proposal; later he had served as liaison between the Bureau of the Budget and the White House staff, and with bureau assistance he had reorganized the Department of Justice during the war.[39] Despite this experience, Rowe told a Bureau of the Budget official that he was in "fundamental disagreement with you reorganizers. You fellows are like the man who is always aching to reach up and put the stars in a straight line."[40] Rowe, who later became a legendary political expert, believed men were more important than organization charts.[41] His political instinct made him sensitive to the impact of organizational change on policy. As a liberal who helped Clark Clifford and others prepare the strategy for Truman's 1948 campaign,[42] Rowe used his talents within the Hoover Commission to defend the administration's interests.

On 17 July, Truman announced his appointments. He named James Forrestal, head of the National Military Establishment, as his Democratic appointee from the executive branch. Forrestal, who had earned a reputation as a good administrator, asked Truman to appoint him to the commission and Truman agreed.[43] Though active in the commission's work in the beginning, his participation declined later, and he suffered a mental breakdown in early 1949. "I had my own experiences with Forrestal—all of which became clear in view of after events," Hoover wrote, referring to Forrestal's mental problems.[44] The commission's last meeting had to be postponed on account of Forrestal's funeral following his suicide.[45]

Truman chose Arthur Flemming, Republican member of the Civil Service Commission, as his second appointee from the executive branch. Born in 1905, Flemming became a college teacher and administrator and a journalist. He served as a member of the Civil Service Commission from 1939 to 1948, when he became president of Ohio Wesleyan University. Although outnumbered by Democrats while he served in the civil service post, Flemming had been a dynamic administrator and had largely controlled the government's personnel program.[46]

George Mead, Truman's Republican appointee from private life, was born in 1877 and educated at Hobart College and the Massachusetts Institute of Technology. Mead revitalized the family business and in 1905 organized what later became the Mead Corporation, a large paper and pulp manufacturing company. In the early 1930s, Mead resembled a typical conservative Republican, enraged by the changes that Roosevelt was inaugurating. One day in the midst of one of his usual complaints about the "goddamn big government," his wife asked, "Why don't you go to Washington and do something about it?" Mead accepted her challenge and began to devote more time to public affairs. As his understanding of government policy and problems grew, he began to change his attitude toward the New Deal.[47] Both Roosevelt and Truman appointed him to various government positions, usually in an advisory capacity so that he could continue his private career.

Truman named Dean Acheson as his second appointee from private life, and Acheson's colleagues elected him commission vice-chairman. Acheson, born in 1893 and educated at Yale and Harvard law school, served as undersecretary of the treasury in 1933, and as assistant and then undersecretary of state from 1941 until he retired in July 1947. Truman respected Acheson,[48] and establishment of the commission provided a good opportunity to keep him involved in public service while affording him an excellent opportunity to examine the organization of the Department of State. Truman appointed him secretary of state while he served on the commission.

These twelve men composed a group that soon came to be universally referred to as the Hoover Commission. Hoover, especially during the first year, dominated it completely.[49] The sources of his power were varied. As a former president, he brought with him prestige that no other commissioner could match. However, since Hoover had to deal with tough-minded, self-confident men who would not subordinate themselves even to an ex-president, other factors also accounted for his control. Hoover believed that this was his last public service, and he intended to leave upon it his personal imprint,[50] a resolve strengthened, no doubt, by his view of the position as an opportunity to vindicate himself after years of neglect and scorn. He concentrated all his time and energy on this task and through sheer hard work he maintained control.[51]

Hard work enabled Hoover to establish the framework within which the other commissioners operated. During the first year, commission meetings consisted largely of progress reports by Hoover to his colleagues. He prepared the agenda, took the initiative in choosing task force (subcommittee) membership and commission staff members, selected subjects for study, and controlled information coming from the task forces to the commission.[52] The commission staff, and most task force members, looked to him for leadership and guidance; all commission activities focused on him. Much of the commission's work consisted of little more than paragraph-by-paragraph revision of reports written by Hoover or his underlings.[53] When people objected, he became tough and stubborn.[54] Asked how the commission resolved disputes, Pollock answered: "The Chairman resolved all these problems—sometimes by just riding roughshod over personalities or any other conflicts."[55]

A major source of Hoover's power, and a constant source of conflict with his colleagues, came from his relationship with the commission's staff. The staff attempted to shield all the commissioners except Hoover from information flowing into the commission and to cut them off from task force activities and investigations. Some commissioners believed that the staff did this deliberately; others believed it simply too incompetent to circulate information efficiently. The fact that several staff members, including executive director Sidney A. Mitchell, were old friends or associates of Hoover exacerbated the problem. They regarded themselves as assistants to Hoover rather than to the entire commission.[56]

Several commissioners, and most task force and staff members, also looked to Hoover for leadership because they shared his political beliefs. Although the commission seldom, if ever, divided strictly along party lines, it was conservative, oriented toward the congressional coalition of Republicans and Southern Democrats.[57] Hoover, becoming more pessimistic and mistrustful of "big government" as he aged,[58] intended to move the commission further in a conservative direction. While choosing a staff he wrote: "The first thing we need is a good counsel—preferably someone who has had experience in the departments and who is surely not a New

Dealer."[59] His biases often shaped the commission's path. For example, he adamantly rejected a request to put labor leaders on task forces, although there were scores of businessmen on them.[60]

This conservative bias extended down to the commission's task forces, which conducted research and prepared reports on specific areas of government. Over three hundred prominent citizens served on these task forces; most were businessmen. "Old Dealers and Republicans" predominated, wrote one observer, who added: "The [task force] investigators were largely drawn from the more conservative elements of our society."[61] These men were often members of pressure groups or were acceptable to such groups. The commission staff cleared the agriculture task force members with conservative farm groups.[62] Insurance companies, engineering and contracting associations, the banking industry, and the like had representatives on the task forces that investigated areas of concern to them.[63]

The greatest source of Hoover's power, and one that provided the greatest danger to the Truman administration, was the widespread assumption that the commission's real task was to prepare a report to guide the new Republican president whom most people expected to take office in January 1949. The commission's findings "were to have been the grand overture of a new Republican era."[64]

Brown, manager of Taft's campaign for the Republican presidential nomination,[65] and Speaker of the House Martin openly acknowledged the role they expected the commission to play. Julius Klein, a friend of both Brown and Hoover, explained Brown's plans to the former president:

Brown. . .asked me to pass along the word to you in strict confidence that he put in the provision that the Committee should report *after* November, 1948, very deliberately so as to lay the groundwork for the expected complete housecleaning that will be necessary at that time.[66]

Martin had similar plans. He believed that after a Republican won the 1948 election, the Hoover Commission would become the instrument of conservative Republican change. He said:

The strategy I had in mind was for the commission to complete its recommendations by the end of 1948. Then we would make these the first order of business in the Eighty-first Congress in January 1949, and enact the whole Hoover plan into law.[67]

It would be the biggest thing that happened in a generation, Martin believed.[68] The commission would make all-out war on "conniving, scheming" federal agencies that, he contended, were attempting to subvert the American form of government.[69]

McGeorge Bundy, whose father was a member of the task force on foreign affairs, provided Stimson with a revealing description of how some intended to use the commission:

> I'm afraid I feel that except in the foreign affairs task force of father and Mr. Rogers, these people are essentially operating as anti-New Dealers, and I do not think that is the right approach to the work of a non-partisan commission. As you know, I am not at all a starry-eyed New Dealer myself, and I think lots of socalled [sic] liberals are silly, but I also think that nothing but harm can come from a partisan approach to the great problem of bureaucracy—I feel sure that these men don't *mean* to be partisan, but I feel equally sure that they are. And I find that father shares my fears. Mr. Hoover is in many ways a wonderful man, but he is terribly scarred by his continuing bitterness at all that came from Franklin Roosevelt.[70]

The Senate Republican Conference also bluntly described the commission as preparing for "a major operation on the sprawling, tax-eating patchwork bureaucracy bequeathed to us by the New Deal."[71]

Thus, Hoover and his supporters intended to lead the commission on a full-scale assault against the New Deal structure erected by Roosevelt. Hoover prepared a policy statement that the commission adopted on 20 October 1947.[72] In this proclamation, the commissioners declared that their task was to study government functions from two viewpoints: the necessity or desirability of a function and the organization and management of the function. The liberal or moderate bloc wanted to concentrate on the latter; Hoover and his followers wanted to focus on abolishing functions they considered unnecessary or undesirable. The policy statement declared:

> There are certain functions which are useful in the development of national life and in the preservation of national ideals. But in all functions, there is the question of priority within national ability to pay. There are still further questions as to boundaries of federal versus state and local functions which jeopardize local government; and there are boundaries in functions by the overstepping of which government begins to stultify the initiative and productivity of the people.

After listing the provisions of the Lodge-Brown act, the commission added:

> Thus it is clear that the Commission is not confined to recommending management or structural changes which improve the efficiency of performance of the executive branch but is clearly directed to exploring the boundaries of government functions in the light of their cost, their usefulness, their limitations, and their curtailment or elimination.[73]

As the commission began its work, Hoover and others often indicated their determination to act on this policy statement. In July 1948, Hoover encouraged task force leaders to list the government functions they were surveying according to their "judgment 'of priority within national ability to pay.' "[74] Sidney Mitchell repeatedly and forcefully told a task force staff member that one of the commission's duties was to "cut down or out" as many government activities as possible.[75] Because of the growing controversy over Truman's national health insurance program, several commissioners asked that the task force on medical activities look into the "evils of socialized medicine."[76] A member of the medical services task force reported that Hoover recently talked at length "about the medical services committee being important because it was the group that had been selected as the opening wedge in those people trying to socialize America."[77]

The commission showed an especial interest in getting into policy matters when it turned to the problem of government "business" activities. In outlining the study of revolving funds and public business enterprises, Hoover suggested one problem to investigate was whether "any of these functions. . .could equally well be conducted by private enterprise."[78] Mitchell instructed the leader of a group looking into the regulatory commissions to determine whether these bodies were exceeding their statutory authority and whether their functions could be better exercised by the states.[79] The task force on lending agencies showed that such agencies competed with private enterprise, that private enterprise could better carry out their activities, that they were obsolete, or that they exceeded the purpose for which Congress created them.[80] The chairman of one task force asserted that the "Sovereign State," not the federal government, had responsibility for such matters as education, housing, and care for the sick, aged, or unemployed.[81]

Despite the plans of the people who created and led the Hoover Commission, the final Hoover reports represented a triumph for the supporters of the New Deal. However, the issue of the liberal reform structure deeply divided the commission and the New Deal victory was not predetermined. Two scholarly observers wrote: "Had the issue gone one way, the Hoover Commission might have become the attempted beginning of a considerable conservative revolution."[82]

Truman's election in 1948 ended the dream of a "conservative revolution." On 5 November 1948, a realistic commission adviser wrote: "I suppose the election results have caused the Commission to readjust some of its plans and its assessment of the future."[83] On 11 November, Hoover publicly capitulated to the Truman administration. A reporter asked to what extent the commission would recommend that the government "back out" of activities it had undertaken in recent years, and Hoover replied:

> Our job is to make every Government activity that now exists work efficiently. . . .It is not our function to say whether it should exist or not, but it is our function to see if we cannot make it work better.[84]

Several years later, a disappointed Republican official contrasted Hoover's surrender on 11 November to the original policy statement the commission adopted in 1947: "It is the *how* that puzzles me. How did October 20, 1947, become November 11, 1948?" he inquired.[85] The answer is complex. Some participants believed that the 1948 election was the crucial event in diverting the commission from its original purpose. Rowe recalled that Hoover simply ignored the arguments of the administration supporters until the first meeting after the 1948 election and then "Hoover flipped over just like that," Rowe said, snapping his fingers.[86] Rowe believed that Hoover was a "very stubborn man" and that it took Truman's upset victory to stop him.[87]

However, the weight of evidence indicated that the story was not that simple. If Taft had won the Republican nomination, the conservative commissioners would probably have completely ignored the liberal bloc, but Dewey's nomination insured that even if the Republicans won the election the new president, a moderate, would not lead a movement to destroy the New Deal structure. His nomination, no doubt, caused the commissioners to begin, even before the election, to waver in their determination to focus on policy issues. In addition, since the commission was a mixed body in terms of political party membership and in ideas, its members found it difficult to reach agreement on matters of policy. If the commission meetings disintegrated into endless bickering over policy questions then nothing would be accomplished. The commissioners also came to realize that they could make significant contributions even with a narrower focus than originally intended.[88]

The commission, therefore, was moving away from the 20 October statement by the time of the 1948 election. Truman's 1948 election campaign victory "rendered inexorable this more limited conception of duty."[89] However, the battle still had not ended. If there would not be a general attack on liberal programs, the conservatives would still try to destroy specific activities. Conflict continued and became worse in late November and December 1948 and reached a high point in February 1949.[90] However, despite these clashes and despite frequent despair among the administration supporters, the tide had turned and the final reports generally stayed out of policy areas.[91]

In addition to his 1948 campaign and victory, Truman and his administration played a more subtle role in shaping the Hoover Commission reports. The administration influenced the commission through its appointees and allies on the commission, through a special relationship that developed between Truman and Hoover, and through a slow intertwining of the administration with the commission.

The administration's interests were protected mainly by the Acheson, Rowe, and Pollock bloc. Pollock, a Republican, had no special relationship with the administration but worked with Acheson and Rowe because he usually agreed with their positions, found them personally likeable, and wished to assert himself against Hoover's attempts to dominate all the commission's activities. Rowe did not regard himself as an administration spokesman, but, as a liberal Democrat with ties to men such as Clifford, he worked closely with the Bureau of the Budget on most questions.[92] It was Acheson who most often acted as a direct spokesman for the administration. He volunteered to assist in any way he could in carrying out the president's wishes regarding the commission's work, and he and Truman met at times to discuss its activities.[93] Rowe referred to Acheson as the "titular leader" of the six Democratic members of the commission.[94] When Truman named Acheson secretary of state, some questioned his remaining on the commission. A Bureau of the Budget official, opposing resignation, explained that Acheson had been the "principal guardian" on the commission of administration interests.[95] Acheson did not resign, although he increasingly followed Rowe's lead on questions before the commission.[96]

"The last two days have been frightful and you are lucky indeed that you are not here," Rowe wrote Pollock concerning commission meetings. He added:

> It gets worse and worse. You and Dean and I really should have decided to file concurring reports on all these subjects and would have saved ourselves much useless agony.[97]

Although Hoover's willingness to take suggestions at first impressed Pollock,[98] he soon changed his mind. When Acheson became secretary of state, *Life* magazine carried his photograph on its cover. Pollock asked Acheson to autograph the picture and added:

> I have seen you many times in exactly that position, and I have often wondered as you looked at the Chairman [Hoover] whether you were saying in your own mind—Is he really thinking or just rearranging his prejudices?[99]

Acheson also complained about Hoover to David E. Lilienthal: ". . .he didn't see how any man could be so wrong about so many things—how to go about a job, people appropriate for things to do, etc.—as Hoover has been."[100]

As this relationship between Hoover and the administration supporters deteriorated, Truman began a friendship with the former president that helped protect the administration interests. Roosevelt had ignored Hoover after he left office in 1933, but Truman quickly brought him back into public life. The two men first met in late May 1945. After the meeting, Hoover wrote: "My conclusions were that he was simply endeavoring to establish a feeling of good in the country, that nothing more would come of it so far as I or my views were concerned."[101] Truman, however, was not engaging in empty gestures. He soon sent Hoover on foreign missions to investigate and report on food shortages in the European nations. From November 1946 to June 1947, Truman found at least eight public occasions to compliment Hoover.[102]

The two men did not immediately come to like each other. After Hoover saw Truman the first time, he commented favorably on the president but added: "Of course, I had to talk to him in words of one syllable."[103] Truman, equally caustic in his comments about Hoover, described him to Lilienthal:

> He's. . .to the right of Louis the Fourteenth. But he deserves to be treated with respect as an ex-President. Roosevelt couldn't stand him and he hated Roosevelt. But he straightened out the food problem in S. America back there in 1945, and he can do some things. No reason to treat him other than with respect. But he doesn't understand what's happened in the world since McKinley.[104]

The strongest test of their developing friendship came during the 1948 presidential campaign. In October, Truman attacked Hoover directly several times and reminded the people "that under the 'Great Engineer' we backed up into the worst depression in our history."[105] These speeches wounded Hoover, and years later his friends still recalled his hurt puzzlement. Hoover always regarded Truman as two men—as a "fine country squire" and a "Pendergast politician."[106]

While straining the relationship between the two men the campaign did not destroy it. An assistant to one of the commissioners believed that Hoover gave up the idea of using the commission to whittle away at the New Deal administrative structure simply because of his gratitude to Truman—"because he was so goddamn flattered by the president's calling on him for service."[107] Years later, Hoover best expressed his attitude toward the Missourian when he wrote Truman a letter in which he uncharacteristically revealed his inner emotions. After thanking Truman for a gift, he added:

This is an occasion when I should like to add something more, because yours has been a friendship which has reached deeper into my life than you know.

I gave up a successful profession in 1914 to enter public service. I served through the First World War and after for a total of about 18 years.

When the attack on Pearl Harbor came, I at once supported the President and offered to serve in any useful capacity. Because of my varied experience during the First World War, I thought my services might again be useful, however there was no response. My activities in the Second World War were limited to frequent requests from Congressional committees.

When you came to the White House within a month you opened the door to me to the only profession I knew, public service, and you undid some disgraceful action that had been taken in the prior years.

For all of this and your friendship, I am deeply grateful.[108]

The Truman administration also helped to shape the Hoover report and to keep it from being an anti-New Deal document by subtly intertwining itself with the commission. Executive branch officials fully cooperated with the commission, partly because Truman ordered them to and partly to promote their own organizational goals or to protect themselves from reorganization.[109] Several departments had persons working full time to supply whatever material the commission wanted.[110] Some agencies allowed their employees to act as expert advisers to various task forces,[111] and most appointed liaison representatives and maintained informal contacts with the commission.[112]

The administration often had a chance to influence the commission by previewing and commenting on its preliminary reports before it took final action. For example, officials of the National Labor Relations Board read and commented on a staff report to the regulatory agency task force before it made its final recommendations to the commission.[113] Hoover encouraged the comptroller general, secretary of the treasury, and director of the Bureau of the Budget each to appoint a person to serve on an advisory committee to the task force on fiscal, budgeting, and accounting functions.[114] The Department of Treasury had an opportunity to comment on both the task force and the preliminary commission reports in the fiscal, budgeting, and accounting area.[115]

To a greater extent than leaders of other executive agencies, the Bureau of the Budget officials developed important relationships with the commission. The bureau did a good deal of the commission's staff work.[116] Some of its own staff members served as expert advisers to the commission. For example, its Division of Statistical Standards assigned four employees to the task force on procurement functions. Two budget officials served as assistants to Acheson and Rowe. A bureau agricultural expert acted as director of research for the agricultural task force.[117] It also provided the commission with factual material and with suggestions for personnel for various commission staff positions.[118] One Budget Bureau official drafted a commission report and then aided commissioners in preparing dissents against the same report.[119] It also reviewed certain reports. In one instance, when the commission began to consider a draft report on administrative services, Hoover commented that it had been "recast" in view of the latest discussions with the budget director.[120]

Most bureau activities were less overt, though perhaps just as important in shaping the final commission report. There were constant, varied contacts between officials of the bureau and the commission, and there were regular meetings between the budget director and Hoover and other commissioners.[121] The bureau kept a running check on the various commission studies,[122] thus allowing it to deal with problems before they got out of hand.

The bureau's greatest concern was to put across its concept of reorganization as a continuous process that could be dealt with most effectively by creating facilities and increasing authority to allow improvement of departmental management and by developing central staff facilities for organizational improvement. The bureau prepared several extensive memoranda on the subject for the commission and carried on negotiations to get the commission to develop an effective study.[123] These efforts were successful and the commission's report on management and control was probably the most satisfactory part of the study from the bureau's point of view.[124]

The reports varied a good deal in quality, largely depending on the soundness of the task force reports.[125] Analysts found, generally, that the commission stayed out of policy areas or, more accurately, usually did not recommend change in existing policy.[126] On the problem of management of the executive branch, which had been of great concern to Truman and to the Bureau of the Budget, the commission's recommendations echoed those of the President's Committee on Administrative Management, the Brownlow Committee of the 1930s. The thrust of the proposals of both bodies was to increase the authority of the president over the executive branch and to strengthen his staff services to enable him to carry out his responsibilities.[127]

Hoover's conflicts with Acheson, Rowe, and Pollock obscured important areas of agreement he shared with them. In the late 1930s, Roosevelt had attempted to establish on a statutory basis a strong, institutionalized presidency. Republicans, joined by many conservative Democrats, had risen in fury to prevent what they had charged was an attempt to establish executive dictatorship. Yet the Republican presidents who took office after World War II assumed the managerial presidency without protest and even expanded its powers. In trying to account for this rapid change in the Republican attitude, one scholar recently argued that the Hoover Commission took the "critical, final step" toward the bipartisan acceptance of the strong presidency.[128]

Hoover did not have to undergo an abrupt change in his views to accept this concept. He had never been the conservative leader that New Dealers had imagined, and although he had attacked big government in the 1930s, he had approved the institutional changes Roosevelt and Truman had made in the presidency. He viewed the problems of the presidency as organizational ones disassociated from the politics of the New Deal. He believed the manager of the executive branch, like any other manager, had to be given authority to carry out his responsibilities.[129]

Don K. Price, who acted as Hoover's assistant on the study of the presidency and who was a scholar with many contacts in the academic and governmental communities, brought him into contact with a generation of scholars who were developing a new model of the presidency. This helped expand and make more flexible Hoover's orthodox theory.[130] Price said Hoover "really contributed to something approaching a workable theory on the fundamental nature of the Presidency."[131] One scholar concluded: "In the end, Hoover and his Commission provided the bridge over which the congressional opponents of the Brownlow Committee recommendations and the old political enemies of Franklin Roosevelt could now embrace the managerial Presidency."[132]

Acheson, Pollock, and Rowe at one point feared that the commission's report would be so bad that it would endanger their reputations. But at its conclusion, they regarded the commission's work with pride.[133] They changed their views because the final reports were much closer to their own and the administration's original position than they had anticipated.[134] Neustadt wrote: "The first Roosevelt Administration broke into virgin territory; the Truman Administration had to deal with the demand for its consolidation and development."[135] He argued that Truman's role "as protector, as defender" of the New Deal was one of his important accomplishments.[136] Thus, Truman's work with the Hoover Commission enabled him in 1949 and 1950 to achieve numerous organizational reforms, but perhaps more importantly it provided one of the important examples of his successful attempt to check conservative onslaughts against the New Deal reforms.

Chapter 8

The Reorganization Act of 1949

Truman's spectacular victory in the 1948 presidential campaign convinced many people that he would be invincible in his second term. Speaker of the House Martin, filled with emotion, told reporters that there was no way to prevent enactment of Truman's entire legislative program.[1]

Martin's despair soon proved premature as the president's domestic program bogged down. However, it still seemed that reorganization would be an exception to the administration's general pattern of failure and defeat and that Congress would quickly grant Truman new and better legislation to replace the Reorganization Act of 1945, which terminated in 1948. Not only had Truman won the election, along with a Democratic Congress, but Hoover and eleven other distinguished members of the Hoover Commission also supported his reorganization program. In addition, because of the commission reports and Truman's reorganization in general, public support increased greatly.

Despite these advantages, Congress delayed so long in renewing Truman's reorganization authority that it almost prevented the administration from submitting any plans in 1949. It also modified the legislative-veto procedure in a way that ended the long evolutionary process of giving the president increased authority over the organization of the executive branch. This modification, allowing reorganization plans to be vetoed by only one house of Congress, rather than both, was a setback not just for Truman but also for future presidents because the Reorganization Act of 1949 set a precedent for later legislation.

The Reorganization Act of 1945 expired on 31 March 1948, and the administration, backed by the Hoover Commission, began to pressure for renewal of its reorganization authority later that year.[2] On 17 January 1949, after Congress received messages from Truman and Hoover requesting reorganization legislation,[3] McClellan and Congressman William Dawson (a Democrat from Illinois) introduced respectively S.526 and H.R.1569, both drafted by the administration.[4] Bureau of the Budget personnel had discussed the bills since early 1948. They had based early drafts on the assumption that agency exemptions and other restrictions would be necessary.[5] However, Truman's surprising victory in 1948 and growing public support for the Hoover Commission made the bureau more optimistic. In contrast to the 1945 act, the administration's final draft of the 1949 bill contained no termination date, included neither specific nor general exemption of agencies, eliminated the clause calling for a cost saving of 25 percent, and permitted the creation of new departments.[6]

In late January, the House Committee on Expenditures in the Executive Departments began hearings on the bill. Dawson, a Black representative from Chicago, served as its new chairman. Democrat Chet Holifield (California) headed the committee's subcommittee on reorganization and, with strong support from Dawson and Democratic Majority Leader John McCormack (Massachusetts), spearheaded the administration's program in the House of Representatives. During Truman's first term, the House, following this committee's leadership, had rejected six out of seven of Truman's plans; during Truman's second term, after makeup of the committee changed and became more liberal,[7] the House voted against only one out of forty-one plans.

Another newcomer to the field of reorganization was Frank Pace, Jr. In January 1949, Truman named his trusted budget director, James Webb, as undersecretary of state.[8] Webb had groomed Pace as his successor and by December 1948 Pace had already assumed many of Webb's duties.[9] Although Director Pace basically followed the path worked out by his more innovative predecessor,[10] he did seem to have the initiative needed to help get a reorganization bill through Congress. He thoroughly enjoyed politics and established close relationships with powerful figures in the executive and legislative branches.[11]

During his year in office, Pace relied heavily on Assistant Budget Director Frederick Lawton; few people in Washington equaled Lawton's knowledge of government operations. He testified first when Dawson opened hearings on 24 January. Continuing organizational problems and the inability of Congress to deal with them through regular legislative methods made the bill necessary, Lawton held. He reviewed the achievements attained under the Reorganization Acts of 1939 and 1945 and concluded that more organizational improvements had been obtained in four years under those acts than had been achieved in the entire previous generation by other means.[12]

After a few days of recess, the committee met again on 28 January, and for the first time opposition to the bill surfaced. Whittington testified first.

He was the powerful chairman of the Public Works Committee and national vice-president of the influential pressure group, the National Rivers and Harbors Congress. In 1945, Whittington had been a strong and important supporter of reorganization, but now he spent about half of his time defending the Army Corps of Engineers. He admitted that the bill would be more effective if Congress did not exempt an agency such as the Army Corps but added: "We are realistic."[13]

This began the major controversy surrounding the 1949 bill. Rumors indicated that the Hoover Commission intended to recommend transfer of the civil functions of the Army Corps to a civilian agency, and the committee members felt the pressure. Democrat Porter Hardy (Virginia) said that opponents of the transfer had besieged him with an "avalanche" of protests.[14] Dawson noted that judging from the telegrams flooding the committee "hysteria" was developing in the minds of some people.[15] Henderson Lanham (a Democrat from Georgia) held that since the people "at home" had no knowledge of any threat to the Army Corps, this was not a grass-roots movement but represented activity by the corps and interested groups.[16]

On 31 January, Democrat Carl Vinson (Georgia), one of the most powerful members of the House of Representatives, testified before Dawson's committee. Vinson, chairman of the House Armed Services Committee, said that the bill's authors did not "adequately recognize the singular importance of the National Military Establishment today, nor the constitutional responsibility of Congress relating to such matters." He objected to the proposal because it allowed the president to combine a desirable non-military reorganization with an undesirable military one. He therefore recommended giving the military services single-package status—for example, a plan on the Army Corps could affect nothing but the corps. His entire committee agreed on this recommendation, Vinson said.

Dawson, sensing a way out of the controversy, said that if he accepted Vinson's amendment he hoped that the thirty-four members of the Armed Forces Committee would then support the entire bill. Realizing that he and Dawson understood each other, Vinson replied: "It is always my policy as chairman of a committee to back up other chairmen, because if you do not you are sowing bad seed."[17]

The committee submitted its report in early February. It modified the administration's bill by prohibiting creation of departments by reorganization plans and by giving single-package status to the National Military Establishment, the Board of Governors of the Federal Reserve System, the Interstate Commerce Commission, and the Securities and Exchange Commission.[18] The committee presented a new bill, H.R. 2361, which incorporated those changes.

The attention and approval given to the Hoover Commission report by the public helped get H.R. 2361 through the House debate, which was held on 7 February, with minimum difficulty. One congressman after another, including Republicans, supported the bill. Some believed that Truman would accomplish little, but they wanted to place responsibility for action on him. Generally, the speakers urged that everything possible be done to speed enactment of the Hoover Commission reports.[19]

Democrat Dwight L. Rogers (Florida) introduced an amendment to prevent a plan affecting the Army Corps from going into effect until both houses of Congress passed a concurrent resolution favoring such a reorganization. Hale Boggs (a Democrat from Louisiana) and others supported Rogers, but Vinson came to Dawson's aid and opposed the amendment. He argued that single-package treatment provided adequate protection. Whittington, who was absent, sent word that he also supported the bill as reported from the committee. The amendment failed 143 votes to 82.[20]

A move to substitute the one-house for the two-house veto failed,[21] and the bill then passed 358 votes to 9.[22]

It had taken the House only three weeks following Truman's 17 January message to pass a strong bill. Since McClellan had already opened Senate hearings, it seemed that Truman would soon have an acceptable bill ready for his signature. However, conflicts developed, especially over the Army Corps, that delayed action for months and seriously weakened the final bill.

Secretary of Interior Harold Ickes described the Army Corps as "the most powerful and most pervasive lobby in Washington."[23] The corps exercised tremendous power because it had developed a network of supporting pressure groups from the local to the national level. This network consisted of municipal, county, and state officials, local industries, chambers of commerce, boards of trade, flood-control district officials, municipal engineers, and individual citizens who benefited from the agency's activities.[24] Its engineering projects were important in the districts and states of numerous representatives and senators. A major project often stretched on for years, funneled vast amounts of money into a legislative district, provided jobs for constituents, and continued to provide long-term economic benefits to powerful groups years after its completion.

This power base allowed the corps to become largely independent of executive branch control, and it used its tremendous influence with Congress to fight any attempt to integrate it into the executive branch. Especially under Roosevelt and Truman, the corps fought to prevent its civil functions from being transferred into the Department of Interior.[25]

John McClellan, who served on the Hoover Commission and chaired the Senate Committee on Expenditures in the Executive Departments, began his move to protect the corps well before the reorganization bill came to his committee. In November 1948, McClellan let it be known that the Hoover Commission might propose transferring the civil functions of the Army Corps to a civilian agency.[26] In January 1949, after the commission decided to make such a recommendation, McClellan "went up and down the Senate office building sounding the alarm."[27]

McClellan's campaign began to have an effect. The Hoover Commission had intended to delay submitting its reports until Congress had passed the reorganization bill, because each report would frighten additional pressure groups into trying to weaken the bill.[28] However, on 19 January James Rowe, one of the most politically astute men in Washington, told Hoover that he believed that the commission had to release its report on the Army Corps to prevent it from being exempted before the public discovered the conflict and waste that existed in its activities.[29] On 11 February, Rowe again suggested releasing its information on the Army Corps. Pressure on congressmen was "terrific," he said: "As of now we have no chance of preventing an exemption for the Engineers."[30]

Finally, in mid-March the commission released its reports. Its task force report on natural resources traced the development of conflicts between the Bureau of Reclamation and the corps. In the beginning, the corps had mainly been responsible for navigation work and the Reclamation Bureau for irrigation projects. This had changed, especially in the 1930s, as the jurisdiction of both had been expanded to cover new responsibilities:

> . . .the one agency working upstream met the other coming down. Now we are witnessing the spectacle of both agencies contending for the authorization, construction, and operation of projects in the same river basins, for example in the Central Valley, Columbia, and Missouri Basins.

This overlapping wasted public money because of duplication of expensive surveys and investigations, but even more because of hasty planning. The report added:

> Each. . .not unnaturally tries to stake out claims in advance of the other. Each completes its basin surveys as quickly as possible, and proposes its development plans for authorization. The Executive and the Congress are presented with conflicting proposals prepared by agencies with different water-use philosophies.

Such conflicts led to ill-conceived projects in some cases, to delay of needed projects in others.[31]

Because of the findings of this task force, the commission, with McClellan and Manasco dissenting, recommended transfer of the corps' civil functions to the Department of Interior. Its report included long quotations from the task force study to illustrate the conflict between the Reclamation Bureau and the corps.[32] These reports gave the administration supporters a weapon with which to attack those who wanted to weaken the bill.

However, proponents of a strong bill had to face a very powerful and stubborn man. For many years, the executive and legislative branches had steadily improved and expanded the legislative-veto procedure as a tool to achieve organizational reform. Now, due to McClellan the process was at a halt.[33] As a conservative, he believed in economy in government, except when it involved expenditures for agencies such as the Army Corps. He was not a hypocrite; rather he was a "concrete and steel man." He was a man who was pessimistic about the nature of humanity. He believed social reform expenditures wasted public funds but that investments in concrete and steel, flood projects for example, benefited the people. He felt that government could not change and improve people's nature through welfare expenditures, but by building dams, which prevented natural disasters and provided jobs and contracts for his constituents, it could improve the way they lived.[34]

This Arkansas senator, who also served as president of the National Rivers and Harbors Congress in 1949, regarded the projects of the corps as a benefit for his underdeveloped state, and he realized that these projects aided him politically. He knew that to be successful in getting such projects one had to cooperate with the corps. It had helped McClellan in the past, and he expected it to be useful in the future.[35] It was to his interest, therefore, to block the Hoover Commission recommendations because they threatened to reduce congressional control over the Army Corps.[36]

McClellan, a conservative who still talked of states' rights, may also have had sincere doubts about the constitutionality of the legislative veto,[37] but in any case he guarded congressional power and did not want to grant the president increased control over executive branch organization.[38] Nor did any good feelings exist between McClellan and Truman that could help moderate the senator's hostility toward the president's use of the legislative-veto procedure. McClellan had once proudly claimed that he was the first prominent Democrat to predict publicly that Truman could never win the 1948 election.[39] One study of 106 selected roll-call votes in 1949 and 1950 revealed that McClellan voted against the administration 96 times.[40] In early 1949, while his committee had the reorganization bill before it, McClellan and other Southerners angrily battled with Truman over the administration's civil-rights program. McClellan urged Truman to compromise to avoid a prolonged fight.[41] Truman refused, and on 28 February 1949 a filibuster began over civil-rights legislation while other bills piled up.[42] This battle made McClellan even more unwilling to compromise on the reorganization bill. He increasingly viewed the one-house veto, rather than the two-house veto of the 1939 and 1945 acts, as the most effective means of protecting the Army Corps.

McClellan opened hearings on S.526 on 2 February. The problem of the Army Corps took up most of the committee's time. Lt. Gen. R. A. Wheeler, chief of engineers, testified that he did not believe that the House's single-package provision fully protected the Army Corps nor did he agree that exemption of the corps would be disastrous to reorganization.[43] Wheeler, prompted by McClellan, testified at length about the operations of the corps and provided plenty of ammunition for those who wanted to exempt the general's agency.[44] Maj. Gen. Lewis A. Pick, scheduled to replace Wheeler shortly, submitted a written statement in which he, even more openly and arrogantly than Wheeler, defied his commander-in-chief.[45] The committee's report included a letter from retired Lt. Gen. Leslie R. Groves, who had commanded the Manhattan Engineer District's atomic bomb project during the war. Groves said that if the Army Corps had been in the Department of Interior at the beginning of World War II military construction would have bogged down. "I can also tell you that he atomic bomb would never have been produced under such conditions," Groves averred.[46]

Hearings closed on 15 February, and the administration, still confident, drew up a statement for Truman to make when he signed the final bill.[47] The fight, however, had just started. Not until six weeks later did the committee submit its report, and it would be months before Truman could make his statement.

These six weeks were important in the history of reorganization but impossible to re-create in detail. Although honest disagreement over legislative policy toward reorganization existed, some "artful camouflage of actual intent" also took place.[48] McClellan intended, perhaps, in the beginning, to hold the reorganization bill as ransom to prevent the Hoover Commission from finally recommending transfer of the Army Corps. The delay may also have been an expression of the senator's irritation with Truman's civil-rights program. McClellan may even have been toying with the idea of killing the bill altogether,[49] although that became impractical because of the rapidly developing public support for the Hoover Commission reports.

Basically, however, the delay came because senators wanted to find an arrangement to protect their favorite agencies, with McClellan especially intent on finding a foolproof way to protect the Army Corps. On 3 March, James K. Pollock notified Hoover that he had talked with Republican Arthur Vandenberg (Michigan), a member of McClellan's committee. The situation was "very bad," Pollock wrote, because the committee intended to recommend the one-house veto. He added:

> This provision must be kept out of the Bill at all costs, and since Senator McClellan is now very much irritated with the President, I believe the only hope is for you to appeal to him personally.[50]

A few days later, Rowe also reported to Hoover that the Senate committee desired to recommend the one-house veto. If so, Rowe asserted, the commission recommendations were dead. He urged Hoover to make a statement to that effect.[51] Hoover, who still had strong influence with the Republican congressional leadership,[52] checked on the situation and replied to Rowe:

> The important Republicans are supporting the Commission's recommendations in toto. The trouble is the Democratic side where, of course, I can have no weight. That rests with the President.[53]

Rowe passed Hoover's message to Clifford, Acheson, and other top presidential advisers and added: "From where I sit, gentlemen, it appears to be your move!"[54]

On 29 March, Rowe notified Hoover that Truman was confident that something could be done and would take the matter up with the legislative leaders.[55] Also, the Bureau of the Budget, which had expected the fight to revolve around agency exemption, now recognized this new threat of the one-house veto. The bureau began to plan its strategy and to establish contact with Democrat Hubert H. Humphrey (Minnesota) and other Democratic members of the committee who might favor the administration's position. The bureau officials, who realized the importance of having Hoover work with the committee Republicans, wanted Truman to cultivate Hoover as well as the Senate leadership. They also began to consider acceptable compromises.[56] However, the Bureau of the Budget conceded that it would be a difficult problem to deal with. Three of the seven Democratic members, all Southerners, would almost certainly support the one-house veto,[57] and it was by no means certain that the administration would get the backing of the other four.

To be successful, the administration had to have some Republican support, but at the end of March committee Republicans began to waver. Vandenberg said that he had told McClellan repeatedly that he wanted a bill that would not jeopardize the chances of reorganization, but, he told Pollock, the matter was complex:

> For example, I carry a special responsibility to protect and preserve the Federal Deposit Insurance Corporation in its present indispensable character of independence. If *none* of our fiscal institutions are given exemptions or limitations, I am quite willing to take my chances on the FDIC. But if *any* of them get exemptions or limitations (as does the Federal Reserve in the House Bill) then I must seek similar identification for the FDIC. This is a typical example of the danger involved in *starting* the business of limitations or exemptions.[58]

Thus, the Republicans came under increasing pressure to give in to McClellan, and they collapsed under this pressure at the end of March. Hoover had helped organize a pressure group to work for the enactment of the Hoover Commission reports, and this organization, the Citizen's Committee for the Hoover Report (CCHR), was "going like a wild fire" by mid-March.[59] In March, Vandenberg asked CCHR officials if they preferred a bill with the one-house veto and no agency exemptions or the two-house veto with exemptions.[60] On 31 March, Hoover telegraphed one of these officials that the Hoover Commission had opposed exemptions and that as a member of the commission he had "neither authority nor desire to enter or encourage compromises of any kind. Nor should. . .[CCHR] make any such undertakings. These are matters for the Congress and the President."[61]

However, at the end of the day, perhaps before they received Hoover's telegram, the CCHR officials told Vandenberg that they wanted the one-house veto with no exemptions.[62] One of the participants wrote later:

> I still wonder whether or not we did right about the Reorganization Act. Only time will tell. It was a tough decision for a couple of political kittens like Bob Johnson and me to make suddenly.[63]

The Republicans on McClellan's committee, guided by the CCHR, unanimously supported the one-house veto.[64]

Finally on 16 May, Democratic Majority Leader Scott Lucas (Illinois) brought S.526 to the floor. McClellan, opening debate, said it was essential to reorganize the executive branch to enable it to deal with modern problems. He described the difference between S.526 and the House version and proudly proclaimed that his committee was submitting to the Senate a "clean bill," one without exemptions.[65] Vandenberg congratulated McClellan. He said he knew that McClellan wanted one or two agencies exempted, just as Vandenberg wanted FDIC exempted, but McClellan had courage to resist.[66] Lodge, a strong supporter of reorganization in the past, complimented McClellan for the manly way he approached the bill and agreed with Vandenberg that S.526 marked a great step forward.[67] Lucas punctured this image of McClellan courageously pushing for a clean bill by forcing him to admit that even if the House agreed to eliminate all exemptions he still would insist on the one-house veto. McClellan did not just want a clean bill but rather wanted a way to limit the president's reorganization authority.[68]

The clerk then began reading the bill for amendment. Without debate, the Senate agreed to all the committee amendments, including the one-house veto.[69] The Senate then passed S.526 and accepted a motion by McClellan that the Senate insist on its amendments in the conference committee.[70]

The Senate and House appointed members to a conference committee to work out an acceptable bill. Democrats Dawson, Holifield, and McCormack, and Republicans Hoffman and Harold Lovre (South Dakota) served from the House. McClellan led the Senate conferees, joined by his Democratic colleagues James Eastland (Mississippi) and Clyde Hoey (North Carolina), and Republican Irving Ives (New York).

The three Democratic House members, who represented the administration's position, fought gallantly for a month but finally failed. The administration first tried to trade agency exemptions to gain the two-house veto. Exemption of the Army Corps did not represent a "real loss," wrote a Bureau of the Budget official, because obviously it could not be reorganized anyway. Nor would exemption of such major regulatory agencies as ICC, FTC, and SEC seriously hurt the reorganization program, especially if compromise on these prevented exemption of the Maritime Commission, which would block an important reorganization. The bureau would also accept single-package status for FDIC, the three railroad regulatory agencies, and the U.S. Tariff Commission.[71]

However, McClellan refused to compromise. He intended to get the one-house veto, and if the administration offered exemptions he would gladly take those also. The heated debate within the conference room indicated that the issue would not be easily settled.[72] The administration considered vetoing, or threatening to veto, any bill that included the one-house veto.[73] It also proposed other compromises, such as allowing a plan to be killed by a two-thirds vote of one house.[74]

The administration still underestimated McClellan's intransigence, and the deadlock continued. On 26 May, the Hoover Commission gathered at the White House to submit its final report to the president. Truman remarked that when Congress passed the reorganization bill he would begin to submit plans based on the commission's recommendations. McClellan guilelessly said that he believed Congress was making reasonable progress. He had never seen Congress so busy, McClellan remarked, intimating, perhaps, that Truman's civil-rights programs had delayed other legislation that the president wanted.[75] After the meeting, Truman publicly announced that he had several reorganization plans ready to submit as soon as Congress passed the bill.[76]

The administration finally realized that if it continued to resist McClellan there would be no reorganization plans submitted in 1949. Nor did presidential veto of a bill containing the one-house veto now seem desirable. No evidence existed that McClellan would ever give way, despite the cost to the president's program and to the Hoover Commission's recommendations. A new bill would probably also contain the one-house veto and might even be worse than the present bill because increasing fear among the executive agencies could result in an uncontrollable drive for exemptions.

Truman finally admitted defeat and had the House conferees yield.[77] The House gave way on almost every point of contention. The conference committee eliminated the House provision for single-package status for the various agencies, accepted the Senate provision allowing creation of departments, and set a termination date of 1 April 1953. On the one-house veto issue, the Senate compromised to the extent that it allowed a majority of the authorized membership of either House (49 in the Senate, 218 in the House) to kill a plan.[78] This compromise helped prevent the one-house veto from being the total disaster that some feared.

On 16 June, both houses, after short debate, accepted the conference report.[79] On 20 June, Truman signed the bill. Although it did not comply with his wishes, he was glad to be able to proceed, he said, and announced that he was immediately submitting seven plans under the act's authority.[80] Asked about the one-house veto a few days earlier, Truman said: "I can't answer that. I don't know. We will have to see how it works."[81]

Truman's role in passage of the 1949 act indicated his changing attitude toward reorganization. He had played the central role in passage of the 1945 act and had performed brilliantly. In 1949, he said the right things at press conferences and signed letters to legislative leaders but did not personally guide the bill through the legislature as he had in 1945. There were several reasons for this—his relationship with Congress had changed, for example—but most importantly, Truman's attitude toward reorganization had altered. After talking to Truman, Hoover, in December 1948, told the commission: "the President did not appear to have a strong interest in reorganization authorities [*sic*] or perhaps felt that the reorganization authority was not too important an issue."[82] In 1945, Truman believed his success as president depended on reorganization of the executive branch. By 1949, he had a more realistic attitude toward reorganization. He realized now the difficulty of achieving reorganization and that in any case administrative reform would not solve his basic problems as president.

Chapter 9

The Reorganization Plans of 1949

Although many experts believed that the one-house veto provision in the Reorganization Act of 1949 threatened Truman's reorganization program, Congress accepted more such plans in 1949 and 1950 than anytime before or since. Tremendous public interest in and support for the Hoover Commission recommendations enabled Truman to overcome, partially, such obstacles as the one-house veto and to gain acceptance of twenty-six plans in two years.

The Hoover Commission did not break new ground, as the Brownlow Committee had done during the Roosevelt administration. Rather, it made its greatest contribution by adroitly generating public support for its proposals. Few peacetime government programs have ever received support from a publicity campaign which equaled that surrounding the Hoover Commission reports in 1949 and 1950. From the beginning of their work, the commissioners recognized the importance of publicity.[1] They hired a public-relations firm that outlined a publicity campaign but later decided to handle the matter themselves.[2] Hoover's circle of friends included many well-known journalists and publishers.[3] He cleverly cultivated reporters, whetting their appetites for what would come.[4] *Life* did a picture layout; commission reports went directly to John Davenport of *Fortune;* by December 1948, the *Reader's Digest, Saturday Evening Post, Collier's,* and others planned to produce articles on the Hoover Commission's work.[5]

As the commission finished its work, its publicity chores were assumed by the Citizen's Committee for the Hoover Report (CCHR). "Without this group," wrote Commissioner Pollock, "a very small part of the report would have been implemented."[6] As early as mid-1948, Hoover and his colleagues began to discuss the possibility of forming such an organization,[7] and in February 1949 Hoover selected Robert Johnson, president of Temple University, to head CCHR. Hoover reviewed for Johnson the failure of previous reorganization attempts and warned that this new committee would also fail unless the people were informed of the significance of the commission's findings.[8] Johnson acted as spokesman for CCHR, and

Charles Coates and Robert L. L. McCormick, perhaps the two most important members of the organization, administered it on a day-to-day basis. Hoover himself served as the ultimate authority on broad policy questions and often on political tactics.

CCHR officials intended to build the organization's power by mobilizing public opinion behind it. It organized quickly at the national level and by November 1949 had established thirty-seven state organizations. To keep its members and the general public informed, the committee published various publications, such as *Action Sheets, Washington Watchdog,* "Here's How" pamphlets (*Here's How We Can Get Better Federal Medical Service*), the "Heart" series (*The Heart of the Hoover Report in Personnel Management*), and the *Committee Report,* a monthly newspaper. These publications were to mobilize rapid support for specific legislation.

CCHR also dealt with independent presses. McCormick, for example, in July 1949 submitted to a reporter on the *New York World Telegram* material designed to undercut executive branch criticisms of the Hoover report.[9] He persuaded a writer from the *New Republic* to moderate his critical article on the commission reports and to mention CCHR in a favorable way.[10] He helped edit a series of twenty-five columns that the *New York Herald-Tribune* syndicated.[11] CCHR officials often wrote editorials and articles for others to sign or supplied facts and material. Many newspapers also cooperated by writing favorable editorials on CCHR.[12]

CCHR also garnered support from many other groups. By August 1949, the committee claimed that national organizations with membership exceeding twenty-five million supported its program.[13] In cooperation with the Advertising Council, and aided by the free services of the J. Walter Thompson public-relations firm, CCHR by 1951 had developed a publicity campaign that included free space in hundreds of newspapers and magazines, fifty thousand cards in buses and streetcars, and frequent spot announcements on radio. By 15 March 1951, 389 newspapers were using 3,087 advertisements ranging from single columns to full pages.[14] Various corporations also participated. Three hundred companies, with a total of two million employees, printed and distributed a CCHR series entitled "Employees Information Series."[15] Insurance companies sent nearly a million pamphlets to policyholders and employees.[16] Westinghouse Corporation mailed eighty thousand CCHR pamphlets to its stockholders. Several hundred companies distributed or reprinted articles written by Johnson.[17]

Actively supporting the Hoover Commission reports became a new fad.[18] In June 1949, a Detroit newspaper estimated that it had received twelve thousand petitions supporting the Hoover Commission report.[19] In

June, Republican Congressman Frank Keefe (Wisconsin) said he had received hundreds of letters championing the Hoover report; Sen. Theodore Francis Green (a Democrat from Rhode Island) received 1,537 responses in one month in mid-1949; by 16 August 1949 Democratic Sen. Scott Lucas (Illinois) had received no fewer than fifteen thousand letters urging him to support Hoover Commission recommendations. On 21 September 1950, the White House mailroom dispatched to the Bureau of the Budget 45,600 newspaper poll clippings and petitions urging favorable action on the Hoover Commission reports.[20]

The public had been generally interested in administrative reform since 1945, but now its support seemed at times fanatic. The government had expanded rapidly during the depression and World War II, and many organizational dislocations stemming from its attempts to cope with those crises still existed. Organizational problems aside, the public had not completely adjusted to the government's intrusion into new areas, to increased government expenditures and higher taxes, and to a high national debt.[21]

A world that had been torn by crises throughout the twentieth century became more confusing and frightening as it entered the atomic age followed by the Cold War. Reorganization seemed to many people a way to escape various, often unnamed, terrors. "Our nation is in great danger of being taken over by a lot of things," one woman wrote Hoover, congratulating him on the commission's work.[22] Pollock wrote: "I am firmly convinced that we must reorganize the Executive Branch, otherwise we will go under sooner or later."[23] "We have travelled a long way down the road toward socialism," wrote one of Rayburn's constituents, who believed the Hoover Reports could halt that development.[24] Dr. F. L. McCluer, president of Lindenwood College, said that many "feel that we are caught in the onrush of catastrophe, are faced with problems that are too great for us, and that in anxiety and doubt we surrender to our fears." McCluer believed that the struggle to enact the Hoover Commission recommendations helped people cope with the fears of the "age of anxiety." Confidence and renewed hope could be found by fighting and winning reorganization battles.[25]

Fear of communism was another important reason for the Hoover Commission's popularity. Since the creation of the Hoover Commission, some had viewed its work as important in its international impact as in domestic matters. Many believed that the United States, challenged by totalitarianism, had to show the rest of the republics that its democratic government could effectively meet the needs of its people. Reorganization transcended domestic American issues, wrote Herbert Emmerich: "It is a problem of global dimensions and upon its solution may depend the survival of free government everywhere."[26] By 1949, Americans had become aware of the significance of the Cold War. In the minds of many people, the two became intertwined—the commission reports became Cold War action documents. The U.S. had to get the executive branch, especially the military, in shape to face new threats. Inefficiency and waste threatened national security. The *Detroit Free Press* claimed Stalin rejoiced because the structure of the United States faced destruction through its own inefficiency. The Hoover Commission report promised salvation, an editorial stated in classic Cold War style:

> Facing the Communist horde, surrounded as we are by darkness and chaos across the world, this [fight for the commission report] must be a holy crusade, a fight for God, for Country, and for humanity.[27]

The dream of saving billions of dollars by reducing government waste and inefficiency constituted the most important reason for public enthusiasm for the commission reports. Though many experts derided the possibility of saving large amounts through reorganization,[28] economy remained the main theme in most expressions of public support.[29] Economy meant quite different things to different supporters. Some reformers regarded reorganization as a way to save money that could then be used for expensive welfare legislation; some conservatives viewed reorganization as a means to save money by eliminating or reducing such programs.[30] Some hoped to use this money to meet new international responsibilities, such as rearming European allies;[31] others hoped such savings might be returned to the pockets of the American citizens through tax cuts.[32] Hoover claimed that savings could amount to four, possibly five, billion dollars a year.[33] Putting the matter in terms most appealing to the average citizens, a CCHR official said savings could yield a reduction of 10 percent of each tax dollar.[34]

This great public interest gradually helped to reconcile the American people to changes within the government. In the late 1940s and early 1950s, many people seemed to have an almost hysterical fear of "big government." The Hoover Commission spent two years studying government organization, and for four more years plans, bills, and administrative actions carrying out its recommendations flowed from the executive branch and Congress. Big government did not go away, but unlike many other modern problems it seemed to be one danger that people could do something about. "This deep interest [in the Hoover reports] on the part of the people is very encouraging," a constituent wrote Rayburn and added: "It makes a fellow feel that maybe our country isn't going to hell after all."[35]

CCHR successfully completed its first assignment of mobilizing public opinion, but it had another difficult task in influencing the administration to take the lead in carrying out the Hoover Commission recommendations. CCHR could bring to bear pressure because of its ability to mobilize public opinion. It could also influence Truman's officials by giving or withholding approval of reorganization plans that the administration considered desirable. The administration was not passive, however. A large percentage of the Hoover Commission recommendations could be effected by administrative action, many more could be submitted to Congress in presidential reorganization plans, and administration endorsement would even aid those that required legislation. Both the administration and CCHR, therefore, would benefit by being cooperative.

Since the national CCHR leaders—Hoover, Johnson, Coates, and McCormick—belonged to the Republican party, and Republicans usually dominated local and state CCHR organizations, cooperation sometimes became difficult.[36] Some critics charged that CCHR acted as a partisan organization,[37] and Hoover at times seemed to regard it as a partisan, or at least an anti-New Deal organization. He wrote a friend that "President Johnson's committee is going like a wild fire and I do not believe our New Deal opponents will have a chance before the sweep this committee will make in the country."[38] In several cases, in 1949 and 1950 CCHR allowed political considerations to influence its stand on reorganization plans. However, for the most part Hoover and other officials tried to keep CCHR politically neutral, although Hoover admitted that "these nonpartisan clothes cramp one's style."[39]

Generally, relations between CCHR and the White House were satisfactory, though neither entirely trusted nor fulfilled the expectations of the other. Truman, for example, refused to endorse fully all the Hoover Commission recommendations.[40] If the White House strongly disagreed with a commission recommendation, it tried to avoid developing reorganization plans in that area altogether. This tactic avoided a direct confrontation that it would probably lose in view of the legislators' constant search for respectable justifications for opposing reorganizations. When the administration agreed with a Hoover Commission recommendation and submitted a plan, it tried not to deviate from the commission reports.[41]

On 20 June, while the CCHR was organizing, Truman submitted seven plans to Congress.[42] Plan one proposed creation of a department of welfare to perform the functions that were administered by the FSA. Even opponents of this plan usually conceded the need for such a department. Truman said that President Harding, Franklin D. Roosevelt's Brownlow

Committee, and the Hoover Commission had all recommended such a department. He pointed out that FSA exceeded in size many existing departments and that its activities included some of the government's most important new functions.[43] The plan, which gave belated organizational recognition to the arrival of the welfare state, would increase the effectiveness of the spokesmen for health, education, and welfare functions in dealing with other executive branch agencies, Congress, and the public.[44]

With Plan two, Truman turned once again to his task of rebuilding the Department of Labor. He had tried twice, unsuccessfully, to move the U.S. Employment Service (USES) permanently from FSA to the Department of Labor. In 1945, he had placed USES in the Department of Labor temporarily, and in 1947 and 1948 he had submitted plans designed to keep it there permanently. Congress had defeated these plans and in 1948, overriding Truman's veto, had returned USES to FSA.[45] His election in 1948 had allowed him to renew his pledge to rebuild the department.

Now he had additional support from the Hoover Commission. In determining the proper location of BES, which included both unemployment compensation and the employment service, the commission decided that the employment service administered the primary function of finding jobs and should be in the Department of Labor. Since unemployment compensation related so closely to the employment service, it also should be moved to that department.[46] Plan two, therefore, transferred BES to the Department of Labor. It also shifted the functions of the Veterans' Placement Service Board to the secretary of labor and abolished the board.[47]

Plans three and four proved to be relatively noncontroversial. Plan three carried out one of the administrative principles most emphasized by the Hoover Commission—that cabinet officers must have authority to reorganize and control their departments.[48] Plan three transferred to the postmaster general the functions of all subordinate officers and agencies of the Post Office Department and created the offices of deputy postmaster general and four assistant postmasters general.[49] Plan four rounded out the Executive Office of the President. Roosevelt had created the executive office by bringing together several staff agencies such as the Bureau of the Budget. Congress later had created two new agencies—the National Security Council and the National Security Resources Board. In line with a Hoover Commission recommendation, plan four transferred both agencies to the Executive Office of the President.[50]

Plan five reorganized the Civil Service Commission (CSC). This move partially carried out a reform that had long interested Truman but that had remained politically unfeasible until the bipartisan Hoover Commission reported. The commission charged that centralizing personnel transactions in CSC and in departmental personnel agencies resulted in unjustifiable delays in personnel matters. Recruitment took too long and often failed to match adequately people and jobs. The level of salaries remained too low, the system of rewards and punishment too ineffective, and termination procedures too slow.[51]

The Bureau of the Budget agreed with the commission's criticism of the personnel system. Many of the commission's solutions for these problems could not be accomplished by reorganization plan, but the bureau did decide to support the Hoover Commission's proposal to increase the CSC chairman's authority.[52] The bureau believed that a strong chairman could exert energetic and decisive leadership by making decisions without the need for full commission meetings and by rapidly adjusting operations to meet changing conditions.[53]

Therefore, plan five transferred to the chairman of the CSC, whom the president would name, the functions of CSC president, executive director, chief examiner, and secretary. It also transferred to him responsibility for the direction of CSC employees, for preparation of budget estimates, for use and expenditures of funds, and for execution and enforcement of the civil service rules and regulations of the president, CSC, and Congress.[54] The commission at first opposed such a plan,[55] but Truman personally succeeded in convincing its members of its necessity.[56]

Plan six dealt with the U.S. Maritime Commission, another agency with long-standing organizational problems. In 1950, Truman would submit plans reorganizing the other regulatory commissions, but the Maritime Commission was in such desperate condition, with revelation of scandal threatening, that Truman decided to act immediately to give the commission the executive authority it totally lacked.[57] Therefore, plan six simply vested in the Maritime Commission's chairman the executive and administrative functions of the agency. It made him responsible for the appointment and supervision of all commission personnel, for distribution of business among the personnel and organizational units of the commission, and for expenditure of funds for administrative purposes.[58]

Plan seven transferred the Public Roads Administration (PRA) from the Federal Works Agency to the Department of Commerce, consistent with the administration's and the Hoover Commission's desire to concentrate transportation functions in one agency.[59] This plan's background, which raised some peculiar legal problems, will be discussed later.

Newspapers reacted well to Truman's plans,[60] and immediate congressional reaction also seemed favorable. No one submitted resolutions of disapproval against plans three, four, five, and six, and they went into effect automatically on 20 August 1949. These plans were not insignificant, and in the past all would have been contested. Congress, in effect, had delegated to the Hoover Commission "clearance responsibility" in cases where Congress did not have "pronounced sentiments" itself.[61]

Hoover seemed disappointed with Truman's plans,[62] but he realized that without the president's cooperation little could be accomplished. When Hoover testified before McClellan's Committee on Expenditures in the Executive Departments, he carefully avoided criticizing the president:

> I wish to say at once that the seven plans are all steps on the road to better organization of the administrative branch. They are, insofar as they go, substantially in accord [with commission recommendations].[63]

CCHR faced the same problem as Hoover. There was not enough enthusiasm about the plans for the committee to want to get involved in the "cat fight,"[64] but it did realize that it needed the administration's cooperation. A CCHR official informed Hoover: "We have not been beating the drum either for Plan Number 1 or for Plan Number 2, but more and more heat is being put on us to do so as the possibility of their defeat becomes more imminent."[65] Johnson gave the plans a rather halfhearted endorsement, commenting tersely: "To the extent that the above mentioned measures conform to the Commission's recommendations, the Citizens Committee joins in their endorsement."[66]

New problems and dangers also developed. Opponents always looked for respectable reasons for opposing reorganization plans. In 1949 and afterwards, they used any deviation from a Hoover Commission recommendation as a weapon with which to destroy plans. This tactic threatened the administration's control of its own reorganization program. If it suited a legislator's purpose, he could substitute the Hoover Commission's judgment for that of the Truman administration, whether or not he really supported the commission's proposal. In addition, since supporters of the commission made unwarranted claims about great savings resulting from its recommendations, the administration's inability to claim such savings left plans open to criticism. As in past years, lack of savings continued to provide a major argument for those who wanted to destroy the plans.

The attack focused first on plan one, which provided a department of welfare. Some supporters regarded plan one as especially important because it marked the beginning of the crusade to enact the Hoover Commission report; others supported it because it gave cabinet status to functions that symbolized the New Deal. Since it simply raised an existing agency to departmental status without transferring other units into it or away from it, there seemed to be good reason to believe Congress would accept plan one.

However, controversy soon developed because the plan became entangled in the fight over national health insurance. Since the beginning of his political career, Truman had been interested in public health matters.[67] In the first few weeks of his administration, he had decided to make health care reform part of his general program,[68] and in November 1945 he had publicly endorsed national compulsory health insurance and other health care proposals.[69] The administration had supported these proposals in the Seventy-ninth and Eightieth Congresses but had made little progress. A major setback occurred when the medical program had come to be termed *socialized medicine.*[70] Using these scare words as a weapon, the American Medical Association quickly assumed leadership in the fight against compulsory health insurance, and in 1948 its House of Delegates assessed each of its members twenty-five dollars to fund a three and a half million dollar attack on Truman's health care design. It had also hired a public-relations firm to begin a campaign to "educate" the people to the dangers of the program.[71] This firm developed the "most impressive job of naked persuasion in American history."[72]

The Hoover Commission foresaw the danger of a welfare department plan becoming enmeshed with the insurance controversy. Since top FSA officials led the fight for the administration's health proposal, raising FSA to departmental status would give advocates of the program more power and prestige. Commissioner Manasco warned against placing health functions in a department of welfare because of the "head-on" fight between proponents of compulsory health insurance and the AMA. "If we go into that," he warned, "we will be splattered all over before we get started."[73] The Hoover Commission thus proposed taking health activities out of the FSA altogether in favor of creating a new independent agency called the United Medical Administration.[74] It then recommended a new department to include only education and social-security functions.[75] While this strategy promised to separate the welfare proposal from the health insurance fight it also violated one of the commission's basic principles: that all executive branch activities belonged in the departments.

FSA administrators "unalterably opposed" a United Medical Administration,[76] and since creation of the new agency would require stripping the military services and Veterans' Administration of their medical functions, any such attempt promised to raise immense political opposition.[77] Plan one, therefore, deviated from the Hoover Commission's recommendation by retaining FSA's health functions in the new department. Truman assured Congress, however, that passage of this proposal would not foreclose future establishment of an independent health agency.[78] Still, opponents used this deviation to attack the plan, though most of them, including AMA, would have opposed the Hoover Commission recommendation as well.[79]

Another political problem, also directly related to the controversy over the health program, developed from peculiar features of the internal structure of the department. The FSA was a "holding-company" type organization, with its constituent units, like the Public Health Service, retaining a great deal of independence. In drafting plan one, the administration could continue the "holding-company" organization or could give the secretary complete authority over his department. Individuals and groups who feared increasing the secretary's authority opposed the latter approach. Educational and medical groups especially resisted subordination of "their" agencies to a central authority because it threatened their influence with these agencies. However, in line with Truman's firmly held belief in centralization of administrative authority, the plan consolidated all the functions of the new department and of its constituent units in the secretary's office.[80]

The recipient of the power, Federal Security Administrator Oscar Ewing, transformed hostility to the health program into opposition to plan one.[81] Plan one provided that Ewing, as federal security administrator, would become temporary secretary of the new department, and everyone assumed that Truman also intended to appoint him permanent secretary. Ewing ardently supported Truman's health program—Hoffman described him as "a shameless propagandist for socialized medicine and compulsory health insurance."[82] When the Senate began debating plan one, Ewing often seemed to be the real issue. Seventeen speakers mentioned his name seventy-one times.[83]

Ewing's strong support for the administration's civil-rights program also irritated Southern senators, who were already angered after a long fight and filibuster over the issue. One Southern senator explained his opposition to plan one in these terms:

> I realize that Jack Ewing [sic] is no Communist, as some of them write and tell me. I also understand the political wisdom of his fight for Negro rights. But I'll be darned if I'm going back home and explain all that. I'll just vote to kill the plan.[84]

Ewing had remained loyal to Truman in 1948 and had worked hard for his election. The president now rewarded this loyalty and refused to "ditch" Ewing even to save the plan.[85]

When McClellan opened hearings on plan one on 21 July, the AMA gave it unenthusiastic approval. An AMA representative testified that the association wanted, as first choice, a separate health department or, as second choice, the Hoover Commission's proposal for a United Medical Administration. However, failing that, he said, AMA would accept plan one with the understanding that a separate medical unit would be preferable ultimately.[86] However, on 29 July, the last day scheduled for hearings, Dr. Francis F. Borzell, speaker of the AMA House of Delegates, appeared before the committee. He contended that the activities and philosophies of the top officials of FSA regarding compulsory health insurance indicated that they were not "fully cognizant of the real medical problems of the country and that the medical profession would find itself in the position of subordination to a group or an agency who do not know medical problems."[87] Thus, the AMA changed its position and now opposed plan one even as a third choice. The AMA perhaps devised this strategy to lull the plan's supporters into inactivity.[88]

On the same day that Borzell testified, Sens. J. William Fulbright (a Democrat from Arkansas), Robert Taft (a Republican from Ohio), and Democrat Lester Hunt (Wyoming) sponsored a Senate resolution rejecting plan one. McClellan briefly reopened the hearings to receive their testimony. Two years earlier, Taft and Fulbright had sought to establish a department of health, education, and welfare. Their bill had left the agency's constituent units largely independent of top management control. They now opposed Truman's plan because it integrated the constituent units into the departmental structure and subordinated them to the secretary.[89]

McClellan's committee recommended rejection of the plan.[90] It then came before the Senate for debate on 16 August. Truman called in six Democratic senators to urge their support[91] and sent a long public letter to Vice-President Alben W. Barkley urging passage of both plans one and two. He said that with its vote on this plan the Senate provided the first test as to whether any group fancying its interests adversely affected could block the effort to achieve economy and efficiency in government. The president argued that the Hoover commissioners unanimously approved the proposals included in both plans. He also informed the Senate that Hoover shared Truman's concern that rejection of the plans would seriously blunt the reorganization drive.[92]

During the debate on plan one, Taft attacked Truman's letter as an intervention in the legislative process and challenged the idea that the plan's defeat entailed, in anyway, a rejection of the Hoover Commission reports. Rather, Taft argued, the plan's adoption would make it impossible to carry out other Hoover Commission proposals because Ewing, and presumably the president, opposed creation of a United Medical Administration.[93] Taft, joined by Fulbright, also attacked the plan because it made the secretary "dictator" over health, education, and welfare functions.[94] Legislators repeated these general arguments over and over, along with attacks on Ewing and "socialized medicine."

Supporters like Hubert H. Humphrey and Democrat James Murray (Montana) attacked AMA lobbying. The vote on plan one, said Murray, tested whether the U.S. government could be purchased.[95] Estes Kefauver (a Democrat from Tennessee), Scott Lucas (a Democrat from Illinois), and Margaret Smith (a Republican from Maine) ridiculed the idea that socialized medicine or Ewing should be an issue in the debate on plan one.[96] George Aiken (a Republican from Vermont), speaking as a member of the Hoover Commission, rejected the charge that the plan deviated from the commission's report. Every item in it, he said, carried out a Hoover Commission proposal.[97]

Despite well-argued defenses by some of the Senate's most capable members, the Senate defeated plan one on 16 August by a vote of 60 against and 32 for.[98] Southern Democrats (from former Confederate states) united with Republicans against the plan. Sixty-eight percent of the Southern Democrats opposed it as did 86 percent of the Republicans.[99]

The Senate next voted on plan two, which transferred BES, composed of the unemployment compensation and the employment services, from FSA to the Department of Labor. As with similar plans that Truman had submitted in 1947 and 1948, opponents stressed two main themes: that the Department of Labor's bias would destroy employer confidence in BES and that the department would try to destroy merit rating or experience rating (a system that allowed employers to reduce their unemployment compensation tax rate by maintaining a stable employment level) because organized labor disliked the system.

Truman's earlier plans had always received rougher treatment in the House than in the Senate, but now strong leadership from Democrats William Dawson (Illinois), Chet Holifield (California), and John McCormack (Massachusetts) swung the Committee on Expenditures in the Executive Departments behind the plan.[100] On 11 August, the House passed plan two by voice vote.[101] In contrast, McClellan's committee rejected the plan.[102]

The Senate debated it on 17 August. The debate consisted of a rehash of arguments heard for the past three years. As Sen. Elbert Thomas (a Democrat from Utah) put it: "This is the same old song, being sung by the same chorus, with slight variations."[103] Opponent Irving Ives summarized that "same song": that employers feared the BES transfer because of the Department of Labor's opposition to merit rating, that the department favored workers while BES functions equally concerned employers, and that the plan gave no indication that it would improve the economy.[104]

Democrat Burnet Maybank (South Carolina), Wayne Morse (a Republican from Oregon), Humphrey, and others supported the plan. They also used the old arguments: that BES's most important function was to find jobs that could best be achieved in the Department of Labor, that support of Truman and of the Hoover Commission meant that every presumption should be made in the plan's favor, that governmental efficiency and economy would be increased, that the various fears expressed regarding the proposal were unjustified and unsupported.[105]

The arguments were old, but after years of disappointment Truman finally transferred BES to the Department of Labor. Plan two passed with a vote of 57 to 32.[106] This congressional action was "principally a reflection of the unparalleled prestige of the Hoover Commission as a source of wisdom on matters of reorganization."[107]

The Republicans did not oppose the plan as strongly as they had in previous years, partly because they disliked opposing a Hoover Commission proposal,[108] and partly because they enjoyed removing an agency from Ewing's domain.[109] Fifty-six percent of the Senate Republicans voted against the plan (compared to 76 percent against it in 1948); 33 percent voted for it. However, the Hoover Commission reports influenced the Democrats more than the Republicans. Ninety-seven percent of the non-Southern Democrats voted for the plan; not one of this group voted against it. Fifty-nine percent of the Southern Democrats voted for the plan; 36 percent voted against it. Both Southern and non-Southern Democrats supported the plan to a greater extent than they had supported similar ones in 1947 and 1948.[110]

This reorganization did not solve the problems of BES. In succeeding years, Congress, with the support of employer groups and state employment security agencies, passed laws limiting the secretary of labor's control over state operations of the employment security program. This action demonstrated the ability of Congress, backed by powerful interest groups, to oversee and develop national policy regarding an agency, irrespective of its location. Plan two had little impact on the structure of power organized around BES functions. It "proved to be of little more significance than a change of address, since the entrance of the Secretary of Labor into the structure of employment security operations did not seriously disturb the equilibrium that existed before the reorganization had occurred."[111]

Other problems also developed. Despite the plan, BES became autonomous within the Department of Labor, operating outside the hierarchy of control.[112] The employment service particularly suffered under this arrangement. Unemployment insurance became the dominant activity and diverted work, thought, and energy from employment functions.[113] Because its chief function became that of servicing compensation claimants, the employment unit acquired the image of "unemployment office" and lost the confidence of many job applicants and employers. Its domination by the unemployment compensation function had the paradoxical effect during times of rising unemployment of causing the employment service personnel to focus on processing increased claims loads rather than intensifying efforts to find jobs.[114] The more people needed its help in finding jobs, the less it could do to meet those needs. From the passage of plan two until 1960, the employment service's regular job placements and its "potential for service" declined.[115] In 1958, the secretary of labor said that the employment agency assisted such a small proportion of the nation's population that its continued existence was questionable. He bluntly charged that the agency personnel concentrated so much on insurance claims that it neglected its main purpose—finding jobs for the unemployed.[116] In the 1960s and 1970s, the employment service continued to have difficulties, especially in adjusting to new poverty programs.[117]

Ordinarily, plan seven would not have been unusually controversial, but it generated conflict because the plan's passage angered Democrat Carl Hayden (Arizona), one of the Senate's most powerful members. Hayden attacked plan seven's unusual background to develop legal arguments that cloaked other concerns.[118] Plan seven transferred the PRA from the Federal Works Agency (FWA) to the Department of Commerce. But before Truman submitted plan seven, the House passed the Federal Property and Administrative Services bill and the relevant Senate committee reported the bill favorably. The measure created the General Services Administration (GSA) and transferred to it all the units and functions of the Federal Works Agency, including PRA.[119] As the administration anticipated, the bill passed before the plan went into effect, thereby eliminating the Federal Works Agency and placing PRA in the GSA. In his message, Truman took notice of the pending bill and said that the plan would go into effect even if Congress passed the bill and the FWA no longer existed.[120] As it turned out, plan seven transferred PRA from GSA rather than from the Federal Works Agency.

Hayden, who chaired the Appropriation Committee's subcommittee with jurisdiction over PRA, submitted a resolution of disapproval on 15

August, only five days before the plan was scheduled to take effect.[121] McClellan's committee reported the plan without holding hearings and without making a recommendation for or against it.[122] Hayden then brought it up for debate on 17 August. When Hayden took the floor, it was only the second time he had made a speech in the Senate since the 1920s.[123] He argued that the plan was illegal and that the Hoover Commission and the administration failed to understand that the PRA administered public works rather than transportation functions. He implied that Truman did not want the plan to go into effect but could not withdraw it without discrediting the Hoover Commission and the attorney general who had given the plan legal clearance. However, he said, even if the plan was legal he did not approve of transferring the PRA to the Department of Commerce.[124] This indicated that Hayden's legal argument only concealed his other reasons for opposing the plan, such as fear of losing jurisdiction over PRA.

After a very short debate, the Senate upheld the plan by a vote of 47 to 40.[125] Plan seven passed only because of Republican support. Only 43 percent of the Democrats voted for it, compared to 56 percent of the Republicans. On this occasion, Democrats from the states west of the Mississippi, motivated by their desire to locate PRA in the Department of the Interior because of their special interest in public works, constituted the key to the Democratic vote. Sixty-three percent of that bloc voted negatively.[126]

Truman could regard congressional treatment of his 1949 plans with a good deal of satisfaction. Although he failed to establish a welfare department, he did take a significant step toward rebuilding the decimated Department of Labor by transferring to it unemployment compensation and employment service functions. He moved further toward the institutional presidency by moving to the Executive Office of the President the National Security Resources Board and the National Security Council. By placing the Public Roads Administration in the Department of Commerce, he took a first step toward gathering transportation functions in one place. Through this and several additional transfers in 1950, Truman prepared for the establishment of the Department of Transportation, which occurred in 1966. Truman also made several undramatic but significant moves to provide for continuous management improvement by centralizing executive and administrative functions in the "strong" chairman plans for the Civil Service Commission and the Maritime Commission and by centralizing all functions of subordinate officials and agencies of the Post Office Department in the postmaster general.

Chapter 10

The Reorganization Plans of 1950: Phase One

At the close of his presidency, Truman announced that he had done more about reorganization than all other chief executives combined. The twenty-seven plans he submitted in 1950 enabled him to make that claim. But it was not an accomplishment of his administration alone; it was his alliance with Hoover that allowed Truman to make this record. In 1950, his administration caught the crest of public support for the Hoover Commission recommendations. Still, it appeared that even that support would not prevent disaster as the Senate began voting on Truman's twenty-seven plans and as pressure groups gathered courage enough to defy public opinion by opposing Hoover Commission proposals.

During most of 1950 and throughout the rest of his administration, a very able new budget director headed Truman's reorganization program. On 30 March, Truman announced that Pace would become secretary of the army and that Lawton would replace Pace as director.[1] Lawton, an influential Bureau of the Budget official for many years, had a long association with Truman.[2] During Lawton's tenure, reorganization plans emerged from the executive branch with less controversy and confusion than in the past. He accomplished this largely because of his knowledge and experience: "He knew the Bureau like a piano and could make it play any tune he wanted."[3] Lawton also viewed the bureau's role as that of conciliator among other executive branch agencies. If agencies clashed over a program, Lawton acted as a compromiser. Further, he developed an unusually good relationship with Congress and with the White House staff, thus allowing him to represent the president on reorganization matters with "unusual effectiveness."[4]

On 13 March, Truman presented twenty-one plans to Congress, the first of three groups submitted in 1950. As in the past, the administration dropped such controversial proposals as transferring the civil functions of

124

the Army Corps of Engineers. In a general message, Truman said that the administration designed the proposals to effect specific Hoover Commission recommendations or to apply principles set forth by the commission.[5]

Over the years, Congress had fragmented authority within the executive branch by placing activities, by statute, directly in subordinate officials and bureaus. Plans one through six transferred all functions and activities within six departments to their respective secretaries. The secretaries would be responsible for all activities within their departments and could make organizational adjustments when necessary. The plans provided for administrative assistant secretaries in each department and for additional assistant secretaries in inadequately staffed departments. These proposals, Truman claimed, provided clear lines of responsibility from the president through the secretaries down to the lowest level within each department.[6] Plan one reorganized the Department of Treasury, plan two the Department of Justice, plan three the Department of the Interior, plan four the Agriculture Department, plan five the Department of Commerce, and plan six the Labor Department.[7] Congress had carried out similar reorganizations in the Departments of State, Defense, and Post Office the year before.

The administration designed plans seven through thirteen to improve internal administration of regulatory agencies. They vested in the chairmen, who would be chosen by the president, responsibility for appointment and supervision of personnel, for distribution of business among the personnel and among the commissions' administrative units, and for the use and expenditures of funds. The commissions retained their authority to make regulatory decisions, to establish general policies, to revise budget estimates, and to distribute funds among major programs.[8] Plan seven reorganized the Interstate Commerce Commission, plan eight the Federal Trade Commission, plan nine the Federal Power Commission, plan ten the Securities and Exchange Commission, plan eleven the Federal Communications Commission, plan twelve the National Labor Relations Board, and plan thirteen the Civil Aeronautics Board.[9]

Plan fourteen authorized the secretary of labor to prescribe regulations and procedures with respect to the administration of labor standards under various laws relating to federal construction of public works and to construction with federally financed assistance or guarantees.[10]

Plans fifteen, sixteen, seventeen, and eighteen continued the process of making the new General Services Administration (GSA) into a central service agency. Plan fifteen moved the administration of the public works programs of Alaska and the Virgin Islands from GSA to the Department of Interior. Plan sixteen transferred responsibility for financial assistance to public-school districts and for grants and loans for water-pollution control from GSA to FSA. Plan seventeen moved administration of advance planning of non-federal public works and the management and disposal of certain wartime public works from GSA to the housing and home finance administrator.[11] Plan eighteen transferred to the general services administrator the functions of various federal agencies with respect to leasing and assigning general purpose space in public buildings and the operation, maintenance, and custody of public office buildings.[12]

Plan nineteen transferred from FSA to the Department of Labor the Bureau of Employees' Compensation and the Employees' Compensation Appeals Board and their functions. Since both agencies administered labor functions, they should be in the Department of Labor, Truman explained.[13]

Since 1789, the Department of State had administered certain routine secretarial and record-keeping functions that had little or no connection with foreign affairs. Since the National Archives and Records Service of GSA was equipped to administer activities of that sort, plan twenty transferred those duties to GSA.[14]

Plan twenty-one, an especially complicated proposal, reorganized the U.S. Maritime Commission. Truman argued that this body suffered from serious administrative defects because it administered two different types of functions that needed two different types of organization. It regulated rates and services of water carriers, passed on agreements among carriers, and protected shippers against unfair and discriminatory practices; these were regulatory activities best administered by a commission or board, Truman said. However, the Maritime Commission also administered various promotional and business programs relating to the merchant marine, which Truman judged could best be carried out by a single executive. Plan twenty-one, therefore, abolished the Maritime Commission and transferred its regulatory functions to the Federal Maritime Board, a new agency within the Department of Commerce, and shifted its promotional and business functions to the secretary of commerce to be administered by another new unit, the Maritime Administration. To provide coordination and to prevent division of personnel, the chairman of the Federal Maritime Board would also head the Maritime Administration.[15]

On 9 May, Truman submitted four more plans to Congress. Three of these affected the Reconstruction Finance Corporation (RFC). Plan twenty-two transferred the Federal National Mortgage Association (FNMA) from RFC to the Housing and Home Finance Agency.[16] Plan twenty-three transferred from RFC to the Housing and Home Finance

Agency functions relating to production and distribution of prefabricated houses and housing components.[17] Plan twenty-four transferred RFC to the Department of Commerce and made its board of directors subject to the secretary's supervision, coordination, and policy guidance.[18]

Plan twenty-five transferred the functions of the National Security Resources Board to its chairman, making that body merely advisory to its head. Administration by committee had made it difficult for NSRB to act rapidly and efficiently, a lack that Truman believed reorganization would remedy.[19]

On 31 May, Truman submitted his final two plans. By that time, Congress had already defeated plan one because it transferred the functions of the comptroller of the currency to the secretary of treasury. Plan twenty-six duplicated plan one, except that it exempted the comptroller of the currency from its provisions.[20]

Plan twenty-seven proposed creation of a department of health, education, and security and transferred to it the functions of FSA. The president declared that in this new plan he tried to meet the objections opponents had raised against the defeated 1949 proposal. Plan twenty-seven allowed the surgeon general and commissioner of education to retain their current statutory authority, independence, and duties.[21]

No one introduced resolutions of disapproval against plans two, three, ten, thirteen, fourteen, fifteen, sixteen, nineteen, twenty, twenty-three, twenty-five, and twenty-six. These twelve plans went into effect without debate or a vote.

Other plans faced strong opposition. The first proposal Congress dealt with generated one of the harshest fights in reorganization history. Plan twelve incorporated the "strong chairman" provision included in plans seven through thirteen, but it became controversial because it also eliminated the Office of the General Counsel of the National Labor Relations Board (NLRB) and transferred its functions to the chairman of NLRB.

Since the late 1930s, critics of NLRB had charged it with actions and decisions unfair to management. When the Republicans had taken control of Congress in 1947, they, with much Democratic support, had passed the Taft-Hartley act over Truman's veto. The authors of the Taft-Hartley act had created the Office of General Counsel with complete control of the "flow" of unfair labor practice cases to the board. They had intended the general counsel to be a new source of power to balance that of the board. Congressman Hartley referred to the office as "the all-important post."[22] The authors intended this rival power center to prevent the board from disregarding and misinterpreting the spirit of the Taft-Hartley act.[23]

After Congress overrode Truman's veto, his administration had to enforce an act that he had promised to have repealed. Choosing a general counsel posed a special problem. Since Truman did not want to be blamed for placing administration of the Taft-Hartley act in unfriendly hands,[24] he nominated Robert Denham as general counsel, who had been an NLRB trial examiner since 1938. Denham, a conservative Republican, had characterized the New Deal-Fair Deal social program as an attempt "to relieve the lazy and indifferent ones—the failures and the drones—of their responsibility for themselves." Management oriented, he claimed union benefits and pensions threatened to undermine the economy.[25] He thoroughly agreed with the goal of the Taft-Hartley act because he believed that the NLRB had been pro-union.[26]

Both the board members and Denham realized that divided authority, with different pressure groups gathering behind each center of power, posed great problems.[27] To try to avoid warfare, the board met with Denham to draw up an agreement delegating certain functions to the general counsel. For several months, the agency performed well.[28] However, differing political philosophies combined with divided functions soon generated friction, which quickly turned into open warfare.[29]

In 1949, the administration attempted to fulfill its promise to labor to repeal the Taft-Hartley act. To accomplish such action, it supported the Thomas-Lesinski bill, but the measure languished in Congress and the administration began to consider other ways to deal with the deepening split within the NLRB.[30] On 24 October, White House aide Stephan J. Spingarn wrote a memorandum calling for Denham's removal. He showed it to Charles Murphy, another aide, who suggested that the removal could be done by a reorganization plan, already under consideration, to abolish the Office of General Counsel.[31]

During the winter the conflict escalated,[32] and finally on 13 March Truman sent plan twelve to Congress. He submitted it, he said, to end the division and confusion of responsibility in the NLRB by abolishing the Office of General Counsel and restoring unified authority to the agency.[33]

Despite these defenses based on administrative grounds, the plan generated instant controversy because the administration intended to use a reorganization plan to change the nature of the Taft-Hartley act. To make matters more difficult for Truman, the Republican-dominated Citizens Committee for the Hoover Report (CCHR) refused to support it. The Hoover Commission had made no specific suggestion regarding the general counsel, but one of its basic recommendations had called for centralization in the chairmen of the regulatory commissions responsibility for administrative and executive functions. Although a CCHR official admitted that the plan was in harmony with the commission recommendations, his organization later decided that although the plan conformed to the commission's general principles, it involved policy as well as organizational issues.[34] "It is very wise to sit on top of the fence," another CCHR official wrote regarding plan twelve.[35] This opinion revealed CCHR's Republican bias and violated its promise to support plans that conformed to the Hoover Commission recommendations.

The business community carried the major burden of opposition to plan twelve. "The drums are being beaten violently to 'save Denham,' " wrote one of NLRB Chairman Paul Herzog's friends.[36] Within a week after Truman submitted the plan, business-dominated interest groups began mobilizing against it. "A drive for votes on the reorganization proposal is under way," said the *NAM News*.[37] The Associated Industries of Georgia sent out an ACTION FLASH letter urging its members to contact congressmen. The U.S. Chamber of Commerce dispatched an ACTION NEEDED letter. The American Trucking Association issued a CALL TO ACTION.[38] The California Association of Employers, Associated Industries of Maryland, Ohio Newspaper Association, and the Georgia Press Association all summoned their constituents to action.[39]

The Committee on Expenditures in the Executive Departments opened hearings on 14 April following favorable action by the House committee.[40] Robert Taft testified first. In 1949, Taft had successfully led a fight to amend the Thomas bill to eliminate the Office of General Counsel, though the bill did not finally take effect.[41] Although it seemed that plan twelve incorporated his amendment, he led the Senate fight to defeat it. Taft wrote Denham: "The motives behind this Plan were both to sabotage the law and to get rid of yourself because you will not yield to the pressure of labor politicians."[42] In his testimony, Taft claimed that the plan did not stem from any Hoover Commission recommendation. He quoted from a telegram that Hoover had just sent him in which the ex-president said he could not recall the commission ever discussing the subject of the general counsel of the NLRB.[43] Taft argued, basically, that the administration wanted to use the plan for the political purpose of nullifying the Taft-Hartley act.[44]

Despite a well-argued defense by Lawton, McClellan's committee voted to reject the plan.[45]

The administration mobilized to save plan twelve. On 3 May, a group composed of White House staff members, Democratic National Committee officials, representatives of the Americans for Democratic Action, and labor union leaders met to plan a strategy. The group laid out a detailed lobbying scheme intended to prevent its opponents from garnering the forty-nine votes they needed to kill the plan.[46] The unions coordinated their lobbying activities with the administration. A White House official reported that they "are working feverishly and Secretary Tobin is cooperating 100%." However, the situation had deteriorated by 9 May when the group met again. A few days earlier they had labeled the votes of thirty-seven senators as "hopeless"; now they listed forty-eight as hopeless and six more as probably opposed.[47] After the meeting, an administration official estimated that the proponents needed to change five to eight votes.[48]

Just before the vote, Truman sent a long public telegram to the president of the Senate. He asserted that plan twelve would correct an administratively unworkable setup and would eliminate a "two-headed freak." The plan neither involved personalities nor went to the substance of the controversy over Taft-Hartley. Truman further charged opponents with being motivated more by politics than by the merits of the plan. In 1949, the Senate had passed a bill that abolished the Office of General Counsel and transferred its functions back to the board; plan twelve did exactly the same thing, Truman said. He then quoted extensively from a 1949 Taft speech in which the Republican leader had explained the necessity of abolishing the Office of General Counsel.[49]

Bitter conflict characterized the Senate's first discussion of the plan on 10 May, but debate calmed considerably the following day, mainly because the supporters of the plan had become reconciled to its defeat. Opponents did not waste energy on verbal overkill. Democrat Allen Ellender (Louisiana) observed that he had not voted against any proposal presented pursuant to the Hoover Commission reports but that the commission did not recommend the changes incorporated in this plan. It struck at the very heart of the Taft-Hartley act because the general counsel's conflict with the board resulted from the board's refusal to enforce the act as passed by Congress.[50] Taft dealt directly with the argument that in 1949 he had supported the same changes that the administration incorporated in plan twelve. Truman's plan, unlike his own 1949 proposal, Taft said, did not just eliminate the Office of General Counsel but transferred its functions to the chairman of NLRB rather than to the board itself. Taft objected to this provision because it threatened to create a setup worse than the original Wagner act.[51]

The Senate vetoed the plan by a margin of 53 to 30.[52] Eighty-three percent of the Republicans voted against it, as did 59 percent of the Southern Democrats. Sixteen percent of the non-Southern Democrats voted against it.[53] Of eighteen Democrats who opposed the plan, only Guy Gillette (Iowa) came from outside Southern or border states. Hostility to labor and the plan's entanglement with an FEPC filibuster that was taking place at the same time probably accounted for the Southern vote.[54]

Although a coalition of Republicans and Southern Democrats vetoed plan twelve, one of Truman's own cabinet officers killed the next proposal brought up for vote. Plans one through six transferred all statutory authority and functions placed in subordinate departmental bureaus and officials to the heads of those departments. Although the department heads would normally delegate the authority and functions back to the bureaus, no subordinate would have authority separate from his superior and the superior would clearly have authority to organize his department as he believed necessary.[55]

Those plans carried out a fundamental Hoover Commission recommendation, but they faced potential opposition on several accounts. Some opponents believed that they concentrated too much authority in the chief executive. One major reason for the fragmented nature of the executive branch was that Congress, or rather congressional committees, placed separate authority in bureaus in order to increase congressional power over executive functions. These reorganization plans threatened that arrangement. A CCHR official summarized this executive-congressional conflict aptly:

> The President's efforts in reorganization have almost entirely been devoted to clarifying lines of authority and affixing responsibility. His interest in this matter is natural because he is both a politician and a management man. The reforms he can put through in this field make him more effective as a political figure because he can control his own bailiwick and also make it easier for him as a manager because he can run the operation a lot easier. . . .The opposition to these Plans was based upon the desire of the Republicans and the conservative Democrats to prevent this assertion of authority so that the agencies concerned would deal directly with Congress and, hence, with the coalition majority in it.[56]

Many pressure groups also opposed this series of plans because strengthening hierarchical control over subordinate bureaus threatened to disturb special relationships that existed between these groups and the bureaus. For example, a CCHR official found that banking organizations strongly opposed certain Hoover Commission recommendations. He wrote:

> The essence of their argument in this respect is very simple. The more confused the Federal organizations that supervise them, the better the

chances that they will be able to do just what they please.[57]

Bankers specifically opposed plan one, which reorganized the Department of Treasury. They focused their opposition on a provision that transferred the functions of the comptroller of the currency to the secretary. Before Truman submitted the plan, a Bureau of the Budget official warned that bankers would "strenuously" object to any weakening of the comptroller's independence.[58] The bankers believed they could more easily influence the comptroller than the secretary of treasury.[59]

The administration anticipated opposition from banking organizations, but Secretary of Treasury John W. Snyder, representing the banks, killed the plan himself. In 1930, Snyder had held a job in the Office of the Comptroller of the Currency.[60] Later as a minor banking official, he envisioned that agency as an arm of the private banking system operating to protect the bankers, rather than as a public body operating to protect the public. Snyder bluntly described the community of interest between bankers and the federal body that affected their business:

> The operations of the Office of the Comptroller of the Currency are closely integrated with those of the banking system, and there is considerable movement of personnel from banks to the Comptroller's examining staff and vice versa—so much so that persons on the Comptroller's staff regard their activities as being in the banking field rather than as government employment. Examiners and assistants who leave the Comptroller's service usually do so to accept positions as officers of banks. . . .[61]

Rather than regarding such a compromising situation as a solid justification for reorganization, Snyder went along with the banking interests' opposition to the plan. Before Truman submitted it, the secretary warned that he intended to give his support only if it exempted the comptroller.[62] The bureau refused to make an exemption because it would open a floodgate of demands from other agencies for similar treatment.[63] Snyder, therefore, notified McClellan on 7 April 1950 that he accepted plan one except for its provision regarding the comptroller of the currency. Since the plan could not be amended, Snyder, in effect, asked for defeat of the plan.[64]

When McClellan opened hearings on 11 April, several senators spoke against plan one. Democrat Burnet Maybank (South Carolina), chairman of the Committee on Banking and Currency, revealed that every member of his committee had voted to oppose the plan. Sens. A. Willis Robertson (a Democrat from Virginia) and Republican Homer Capehart (Indiana), each of whom submitted resolutions of disapproval, both argued that the plan threatened the comptroller's independence and paved the way for "political" influence on banking policy, portending unsound credit policies. Both senators held seats on the Committee on Banking and Currency.[65]

The committee received three hundred and seventy-six communications, mostly from bankers, dealing with plan one, all but one of which opposed it.[66] Many bankers also appeared personally before the committee. Former Congressman D. Emmert Brumbaugh, now an official of the National Association of Supervisors of State Banks, urged that nothing be done to weaken the dual national-state banking system. He opposed any compromise with the independence of the Office of the Comptroller of the Currency, the Federal Deposit Insurance Corporation, or the Federal Reserve System. Brumbaugh charged that plan one presaged a plan to move FDIC and the Federal Reserve System under the control of the secretary of treasury. He frankly admitted that he desired disunity in the area of banking regulation.[67] In response to the bankers' pressure, the committee reported plan one unfavorably.[68]

On 11 May, the Senate debated plan one. Truman had refused to withdraw the plan partly because he wanted to force congressmen to face a roll-call vote on reorganization issues.[69] Actually, Congress had little fear of opposing the president's proposal. Following a brief debate, the Senate defeated plan one with a vote of 65 to 13.[70] This outcome shocked and frightened CCHR because even though the plan conformed to the Hoover Commission recommendations, it attracted only thirteen supporters.[71]

The next two plans brought to the Senate floor were inherently controversial. Plans seven and eleven reorganized the Interstate Commerce Commission and the Federal Communications Commission, respectively. These proposals transferred executive and administrative functions of the regulatory commissions to their chairmen and gave the president authority, when he did not already have it, to appoint them.

These plans responded to increasing criticism of the entire regulatory system. Many of the problems with regulatory commissions resulted from the government's changing economic and social role. As the federal government expanded its functions to insure economic stabilization, as defense needs became increasingly intertwined with economic policy, and as poverty programs and other welfare activities gained importance, the role of regulatory commissions changed. Since almost all of these new activities took place outside the commissions, it became increasingly important to coordinate regulatory policy with general government policy.[72] But the president found it difficult to achieve such coordination. The commission system dissipated his ability to guide development and execution of public policy.[73] Increasing the authority of the chairmen and allowing the president to nominate them would allow the administration to exert more authority in this area.

Therefore, additional serious problems had developed. Reformers had once hoped that the regulatory commissions would effectively cope with problems that had emerged as the United States moved toward an oligopolistic economy. They had anticipated that regulatory commissions would provide the protection for the public that the competitive marketplace had decreasingly exerted. As early as 1897, Attorney General Richard Olney had predicted what would really happen. He reassured a railroad president who wanted to abolish the ICC:

> The older such a commission gets to be, the more inclined it will be found to take the business and railroad view of things. It thus becomes a sort of barrier between the railroad corporations and the people and a sort of protection against hasty and crude legislation hostile to railroad interests. . . .The part of wisdom is not to destroy the Commission, but to utilize it.[74]

A half century later, Marver Bernstein confirmed Olney's insight:

> The close of the period of maturity [of the commission] is marked by the commission's surrender to the regulated. Politically isolated [since they were arms of neither the president nor Congress], lacking a firm basis of public support, lethargic in attitude and approach, bowed down by precedent and backlogs, unsupported in its demands for more staff and money, the commission finally becomes a captive of the regulated groups.[75]

Truman viewed regulatory ineffectiveness as largely an administrative problem and had long opposed administration by boards or committees. He strongly believed that one person should exercise administrative responsibility. "He believed that you could not effectively conduct day-to-day business in a town meeting," recalled one of Truman's advisers.[76] He hoped that a shake-up of the administrative structure would enable aggressive chairmen to solve the problems that had destroyed the effectiveness of the regulatory system.

Despite widespread criticism of the commissions, reorganization proposals affecting them—even the mild changes Truman proposed—confronted tremendous obstacles. In addition to all the usual problems with reorganization, these revisions faced special difficulties because both Congress and the clientele groups—that is, the regulated industries—regarded the commissions as peculiarly their own.[77] Speaker of the House Rayburn once cautioned an FCC chairman: "Just remember one thing, son.

Your agency is an arm of the Congress, you belong to us. Remember that and you'll be all right."[78]

Congressional committees, always trying to subordinate executive agencies to themselves, guarded independent regulatory commissions jealously and blantantly.[79] One committee, the Committee on Interstate and Foreign Commerce, assumed the dominant role in this relationship. Former Sen. Paul Douglas described this particular relationship:

> Membership on the Senate's Committee on Interstate and Foreign Commerce, which handled all legislation for most of those bodies [regulatory commissions], was second only to the Appropriations Committee for those wanting raw power. With special eagerness, the commissioners generally toadied to these men. One Senator represented the airlines, a few the railroads, some the power companies, while nearly everyone was concerned with the franchises doled out gratuitously for radio and television stations. Legislators were constantly begged to intercede on behalf of some special interest. Republican firms hired Democratic lawyers and "lame-duck" men of influence to represent them. It was commonly said that Republicans did not mind letting Democrats have 10 per cent of the plunder if they could keep the remaining 90 per cent. Some of those who objected publicly to such practices possessed subterranean channels of influence into the very bodies which they did not want to have the politicians intrude upon.[80]

In 1950, Sen. Edwin C. Johnson (a Democrat from Colorado) headed this powerful committee. Johnson had "developed a personal legend of an almost supernatural political skill" and was almost totally "unpartisan," a journalist recalled.[81] Less kindly, Truman said: "He votes with the Republicans much oftener than he does the Democrats, although he poses as a Democrat."[82] Johnson generally distrusted executive power and regarded the regulatory commissions as arms of Congress.[83] He viewed Truman's plans as threats to his "personal domain."[84]

Johnson submitted resolutions of disapproval against plans seven, eight, nine, and eleven, and on 24 April McClellan's committee began reviewing them.[85] In his testimony, Johnson said that a majority of his committee opposed the four plans because the regulatory agencies were arms of Congress and should not be modified by the chief executive.[86]

The railroad industry strongly backed Johnson's resolutions of disapproval, concentrating its opposition against plan seven on the Interstate Commerce Commission. Rumors of administration plans to centralize policymaking functions regarding transportation in the Department of Commerce made industry leaders nervous.[87] Truman's plan for the ICC, which was influenced by leaders in the railroad business, would improve the administration's chances of winning a hearing for its policies on transportation within the agency. The trucking industry opposed the plan and called for further study and comprehensive legislation.[88] Water carriers apparently did not oppose the reorganization.[89] They could benefit from increased administration influence over ICC because such a change was likely to dilute railroad control of the agency.

Lawton tried to defend the plan by wrapping it in the Hoover Commission mantle and by stressing the limitations on the chairman's power under the plan.[90] Rowe and Pollock, two former Hoover commissioners, supported Lawton's position.[91] Harold Leventhal, representing CCHR, endorsed the plan on the grounds that it improved administration. He alleged that the railroads did not want ICC to operate efficiently because delays operated in their favor. Leventhal cited the notorious instance of an ICC case that threatened to make barge lines more competitive with railroads but that had been pending for twenty years. Leventhal also pointed out that plan seven opened lines of communication between the White House and ICC. He also added: "They may and rightfully should give consideration to the President's views on national policy, without in any way being bound by those views."[92]

Despite strong opposition, the Senate committee divided rather evenly. The plan was rejected by a vote of 6 to 5. McClellan led four committee Republicans and one Democrat on the negative side.[93]

On 17 May, Johnson brought plan seven up for vote. He said he opposed the plan for two main reasons. First, it would create a one-man commission by giving too much power to the chairman. Second, permitting the president to appoint the chairman would make the ICC part of the executive branch rather than allowing it to remain as an arm of Congress.[94] John W. Bricker (a Republican from Ohio) charged that the plan threatened to establish executive dictatorship:

> It is a part of the whole, over-all policy of the totalitarian philosophy of government. It may not be a long step, but it is a step directly in that direction.[95]

Benton and Humphrey argued for the plan. Benton ridiculed the idea that opponents rejected the plan simply because it violated the independence of the regulatory commissions. He pointed out that McClellan's committee approved the plans that applied the same organizational pattern to three other commissions. It turned down plan seven, Benton charged, only because of opposition from powerful interest groups.[96]

Without further debate, the Senate overwhelmingly voted against the plan with a count of 66 to 13.[97] "The alliance of the ICC with pressure groups representing its regulated clientele was sufficiently powerful to defeat Plan No. 7."[98]

Johnson immediately moved to take up plan eleven, which reorganized FCC. McClellan's committee had held hearings on it jointly with plan seven. Although most testimony had dealt with plan seven, some witnesses did concentrate on the FCC. The Federal Communications Bar Association and the National Association of Broadcasters opposed it, as did members of Johnson's committee.[99]

Despite its similarity to plan seven, McClellan's committee reported favorably on plan eleven.[100] However, Johnson confidently moved to take up plan eleven immediately after the Senate defeated plan seven. With little debate, the Senate rejected plan eleven by a vote of 50 to 23.[101] A CCHR official termed this defeat a fluke that occurred because plan eleven came up at the same time as plan seven when momentum was against it.[102] In addition, consistency seemed to dictate that if the Senate killed one plan it should also kill the other identical proposal.

Republicans continued to reject the proposals of the Republican-created Hoover Commission. Only 5 percent voted for plan seven and 19 percent for plan eleven. Nine percent of the Southern Democrats agreed to plan seven and 14 percent voted for plan eleven. But again, as with plan one, surprising numbers of non-Southern Democrats rejected the president's plans. Only 28 percent voted for plan seven and 37 percent for plan eleven. Several interrelated circumstances had thwarted the administration's scheme. Congress demonstrated again its long-standing distaste for any increase in executive power over commissions, and the FEPC debate had diminished some segments of potential legislative support. Yet, the Senate later approved two plans similar to the defeated ones. That eventual victory signified that pressure from the railroad, television, and radio industries was the distinctive reason for Truman's failure to reorganize the ICC and FCC in the battles of May.[103]

The Senate next voted on plan four, which transferred USDA functions to the secretary of agriculture. It faced stronger opposition than any other plan. More than in any other department, proposed organizational changes in USDA created great controversy. Political scientist Grant McConnell found that interested groups regarded agricultural organization as important as the substance of agricultural programs.[104]

All the major farm organizations opposed plan four, one of the few issues on which they agreed.[105] The Senate yielded to this pressure. No one spoke in favor of the plan, not even Benton, who had emerged as the strongest defender of Truman's plans, and only one senator voted for it. Even important executive branch officials gave minimal support. The secretary of agriculture did not regard the plan as crucially important because he already had authority over many agencies in his department, and he probably realized that he could not use the power the plan would grant to make organizational changes. The administration also did not regard it as worthy enough to make the same effort for this plan as it had done for the others.[106]

The reasons for opposition to the plan were varied and complex, entangled in the almost impenetrable maze of agricultural politics. Much of the opposition stemmed from the fact that the plan would increase Secretary of Agriculture Charles F. Brannan's power. Brannan, a disturbing figure in farm politics, projected a liberal image in an area generally dominated by conservative pressure groups. To many he symbolized the unsettling shift from rural to urban dominance, and agricultural leaders resented him because he refused to give even lip service to their values and symbols.[107] The farm organizations feared Brannan. A CCHR official wrote:

> Brannan is a formidable and competent person. He has a large and well-appointed organization. It is with good reason that they fear him and are reluctant to upset the status quo, because they fear that Brannan can take advantage of the flux to strengthen his office vis-a-vis the farm organizations to which he is opposed. In my opinion, he most certainly would attempt this; therefore, their fear is probably fairly well justified.[108]

The farm organizations also feared various schemes that they believed Brannan would undertake if he had the opportunity. The Brannan plan, which involved making changes in the farm price support system, especially created apprehension. In 1953, Sen. Clinton Anderson (a Democrat from New Mexico), a former secretary of agriculture, while testifying on a plan similar to Truman's plan four, recalled the situation in 1950:

> There was a very hot controversy going on at the time the other reorganization plan came up. It involved a somewhat different concept of price supports than had been established by the country over a period of years. And I think it was due to that fact that the Senate, at least, was as divided as it was.[109]

Other complex, often half-hidden, sources of opposition existed. For example, Anderson said a "personal situation" between himself and the department in 1950 prevented him from being "enthusiastic" about any proposal that came from it.[110] Some experts believed Congress rejected the plan because of fear that Brannan intended to move various departmental functions to the Production and Marketing Administration;[111] others believed the major opposition specifically resulted from fear that Brannan would eliminate the independency of the Farm Credit Administration;[112] still others, regarded the problem of the relationship between the PMA, Soil Conservation Service, and Extension Service as the specific key to the plan's defeat.[113]

McClellan's committee voted against plan four 7 to 5, with Humphrey, Leahy, and Benton submitting a minority report.[114] But not even these men defended the plan when it came up for a vote by the Senate on 18 May. The special circumstances surrounding the plan, with defeat almost certain, made it difficult to support it, a Bureau of the Budget official reported.[115] Humphrey, generally one of the staunchest reorganization proponents, declined even the "dubious honor" of controlling debating time for supporters of the plan.[116] After a short debate, with no one speaking for the plan,[117] the Senate voted by voice vote. Sixty-four members answered a quorum call, but observers heard only one man, Harley Kilgore (a Democrat from West Virginia), vote for the plan.[118]

Despite unprecedented public interest in reorganization, Truman's 1950 program seemed headed for disaster. It did not surprise knowledgeable observers that the Senate killed plan twelve, because by eliminating the Office of the General Counsel of NLRB the administration attempted to disturb the organizational balance of power created by the Taft-Hartley act. However, many observers were surprised when the Senate rejected plans one and four, transferring functions of the Departments of Treasury and Agriculture to the respective department secretaries, and plans seven and eleven, creating "strong" chairmen for the Interstate Commerce Commission and the Federal Communications Commission. On the surface, these plans were simple, noncontroversial attempts to give executive officials continuing authority to manage and reorganize their agencies. Underneath, however, these plans would have given agency officials potential authority to disturb the power relationships that had evolved between executive units, congressional committees, and interest groups.

Thus, the Senate had killed the first five plans it had considered. Not only did Truman's 1950 program appear to be endangered, but since it was doubtful that any future program would have such favorable conditions, the future of the movement for organizational reform seemed dim.

Chapter 11

The Reorganization Plans of 1950: Phase Two

In a one-week period, the Senate killed the first five plans it considered of the twenty-seven that the president submitted in 1950. Fortunately for Truman, the political situation began to shift. Despite that one disastrous week, twenty of his plans eventually took effect.

On 18 May, the House turned its attention to plan six that reorganized the Department of Labor. Democratic Congressman Wingate Lucas (Texas) led the opposition to the measure. In 1949, Lucas had persuaded Congress to accept a proposal that confirmed the independence of the wage and hour administrator within the Department of Labor.[1] He apparently regarded plan six, which transferred all functions within the Department to the secretary, as a personal affront because Truman had ignored a congressional decision made only six months earlier.[2]

Dawson's Committee on Expenditures in the Executive Departments held hearings and reported the plan favorably.[3] After a brief debate, the House passed plan six without a roll-call vote.[4] McClellan's Senate committee reported it favorably,[5] and it went into effect without further challenge. Truman had achieved his first victory of 1950.

The passage of this plan and plan two of 1949, as well as other actions stemming from the Hoover Commission recommendations, made the Department of Labor stronger than it had ever been in its history.[6] From the earliest days of his presidency, Truman had worked to rebuild that department. Its restoration was one of the legacies of the Fair Deal.

In 1949, Congress had accepted Truman's "strong chairman" plan for the U.S. Maritime Commission, but it soon became apparent that it needed further, more drastic reorganization. In October 1949, a Bureau of the Budget official warned that serious problems still existed. The commission, he said, had "put ends above means" in its determination to develop the American merchant marine. The bureau believed that the matter was serious enough to warrant the president's concern. In a recent investigation, a House committee characterized the Maritime Commission as "hostile" or "uncooperative" and suggested transferring it to an executive department.[7] The General Accounting Office also found many irregularities, and some illegalities, in its subsidy activities.[8] Both the Hoover Commission and the President's Advisory Committee on the Merchant Marine also recommended drastic reorganization.[9]

Thus, plan twenty-one abolished the Maritime Commission and transferred its functions to two newly created Department of Commerce agencies, the Federal Maritime Board and the Maritime Administration. The secretary would control all functions except two: regulatory powers remained independent of his office, and he had no control over board subsidy decisions.[10] The plan was "fearsomely complicated," a CCHR official warned Hoover.[11]

Republican Owen Brewster (Maine), a Senate leader on maritime affairs and a member of the Committee on Interstate and Foreign Commerce, testified against plan twenty-one when McClellan's committee began hearings on 8 May. He charged that the transfer threatened the merchant marine because the Maritime Commission devoted itself to rebuilding American maritime strength, while other officials in the "upper echelons" of the administration wanted to allow foreign allies such as England to earn dollar exchange through expansion of their own shipping services. Brewster feared that the Department of Commerce would sacrifice the American merchant marine in the interest of these broader concerns.[12]

Brewster touched on another major theme developed by the plan's opponents. Noting that Truman had ordered Secretary of Commerce Charles Sawyer to study the feasibility of a transportation department, Brewster revealed that he had reliable information that Sawyer intended to recommend consolidation of transportation functions within his department. Brewster suggested that Congress should also thoroughly consider its policy toward such consolidation, rather than move toward it in piecemeal fashion with this plan.[13] In his message on plan twenty-one, Truman had described it as a "long step forward" toward integration of government transportation functions. He had announced that he would look to the secretary of commerce for leadership in transportation matters and for that reason the plan provided for an undersecretary of commerce for transportation.[14] This provision caused transportation interests in general to oppose the plan.

When the hearings started, only two groups directly connected with water transportation testified against it. The shipping industry's failure to oppose the plan openly did not surprise former Congressman John J. O'Connor, who represented the Isbrandtsen Company, the largest independent, non-subsidized, American flag steamship owner and operator. He said that the industry intended to scuttle the plan but feared attacking it openly. Opposition to the plan came from the twelve big companies that received most of the subsidies and other favors from the Maritime Commission, he said. Congress established the agency to regulate the industry, but the industry controlled the agency and regulated itself.[15] The big companies opposed the plan because they did not want anything to disturb their relationship with the Maritime Commission.

O'Connor also opposed the plan but on the grounds that it did not carry reorganization far enough. The shipping industry had already corrupted the Maritime Commission, he held. Many of its staff members came from the big shipping companies, for example, and the plan gave little promise of eliminating this problem. According to the blunt-spoken former congressman:

> To dig out this Maritime Commission. . .and replant it bodily, personnel, and what not. . .is like transplanting a badly tainted tree, merely to some new location, without even spraying it, or pruning it. It will still be the same old eyesore. The jungle of the Commerce Department will be penetrable to all who need approach the new Maritime Board of three [members], merely reduced from five. They will not even leave the building they are now in, or even the corridors now cluttered with the bowing and scraping contact men of the chosen.[16]

O'Connor advocated placing the Maritime Commission within a transportation department.[17]

The shipping industry did not have to oppose the plan publicly because the rest of the transportation industry carried the lobbying burden. Representatives of railroad, airline, trucking, and other transportation and shipping associations testified against it. These groups feared that plan twenty-one established a pattern that the administration intended to apply to the rest of the industry, by transferring transportation activities from agencies like the Interstate Commerce Commission into the Department of Commerce to strengthen presidential influence over these functions.[18] These groups, which controlled the public bodies that supposedly regulated them in behalf of the public, now sensed a threat to their traditional power base.

The plan received strong supporting testimony from several executive officials, but the administration also needed CCHR support because the plan deviated from the Hoover Commission recommendation to place the

Maritime Commission's nonregulatory functions in the Department of Commerce and to leave its regulatory functions in an independent agency. The Bureau of the Budget wisely submitted the reorganization proposal to the CCHR before sending it to Congress. A CCHR official, who recommended that his committee support the plan, told Hoover that the administration wanted to circumvent a fast-growing scandal. He explained that when the administration began to work out organizational details it proved impossible to divide the functions exactly as the Hoover Commission envisioned but that plan twenty-one carried out the spirit of the commission's recommendations. He advised Hoover that if the CCHR did not support the plan the administration probably would not submit it because even with CCHR support its enactment would be "nip and tuck."[19] Therefore, with Hoover's silent consent the CCHR representative appeared before McClellan's committee and stated that the CCHR strongly supported the plan as a "practical generalized" application of Hoover Commission recommendations.[20]

McClellan's committee reported the plan with no recommendation for defeat or passage,[21] and on 19 May the Senate began its debate. Republican Sen. George Malone (Nevada) had passed along to a Republican official that the Senate would probably defeat plan twenty-one that afternoon.[22] However, after a short discussion, the Senate accepted the plan with a vote of 59 to 14. This was one of the few times that a majority of Republicans, Southern Democrats, and non-Southern Democrats voted for a plan.[23] It passed because of unusually persuasive administrative arguments for it. McClellan and other committee members did not speak against it, perhaps because of the knowledge that scandal could erupt at anytime.

Since the White House designed plan twenty-one to correct critical administrative problems, it constituted an unusual case. The real test for the success of Truman's 1950 program in the Senate came on Monday, 22 May, when Congress debated plans eight and nine, which centralized authority in the presidentially appointed chairmen of the Federal Trade Commission and the Federal Power Commission. The Senate had already struck down five plans containing comparable shifts of authority.

McClellan had combined hearings on these two plans with those on plans seven and eleven. Aside from general opposition of men such as Sen. Edwin Johnson (a Democrat from Colorado) and general support from witnesses like Budget Director Lawton, little testimony related directly to FTC and FPC. Plans eight and nine duplicated plans seven and eleven, but McClellan's committee reported them favorably, despite its chairman's opposition.[24]

When plan eight came up for debate on 22 May, Benton provided the drama.[25] Benton, the Senate's newest member and one of the president's most steadfast admirers, fully devoted himself to the passage of Truman's 1950 reorganization program. "I have no higher priority in the Senate than this," he wrote.[26] He became deeply interested in reorganization because of his experience in business and government, especially his tenure as assistant secretary of state when he saw the need for administrative efficiency and economy.[27] In addition, Connecticut Gov. Chester Bowles had appointed his friend Benton to fill out an uncompleted senatorial term, and Benton faced a difficult special election in 1950. According to a scholar, he became the Senate's leading advocate of the Hoover Commission proposals because he thought this issue would help him establish rapport with Connecticut's business community.[28]

Benton, with his good friend Humphrey, had led the fight during the battles for the first few plans. After watching the Senate kill five of them, he became alarmed and began to try to force the White House, the Bureau of the Budget, Hoover, and others to exert more leadership.[29] While defending plan eight, Benton, frustrated at this point, delivered an excellent speech explaining the political difficulties reorganization faced. He said that he finally understood why the Senate "knocked off" five of the first six plans "like clay pigeons in a shooting gallery." Obviously strong opposition came from special interest groups, Benton lectured, but the important question was why they succeeded. Benton offered three major and two minor explanations. First, the administration did not undertake sufficient preparatory work with Congress. It failed to consult key senators most concerned with activities affected by the plans. Nor did the administration explain adequately the reasons for the plans, which meant that the arguments of the special interest groups carried more weight. Second, said Benton, Senate leaders such as Lucas, Taft, McClellan, and others did not provide effective support for the plans, though both parties loudly proclaimed approval of Hoover Commission proposals. Third, the public did not make its support felt. CCHR did not have resources to offset special interest opposition, and Hoover failed to use his great prestige to enter publicly the "cat fight" for these plans. He said he understood that behind the scenes Hoover and one of the CCHR high officials had even opposed one or more of the reorganization plans. Two secondary reasons also contributed to the plans' failure, Benton charged. First, the fact that this was an election year made pressure groups more effective than usual. Second, the current debate over FEPC created antagonism and cost some crucial votes.[30]

Johnson again tried to mobilize the Senate to kill this plan, as it had similar ones a few days earlier.[31] However, Benton had his reward and the plan passed 34 votes against and 37 votes for.[32] Again McClellan and his committee did not fight the plan on the floor.

Johnson said he did not object to the Senate immediately voting on plan nine. Long and Capehart made a few remarks against it and O'Conor briefly spoke in favor of it.[33] Then the Senate accepted the plan 37 votes against and 36 for.[34] Although the majority of those voting opposed the plan, the requirement for a constitutional majority of forty-nine for veto saved it. Fewer than 45 percent of all Democrats voted for the plans. This made the high absentee rate crucial. In view of the forty-nine vote requirement to kill plans, failure to cast a vote was, in effect, a vote for the plan.

The tide had now turned in favor of the plans and several political figures received credit. *Newsweek* entitled an article "Bill Benton Blitz" and gave him credit for single-handedly changing the Senate's attitude.[35] However, the situation was more complex than that. There seemed to be a general awakening to the fact that Senate action had endangered a popular reorganization program, based on the Hoover Commission reports. Various individuals began pressuring for passage of the plans, and, after CCHR and others stirred up public reaction, a "deluge of letters" hit Congress.[36] In addition, Hoover encouraged Republican leaders, including Taft, to support the plans. "Has Mr. Truman offered to make you a member of the Grand Order of St. Louis for having pulled his chestnuts out of the fire?" a CCHR official asked Hoover.[37]

Truman also began to look after his program himself. "Whip cracked on recalcitrant Senator at Blair House," a CCHR official telegraphed, referring to a meeting between Truman and McClellan.[38] According to a report in *Newsweek*, Truman used charm rather than force, reassuring McClellan that he had not attempted a power grab through his reorganization program. According to the report, McClellan apologized for angry remarks he had made about Truman's motives and later told some colleagues that if the meeting had taken place a month earlier the results of the Senate action might have been different.[39]

Another element in this political shift came on Friday, 19 May, when the Senate voted on and defeated a move to close the FEPC filibuster. In discussing the legislative history of the first twenty-one plans, a Bureau of the Budget official noted that Congress defeated all plans voted on before the FEPC cloture vote and passed all that came up after the vote.[40]

Three others of the first twenty-one plans remained to be considered by

23 May, before the sixty-day waiting period ended. Plan five, debated immediately after the disposition of plan nine and voted on the next day, transferred functions of the Department of Commerce to the secretary. The Bureau of the Budget correctly anticipated that a major problem would arise over transferring Patent Office activities to the secretary.[41] The question of whether that unit should be in a department had been debated for over a century.[42] The administration expected patent lawyers to fight the plan, but discord within the Department of Commerce allowed this rather small pressure group to exert great influence. Secretary of Commerce Sawyer, who described himself as "an unashamed partisan of business,"[43] originally wanted the plan to include the Patent Office, but one of his assistants convinced him that the transfer was inappropriate because the Patent Office administered quasi-judicial functions.[44]

Dawson's committee approved the plan, but Hoffman submitted a minority report in which he reminded his colleagues that Henry Wallace had been secretary of commerce and declared ominously that anyone who advocated killing little pigs should not have control of the patent system.[45] On 18 May, immediately after passing plan six on the Department of Labor, the House voted on plan five. After only a few minutes debate, it accepted the plan.[46]

The crucial vote again came in the Senate. McClellan's committee opened hearings on 27 April, when Republican Alexander Wiley (Wisconsin) testified against the plan. Although Wiley belonged to the Republican party, he chaired the subcommittee on patents of the Committee on the Judiciary. The senator posed questions about a scheme that would destroy the foundation that supported the free enterprise system:

> I understand the Secretary does not want it. I understand the people in the Patent Office do not want it. Who, for Heaven's sake, wants it then? Why is it done?

Wiley implied that there was mysterious forces involved, men with "synthetic notions" who wanted to destroy the system.[47]

McClellan's committee reported the plan without any recommendation regarding its passage.[48] When it came before the Senate on 22 May, just after plans eight and nine passed, Wiley led the fight to kill it. He did not object to any part except that which affected the Patent Office. He reminded the Senate that Sawyer had opposed this provision once also.[49] On 23 May, the plan passed with 43 votes for it and 23 votes against.[50] About 60 percent of both wings of the Democratic party voted for the plan, compared to 24 percent of the Republicans. The relatively high support from Southern Democrats (59 percent for the plan) probably reflected their faith that the conservative Sawyer would not abuse the authority granted to him.

The Senate then turned to plan seventeen, which transferred advance planning of non-federal public works from the General Services Administration to the Housing and Home Finance Agency. Of all the contested plans, it drew the least opposition from private organizations, but Aiken attacked the plan when McClellan held hearings on 16 May. Aiken argued that Congress, after full deliberation, placed advance planning in the GSA in October 1949, which was after the Hoover Commission reported. He believed that the administration unfairly used the legislative veto to negate a congressional action.[51]

McClellan's committee reported the plan without recommendation,[52] and the Senate limited debate to one hour. Aiken attacked the plan, but, recognizing the hopelessness of the fight, he spent most of his time joking about bureaucratic jargon.[53] The plan passed with 43 votes for and 29 against.[54] The Democrats supported the plan (55 percent of the Southern Democrats and 66 percent of the non-Southern Democrats), but 60 percent of the Republicans voted against it.

The Senate also voted on plan eighteen on 23 May, the third plan to be voted on that day. This plan, technical in its provisions, transferred from other agencies responsibility for leasing and assigning space in most public buildings to the General Services Administration and transferred operation, maintenance, and custody of most of these structures to the GSA.[55] Opposition developed because the plan transferred from the Post Office Department to the GSA several thousand custodial workers who feared losing a certain amount of pay and other benefits.[56] The House committee held hearings and reported the plan favorably, but its opponents never brought it to the House floor, evidently because they had no hope of defeating it.[57]

In the Senate, Democrat Olin Johnston (South Carolina), a member of the Post Office and Civil Service Committee, introduced a resolution against the plan. Johnston and representatives of several unions testified against the plans when McClellan held hearings on 16 May. They argued that the plan penalized maintenance employees.[58]

Plan eighteen received stronger institutional support than most other plans, perhaps because the plan offended only low-income custodial workers rather than officials of big business organizations. Representatives of the Bureau of the Budget, Post Office Department, GSA, Civil Service Commission, and Public Buildings Administration tried to reassure the custodial workers that the administration intended to do everything possible to safeguard their interest. Administrators also defended the plan strongly in terms of economy and efficiency.[59] After this campaign for the plan, the AFL moderated its opposition somewhat.[60] The committee reported the plan without recommendation, but the thrust of its report favored the plan.[61]

When the plan came up for debate on 18 May, Johnston was absent and another congressman, who had cosponsored the resolution against the plan, admitted that he now supported it.[62] After some discussion, the Senate passed it with 69 votes for and 7 votes against.[63] In an unusual vote, 74 percent of the Republicans voted for the plan, along with 63 percent of the non-Southern Democrats and 82 percent of the Southern Democrats. This strong support probably reflects the fact that the chief pressure group opposed to the plan was composed of lowly custodial workers, many of whom were Blacks.

Plan twenty-four, which attempted to end the Reconstruction Finance Corporation's (RFC) independency by placing it in the Department of Commerce, grew from administration attempts to develop a small business program. Truman called for this program in his 1950 State of the Union message,[64] and on 14 February Secretary of Commerce Sawyer outlined tentative plans for insuring loans to small businesses and for taking other steps to improve capital and credit resources.[65] Truman encouraged Sawyer to quickly develop a broad program and asked him to work with White House aide Stephen J. Spingarn and other members of the executive office. Spingarn asked the Bureau of the Budget for its recommendations and explained that the present opinion was to place such programs in the Department of Commerce. He added that Sawyer believed that reorganization should place RFC there also.[66]

The Bureau of the Budget, evidently concerned about a congressional investigation of RFC, had already drawn up a plan to transfer that agency either to the Department of Commerce or, as recommended by the Hoover Commission, to Treasury.[67] In response to Spingarn's request, a budget official said that the transfer of RFC to Commerce conformed to the bureau's long-term organizational objectives and that the goals of the RFC business loan programs coincided with those of the Department of Commerce. The bureau official tentatively recommended inclusion of the transfer in the small business program legislation.[68]

On 5 May, Truman submitted his special message to Congress calling for passage of a small business program, including transfer, by a plan to be submitted later, of RFC to the Department of Commerce.[69]

In mid-June, Dawson's and McClellan's committees held hearings on plan twenty-four. The House committee reported the plan favorably.[70] When the plan came up for vote only 232 members answered the roll call. Since it took 218 votes to kill it, the plan passed.[71]

In the Senate, Senator Fulbright, who headed a subcommittee that had RFC under investigation, provided the main opposition. The senator's opposition to this plan "could be described as a scientific interest in holding the subject constant until the nature of its sickness, and the best possible remedy, could be thoroughly explored."[72] Perhaps Fulbright also wanted to reap the full rewards of publicity before the president acted to correct the investigated problem.[73]

Fulbright appeared before McClellan's committee when it opened hearings on 14 June. He wanted no changes made until his subcommittee finished its study. The senator held that the major question was not whether to transfer RFC to the Department of Commerce or to leave it independent but whether to retain the agency at all. If his subcommittee decided that RFC needed to be transferred, it could be accomplished by legislation. Fulbright indicated, however, that he believed RFC should remain as an independent agency.[74]

Since it lacked a quorum, the committee reported the plan without recommendation, though the majority of those present expressed disapproval. The committee directed the thrust of its report against the plan.[75] During the debate on 6 July, Fulbright spoke against the plan, arguing that nothing should be done until he completed his investigation.[76] Many senators then argued that the plan should be defeated so that RFC would be undisturbed until Fulbright finished his work.[77] For example, Humphrey, a strong advocate of Truman's program, failed to support this plan. His assistant notified the administration that Humphrey feared that if he publicly supported it he would appear "to slap Fulbright's face." A White House aide added: "This is a matter of senatorial courtesy rather than any substantive disagreement with the plan."[78]

Only Sen. Francis J. Myers (a Democrat from Pennsylvania) defied this senatorial tradition during the debate. He supported the plan because he regarded it as an integral part of the small business program.[79] However, with seventy-nine senators present the Senate defeated the proposal without a roll-call vote.[80]

Immediately afterwards, the Senate debated plan twenty-two, which carried out a Hoover Commission proposal to transfer the Federal National Mortgage Association (FNMA) from the RFC to HHFA.[81] FNMA provided a secondary market for FHA and VA insured home loans. Transferring it from RFC further emphasized RFC's business, as opposed to housing, functions. The administration had hoped this plan, along with plan twenty-three on prefabricated housing, would make the RFC transfer to the Department of Commerce easier.[82]

When McClellan's committee opened hearings on 28 June, it appeared that strong antagonism to the mortgage funding scheme had developed. CCHR Director Robert Johnson said that real estate and veterans groups had the plan under "heavy fire."[83] Sens. Walter George (a Democrat from Georgia) and Harry P. Cain (a Republican from Washington) introduced a resolution against it, and Cain, described by one historian as a "leading spokesman for the real estate lobby,"[84] testified against the plan. He held that FNMA administered credit and banking rather than housing functions. If the administration wanted to transfer FNMA, he said, it might just as well place it in the Veterans' Administration because in recent months 90 percent of the new mortgage loans FNMA acquired were home loans guaranteed by VA. He also declared that if HHFA acquired FNMA the housing administration might be biased toward Federal Housing Administration at the expense of VA.[85]

Sen. John J. Sparkman, chairman of the subcommittee on housing and rents of the Committee on Banking and Currency, testified for the plan. The Senate, he said, had passed two bills transferring FNMA to the housing agency, and congressional studies as well as the Hoover Commission had concluded that it should be there. Sparkman also argued that the plan would allow needed policy changes to gear FNMA to housing activities more effectively.[86] Raymond Foley, housing and home finance administrator, testified along the same lines.[87] McClellan's committee reported the plan without recommendation.[88]

When the Senate debated the plan on 6 July, Sparkman spoke for it and Cain opposed it but weakened his argument by saying that he and the others opposed it mainly because it did not provide for economy.[89] After an extremely short debate, the plan passed with 30 votes against it and 43 votes for it.[90] Fifty-five percent of the Southern Democrats supported the plan and 59 percent of the non-Southern Democrats (41 percent of the latter were absent). Fifty-five percent of the Republicans voted against it.

In 1949, Truman had submitted a plan to change the Federal Security Agency into a department of welfare. Congress had defeated the measure, but Truman still believed that the FSA functions deserved departmental status and would benefit by having increased public attention focused on them.[91] Truman also felt obligated to Ewing. Ewing, a capable political strategist, worked hard for many programs Truman regarded as central to the Fair Deal and loyally supported Truman when many people, identified with the liberal wing of the Democratic party, looked to others to carry on the work of their hero, Franklin D. Roosevelt. Truman submitted plan twenty-seven, giving FSA departmental status, because of the urging of his loyal secretary. Lawton described Truman's attitude as "inclined to go along with the plan, although not too enthusiastically."[92]

At first the administration had wanted to rely on legislation rather than to submit a new plan.[93] However, in mid-February, Ewing initiated a meeting with interested senators to discuss the possibility of offering another plan.[94] A lobbyist for the American Parents Committee, who had correctly predicted the 1949 plan's defeat, warned the administration that Congress would reject the new measure; the problem, she said, stemmed not from the internal organization of the proposed department but from hostility to Ewing himself.[95] However, the administration acquiesced in Ewing's desire to use the legislative-veto procedure. It offered a new plan and tried to avoid defeat by responding to criticism leveled at the 1949 scheme.[96] Opponents attacked the 1949 plan because it centralized all FSA functions in the secretary of the proposed new department. The 1950 plan continued FSA's "holding company" type organization, allowing the agency's constituent units to retain a good deal of independent authority. This violated Bureau of the Budget organizational principles but the bureau knew it had to compromise to give the plan a chance of passing. "The present Plan 27 is an example of an evenly compromised plan," a budget official wrote.[97]

On 15 June, the House Committee on Expenditures in the Executive Departments opened hearings on Hoffman's resolution against plan twenty-seven. The AMA, as in 1949, deployed its full force against the plan. It was more active politically in 1950 than at anytime during its history and spent two and one-half million dollars on lobbying.[98] The physicians' association opposed the plan partly because it believed that commingling health, education, and welfare functions threatened to lead to socialized medicine but mainly, said the AMA representative, because it wanted Congress to create a department of health with cabinet rank as the first step toward the AMA's twelve-part program for medicine. Plan twenty-seven would make it difficult to establish such a department.[99]

The House had not killed any plans in 1949 and 1950, and the House committee, unlike McClellan's, had approved plan twenty-seven.[100] The Senate thus seemed to be the major threat to the plan, and the president, the Bureau of the Budget, and Ewing concentrated their activities on the upper house.[101] As the deadline for voting neared, a White House aide wrote a memorandum suggesting final strategy for dealing with the Senate and only in passing mentioned that the House intended to vote on the plan that day, which was 10 July.[102] Ewing later admitted that the administration had "slipped," because the showdown came not in the Senate but in the House. Brown gloated to Ewing: "We sort of misled you there."[103]

When the plan came up for vote, Holifield and a few others defended it, but Dawson delivered the most impassioned defense. He recalled FSA's role in World War II and said that with the developing conflict in Korea, agencies dealing with human resources needed departmental status. Opposition, he said, came from organized medicine, which intended to block the plan until it got a department of health: "Like a dog in a manger, they stand there; they cannot eat the hay but they will not let the horse eat it because they cannot eat it." He claimed that for every doctor who opposed it, three hundred citizens supported the plan. Dawson reminded Democrats that the measure conformed to the party's 1948 campaign promises. When someone suggested that the plan threatened to lead to socialized medicine, Dawson said such charges provided a smoke screen to hide other motives for opposition.[104]

Brown now rose for the first time during the Eighty-first Congress to oppose the plan. He did so on the grounds that it deviated from the Hoover Commission recommendations.[105] Halleck also spoke against it and reminded his colleagues of the fall elections: "Now, mark it well, your vote on this proposition is going to put you on one side or the other of this great issue of socialization of medicine."[106] Hoffman attacked the plan because it increased Ewing's power over medicine and education.[107] Speaker after speaker repeated these arguments.[108]

McCormack took the floor, evidently trying deliberately to raise partisan feeling in order to hold the Democrats in line.[109] However, the House defeated the plan by 249 votes to 71.[110] AMA's Washington office reminded doctors to reward these opponents because many had disrupted their campaigns to return to Washington to vote against the plan.[111] Not one of the Southern representatives supported the plan. Probably Ewing's support of civil rights and national health insurance determined the outcome of the vote.[112] Truman now gave up his attempts to create a welfare department; not until both he and Ewing were gone did Congress create the department.

In summary, congressional treatment of Truman's 1950 reorganization program left a mixed record. With the defeat of plans one and four, he failed to transfer the functions of the Departments of Treasury and Agriculture to their respective secretaries. However, these defeats were partly offset by an earlier reorganization that had already vested most department functions in the secretary of agriculture[113] and by the passage of plan twenty-six that, with the exception of the Office of the Comptroller of the Currency, transferred Treasury Department functions to that secretary. The defeat of plans seven, eleven, and twelve prevented the establishment of "strong" chairmen within the ICC, FCC, and NLRB, respectively. The defeat of plan twelve also prohibited the elimination of Denham's Office of General Counsel. Truman soon "purged" Denham, but a 1960 investigation concluded that divided authority continued to hamper the enforcement of the national labor relations legislation.[114] The defeat of plan twenty-four left RFC as an exposed independent agency rather than placing it in the Department of Commerce. This controversial agency never recovered from the onslaught that began against it as scandals were uncovered during the last years of Truman's administration. The defeat of plan twenty-seven delayed creation of a health, education, and welfare department. However, earlier actions by Roosevelt and Truman had paved the way for such a department, and Eisenhower took the final step in 1953.

Truman got twenty plans through the Congress. Although they varied in significance, many of them were "Rooseveltian in their concepts of Presidential power."[115] Plans two, three, five, and six transferred the functions respectively of the Departments of Justice, Interior, Commerce, and Labor to their secretaries. Similar legislation and plans had already accomplished this in the Departments of State, Defense, and Post Office. The plans also provided for additional assistant secretaries. The administration designed these plans to allow managers to deal flexibly and speedily with administrative problems. Truman believed that these proposals would enable government to be responsive to the rapidly changing conditions and problems that characterized modern society. They also allowed Truman to put into effect administrative principles—centralizing and clarifying channels of authority—that he had believed in throughout his public career.

Such plans did allow for more flexibility and responsiveness. However, the executive branch had not been fragmented by accident. Executive agencies, with the support of their allies in Congress and among their constituencies, had won independence from superiors in the hierarchy above them. The 1950 plans reversed the process in many departments but did not change the structure of power that created the division. Therefore, the process started again. Truman's victories were not final ones but part of a continuing struggle of the chief executive to attain mastery of the executive branch.

Furthermore, even if subordinate officials did not have statutory authority separate from the secretary and president, they often had a good deal of informal independence from their superiors. The president often had less real authority over legal subordinates than his influence gave him over legally independent agencies. Therefore, these plans, which gave the president and secretaries authority over the activities and agencies of the departments, were seldom fully effective.[116] Department heads were rarely able to use freely the authority they had over bureau chiefs.[117] For example, after the passage of plan six, the Department of Labor remained "a loose-knit confederation of agencies," so divided that an "acrimonious controversy" developed over whether some of the labor bureaus would even allow their telephone calls to be handled through the department switchboard.[118]

Organizational principles similar to those that led to the first six proposals also spawned plans eight, nine, ten, and thirteen, which vested in chairmen chosen by the president the executive and administrative functions of the Federal Trade Commission, Federal Power Commission, Securities and Exchange Commission, and Civil Aeronautics Board, respectively. Similar reorganizations had been accomplished the previous year for the Civil Service Commission and the Maritime Commission. This series of plans suffered from the same weaknesses as the departmental plans. The problems of the regulatory commissions were not organizational but stemmed from causes rooted deep within the power structure of the nation.[119] The commissions placed special interest above the general interest because of power relationships, not because of organizational accidents and anomalies. These plans did not affect the real problems with regulatory commissions: That although they were supposedly designed to regulate private economic interests on behalf of the public, they actually operated in behalf of particular interests often to the detriment of the general public. The problem was not that the agencies were unresponsive; they were responsive to the powerful groups within the capitalist system, but not to the general population.

Scholars disagreed in their evaluation of these "strong chairmen" plans. Political scientist Marver Bernstein believed that in agencies where the chairmen had "taken hold" there had been signs of improvement in internal management.[120] James M. Landis, who had chaired a commission and served on others, argued in a 1960 report to John F. Kennedy, that the plans had "strangely missed fire." He concluded: "The obvious design of this provision of the various reorganization plans was to make the chairman the contact for agency affairs with the office of the President and, by enhancing his powers, to increase his prestige and to put him in a real position of leadership with reference to his agency. The measure has failed to achieve this purpose."[121] Chairmen had not used the power given to them by the plans, nor had the presidents attempted to exercise authority over the regulatory agencies.[122] However, another investigator concluded that the plans had caused changes, but not in the way Truman had intended. He believed that the extension of presidential power to the chairmen had politicized the commissions from top to bottom. Loyalty to the president had become necessary, and politics had eroded the expertise that supposedly had provided the foundation of the commissions.[123]

Plans fourteen and nineteen strengthened the secretary of labor and added to the Department of Labor the Bureau of Employees' Compensation and the Employees' Compensation Appeals Board. These plans, along with plan two of 1949, which transferred the Bureau of Employment Security to the department, allowed Truman to achieve one of his strongly held personal goals—strengthening the Department of Labor.

Plans fifteen, sixteen, seventeen, eighteen, and twenty continued the process of creating a central service agency by transferring various functions to the new General Services Administration or moving inappropriate functions from it. Plans twenty-two and twenty-three transferred housing functions from RFC to the Housing and Home Finance Agency in order to strengthen HHFA and to prepare RFC for transfer to the Department of Commerce, although defeat of plan twenty-four prevented that. Plan twenty-five transferred the functions of the National Security Resources Board to the chairman and made the board an advisory body.

One of the most drastic organizational changes occurred through plan twenty-one that abolished the Maritime Commission and transferred its functions to the Department of Commerce. This plan, along with plan seven of 1949, which transferred the Bureau of Public Roads to the Commerce Department, began the process of centralizing transportation functions in one agency. This particular plan prepared the way for the Department of Transportation, which Congress created in 1966. Truman symbolized this by providing for an undersecretary of transportation in plan twenty-one. The proposal also furnished a rare instance in which Congress allowed abolition of an independent commission. Congress took this drastic step because of the serious administrative problems suffered by the Maritime Commission.

Plan twenty-one did help the maritime agencies cope more effectively with their duties,[124] but this plan also demonstrated the difficulty of attempting to solve deep-rooted problems by organizational change. In 1961, Congress re-created an independent commission, the Federal Maritime Commission, and undid part of the 1950 plan by transferring the maritime regulatory functions from the Department of Commerce to it. From 1946 to

1964, five different agencies administered maritime promotional functions.[125] One scholar concluded that while observers disagreed on the causes of the present unsatisfactory situation, all of them agreed that the government shipping program had not adequately met postwar needs. He found specifically that plan twenty-one had failed to achieve its purposes. The plan had attempted to separate regulatory, quasi-judicial, and administrative functions, but by 1959 the functions had blended to such an extent that the chairman-administrator, who administered both the Federal Maritime Board and the Maritime Administration, had to sign all correspondence and orders in both capacities to be sure that his action would not be challenged on the grounds that it had been based on the wrong authority. Difficulties also developed between the maritime agencies and the Department of Commerce officials. Regulatory functions were almost entirely eclipsed within the action-oriented department. In addition, the plan created even closer ties between the maritime agencies and the maritime industry because the plan removed the prohibition against appointment of industry personnel to the agencies.[126]

Chapter 12

Reorganization, 1951–1952

During his last two years in office, Truman's popularity and credibility deteriorated to such an extent that his ability to govern seemed threatened. Controversies resulting from the Korean War and from corruption within the executive branch gave birth to several reorganization proposals, but also eroded Truman's ability to get those plans through Congress.

The Korean War started too suddenly for Truman to undertake the sort of administrative preparations that Franklin D. Roosevelt had begun well before the United States entered World War II. Truman at first seemed confident that the existing machinery could handle any problems that arose.[1] However, as mobilization proceeded the administration gave more thought to government organization. On 18 December 1950, Truman informed congressional leaders that the critical world situation called for the use of a number of emergency powers. Existing authority provided a reservoir for most requisites, but the president asked Congress to reenact immediately Title One of the First War Powers Act of 1941, which would allow him to make rapidly any organizational changes that Defense Mobilization Director Charles Wilson found necessary.[2]

However, to the surprise of the administration, the House denied Truman even a modified version of this emergency reorganization proposal. This occurred for a number of reasons—Republican displeasure with Truman's handling of the Korean War, for example—but the defeat generally reflected the increased influence of the "conservative coalition" in the Eighty-second Congress and the growing feeling in Congress that executive power was expanding too rapidly.[3]

Despite the defeat of the emergency reorganization bill, the administration still had the regular authority granted by the Reorganization Act of 1949. However, it soon decided to make only limited use of that authority. That decision reflected Truman's slackened interest in administrative reform, which his success in 1950 did not change, and his growing concern with other problems, particularly Korea. It also reflected the Bureau of the

157

Budget's belief that since the 1950 proposals had placed reorganization authority in the departmental secretaries, most management improvement could take place through their actions rather than by new plans.[4]

However, other forces came into play. Most of the six plans Truman submitted in 1951 and 1952 stemmed directly or indirectly from the scandals that marred the last two years of his administration. In 1949, "the mess in Washington" began attracting public attention as the Senate looked into the activities of "influence peddlers." The investigation soon touched the White House because of the involvement of one of Truman's friends— Gen. Harry Vaughan.[5] The first scandal to affect the reorganization program involved the RFC. Stuart Symington, whom Truman later appointed to head RFC, said it was a "horrible mess": "I've seen some bad ones, but this is the worst in my experience."[6] In 1932, Congress had created RFC to counter the depression and had strengthened and expanded it during the New Deal and World War II. RFC lending soared in the postwar period, encouraged by an administration that feared a depression and that wanted to take political advantage of its loan-making ability. Since RFC had no real criteria to guide it in making loans, administration figures increasingly overrode the business judgment of its officials.[7]

In 1949, RFC made several highly publicized loans that demonstrated faulty judgment. While examining these cases, Fulbright found that some RFC employees had gone to work for companies that had received money from the agency and that RFC directors were evasive about certain of the organization's practices. In early 1950, Fulbright, as chairman of a subcommittee of the Committee on Banking and Currency, proceeded to investigate the agency. The subcommittee included Fulbright, Democrat Paul Douglas (Illinois), and Charles Tobey (a Republican from New Hampshire).[8]

Fulbright did not desire to destroy RFC; he wanted to investigate existing conditions and then to make any needed corrections in agency operations. But Truman opened the way for disaster for the agency by acting unwisely, as he often did when people attacked his subordinates. As the Fulbright subcommittee uncovered various scandals attention increasingly focused on the RFC. In August 1950, Truman fired three of its five directors. However, the Fulbright subcommittee believed that the two retained were Donald S. Dawson's followers, a White House aide whom the subcommittee regarded as one of the corrupting influences. The senators believed that Dawson handpicked Truman's three new appointments to replace directors who had proved too independent. Fulbright privately informed Truman of his concern in September but the president ignored him. By the end of 1950, the press anxiously awaited a subcommittee report, but Fulbright, with the caution that characterized much of his career, held back. Finally, he requested an off-the-record meeting with Truman. He, Tobey, and Douglas had a congenial conference with Truman on 12 December. They told him that RFC needed a basic reorganization, which to avoid embarrassment could be presented as a move to strengthen RFC administration. The meeting ended on a friendly note and the senators left pleased. But then on 28 December, Truman, without forewarning, resubmitted the names of all the present RFC directors for confirmation by the Senate. Fulbright still delayed. In January, he asked the White House what other actions the president intended to take concerning the RFC; the administration gave him no information.[9]

Finally, in early February 1951, Fulbright released his subcommittee's report. It scathingly attacked previous RFC operations and proposed a bill to replace the five-man board of directors with a single administrator who could be held responsible for RFC activities.[10]

On 8 February, Truman publicly referred to the report as "asinine" and said it was a deliberate attempt to reflect unfavorably on the president himself.[11] After this outburst, which further undermined the administration's position, Truman gave in. White House officials consulted with Fulbright and Senator Maybank,[12] chairman of the Committee on Banking and Currency, and on 19 February Truman submitted plan one of 1951. The plan placed RFC under a single administrator. In his message to Congress, Truman did not refer to the scandals, but he did promise "additional safeguards" regarding loan policy.[13]

Truman still resisted making a full, frank admission that White House and executive officials had committed illegal or unethical acts. Instead, he tried to solve the problem through a public-relations campaign.[14] But Fulbright paid no attention to administration antics. He dropped his restrained manner and announced that his subcommittee would hold public hearings with the limited objective of proving the report was not asinine. He now became "hard, cold and implacable" in his investigation. It was improbable that the agency could recover from his onslaught.[15]

After Hoffman submitted a resolution of disapproval, Dawson's Committee on Expenditures in the Executive Departments held hearings on plan one on 2 and 5 March. The main issue quickly became one of whether RFC should be phased out. Paul Douglas brilliantly argued that the nature of the country's oligopolistic economy justified the existence of RFC. He said that the nation needed the agency because small businesses found it difficult to get private loans for long-term investments and new businessmen found it difficult to get funds for initial operations. He said evidence also existed that big investment houses had agreed to restrict the entrance of new businesses into major industries dominated by a few firms.[16] Only one person testified against the plan, and the committee recommended its passage.[17]

On 13 March, immediately after the House rejected the bill that would give Truman emergency reorganization authority, Dawson brought plan one up for debate. The debate immediately turned into a verbal brawl as each party, conscious of the 1952 elections, prepared a record of indictment against the other side. Republicans charged that the plan would make RFC more susceptible to political influence by centralizing authority in an administrator under control of the political party in power, that the administration designed the plan only to reorganize the way people thought about the men who ran the government, that the White House hastily wrote the proposal to stop the investigation of RFC, that it deviated from Hoover Commission recommendations.[18] Several Republicans argued that RFC should be abolished, not reorganized.[19]

The Democrats were even more overtly political. They supported the plan on the grounds that it corresponded with the recommendations of the Fulbright subcommittee and that it began the process of correcting an important problem. Several claimed that the Republicans opposed reorganization because they wanted the scandals to continue for their own political benefit.[20] Henderson Lanham said that the antics of the Republicans disgraced the political process. "You want to keep the mess smelling to high heaven for political advantage," he charged.[21]

The House voted on 14 March. Two hundred representatives voted against reorganization; 198 for it. It passed because the opposition did not have a constitutional majority.[22]

The Senate began consideration of plan one after Capehart introduced a resolution against it. On 21 March, McClellan began hearings. He appeared more favorable to this plan than most others,[23] perhaps because the scandal damaged the Democratic party. Democrat George Smathers (Florida) and Fulbright offered strong support. Smathers, who won praise even from opponents, argued that poor administration of a law did not render the law bad. He said the private banking system no longer served small businesses. RFC had made five hundred thousand small business loans since 1932; since a business had to be denied private banking help before turning to RFC, this federal service proved that the banking system had not met small business needs. He admitted that legislation might be needed to limit RFC activities to small business but argued that in the meantime Congress should accept plan one to prevent RFC from being "swept away in a tide of indignation."[24]

Fulbright defended RFC and admitted that his subcommittee might have made a mistake by not pointing out the good that RFC had accomplished. He said, for example, that it had helped Arkansas emerge from its colonial, raw material producing economic condition. But he also believed that RFC absolutely required reorganization; that Congress should accept this plan or abolish the agency. He argued that the coalition against the plan contained two diverse elements. One wanted to abolish RFC, a legitimate aim. However, this group must not confuse two different things; the plan should go into effect even if Congress later decided to abolish the agency. The other group wanted neither to abolish RFC nor to reorganize it. It wanted to retain the existing organization until the 1952 elections "as a horrible example of Democratic ineptitude."[25]

The Republican Senate Policy Committee voted to oppose plan one,[26] and four Republican senators testified against it. They argued that RFC should be eliminated entirely, not reorganized. They also enjoyed recounting Truman's antics, such as his referring to Fulbright's report as asinine a few days before incorporating its recommendations in this plan.[27]

The committee voted against the plan seven to six, with Democrat A. Willis Robertson (Virginia) joining six Republicans in opposition.[28]

As the Senate prepared to vote, rumors that Truman intended to appoint highly respected Symington as RFC administrator helped the plan's chances.[29] However, a new problem arose. Truman's reorganization plans had often become entangled with extraneous controversial issues, but few as explosive as with plan one. On 11 April, the nation learned that Truman had fired Gen. Douglas MacArthur. On 12 and 13 April, the Senate debated plan one, or rather it bitterly debated the MacArthur firing with short breaks to discuss the plan.

During the debate supporters relied on the positions developed in the House proceedings and in the Senate hearings. Opponents argued that Congress should abolish RFC.[30] Robertson summed up the problem in an ironic compliment to Fulbright. He said that the Arkansas senator had convinced everyone that RFC should either be reorganized or abolished; Robertson said he believed that adoption of the plan would hinder future attempts to abolish the agency.[31] The Republicans played up the scandals and Truman's erratic actions before he submitted the plan.

When the vote occurred, forty-one senators voted against the plan and only thirty-three for, but it went into effect because opponents lacked the constitutional majority of forty-nine.[32] Sixty percent of the Democrats supported the proposal; 80 percent of the Republicans opposed it. This was an unusual vote in that 68 percent of the Southern Democrats voted for the plan compared to 54 percent of the non-Southern Democrats.

Unfortunately, the plan did too little and came too late. RFC never recovered from the congressional investigations of these scandals. The crucial event had been the defeat of plan twenty-four of 1950. If that plan had transferred RFC to the Commerce Department, it would have been protected from the opposition. But with the agency isolated and exposed, plan one did not end opposition to it. In 1954, Congress voted to terminate it and abolition took place in 1957.[33]

Truman submitted only this one plan in 1951; it seemed that he would not be much more active in 1952. The Bureau of the Budget asked the departments and agencies for reorganization suggestions but few indicated need for further changes.[34] However, the effect of the scandals became more and more serious. A poll in February 1952, indicated that 52 percent of the public believed that widespread corruption existed among high administration officials.[35]

These scandals finally forced Truman to act again. He submitted plans to place under civil service collectors of internal revenue, postmasters, U.S. marshals, and customs collectors. Political leaders regarded these positions as patronage for the party in power. Party officials often made appointments with little regard for the administrative and professional qualifications of the persons selected.[36] A basic provision of Truman's plans eliminated Senate confirmation of these appointments. "There is going to be a howl from the patronage boys all the way down the street. But I will fight for this vital and urgent change," Truman promised.[37]

The Bureau of Internal Revenue (BIR), the present-day Internal Revenue Service, scandals threatened the administration politically because it affected millions of American taxpayers directly and encouraged the Republicans to try to make corruption a major issue in the 1952 elections.[38] These scandals reflected severe administrative problems in BIR. The agency had had a good reputation before World War II, but the war placed it under severe strain. The number of tax returns filed quadrupled from 1940 to 1946, and BIR had to administer many new and complex taxes. By the end of the war, tax refunds took twelve months or more to process; similar delays occurred in investigations of returns.

In 1946, Secretary of Treasury Snyder launched a program to modernize BIR and by 1951 had made many improvements. However, since BIR machinery had not changed much since 1862, it needed a general reorganization. Strong opposition to such a reform existed both outside and inside

BIR. Resistance especially came from "islands of power" gathered around the patronage offices of the collectors.[39] But the scandals ended this resistance.

There were sixty-four collectors; each headed a district and had responsibility for collecting all types of internal revenue within his district. More than half of all BIR employees worked under the collectors.[40] Collectors received their appointments from the president with consent of the Senate, without regard to the Civil Service Commission rules. The president made his appointments on the basis of advice from the senators in the state in which a collector served. If the state did not have a senator of the president's party, the administration chose a person recommended by the state's party organization.[41] The BIR was normally not consulted about these appointments.[42]

Ironically, the disaster that Truman confronted in 1952 was partially of his own making. In 1940, when Truman had seemed certain to lose his race for reelection to the Senate, Robert Hannegan, one of the leaders of the St. Louis Democratic machine, had switched his organization's support to Truman. Truman then proposed Hannegan as collector of internal revenue at St. Louis, and Roosevelt made the appointment in 1942. A year later, Secretary of Treasury Henry Morgenthau selected Hannegan as the outstanding collector in the nation. He became commissioner of BIR in October 1943. Although he served for less than four months, Hannegan, a politico, "began reshaping the Bureau in his own image."[43] Edward H. Foley, undersecretary of treasury, said that Hannegan's standards were different from those that most people had been accustomed to in BIR. Joseph Nunan, whom Hannegan recommended as his successor, continued this political atmosphere from 1944 to 1947.[44]

In December 1947, Sen. John J. Williams (a Republican from Delaware) revealed that embezzlements had been discovered in the collector's office in Wilmington. This disclosure gained Williams the confidence of BIR employees and others, and they began to supply him with further information. Williams investigated many months before making additional charges. Then in June 1950, he exposed improprieties in collectors' offices in several major cities, prompting formal Senate and House investigations.[45] Democrat Cecil R. King (California), who chaired a subcommittee of the House Ways and Means Committee, undertook the most important inquiry.

As a result of such investigations, Snyder fired a dozen collectors and two hundred other BIR employees; many had taken bribes, embezzled government funds, or had not paid their own taxes. Investigation also uncovered Justice Department laxity in prosecuting BIR corruption, and in late 1951 Truman fired T. Lamar Caudle, assistant attorney general in charge of the tax division within the Justice Department.[46]

By mid-1951, it seemed obvious that BIR troubles calledfor someone who would make extensive changes in the bureau. Snyder recommended Brig. Gen. John B. Dunlap, who then received complete authority from Truman and Snyder to clean up the agency. He took many steps to improve administration but soon found that he had to have statutory authority to make two fundamental changes: to bring politically chosen collectors under civil service and to reorganize the field offices of the bureau along functional lines with a clear chain of authority from the top down through the field organization.[47]

Truman was not eager to use his reorganization authority to deal with these problems,[48] but pressure mounted as the scandal continued to expand. On 13 October, a former St. Louis collector surrendered under an indictment charging him with conflict of interest and acceptance of bribes. Two weeks later, Frances Perkins, Democratic member of the Civil Service Commission, demanded that Congress place collectors under civil service. On 30 October, this suggestion received the backing of Kefauver, who had emerged as a rival to Truman for the Democratic nomination.[49] On 1 November, Frank McKinney, the new chairman of the Democratic National Committee, publicly recommended placing collectors under civil service.[50]

Truman finally had to act. A White House aide recalled that BIR reorganization deeply interested the Democratic National Committee. The Republicans had made a partisan issue of corruption "and that was a matter of great concern to the Democratic party as to. . .what *could* be done about it. The Internal Revenue Reorganization was one phase of that—of doing something about it."[51] As an indication of the urgency of the political situation, Truman violated his usual procedure of keeping a plan secret until he submitted it to Congress. On 2 January 1952, he announced that he intended to institute a sweeping reorganization of BIR.[52] In press conferences held in the next two days, Truman and Dunlap stressed that the plan stemmed from several years of planning and study, that the administration had not hastily slapped it together to quiet agitation over the scandals.[53]

Finally on 14 January, Truman submitted plan one. He explained that the BIR needed a comprehensive reorganization to increase its efficiency and to provide better machinery for assuring honest and impartial administration of internal revenue law. The "archaic" statutory office of collector remained as the principal barrier to good administration. The president and

Senate should fill major policymaking offices, but positions of a technical nature, such as BIR collectors, should be under civil service, he said. The plan abolished the offices of the collectors and allowed the secretary of treasury to establish up to twenty-five district offices, each headed by a district commissioner responsible to the BIR commissioner but with full responsibility for his district. It also eliminated the Offices of Deputy Commissioner, Assistant Commissioner, Special Deputy Commissioner, and Assistant General Counsel and replaced them with new offices to be filled under the civil service.[54]

Dawson's committee held hearings on plan one beginning on 18 January.[55] No real opposition developed and it easily cleared the House on 30 January.[56]

As the fight shifted to the Senate, Truman had help from outside the administration. The Republican attitude toward the plan was ambivalent, which made Hoover's support vital. He endorsed the proposal, although he suggested that Congress should satisfy itself that the plan did not "blanket" present Democratic incumbents into the new positions without requiring them to satisfy civil service regulations on the same basis as other applicants.[57] CCHR's full support of plan one also helped assuage Republican uneasiness about it. A CCHR official believed that Truman submitted the plan to get himself "off the hook," but concluded: "It's still a Hoover Commission proposal. It still is good in the long run. We must still do our best to put it through."[58]

The ambivalent Republican position stemmed partly from that party's attitude toward Truman. Even Hoover found his partnership with Truman increasingly difficult. To one supporter of reorganization Hoover wrote: "Certainly you do keep up the battle. But my private opinion is that we need a change in administration to succeed. In the meantime, we must keep the subject alive."[59] Other Republicans shared this opinion. Republican Congressman George Bender (Ohio), who reluctantly supported the plan, wrote a constituent: "You say that the plan will materially increase economy and efficiency in government. My friend, nothing will increase the efficiency and economy in the present Administration except a damn good licking for Truman and his gang next November."[60] Republican Sen. George Malone (Nevada) proclaimed: "It is almost as much of a crime to let the current President appoint the new Civil Service people who will administer the Internal Revenue Bureau as it would be to leave it in its present condition."[61] A CCHR supporter discovered that powerful figures in Detroit had pressured Republican Sen. Homer Ferguson to oppose the plan: "This had been urged upon him primarily because the folks here felt that the bureau ought to be reorganized under another administration and not pulled out of the hole at the moment."[62] A CCHR official found that the National Association of Manufacturers had extensive technical reasons for opposing the plan: "They all add up to this: 'If Truman wants it, the Plan can't be any good.' "[63] Many Republicans opposed the plan because they anticipated victory in 1952, and they hoped to fill the offices this proposal would abolish. They also feared that the administration would "blanket" Democrats into the new offices.[64]

McClellan began hearings on 30 January and held six additional sessions, the last of which was on 4 March. Committee members impressed observers with their apparent unfriendliness toward the plan.[65] Even before he began hearings, McClellan told a CCHR official that he intended to oppose the proposal.[66] Oddly enough, McClellan did not have patronage privilege with the administration.[67] He evidently opposed the plan because he viewed patronage solely through the eyes of a congressman and probably regarded himself as fighting for an abstract political privilege. He was also skeptical and pessimistic about human nature. He would not be moved by "good government" advocates, nor by academic arguments.[68]

The scandals helped the proposal's prospects by creating a sense of urgency but endangered it by allowing opponents to charge that the administration had slapped it together just to quiet the public.[69] Administration officials explained that this plan grew from long years of study and management improvement activity,[70] but McClellan was not too impressed. "It took you 5 years to develop a plan that contains 375 words, is that correct?" he asked.[71]

Strongest opposition came from Senator George and Republican Eugene Millikin (Colorado). They dominated the Committee on Finance, to which the Senate referred the nominations of BIR collectors. The great respect George's colleagues had for him made him a formidable opponent, especially on all matters involving taxes.[72]

George claimed that he opposed the plan because it did not conform to the Reorganization Act of 1949, did not specify savings, did not detail what form the future bureau would take, did not guarantee the citizen's right to sue collectors, and did not create another statutory structure to replace the one abolished by the plan.[73] One observer called George's testimony sheer "shysterism,"[74] but a CCHR official commented: "I have a feeling that his statement is a phony, but, if so, it is one of the best documented and formidable phonies I have seen in a long time." This official warned: "In view of Senator George's immense prestige and the quality of this document, he may well have dealt a death blow to the proposed reorganization."[75]

The committee voted against plan one 7 to 5.[76] The Senate debated it on 12 and 13 March. A newspaper poll at the end of February found that forty-five senators intended to vote against the plan.[77] A CCHR survey on 10 March indicated that there were twenty-two sure votes for the plan and thirty-one against it.[78] Truman's prestige fell to one of its lowest points just the day before the debate opened; in the New Hampshire presidential primary Kefauver got nearly 55 percent of the vote to Truman's 44 percent.[79]

However, Budget Director Lawton recalled that the administration really "put the muscle" into the fight over plan one. Truman, at Snyder's insistence, delayed sending up the other plans until Congress acted on the BIR reorganization, and Snyder and other administration officials spent much time lobbying congressmen.[80] Truman increased his own unpopularity because of a letter that he wrote to Vice-President Barkley on 12 March. He explained that the plan formed an essential part of a program to assure honesty, integrity, and efficiency. "Unfortunately, those who find it to their advantage to preserve the present system, or to play politics with the integrity of the public service, have raised specious arguments against the plan that obscure the real issue." He warned that taxpayers would be interested in knowing that political patronage swayed some senators more than good public service.[81] Truman thus took full advantage of the legislative-veto procedure and willingly accepted the personal hatred created by the plan and by his messages in support of it.[82]

After McClellan opened debate, he asked for a quorum call so that all members would be present as George took the floor. George declared that he had been on the Committee on Finance for twenty years and felt that he owed it to his colleagues to explain his position on the plan. He had not reached a hasty decision. He had talked to the secretary of treasury several times but had finally decided to oppose the plan. Truman's attempt to portray opponents of the plan as interested only in patronage especially upset George.

> The most charitable thing I can say of the President is that concerning his personal honesty and personal character I have no comment, but he is the poorest advocate of a cause, good, bad, or indifferent, that the world has ever produced.[83]

Throughout his speech, in which he repeated the arguments he made before the committee, George sarcastically attacked the administration.[84] The *Washington Post* commented that few could remember a more scathing public indictment of a president by a senator of his own party and speculated that the sharpness of this attack resulted from the fact that a week earlier the senator's colleague from Georgia, Richard Russell, had joined the race for the presidential nomination.[85]

Democratic Senators Humphrey, Benton, Monroney, Murray, and Lehman strongly supported the proposal, arguing that the plan had to be accepted in order to solve the existing problem in BIR and to improve confidence of the public in the agency. Humphrey also expressed assurance in the outcome of the vote. He recalled that when it came time to vote on the plan in the House: "The opposition sort of faded away, somewhat after the manner of a great general."[86]

After some further debate, the Senate passed plan one 53 votes for and 37 against.[87] The administration, with CCHR support, had gone all out and had evidently turned the Senate around.[88] An "anonymous but completely authoritative" report said that McClellan had 47 votes against the plan but when it became obvious that he could not get 49, ten senators switched sides. They preferred not to open themselves unnecessarily to charges that they were motivated by desire for patronage; they then switched sides or did not vote.[89]

When Truman made plan one public, favorable reaction encouraged administration officials to consider additional proposals.[90] As part of a "Clean Up Campaign" to counter public concern over the scandals, Truman asked his subordinates to consider placing additional categories of government employees under civil service.[91] On 10 April, he submitted three plans that transferred from the president and Senate to department heads responsibility for appointment of many field officers. The proposals established clear lines of responsibility throughout these departmental organizations, which was a fundamental recommendation of the Hoover Commission. Truman argued that development of national policy was too complex and crushing to allow relations between president and Congress to be further complicated by conflict over selection of non-policymaking officials. The plans would take effect gradually to avoid immediately separating incumbents and giving partisan advantage to either party.[92]

Plan two provided for elimination of presidential appointment and Senate confirmation of postmasters at post offices of the first, second, and third class and placed those positions, which numbered about 21,500, under civil service as the offices became vacant. Plan three abolished the patronage offices of collector of customs, comptroller of customs, surveyor of customs, and appraiser of merchandise. It created new positions under the civil service with incumbents in posts destined for deletion serving out their terms. Plan four gave the attorney general authority to appoint U.S.

marshals under the civil service. The plan abolished existing offices, although again the incumbents would serve out their existing terms.[93]

These plans faced tougher opposition than plan one. Although they stemmed indirectly from the scandals by symbolizing a cleaning up of the government, no specific scandal created a sense of urgency. Also, Truman had lashed out at the Senate in dramatic attacks in order to get the first plan accepted. This created a backlash against the new proposals. In addition, these plans affected many more patronage positions, and they faced opposition from organized labor.

Truman again pushed hard for these proposals. On 2 May, for example, he explained and strongly defended his plans while speaking to the National Civil Service League.[94] CCHR also placed its full power behind the president's proposals. CCHR officials quickly met to plan an extensive program of support, and by 28 April the organization began to apply pressure for their adoption.[95] It admitted that the plans might freeze some Democrats in office but said: "In the judgment of the Committee the merits of the proposal are much more important than the political implications."[96] CCHR officials referred to the plans as the most important federal personnel reforms since the Civil Service Act of 1883.[97]

The main debate revolved around the issue of patronage in the appointment of postmasters; the fate of plan two determined that of the other proposals. These twenty-one thousand positions theoretically were already under civil service but as a practical matter composed the major remaining part of the spoils system. When a vacancy occurred, the Post Office Department asked the congressional district's representative, if he belonged to the party in power, to name an acting postmaster. Months later the government would give a civil service examination; ordinarily, with his on-the-job training, the acting postmaster would rank among the top three in the examination results (if not he could take the test again). When the department learned the results, it allowed the representative to choose from the top three candidates, which meant that he could almost invariably name the acting postmaster. If the representative belonged to the wrong party, the Post Office Department consulted the state's senators or party organization.[98] "This practice is within the letter of the law, but not within the spirit," a White House aide wrote.[99]

Truman's plan did not state that this system of consultation would cease; it simply ended Senate confirmation. Perhaps the plan would have created an appointment system for first-, second-, and third-class postmasters that already existed for fourth class; the postmaster general appointed fourth-class postmasters with congressional advice, but not with Senate confirmation.[100] Real patronage rested with the House,[101] and perhaps the plan would not have disturbed that; in any case, the House did not contest it. Opponents contended that the plan simply transferred patronage to the postmaster general. Their skepticism rested on the assumption that the department would fill vacancies on the basis of examinations (which meant that the postmaster general would choose among the three top candidates) rather than by promotion from within the service, the normal procedure in the civil service.[102] A memorandum circulated in the White House stated that Postmaster General Donaldson and Civil Service Commissioner Ramspeck intended to testify that all political clearance would cease when the plan took effect, but a note added to the bottom of this memorandum said the postmaster general never heard of such a proposal.[103] After the fight ended, the *Washington Post* criticized the administration for playing coy by declining to give assurance that all political clearance would cease.[104]

This confusion gave opponents an easy opportunity to attack the plan. Sen. Styles Bridges (a Republican from New Hampshire) charged that it represented an effort to freeze Democrats in these positions because Truman foresaw a Republican victory in 1952.[105] Republican Sen. John M. Butler (Maryland) explained that he did not vote for it because "I don't see how we could possibly get any better government by taking the appointment away from the Senate and giving it to the Chairman of the National Committee of the party in power."[106] Sen. Margaret Chase Smith (a Republican from Maine) said that plan two would allow the postmaster general to make appointments. Since that official had traditionally been a party manager, the new system would be as political as in the past.[107] Similarly, Sen. Blair Moody of Michigan, who voted for the plan, wrote: "I would have been very much surprised if, had the plans weathered the Senate, the Postmaster General had not continued to informally receive and act upon recommendations from the county chairmen."[108]

Olin D. Johnston (South Carolina), Kenneth McKellar (Tennessee), Matthew Neeley (West Virginia)—all Democrats—and Frank Carlson (a Republican from Kansas), members of the Committee on Post Office and Civil Service, submitted resolutions of disapproval of plan two, and McClellan opened hearings on all three plans on 14 May. Proponents included representatives from the agencies involved, Budget Director Lawton, former Hoover Commissioner Arthur Flemming, James R. Watson, executive director of the National Civil Service League, and J. T. Sanders, legislative counsel of the National Grange. They argued that these plans improved the chain of command by removing presidential appointment from officials far down in the departmental hierarchy. This would improve responsibility and accountability and would protect the affected individuals from political pressure. Postmaster General Donaldson said that his department now consulted political leaders on appointments, but that under the plan the president might be expected, but not legally required, to instruct him to ignore these people.[109]

Strongest opposition came from organized labor. Senator Benton wrote: "I call this a tough vote because so many of the postal workers in my own state, where I am running for reelection, made it abundantly clear to me that they were opposed to this legislation and would be unhappy with my support of it."[110] It seemed strange that unions representing career postal workers would oppose a plan to open twenty-one thousand postmasterships for these employees.[111] The union position reflected the special privileges postal employees had received as a result of their close ties with Congress. This made them "somewhat equivocal with respect to the merit system and modern personnel methods."[112] Donaldson increased the tension between unions and post-office officials because he did not get on well with the labor leaders. As a result, these organizations learned to depend almost exclusively on Congress for solutions to their problems.[113] The reorganization plan threatened to cut that tie by increasing the power of the executive branch.

Therefore, representatives of the National Association of Letter Carriers, Government Employees Council, American Federation of Labor, and National Federation of Post Office Clerks testified against the plan. They argued that the plan would not reduce politics but would simply build an even stronger machine headed by the postmaster general.[114] This powerful opposition caused many senators to look for an acceptable excuse to oppose the plan, and McClellan's committee, with several senators dissenting, recommended its defeat.[115]

On 16 June, McClellan brought plan two up for debate and vote. The political situation remained unsettled. On 17 May, a journalist predicted that the Senate would almost certainly defeat the plan.[116] But on 5 June, a CCHR official said that the "latest informed word" indicated that it would pass.[117] The following day he wrote: "The Budget Bureau boys called up this morning to ask me whether they were suffering from 'hardening of the bureaucratic arteries' in thinking that Plan No. 2 was safe. It begins to look that way but I keep pinching myself."[118] However, as time for the vote approached, it became evident that the proposal was in trouble.[119]

During the debate, Southern Democratic leaders led the opposition against the president's plan. McClellan opened with an attack on the

CCHR, ridiculing its claims of savings obtained through reorganization. He then turned to plan two and said that the only thing that it did was to remove the requirement for Senate confirmation. The postmaster general would still select postmasters from among three eligible people; he could still consult with anyone but would not send the choice to the Senate for confirmation.[120] Johnston, Eastland, Stennis, and George all expressed similar sentiments. They argued that the plan would not decrease politics but would allow the executive branch to build a political machine.[121]

Humphrey, Herbert R. O'Conor (a Democrat from Maryland), and Monroney spoke for the plan but said little more than that the spoils system was bad and inefficient and that the plan would eliminate patronage by ending Senate confirmation.[122] They did not answer the specific objections of the opponents.

The Senate then rejected the plan by 56 to 29 votes.[123] No scandal existed to create a sense of crisis nor did Truman make a highly personalized challenge to the opposition, while resentment lingered for his having done so in the case of plan one.[124] Snyder also hurt the plan by forcing the administration to hold it back until after the vote on plan one. Some senators who supported plan one voted against plan two because they considered it less important for the administration and for the Democratic party and wanted to get back in the good graces of their colleagues.[125] CCHR officials claimed that the Truman administration received good publicity for having introduced the plans but then abandoned them and kept the patronage.[126]

The Senate quickly turned to plans three and four. The "herd instinct" then took over;[127] Smith said plan two's weaknesses "set" the opposition to the other two plans.[128] Humphrey and McClellan asked the Senate to limit debate on plan three to ten minutes. After short discussion, the Senate rejected it with a vote of 51 to 31. After similarly short debate on plan four, the Senate defeated it 55 to 28.[129]

On 1 May, Truman submitted his last reorganization plan. For many years he had sought unsuccessfully to persuade Congress to provide home rule for the District of Columbia.[130] Plan five, however, effected an improvement in the existing government structure. In 1951, both the Bureau of the Budget and the Board of Commissioners of the District of Columbia drew up schemes for district reorganization. Since they could not work out a compromise, they appealed to Truman to choose between their measures.[131] The budget plan provided a city manager-council form of government. The board's plan retained the commission model and attempted to improve it by transferring to the board all the functions of more than seventy district agencies.[132] One survey indicated that thirty-six district groups supported the board plan and three the Bureau of the Budget scheme.[133] Truman talked to numerous "responsible" district citizens and found them unanimous in their opposition to the budget plan.[134] Lawton recalled that Truman favored the budget reorganization proposal but decided that there was so much opposition to it that "the game wasn't worth the candle."[135] He, therefore, decided to support the board.

In his message to Congress, Truman said that the district needed both home rule and reorganization, but the Reorganization Act of 1949 forbade submitting a home rule plan under its authority. Instead, plan five would bring about a basic simplification of district government by transferring to the board the functions of most existing agencies.[136]

McClellan's committee held hearings on the plan. Almost no one opposed it, although a few offered only minimal support because it did not go far enough.[137] The committee reported it favorably.[138] No one introduced a resolution against the measure and it went into effect without a vote.

Truman's reorganization program ended in the ambivalent manner that characterized his drive for administrative reform from 1945 to 1953. In this final session of Congress, he failed to expand his reorganization authority and to extend real civil service coverage to thousands of government employees. He reorganized RFC but accomplished this too late to prevent it from being terminated several years later after being weakened by the scandals of his administration. He reorganized the governmental structure of the District of Columbia but admitted that the plan he submitted was inferior to the one the Bureau of the Budget devised and that both did not meet the real need—home rule.

However, by getting plan one of 1952 into effect Truman did improve one of the key agencies of the federal government, the Internal Revenue Service. This was a major reform. The health of the entire government system depended, to a considerable extent, on a favorable public image of IRS. The agency's reputation had been badly tarnished in the 1940s, but with the important changes brought about in 1951 and 1952, its image improved and remained high for many years. In 1957, Congressman Wilbur Mills, aided by an advisory group of lawyers and accountants, conducted a "critical review" of the IRS and found that the organizational structure developed by the 1952 plan was sound.[139]

Conclusion

In 1952, Truman brought his reorganization program to a close. He had designed his campaign for administrative reform to correct persistent organizational problems, many of which had concerned him long before he became president. Truman's plans also served another purpose not directly related to management improvement. In the confusion and self-doubt that he felt during the weeks following Roosevelt's death, reorganization provided Truman with a program that he had been interested in for more than twenty years, that he believed he could handle more competently than Roosevelt, and that he could initiate immediately. Similarly, the program helped reassure many people who had doubts about Truman's ability to carry out successfully Roosevelt's foreign and domestic programs. His reorganization program attracted a great deal of attention in 1945, and Truman won approval of his handling of reorganization legislation in that year. The program was doubly reassuring because it promised to improve the administration of New Deal programs, which even supporters believed were administratively weak.

Despite the difficulties with reorganization, Truman achieved some important gains. He protected the New Deal reform structure by diverting the Hoover Commission from its initial intention of leading a conservative counterrevolution. He further shored up the New Deal by bringing the commission into the political mainstream where a tremendous public campaign, one of the strongest ever in peacetime, could develop behind its recommendations. This campaign was directed toward making the existing structure work better, rather than destroying it. Truman explained to Winston Churchill that his victory in the 1948 election was not the great political upset that many had assumed: "Really it was not—it was merely a continuation of the policies which had been in effect for the last sixteen years and the policies that the people wanted."[1] This also explained the people's reaction to the Hoover Commission. Support for the commission proposals, which turned into a national fad, allowed the people to ratify the New Deal by trying to insure that its programs were effectively administered. This reorganization movement helped moderate public anxiety with "big government," a concern that posed a threat to the welfare state because conservatives could exploit it.

174

Truman also achieved several administrative reforms that were of special interest to him. From the beginning of his political career, he stressed the need for centralizing administrative authority in those responsible for managing programs. He directed many of his plans to that principle. Truman also achieved one of his most desired goals by rebuilding the shattered Department of Labor. By the end of his presidency, the department was stronger than it had ever been in its history, although it continued to have organizational problems. In addition, Truman prepared the way for several administrative reforms that future presidents carried to completion. He failed to transform the Federal Security Agency into a department of welfare, but because of his various transfers to and from FSA, the final act of giving it departmental status was largely a formality. He also paved the way for the emergence of the Department of Housing and Urban Development and the Department of Transportation when he submitted several plans that furthered the process of centralizing housing and transportation activities.

Perhaps the most useful but undramatic plans were those that transferred authority from subordinates to the departmental secretaries and that placed executive functions in the hands of regulatory commission chairmen. These changes allowed rapid, continuing administrative adjustment to meet problems as they arose. With other necessary but undramatic plans, Truman made permanent many organizational arrangements that had proved beneficial during World War II. These changes helped make an orderly transition from war to peace. Additional plans strengthened the Executive Office of the President by transferring to it the National Security Council and the National Security Resources Board. Truman won approval of several proposals that strengthened and brought order to the new General Services Administration. He improved the obsolete and ineffective government of the District of Columbia. His plan to reorganize the Reconstruction Finance Corporation did not save the agency from termination but many of its functions were later assumed by the Small Business Administration. One of his final victories improved and restored the people's confidence in one of the key agencies of the U.S. government—the Internal Revenue Service.

However, despite these gains, Truman became disillusioned with reorganization and, probably, would have ended his program much earlier if there had not been special pressures. After generating expectations that he would give administrative reform high priority during his presidency, Truman submitted only three plans in 1946, three more in 1947, and one in 1948. If the Hoover Commission had not changed the political situation,

Truman most likely would have made little use of the legislative-veto mechanism in the following years. However, capitalizing on the favorable response to the reports of the Hoover Commission, the president submitted thirty-five plans during the Eighty-first Congress. Yet even in 1949 and 1950, he did not participate in the details of the program as enthusiastically as he had early in his administration, and in 1951 and 1952 Truman used the legislative veto only as an emergency device to deal with political problems because of scandals.

Truman had learned, as did later presidents, that reorganization proposals faced such strong opposition that expenditures of time, energy, and political resources ordinarily make them too costly to be undertaken on a large scale. The combined opposition from executive agencies, congressional committees, and pressure groups were almost impossible to overcome, especially in the case of plans that were most desirable to the executive. When reorganization proposals passed, they often did not change the existing power relationships, and they usually failed to accomplish what the president wanted. Reorganization did not prove to be the magical instrument that some had envisioned to create an effective governmental structure responsive to the president as the representative of the people. One scholar concluded: "In the end, after thirty years, the effort to help the president in making government work has not succeeded."[2]

Presidents increasingly tried to solve administrative problems by working around them, using, for example, White House staff personnel to direct activities normally handled by the permanent bureaucracy or building a supra-cabinet to represent presidential interests more directly. By the end of the 1930s, it had appeared that Congress and the president had developed the legislative veto into a tool that the president could use to control somewhat the executive branch. However, Truman's inability to do that, given both his commitment to reorganization and unusually strong public interest in the program, indicated that a serious problem existed. Government became ever larger and undertook increasingly varied and complex activities, while the president found it increasingly difficult to manage or even to be familiar with more than a limited range of its activities.

An additional problem developed because when reorganization plans succeeded in carrying out their authors' aims, they usually centralized authority at the top of the administrative hierarchy. As one of Truman's reorganization experts admitted, the administrative reformers failed to foresee that they were building instruments of power that could be abused when less trustworthy men got control of them.[3] Different conceptions of democracy were involved in the reorganization struggle. Proponents believed democracy would be furthered by creating a rational, hierarchical structure responsive to the president who represented all the people. Many opponents viewed democracy as arising from a decentralized, competitive decisionmaking structure that provided access to group pressure at many different points.

Thus, Truman's executive reorganization program accomplished specific administrative improvements and prepared the way for several future improvements. It created a government structure as "inherently manageable" as it had ever been.[4] This achievement was somewhat overshadowed because Roosevelt served as the managerial model against which all later presidents were measured, usually unfavorably. This was unfair to his successors because Roosevelt's peacetime administrative establishment was incomparably smaller than that of the recent presidents; bureaucracy swelled during the war but Roosevelt also received more formal and informal administrative authority during this emergency than the chief executives who followed him. Truman's program helped reconcile people to big government and protected the New Deal reform structure. But it also revealed the limitations of such administrative reform. The structure of power resting on the foundation of the triangular relationship among executive agencies, congressional committees, and the interest groups proved to be so formidable that even a president as committed to reorganization as Truman failed to build an administrative structure suitable for dealing with modern needs and problems.

Chapter 1

1. Harry S. Truman, *Year of Decisions*, vol. 1 of *Memoirs by Harry S. Truman*, p. 486.

2. Ibid., pp. 95–96; Harold D. Smith, conference with the president, 26 April 1945, Harold D. Smith Diary, Harold D. Smith papers.

3. Truman, *Year of Decisions*, pp. 226–27; Smith Diary, 4 May 1945.

4. Smith Diary, 4 May 1945; Harry S. Truman, *Public Papers of the Presidents of the United States: Harry S. Truman, 1945*, pp. 69–70.

5. Ed Lockett to Don Bermingham, 1 June 1945, Ed Lockett Reports folder, Frank McNaughton papers.

6. Truman, *Public Papers: 1945*, pp. 278–79.

7. Ibid., pp. 562–63.

8. Smith Diary (this entry based on notes written by Paul Appleby), 19 December 1945.

9. Congress took no action on plan eight of 1949 (providing for a department of defense); the plan was superceded by legislation. In histories of the period, and even in some specialized studies of reorganization, there is a great deal of confusion over the mechanics of reorganization and over the final disposition of the plans. Confusion arose because of the way in which plans were enacted. The basic procedure was that the president submitted a plan that went into effect at the end of sixty days unless rejected by Congress. Under the Reorganization Act of 1945, the plan went into effect unless vetoed by both houses of Congress; under the Reorganization Act of 1949, it went into effect unless vetoed by one house of Congress. The 1949 act required a constitutional majority, rather than a simple majority, to kill a plan. Therefore, several plans went into effect even though a majority of those voting decided against it. Also, instead of voting directly on a plan, under both acts congressmen voted on resolutions of disapproval; therefore, a "nay" vote supported the plan.

10. The *New York Times*, 30 January 1953, p. 8.

11. Harry S. Truman, *Public Papers of the Presidents of the United States: Harry S. Truman, 1952–53*, p. 1117. For an evaluation of Truman's claim see Elmer E. Cornwell, Jr., "The Truman Presidency," in Richard S. Kirkendall, *The Truman Period as a Research Field*, pp. 213–52.

12. Laurin L. Henry, *Presidential Transitions*, p. 640.

13. Transcript of meeting between the president and the Hoover Commission, 26 May 1949, President Truman (meetings—Truman—Pace) folder, Accession No. 5308–10, Bureau of the Budget files, Office of Management and Budget.

14. Avery Leiserson, "Political Limitations on Executive Reorganization," p. 70.

15. Richard Polenberg, "Historians and the Liberal Presidency: Recent Appraisals of Roosevelt and Truman," pp. 20–21; address by Thomas E. Cronin, "The Textbook Presidency and Political Science," pp. 34915–28; Erwin C. Hargrove, *The Power of the Modern Presidency*, pp. 4–12; see also Otis L. Graham, Jr., *Toward a Planned Society: From Roosevelt to Nixon*.

16. Polenberg, "Historians and the Liberal Presidency," pp. 25–35.

17. James W. Davis and Delbert Ringquist, *The President and Congress: Toward a New Power Balance*, pp. 5–9.

18. Polenberg, "Historians and the Liberal Presidency," pp. 25–35; Hargrove, *Power of the Modern Presidency*, pp. 21–28, 79–80; Athan Theoharis, "The Truman Presidency: Trial and Error," pp. 49–52.

19. Hargrove, *Power of the Modern Presidency*, p. 3; see also Dwight Waldo, "Scope of the Theory of Public Administration," in James C. Charlesworth, *Theory and Practice of Public Administration: Scope, Objectives, and Methods*, p. 10; and Vincent Ostrom, *The Intellectual Crisis in American Public Administration*.

20. Address by James Fesler, 12 October 1967, pp. 143–44.

21. Francis E. Rourke, *Bureaucracy, Politics, and Public Policy*, pp. 118–22.

22. U.S., Congress, House, Committee on Expenditures in the Executive Departments, *President's Message [of December 9, 1932] on Consolidation of Government Agencies,* Hearing, 72d Cong., 2d sess., pp. 1–2.

23. F. W. Coker, "Dogmas of Administrative Reform, as Exemplified in the Recent Reorganization in Ohio," pp. 399–411; Harvey Walker, "Theory and Practice in State Administrative Organization," pp. 249–54; William H. Edwards, "The State Reorganization Movement," part 1, pp. 13–30, part 2, pp. 15–41, part 3, pp. 17–67, part 4, pp. 103–37; William H. Edwards, "The Public Efficiency Experts," pp. 301–12.

24. Charles S. Hyneman, "Administrative Reorganization," pp. 66–67, 71–73.

25. Marshall E. Dimock, "The Objectives of Governmental Reorganization," p. 233; David S. Brown, " 'Reforming' the Bureaucracy: Some Suggestions for the New President," p. 166; U.S., Congress, Senate, Committee on Government Operations, *Establish a Commission on the Organization and Management of the Executive Branch,* 90th Cong., 2d sess., p. 107.

26. Milton Musicus, "Reappraising Reorganization," pp. 107–12.

27. Hargrove, *Power of the Modern Presidency,* p. 241.

28. Matthew Holden, Jr., " 'Imperialism' in Bureaucracy," p. 951.

29. Martin Landau, "Redundancy, Rationality, and the Problem of Duplication and Overlap," pp. 348–49, 356.

30. Herbert A. Simon, "The Proverbs of Administration," pp. 53–67.

31. I. M. Destler, *Presidents, Bureaucrats and Foreign Policy: The Politics of Organizational Reform,* pp. 40–41; Peri E. Arnold, "Reorganization and Politics: A Reflection on the Adequacy of Administrative Theory," pp. 205–10; James W. Fesler, "Administrative Literature and the Second Hoover Commission Reports," pp. 135–42.

32. Robert T. Golembiewski, "Organization Development in PublicAgencies: Perspectives on Theory and Practice," p. 367.

33. Harlan Cleveland, *The Future Executive: A Guide for Tomorrow's Managers,* pp. x–xi.

34. Murray Edelman, *The Symbolic aases of Politics,* pp. 63–65.

35. Peter Woll, *American Bureaucracy,* p. 60; Clara Penniman, "Reorganization and the Internal Revenue Service," p. 121; Francis E. Rourke, "Reorganization of the Labor Department" (Ph.D. diss.), pp. 13–14.

36. Dennis R. Eckart and John C. Ries, "The American Presidency," in Leroy N. Rieselbach, *Peoplevs. Government: The Responsiveness of American Institutions,* pp. 63–64.

Chapter 2

1. W. Brooke Graves, *Reorganization of the Executive Branch of the Government of the United States: A Compilation of Basic Information and Significant Documents, 1912–1948,* p. viii.

2. Chong Mo Pak, "The Dynamics of Governmental Reorganization" (Ph.D. diss.), pp. 1–2; Herbert Emmerich, *Essays on Federal Reorganization,* pp. 3–4; Barry Dean Karl, *Executive Reorganization and Reform in the New Deal: The Genesis of Administrative Management, 1900–1939,* pp. 166, 182.

3. Edward H. Hobbs, *Executive Reorganization in the National Government,* pp. 23–25.

4. Ibid., pp. 12–13, 12 (note 1); Pak, "Dynamics of Government Reorganization," pp. 5–7.

5. Oscar Kraines, *Congress and the Challenge of Big Government,* pp. 11, 23–29, 42–46, 53–54; Gustavus A. Weber, *Organized Efforts for the Improvement of Methods of Administration in the United States,* pp. 66–71.

6. Harold T. Pinkett, "The Keep Commission, 1905–1909: A Rooseveltian Effort for Administrative Reform," pp. 297–98; Oscar Kraines, "The President Versus Congress: The Keep Commission, 1905–1909, First Comprehensive Presidential Inquiry into Administration," pp. 5–54. Also see Karl, *Executive Reorganization and Reform in the New Deal,* p. 187.

7. Graves, *Reorganization of the Executive Branch of the Government of the United States*, pp. 1–3; Hobbs, *Executive Reorganization in the National Government*, pp. 14, 16–17.

8. Hobbs, *Executive Reorganization in the National Government*, pp. 18–20.

9. Ibid., pp. 21–23, 27–35; Lewis Meriam and Laurence F. Schmeckebier, *Reorganization of the National Government: What Does It Involve?*, pp. 185–86.

10. Meriam and Schmeckebier, *Reorganization of the National Government*, pp. 187–96; Karl, *Executive Reorganization and Reform in the New Deal*, p. 190; Hobbs, *Executive Reorganization in the National Government*, pp. 36–37.

11. Karl, *Executive Reorganization and Reform in the New Deal*, p. 191.

12. Franklin D. Roosevelt, *Looking Forward*, pp. 71–72.

13. Anne O'Hare McCormick, "Roosevelt's View of the Big Job," p. 2.

14. Louis Brownlow, *A Passion for Anonymity: The Autobiography of Louis Brownlow*, p. 382.

15. Karl, *Executive Reorganization and Reform in the New Deal*, pp. 195–96.

16. Ibid., p. 199.

17. Ibid., p. 247.

18. Ibid., pp. 254–56. Also see the excellent study by Richard Polenberg, *Reorganizing Roosevelt's Government: The Controversy Over Executive Reorganization, 1936–1939*. For studies of the executive theory of reorganization see also Harold Seidman, *Politics, Position, and Power: The Dynamics of Federal Organization*, pp. 3–11; and Nancy Ann Edwards, "Congress and Administrative Reorganization" (Ph.D. diss.), pp. 2–24. For the relationship between reorganization and national planning see Otis Graham, *Toward a Planned Society: From Roosevelt to Nixon*, pp. xiii, 59–63, 106, 112.

19. Andrew J. Wann, *The President as Chief Administrator*, chapter 7.

20. Peter Page Schauffler, "A Study of the Legislative Veto" (Ph.D. diss.), p. 2.

21. Harvey C. Mansfield, "Federal Executive Reorganization: Thirty Years of Experience," p. 341.

22. Frederick J. Lawton, "Some Problems of Governmental Organization," 4 August 1959, Reorganization (miscellaneous) folder, Frederick J. Lawton papers.

23. Schauffler, "Study of the Legislative Veto," p. 233 (note 445).

24. Wann, *President as Chief Administrator*, pp. 93, 96.

25. Franklin D. Roosevelt, *The Continuing Struggle for Liberalism, 1938*, vol. 7 of *The Public Papers and Addresses of Franklin D. Roosevelt*, p. 179.

26. James MacGregor Burns, *Roosevelt: The Lion and the Fox*, p. 345. Also see Lindsay Rogers, "Reorganization: Post Mortem Notes," pp. 161–72.

27. Truman to Herbert C. Hoover, 11 October 1945, Truman correspondence 1945–1946 folder, Herbert C. Hoover papers.

28. Avery Leiserson, "Political Limitations on Executive Reorganization," p. 74.

29. Harry S. Truman, *Year of Decisions*, vol. 1 of *Memoirs by Harry S. Truman*, p. 154.

30. Seymour Scher, "The Politics of Agency Organization," p. 328.

31. Herbert Roback, "Do We Need a Department of Science and Technology" (reprint), pages are unnumbered; also see Paul H. Appleby, "The Significance of the Hoover Commission Report," pp. 8–9. Also see Charles E. Jacob, *Policy and Bureaucracy*, pp. 3–4.

32. Statement by Roback, personal interview.

33. Mansfield, "Federal Executive Reorganization," p. 334.

34. Joe L. Evins, *Understanding Congress*, p. 228.

35. Appleby, "Significance of the Hoover Commission Report," pp. 8–9.

36. Roback, personal interview.

37. Donald C. Stone to James E. Webb, 7 February 1947, James E. Webb papers.

38. Ralph [Gwinn] to Clarence Brown, 24 March 1952, Political-G folder, Clarence Brown papers.

39. U.S., Congress, House, Committee on Government Operations, *To Amend the Reorganization Act of 1949*, Hearing, 83d Cong., 1st sess.

40. Joseph P. Harris, *Congressional Control of Administration*, p. 42.

41. James MacGregor Burns, *The Deadlock of Democracy: Four-Party Politics in America*, p. 262.

42. Meriam and Schmeckebier, *Reorganization of the National Government*, p. 3.

43. Harold O. Lovre to Truman, 25 May 1950, OF (Official File) 285A, Truman papers.

44. Executive officials regarded savings as a secondary reorganization goal. Most believed that large savings could not be achieved by structural reorganization. No "sophisticated" administrator, said Appleby, expected to save over 2 or 3 percent in administrative costs through a reorganization. Thus, major budget cuts had to come by eliminating functions of government. "We can only cut the budget substantially," wrote Republican Congressman John Vorys (Ohio), "by cutting out, or limiting things the government is doing for the people." Therefore, reorganizations that saved the most money ran into the greatest opposition. "The trouble is," Vorys pointed out, "that a great many people who are for economy in general, are against any cut in their particular project, subsidy, etc." Appleby, "Significance of the Hoover Report," pp. 5–6; [John Vorys] to Mrs. Rolland M. Edmonds, 20 February 1950, Hoover Commission-Legislative folder, John Vorys papers.

45. Milton Musicus, "Reappraising Reorganization," p. 108; I. M. Destler, *Presidents, Bureaucrats and Foreign Policy: The Politics of Organizational Reform*, p. 47; Mansfield, "Federal Executive Reorganization," p. 334; Seidman, *Politics, Position, and Power*, pp. 11, 27.

46. Karl, *Executive Reorganization and Reform in the New Deal*, p. 28.

47. Truman to S. A. Story, 24 March 1950, OF 285A, Truman papers.

48. Statement by president on signing Reorganization Act of 1945, 20 December 1945, ibid.

49. George Galloway, *Congress at the Crossroads*, pp. 230–33; Roland Young, *Congressional Politics in the Second World War*, pp. 225, 237; Emmerich, *Essays on Federal Reorganization*, p. 32; Kenneth W. Street, "Harry S. Truman: His Role as Legislative Leader, 1945–1948" (Ph.D. diss.), pp. 155–62.

50. Marion T. Bennett to Carl R. Johnson, 26 June 1946, folder No. 643, File J–1, Marion T. Bennett papers.

51. Evins, *Understanding Congress*, pp. 223–27, also see pp. 60–62, 248.

52. William L. Morrow, *Congressional Committees*, p. 152; Frederick J. Lawton, "Legislative-Executive Relationships in Budgeting as Viewed by the Executive," p. 39; Peter Woll, *American Bureaucracy*, pp. 49–53; J. Leiper Freeman, *The Political Process: Executive Bureau-Legislative Committee Relations*, p. 31; also see Morrow, *Congressional Committees*, pp. 156–57.

53. Donald C. Blaisdell, *American Democracy Under Pressure*, p. 180.

54. Emmerich, *Essays on Federal Reorganization*, pp. 37–38. Departmental secretaries are sometimes said to be "natural enemies" of presidents, but the department heads are often mere "fronts" for the bureaus within them. For discussions of the departments in organizational politics see Thomas E. Cronin, " 'Everybody Believes in Democracy Until He Gets to the White House. . .': An Examination of White House-Departmental Relations," pp. 573–625; Seidman, *Politics, Position, and Power*, pp. 51–53; Richard F. Fenno, *The President's Cabinet: An Analysis in the Period from Wilson to Eisenhower*, pp. 229, 232–34; Paul H. Appleby, "Organizing Around the Head of a Large Federal Department," p. 225; Appleby, "Significance of the Hoover Report," pp. 9–10; Emmerich, *Essays on Federal Reorganization*, p. 40; see the statement by John Gardner in Kenneth R. Cole, Jr., "Should Cabinet Departments and Agencies Be More Independent?" in Charles Roberts, ed., *Has the President Too Much Power? The Proceedings of a Conference for Journalists Sponsored by the Washington Journalism Center*, pp. 129–30.

55. Frederick C. Mosher, "Some Notes on Reorganizations in Public Agencies," in Roscoe C. Martin, ed., *Public Administration and Democracy: Essays in Honor of Paul H. Appleby*, p. 131.

56. Ibid., pp. 139–41.

57. Lawton, "Some Problems of Governmental Organization," 4 August 1959, Reorganization (miscellaneous) folder, Lawton papers.

58. For example, see Jerry Kluttz column in the *Washington Post*, 1945–1946. Secretary of

State James F. Byrnes said: "During the early months of my tenure we made a conscious effort to help the Department recover from an acute attack of 'reorganization jitters.' " James F. Byrnes, *Speaking Frankly*, p. 245.

59. Julius Krug to Truman, 6 May 1946, OF 6D, Truman papers.

60. Francis E. Rourke, *Bureaucracy, Politics, and Public Policy*, pp. 11–12; Norton E. Long, "Power and Administration," in Francis E. Rourke, *Bureaucratic Power in National Politics*, pp. 16–17. See also Harlan Cleveland, "Survival in the Bureaucratic Jungle," in Alan A. Altshuler, *The Politics of the Federal Bureaucracy*, pp. 122–23; Matthew Holden, " 'Imperialism' in Bureaucracy," pp. 943–50.

61. Marshall E. Dimock, "Expanding Jurisdictions: A Case Study in Bureaucratic Conflict," in Robert K. Merton and others, *Reader in Bureaucracy*, p. 285.

62. Rourke, *Bureaucracy, Politics, and Public Policy*, pp. 24–25; Freeman, *Political Process*, p. 96; Harris, *Congressional Control of Administration*, pp. 70–72.

63. Rourke, *Bureaucracy, Politics, and Public Policy*, pp. 27–28.

64. Marshall E. Dimock, "Bureaucracy Self-Examined," in Merton and others, *Reader in Bureaucracy*, pp. 403–5; Stephen Horn, *The Cabinet and Congress*, p. 214.

65. Ernest S. Griffith, *Congress: Its Contemporary Role*, pp. 50–51.

66. Aaron Wildavsky, *The Politics of the Budgetary Process*, pp. 48–49.

67. Kenneth Kofmehl, *Professional Staffs of Congress*, p. 83.

68. See Dennis Chavez to Truman, 30 June 1949, OF 2310E, Truman papers; Morrow, *Congressional Committees*, p. 216; Seidman, *Politics, Position, and Power*, pp. 37–39, 42, 61–63.

69. Roosevelt, *Public Papers, 1938*, pp. 202–3.

70. Christian Herter, "Our Most Dangerous Lobby," p. 5.

71. J. Leiper Freeman, "The Bureaucracy in Pressure Politics," p. 19.

72. Nicholas A. Masters, "Committee Assignments," in Robert L. Peabody and Nelson W. Polsby, *New Perspectives on the House of Representatives*, pp. 50–57.

73. Wildavsky, *Politics of the Budgetary Process*, p. 67. Also see Seidman, *Politics, Position, and Power*, p. 40. For an example of agency power in an election see Richard Bolling, *House Out of Order*, pp. 120–21; and Frank E. Smith, *Congressman from Mississippi*, pp. 284, 286.

74. *Congressional Record (CR)*, 81:1, 1949, vol. 95, pt. 14, p. A4167. Also see address by Sen. William Benton, 18 February 1952, 2d National Reorganization Conference folder, Citizens Committee for the Hoover Report file, Robert L. L. McCormick papers; Herbert Emmerich, *Federal Organization and Administrative Management*, p. 130.

75. Leiserson, "Political Limitations on Executive Reorganization," p. 72.

76. All of these comments apply to regulatory commissions. Additional problems, such as the congressional tendency to regard them as arms of Congress, made the regulatory commissions even more difficult to reorganize. For example, see: Mansfield, "Federal Executive Reorganization," p. 339; Freeman, "Bureaucracy in Pressure Politics," p. 13; R. C. Atkinson, "Nature and Extent of the President's Powers Under the Reorganization Act," 6 September 1946, Reorganization Act of 1945: Legal Opinions and Interpretations folder, Series 39.32, Bureau of the Budget files, Office of Management and Budget; Marver H. Bernstein, *Regulating Business by Independent Commission*, pp. 4–5, 53, 131; Seidman, *Politics, Position, and Power*, p. 57. Also see Bernard Schwartz, *The Professor and the Commissions*.

77. Roback, personal interview.

78. Charles S. Hyneman, *Bureaucracy in a Democracy*, pp. 109–10.

79. Anthony Downs, *Inside Bureaucracy*, p. 7.

80. Wildavsky, *Politics of the Budgetary Process*, p. 66.

81. Rourke, *Bureaucracy, Politics, and Public Policy*, pp. 14–15.

82. Truman to Ernest A. Story, 24 March 1950, OF 285A, Truman papers.

83. E. Pendleton Herring, "Social Forces and the Reorganization of the Federal Bureaucracy," p. 187.

84. Rourke, *Bureaucracy, Politics, and Public Policy*, pp. 1–3.

85. Arnold Miles and Alan L. Dean, *Issues and Problems in the Administrative Organization of National Governments,* p. 8.

86. Robert L. L. McCormick to Herbert C. Hoover, 20 December 1949, CCHR Chrono file, McCormick papers.

87. McCormick to Sidney A. Mitchell, 5 April 1949, ibid.

88. McCormick to Tom Ridgway, 29 September 1949, ibid. Also see Seidman, *Politics, Positions, and Power,* pp. 16–17; Marriner S. Eccles, *Beckoning Frontiers: Public and Personal Recollections,* p. 389.

89. McCormick to Hoover, 9 October 1950, "G" folder, General Correspondence, 1947–1953, Commission on Organization of the Executive Branch papers, Herbert C. Hoover Presidential Library.

90. Appleby, "Significance of the Hoover Report," pp. 7–8.

Chapter 3

1. Harold D. Smith, *The Management of Your Government,* p. 69; Harry S. Truman, *Public Papers of the Presidents of the United States: Harry S. Truman, 1945,* pp. 69–70.

2. *CR,* 76:1, 1939, vol. 84, pt. 11, p. A1105.

3. For discussions of Truman's childhood and his career as a farmer as influences on the development of his administrative ideas and as sources of managerial experience see Richard S. Kirkendall, "Harry S. Truman: A Missouri Farmer in the Golden Age," pp. 467–83; Richard T. Johnson, *Managing the White House: An Intimate Study of the Presidency,* pp. 43–45. For a study that stressed the importance of Truman's background for understanding his presidency, see Dorothy Rudoni, "Harry S. Truman: A Study in Presidential Perspective" (Ph.D. diss.).

4. Henry A. Bundschu, *Harry S. Truman: The Missourian;* Jay M. Lee, *The Artilleryman: The Experiences and Impressions of an American Artillery Regiment in the World War,* p. 32; Dewitt Gilpin, "Truman of Battery D," p. 9; statement by Ted Marks, oral history interview; statement by Edgar G. Hinde, oral history interview.

5. For example see William Hillman, *Mr. President: The First Publication from the Personal Diaries, Private Letters, Papers, and Revealing Interviews of Harry S. Truman,* p. 193.

6. Robert J. Donovan, *Conflict and Crisis: The Presidency of Harry S. Truman, 1945–1948,* p. 23.

7. Dwight Waldo, *Perspectives on Administration,* pp. 35–37.

8. Daniel P. Parker, "Neither Left Nor Right: The Political Philosophy of Harry S. Truman," p. 21. Also see John F. Murphy, *The Pinnacle: The Contemporary American Presidency,* p. 39.

9. Jonathan Daniels, *The Man of Independence,* p. 116. For a study of Truman's early political career see Bert Cochran, *Harry Truman and the Crisis Presidency,* pp. 40–67.

10. Daniels, *Man of Independence,* pp. 109, 112–14; William M. Reddig, *Tom's Town,* pp. 105–6, 269; Lyle W. Dorsett, *The Pendergast Machine,* pp. 71, 91.

11. Dorsett, *Pendergast Machine,* pp. 72, 135–36; Reddig, *Tom's Town,* p. 265; Maurice Milligan, *The Inside Story of the Pendergast Machine by the Man Who Smashed It,* p. 217; Hinde, oral history interview; Hillman, *Mr. President,* p. 174.

12. Statement by Nathan T. Veatch, oral history interview; statement by Walter Matscheck, oral history interview conducted by J. R. Fuchs; Hinde, oral history interview; also see Alonzo L. Hamby, *Beyond the New Deal: Harry S. Truman and American Liberalism,* p. 42.

13. Irving Brant, "Harry S. Truman," p. 577.

14. Hamby, *Beyond the New Deal,* pp. 41–42; Daniels, *The Man of Independence,* pp. 150–51; Greater Kansas City Regional Planning Association, *Results of County Planning: Jackson County, Missouri.*

15. Dorsett, *The Pendergast Machine,* p. 72.

16. For examples see *The Examiner* [Independence], 15 December 1928, 19 December 1928, 6

January 1931, 26 May 1932, pp. 1, 2; 9 September 1932, p. 3; the *Kansas City Star,* 17 November 1932, p. 2; Greater Kansas City Regional Planning Association, *Results of County Planning,* p. 122; editorial, the *Kansas City Times,* 26 May 1930, p. 18; Dorsett, *The Pendergast Machine,* pp. 107–8; Reddig, *Tom's Town,* p. 183; Missouri State Planning Board, *A Preliminary Report on a State Plan for Missouri,* p. iii; Kansas City Chamber of Commerce, *Where These Rocky Bluffs Meet: Including the Story of the Kansas City Ten-Year Plan,* pp. 82–83, 113–26, 157–60, 166–71, 177.

17. "A County Budget?" *Kansas City's Public Affairs* (pamphlet); "Can the County Government be Efficient," *Kansas City's Public Affairs* (pamphlet); "Modernize County Government," *Kansas City's Public Affairs* (pamphlet).

18. Divided authority, for example, led to conflict with county engineer Leo Koehler, a Republican. The conflict delayed the court's work and led Koehler to challenge Truman to a fist fight. *The Examiner* [Independence], 2, 3, 16, 22 January, 6 February, 26 November 1923; Veatch, oral history interview.

19. *Lee's Summit Journal* [Missouri], 12 May 1927, p. 1.

20. The *Kansas City Star,* 7 October 1929, p. 6.

21. *The Examiner* [Independence], 30 October 1930.

22. The *Kansas City Star,* 28 November 1931, p. 2.

23. *Boonville Daily News* [Missouri], 25 February 1932, p. 1.

24. Dorsett, *The Pendergast Machine,* pp. 81, 86; Matscheck, oral history interview conducted by Fuchs; statement by Matscheck, oral history interview conducted by Dorsett. Prof. Lyle Dorsett kindly allowed me to use material from this interview. Also see the *Kansas City Star,* 13 February, p. 1; 23 March 1933, p. 6; *The Examiner* [Independence], 9 March 1933, p. 1.

25. George Baughman to Walter Burr, 9 February 1934, Division of Operations, U.S.E.S., Missouri, Miscellaneous Correspondence U.S.E.S. folder, Burr to Stanley B. Mathewson, 16 May 1934, Missouri: Organization Correspondence U.S.E.S. folder, Record Group (RG) 183, National Archives.

26. Truman to Burr, 21 December 1933, Missouri: Organization Correspondence U.S.E.S. folder, ibid.

27. Truman to Burr, 10 January 1934, ibid.

28. Harry S. Truman, *Year of Decisions,* vol. 1 of *Memoirs by Harry S. Truman,* p. 148.

29. Ibid., pp. 147–48, 156–58; "Compilation of Information and Statements Which May Indicate or Suggest Possible Policies of President Truman," April 1945, OF 79, Truman papers.

30. *CR,* 76:1, vol. 84, pt. 11, p. A1105; Truman, *Year of Decisions,* p. 147.

31. For an early example of this criticism see *CR,* 77:1, 1941, vol. 87, pt. 7, pp. 7117–18.

32. *CR,* 78:1, 1943, vol. 89, pt. 11, p. A3075.

33. Donald H. Riddle, *The Truman Committee,* pp. 99–100, 163.

34. U.S., Congress, Senate, Special Committee Investigating the National Defense Program, *Investigation of the National Defense Program,* S. Rept. No. 480, pt. 5, 77th Cong., 2d sess., p. 62.

35. Ibid., pp. 97–101.

36. Ibid., pt. 6, p. 51.

37. U.S., Congress, Senate, Special Committee Investigating the National Defense Program, *Investigation of the National Defense Program,* S. Rept. No. 10, pt. 1, 78th Cong., 1st sess., p. 4.

38. Ibid., pt. 2, p. 5.

39. Ibid., pt. 3, pp. 13–14.

40. Ibid., pt. 9, pp. 4–5.

41. Ibid., pt. 4, p. 3.

42. John Gunther, "The Man from Missouri," p. 33; Luther Huston, *New York Times,* 15 April 1945, sect. 4, p. 4; Wesley McCune and John R. Beal, "The Job That Made Truman President," pp. 620–21; Harry A. Toulmin, Jr., *Diary of Democracy,* p. 27; Riddle, *Truman*

Committee, pp. 17, 51.

43. I wish to thank Prof. Barton Bernstein for this suggestion.

44. Hillman, *Mr. President*, p. 110.

45. Truman, *Year of Decisions*, pp. 9, 11.

46. Richard S. Kirkendall, "Truman's Path to Power," p. 73.

47. Richard E. Neustadt, *Presidential Power: The Politics of Leadership*, pp. 175–76. Also see James David Barber, *The Presidential Character: Predicting Performance in the White House*, pp. 261–62.

48. Truman, *Year of Decisions*, pp. 119, 121.

49. Ibid., p. 119.

50. Hillman, *Mr. President*, pp. 88, 199; Harry S. Truman, *Mr. Citizen*, pp. 168–70; Harry S. Truman, *Years of Trial and Hope*, vol. 2 of *Memoirs by Harry S. Truman*, pp. 195–205.

51. Richard Rhdes, "Harry's Last Hurrah," p. 53.

52. Hillman, *Mr. President*, p. 13.

53. Rhodes, "Harry's Last Hurrah," pp. 52–53.

54. Truman, *Year of Decisions*, pp. 226a27.

55. Hillman, *Mr. President*, pp. 10, 14.

56. Remarks of the president to a group from the Institute for Teachers of Government and Administration, 23 June 1948, Reorganization of the Executive Branch—Memoranda folder, George Elsey papers.

57. Lady Bird Johnson, *A White House Diary*, p. 82.

58. Truman, *Mr. Citizen*, p. 264.

59. David E. Lilienthal, *Venturesome Years, 1950–1955*, vol. 3 of *The Journals of David E. Lilienthal*, pp. 250–51.

60. Neustadt, *Presidential Power*, p. 174. For a further discussion of Truman's administrative ideas and techniques see Johnson, *Managing the White House*, chapter 3, pp. 51–53; Harold Seidman, *Politics, Position, and Power: The Dynamics of Federal Organization*, pp. 90–91.

61. I wish to thank Professor Bernstein for this suggestion. See Chapter 4 for a discussion of Truman's reluctance to undertake reorganization.

62. Truman, *Year of Decisions*, p. 486.

63. Ibid., p. 96.

64. Ibid., p. 106.

65. Ibid., p. 227.

66. Harold D. Smith, conference with the president, 8 August 1945, Harold D. Smith Diary, Harold D. Smith papers.

67. Truman, *Years of Trial and Hope*, p. 46.

68. Louis Brownlow, "Reconversion of the Federal Administrative Machinery From War to Peace," p. 312; Caleb Perry Patterson, *Presidential Government in the United States: The Unwritten Constitution*, p. 146; foreword by Eric Johnston, in Smith, *The Management of Your Government*, pp. v–vi; Harold Zink, "Government Reform in the U.S.A.," p. 69.

69. Elmo Roper, *You and Your Leaders: Their Actions And Your Reactions, 1936–1956*, pp. 52–53, 60–61.

70. Goodwin Watson, "Bureaucracy as Citizens See It," p. 4; James S. Twohey Associates, *Twohey Analysis of Newspaper Opinion*, 8 September 1945. Also see Robert A. Garson, *The Democratic Party and the Politics of Sectionalism, 1941–1948*, pp. 28–29.

71. Twohey Associates, *Twohey Analysis of Newspaper Opinion*, 8 September 1945.

72. Neustadt, *Presidential Power*, p. 177.

73. Wilfred E. Binkley, *President and Congress*, p. 236, quoted in Andrew J. Wann, *The President as Chief Administrator*, p. 204 (note 3).

74. Wann, *President as Chief Administrator*, pp. 77–78.

75. Truman, *Year of Decisions*, p. 12; also see Harold Ickes Diary, 29 April 1945, Harold Ickes papers.

76. One scholar wrote: "For a good many decades, American students—and probably the citizenry in general—have relied upon reorganization as a principal tool as well as symbol of administrative improvement, i.e., of reform." Frederick Mosher, "Some Notes on Reorganizations in Public Agencies," p. 129.

77. John Fischer, "Mr. Truman Reorganizes," p. 26.

78. Kirkendall, "Truman's Path to Power," pp. 69–70.

79. Ibid., p. 71.

80. Garson, *The Democratic Party and the Politics of Sectionalism*, pp. 13, 33.

81. Kirkendall, "Truman's Path to Power," p. 68; James T. Patterson, *Congressional Conservatism and the New Deal: The Growth of the Conservative Coalition in Congress, 1933–1939*; Roland Young, *Congressional Politics in the Second World War*; John Robert Moore, "The Conservative Coalition in the United States Senate, 1942–1945," pp. 368–76; Mary H. Hinchey, "The Frustration of the New Deal Revival, 1944–46" (Ph.D. diss.), pp. 35–46.

82. Truman, *Year of Decisions*, pp. 86–87.

83. Morrow, *Congressional Committees*, p. 24.

84. Smith Diary, 26 April 1945; Avery Leiserson, "Political Limitations on Executive Reorganization," pp. 81–82. Truman also believed that a consolidated executive agency could unify its clientele groups, which would lessen conflict within Congress and between the executive branch and Congress. See Truman, *Year of Decisions*, pp. 110–11.

Chapter 4

1. Avery Leiserson, "Political Limitations on Executive Reorganization," p. 72.

2. Harold D. Smith, conference with the president, 4 May 1945, Harold D. Smith Diary, Harold D. Smith papers; Harry S. Truman, *Year of Decisions*, vol. 1 of *Memoirs by Harry S. Truman*, pp. 226–27.

3. Harry S. Truman, Message to Congress, 24 May 1945, OF (Official File) 285A, Harry S. Truman papers.

4. By-line article by Allen J. Green, *Washington Daily News*, 25 May 1945, p. 26.

5. By-line article by Robert C. Albright, *Washington Post*, 26 May 1945, Democratic National Committee Clipping File.

6. The *Washington Post*, 29 May 1945, p. 10.

7. W. J. [Hassett] to Truman, 25 May 1945, Hassett to Smith, 25 May 1945, [Smith] to Hassett, 6 June 1945, draft of reorganization act submitted to Manasco and McCarran, 7 June 1945, Hassett to McCarran, 7 June 1945, Hassett to Manasco, 7 June 1945, OF 285A, Truman papers.

8. U.S., Congress, House, Committee on Expenditures in the Executive Departments, *To Provide for Reorganizing Agencies of the Government* [Reorganization Act of 1945], Hearing, 79th Cong., 1st sess., pp. 19, 40; U.S., Congress, Senate, subcommittee of Committee on the Judiciary, *Reorganization of Executive Departments* [Reorganization Act of 1945], Hearing, 79th Cong., 1st sess., pp. 1–3.

9. Helen Fuller, "Manasco, One–Man Bottleneck," pp. 795–96.

10. House, Committee on Expenditures in the Executive Departments, *To Provide for Reorganizing Agencies of the Government*, Hearing, pp. 3–5.

11. Ibid., p. 78.

12. The *Washington Post*, 29 May 1945, p. 10.

13. Statement by Manasco, personal interview.

14. Daily record, Smith Diary, 8 June 1945.

15. The *New York Times*, 11 June 1945, p. 1.

16. Kenneth W. Street, "Harry S. Truman: His Role as Legislative Leader, 1945–1948" (Ph.D. diss.), pp. 108, 139–45.

17. *CR (Congressional Record)* 79:1, 1945, vol. 91, pt. 6, pp. 8230–32.

18. Frank McNaughton to Arthur Monroe, 7 September 1945, McNaughton Reports folder, Frank McNaughton papers.

19. The *Washington Post*, 3 September 1945, p. 7; House, Committee on Expenditures in the Executive Departments, *To Provide for Reorganizing Agencies of the Government*, Hearing, p. 59.

20. "Warren, Lindsay. . . ," *Current Biography: Who's News and Why, 1949*, pp. 624–26; Lindsay C. Warren to Charles Ross, 4 September 1945, OF 285A, Truman papers; Louis Brownlow, "Reconversion of the Federal Administrative Machinery from War to Peace," p. 322.

21. "Payroll Ax Handed to Truman," *Business Week*, pp. 17–18.

22. House, Committee on Expenditures in the Executive Departments, *To Provide for Reorganizing Agencies of the Government*, Hearing, p. 69.

23. For descriptions of Warren, which help explain his effectiveness before congressional committees see: Alexander Pow, "The Comptroller General and the General Accounting Office of the U.S." (Ph.D. diss.), pp. 35–36; Alfred Steinberg, "Watchdog on Washington Waste," pp. 121–24.

24. House, Committee on Expenditures in the Executive Departments, *To Provide for Reorganizing Agencies of the Government*, Hearing, p. 79.

25. Harold Seidman to Fred Levi, 6 September 1945, Reorganization Act of 1945 folder, Series [39.32], Bureau of Budget file, Office of Management and Budget.

26. The *New York Times*, 10 September 1945, p. 32.

27. U.S., Congress, House, Committee on Expenditures in the Executive Departments, *Reorganizations in Executive Branch* [Reorganization Act of 1945], H. Rept. No. 971, 79th Cong., 1st sess., (1945).

28. Smith Diary, 4 May 1945.

29. Alfred Steinberg, *Sam Johnson's Boy: A Close–up of the President from Texas*, p. 314; Joseph G. Feeney, oral history interview.

30. Jack Anderson and Ronald W. May, *McCarthy: The Man, the Senator, the "ISM,"* p. 341.

31. *CR*, vol. 91, pt. 8, pp. 10713–15; McNaughton to Don Bermingham, 3 November 1945, Frank McNaughton Reports folder, McNaughton papers; the *New York Times*, 17 October 1945, p. 1.

32. Senate, Committee on the Judiciary, *Reorganization of the Executive Departments*, Hearing, p. 19.

33. Ibid., pp. 76–79, 81, 103–4, 126–27.

34. Ibid., pp. 91–93.

35. Ibid., pp. 129–30.

36. Ibid., pp. 35, 60–76, 106–13, 114–21, 123–26, 131.

37. Ibid., p. 127.

38. Ibid., p. 89.

39. U.S., Congress, Senate, Committee on the Judiciary, *Reorganization of Government Agencies* [Reorganization Act of 1945], S. Rept. No. 638, 79th Cong., 1st sess., (1945).

40. McNaughton to Jack Beal, 22 June 1945, McNaughton Reports folder, McNaughton papers.

41. Street, "Harry S. Truman," pp. 120–21.

42. Harry S. Truman, *Public Papers of the Presidents of the United States: Harry S. Truman, 1945*, p. 225.

43. Street, "Harry S. Truman," pp. 137, 155–62; McNaughton to Monroe, 7 September 1945 and 15 September 1945, McNaughton Reports folder, McNaughton papers. For a systematic review of the turmoil of Truman's early years in office see Robert J. Donovan, *Conflict and Crisis: The Presidency of Harry S. Truman, 1945–1948*.

44. "Modernizing the Government," the *New Republic*, pp. 557–58.

45. Republican National Committee, Research Division, *Reorganization of the Executive*

188 Bureaucratic Politics

Branch: The Problem Before Congress in 1945 (pamphlet), pp. 6–9.

46. James F. Byrnes, "Why We Must Give the President A Clear Road," pp. 20–21.

47. Smith Diary, 9 November 1945.

48. Ibid., 5 June 1945.

49. David E. Lilienthal, *The Atomic Energy Years, 1945–1950,* vol. 2 of *The Journals of David E. Lilienthal,* p. 3.

50. The *New York Times,* 12 August 1945, p. 1.

51. C. Dwight Dorough, *Mr. Sam,* pp. 261–62.

52. The *New York Times,* 28 September 1945, p. 21.

53. *The Sun* [Baltimore], 13 May 1945, Democratic National Committee Clipping file; Truman, *Year of Decisions,* pp. 95–97.

54. By-line article by Walter Trohan, [Washington] *Times-Herald,* 28 May 1945, Democratic National Committee Clipping file.

55. By-line article by Albright, *Washington Post,* 27 May 1945, ibid.

56. Editorial, *New York Herald Tribune,* 26 May 1945, ibid.; column by Arthur Krock, *New York Times,* 27 May 1945, sect. 4, p. 3; by-line article by Bertram D. Hulen, 3 June 1945, sect. 4, p. 10; Wesley McCune and John R. Beal, "The Job That Made Truman President," p. 621; Richard L. Strout, "Harry S. Truman Sets His Course," p. 18; John Gunther, "The Man from Missouri," p. 32; column by Marquis Childs, *Washington Post,* 31 October 1945, Democratic National Committee Clipping file; John Fischer, "Mr. Truman Reorganizes," p. 26.

57. The *New York Times,* 21 May 1945, p. 10; Jerry Voorhis, *Confessions of a Congressman,* p. 251.

58. Warren to Matthew J. Connelly, 5 October 1945, OF 285A, Truman papers.

59. McNaughton to Monroe, 7 September 1945, McNaughton Reports folder, McNaughton papers.

60. McNaughton to David Hulburd, Jr., 5 October 1945, ibid.

61. McNaughton to Hulburd, 23 November 1945, ibid.

62. *CR,* vol. 91, pt. 7, pp. 9363–64.

63. Ibid., pp. 9339–42.

64. Ibid., p. 9342.

65. Ibid., pp. 9344–45.

66. Robert S. Allen and William V. Shannon, *The Truman Merry-Go-Round,* p. 203.

67. *CR,* vol. 91, pt. 7, pp. 9351–57.

68. McNaughton to Hulburd, 5 October 1945, McNaughton Reports folder, McNaughton papers; *CR,* vol. 91, pt. 7, p. 9427.

69. Richard Polenberg, *Reorganizing Roosevelt's Government: The Controversy Over Executive Reorganization, 1936–1939,* p. 167; McNaughton to Hulburd, 5 October 1945, McNaughton Reports folder, McNaughton papers; Manasco, personal interview.

70. *CR,* vol. 91, pt. 7, p. 9427.

71. Ibid., pp. 9427–36.

72. Ibid., pp. 9434–35; Manasco, personal interview.

73. *CR,* vol. 91, pt. 7, pp. 9435–36.

74. Democrat Schuyler Otis Bland (Virginia), chairman of the Committee on the Merchant Marine, offered an amendment to exempt the U.S. Maritime Commission and Republican Fred Crawford (Michigan), a member of the Committee on Banking and Currency, offered an amendment to exempt the Export-Import Bank. Bland and Crawford, said McNaughton, "were undoubtedly primed by those agencies." Both amendments failed. Other representatives tried to further protect the Veterans Administration and the Army Corps of Engineers but both attempts failed. McNaughton to Hulburd, 5 October 1945, McNaughton Reports folder, McNaughton papers; *CR,* vol. 91, pt. 7, pp. 9440–42, 9449.

75. *CR,* vol. 91, pt. 7, pp. 9442–44.

76. McNaughton to Beal, 22 June 1945, McNaughton Reports folder, McNaughton papers;

Tris Coffin, *Missouri Compromise,* p. 76; Tom Wicker, *JFK and LBJ: The Influence of Personality Upon Politics,* p. 70; Jim Wright, *You and Your Congressman,* p. 153.

77. *CR,* vol. 91, pt. 7, p. 9445.

78. Ibid., p. 9450.

79. Ibid., pp. 9453–54.

80. Daily record, Smith Diary, 1 November 1945; Smith later told Truman that the Bureau of the Budget drafted for Murdock the amendments designed to improve the Senate bill. Smith Diary, 28 November 1945.

81. The *New York Times,* 16 November 1945, p. 1.

82. *CR,* vol. 91, pt. 8, pp. 10271–72.

83. Ibid., pp. 10333–36.

84. Ibid., pp. 10333–36, 10522–29.

85. Allen and Shannon, *Truman Merry-Go-Round,* p. 287.

86. Robert A. Garson, *The Democratic Party and the Politics of Sectionalism, 1941–1948,* p. 101.

87. By-line article by Jack Steele, *New York Herald Tribune,* 6 May 1945, Democratic National Committee Clipping file.

88. Alden Hatch, *The Byrds of Virginia,* pp. 452, 471.

89. Ibid., pp. 479–82.

90. The *New York Times,* 2 November 1945, p. 9.

91. *CR,* vol. 91, pt. 8, pp. 10571–78.

92. Ibid., p. 10713.

93. Dorough, *Mr. Sam,* p. 397; V. O. Key, Jr., *Southern Politics in State and Nation,* pp. 361–62.

94. *CR,* vol. 91, pt. 8, pp. 10719–23.

95. Ibid., pp. 10757–58.

96. Ibid., pp. 10762–63; Peter Page Schauffler, "A Study of the Legislative Veto" (Ph.D. diss.), pp. 119–23.

97. *CR,* vol. 91, pt. 8, p. 10800.

98. Ibid., p. 10268.

99. Arthur Maass, *Muddy Waters: The Army Engineers and the Nation's Rivers,* p. 46.

100. Ibid., pp. 40–43, 45–50, 61–133.

101. *CR,* vol. 91, pt. 8, pp. 10326–28, 10330–31.

102. Ibid., pp. 10331–32; Key, *Southern Politics,* p. 358 (note 13).

103. *CR,* vol. 91, pt. 8, p. 10721; the *New York Times,* 19 October 1945, p. 16.

104. Propeller Club of the United States, "Exemption of the United States Maritime Commission from Reorganization of Agencies," p. 322.

105. *CR,* vol. 91, pt. 8, pp. 10715–19.

106. McNaughton to Hulburd, 23 November 1945, McNaughton Reports folder, McNaughton papers.

107. The *New York Times,* 28 November 1945, p. 19, 1 December 1945, p. 32, 9 December 1945, sect. 5, pp. 3, 4; American Farm Bureau Federation, *Official News Letter,* 14 November 1945, p. 4; *Public Utilities Fortnightly,* 11 October 1945, pp. 6, 8.

108. Smith to Truman, Report on Status of Legislation, 30 November 1945, OF 419–B, Truman papers.

109. U.S., Congress, House, Committee of Conference, *Reorganizations in Executive Branch* [conference report on Reorganization Act of 1945], conference report 1378, 79th Cong., 1st sess.

110. *CR,* vol. 91, pt. 9, pp. 11963–65; Warren to Cochran, 11 December 1945, Bills-misc. folder, Sam Rayburn papers.

111. The *New York Times,* 12 December 1945, p. 28; Truman to Smith, 20 December 1945, OF 285A, Truman papers.

112. Statement by president on signing reorganization act, 20 December 1945, OF 285A,

Truman papers. The act can be found at: U.S., *Statutes at Large,* Public Law 263, 59, part 1, 79th Cong., 1st sess., pp. 613–19.

113. For example see Samuel Lubell, *The Future of American Politics,* p. 22.

Chapter 5

1. Harold D. Smith, conference with the president, 13 September 1945, Harold D. Smith Diary, Harold D. Smith papers.

2. Ibid., 19 December 1945.

3. Harry S. Truman to Jennings Randolph, 29 April 1946, OF (Official File) 285A, Harry S. Truman papers.

4. Truman to Clarence C. Dill, 23 May 1946, ibid.

5. Frank McNaughton to Don Bermingham, 29 June 1946, McNaughton Reports folder, Frank McNaughton papers.

6. Smith Diary, 29 April 1946.

7. Truman to Robert L. Johnson, 1 April 1949, President's Secretary's File, Truman Papers.

8. Smith to Truman, 8 February 1946, Reorganization Program for 1946 folder, Series [39.32], Bureau of Budget file, Office of Management and Budget.

9. For example see Smith Diary, 28 February 1946, 2 May 1946.

10. "Procedure Followed in the Development of Plans 1, 2, and 3 of 1946," Reorganization-Items 1 through 6 folder, James E. Webb papers.

11. Demetrios Caraley, *The Politics of Military Unification: A Study of Conflict and the Policy Process;* Paul Y. Hammond, *Organizing for Defense: The American Military Establishment in the Twentieth Century.*

12. Paul H. Appleby, "Harold D. Smith—Public Administrator," pp. 77, 79. Also see John W. Ramsey, "The Director of the Bureau of the Budget as a Presidential Aide, 1921–1952: With Emphasis on the Truman Years" (Ph.D. diss.), p. 92; Robert E. Sherwood, *Roosevelt and Hopkins: An Intimate History,* p. 72.

13. "Smith, Harold. . . ," *Current Biography: Who's News and Why 1943,* pp. 710–13.

14. Louis Brownlow, *A Passion for Anonymity: The Autobiography of Louis Brownlow,* pp. 415–16. For a study of the evolution of the Bureau of the Budget see Dan Biederman, "Harold Smith and the Growth of the Bureau of the Budget, 1939–1946" (senior thesis).

15. Herman M. Somers, *Presidential Agency: OWMR, the Office of War Mobilization and Reconversion,* pp. 1–2, 80.

16. Ibid., p. 66; Ramsey, "Director of the Bureau of the Budget," p. 34.

17. Statement by Roger W. Jones, oral history interview.

18. Ramsey, "Director of the Bureau of the Budget," pp. 126–27, 129, 129 (note 33), 139–40; "Mr. Smith Stays in Town," *Newsweek,* p. 29.

19. Truman to Smith, 4 October 1945, OF 79C, Truman papers.

20. Ramsey, "Director of the Bureau of the Budget," p. 138.

21. "Statement by President on Signing Reorganization Act," 20 December 1945, Harry S. Truman, *Public Papers of the Presidents of the United States: Harry S. Truman, 1945,* p. 562; Smith to M. C. Latta, 19 December 1945, White House Bill file, Truman papers.

22. "Procedure Followed in the Development of Plans 1, 2, and 3 of 1946," Reorganization-Items 1 through 6 folder, Webb papers.

23. John R. Snyder to Smith, 12 January 1946, Reorganization Program of 1946 folder, Series [39.32], Bureau of Budget file, Office of Management and Budget.

24. Truman to Smith, 14 January 1946, Smith to Snyder, 15 February 1946, ibid.

25. Smith Diary, 21 January 1946.

26. Ibid. See also Smith to Snyder, 15 February 1946, Reorganization Program for 1946 folder, Series [39.32], Bureau of Budget file, Office of Management and Budget.

27. Statement by James Webb, personal interview.

28. Smith Diary, 15 May 1946.

29. Harold Ickes Diary, 6 September 1945, Harold Ickes papers.

30. Smith Diary, 8 February 1946; Richard E. Neustadt, *Presidential Power: The Politics of Leadership*, p. 174.

31. David E. Lilienthal, *The Atomic Energy Years, 1945–1950*, vol. 2 of *The Journals of David E. Lilienthal*, pp. 2–4.

32. See Chapter 5.

33. Smith Diary, 29 April 1946.

34. Truman, *Public Papers, 1945*, pp. 562–63.

35. Truman to Kenneth McKellar, 31 January 1946, OF 285C, Truman papers.

36. "Reorganization Proposals Received from Departments and Agencies [and] Budget Bureau Staff," 8 May 1946, untitled folder marked F2–51, F2–50, Series [39.32], Bureau of Budget file, Office of Management and Budget.

37. For example see Donald C. Stone to [Appleby], 14 October 1945, Smith to Truman, 8 February 1946, Reorganization Program for 1946 folder; R. C. Atkinson, "Conference with Appleby et al on Reorganization Proposals, October 24, 1945," 28 December 1945, untitled folder with material in it marked F2–50–51–52, Series [39.32], Bureau of Budget file, Office of Management and Budget.

38. Harry S. Truman, *Public Papers of the Presidents of the United States: Harry S. Truman, 1946*, pp. 249–55. *Public Papers* contains only the message to Congress explaining the plans. For copies of the message and plan see U.S., President, 1945–1953 (Truman), *Message from the President of the United States Transmitting Reorganization Plan No. 1 of 1946*, pp. 1–13. The plan included the following additional reorganizations: transferred to the Secretary of State certain functions of the Office of Inter–American Affairs, transferred from the Attorney General to the Commissioner of Internal Revenue some activities relating to the enforcement of the National Prohibition Act, abolished the Office of the United States High Commissioner to the Philippine Islands, transferred to the director of war mobilization and reconversion the duties of the Director and the Office of Contract Settlement, made permanent the transfer of the credit union functions from the Farm Credit Administration to the Federal Deposit Insurance Corporation, and reorganized the research programs of the Department of Agriculture to continue and extend further a consolidation process started by Roosevelt.

39. Barton J. Bernstein, "Reluctance and Resistance: Wilson Wyatt and Veterans' Housing in the Truman Administration," pp. 47–48.

40. Samuel E. Trotter, "A Study of Public Housing in the United States" (Ph.D. diss.), pp. 180–82.

41. See the cartoons and text in Bill Mauldin, *Back Home*, pp. 61–69; Richard O. Davies, *Housing Reform During the Truman Administration*, p. 40.

42. Davies, *Housing Reform During the Truman Administration*, p. 29.

43. Truman, *Public Papers, 1945*, pp. 290–92.

44. Davies, *Housing Reform During the Truman Administration*, pp. 33, 42, 46, 49.

45. Raymond M. Foley to Truman, 14 November 1945, OF 63, Truman papers; Atkinson, "Conference with Appleby et al on Reorganization Proposals, October 24, 1945," 28 December 1945, untitled folder with material in it marked F2–50–51–52, Series [39.32], Bureau of Budget file, Office of Management and Budget.

46. Smith Diary, 15 May 1946.

47. Truman, *Public Papers, 1946*, p. 252.

48. Harry S. Truman, *Year of Decisions*, vol. 1 of *Memoirs by Harry S. Truman*, p. 227; Smith Diary, 4 May 1945.

49. Truman, *Public Papers, 1946*, pp. 255–59. The message and plan are also contained in U.S., President, 1945–1953 (Truman), *Message from the President of the United States Transmitting Reorganization Plan No. 2 of 1946*, pp. 1–8. The plan also carried out the following additional

reorganizations: directed FSA to establish, when possible, uniform standards and procedures and to permit each state to submit a grants-in-aid single plan of operation for its related grants-in-aid programs, abolished the Federal Board of Education and its functions, transferred to the federal security administrator the vital statistics functions of the Census Bureau, transferred supervision of the vending stand program for the blind from the Office of Education to the federal security administrator, abolished the Board of Visitors of St. Elizabeth's Hospital, and abolished the Office of Assistant Commissioner of Education and transferred its activities to the Office of Education.

50. Truman, *Public Papers, 1946,* pp. 256–58.

51. "Memorandum Concerning Recent Reorganization Plans," 17 July 1946, Budget Bureau Procedure for Formulation, Presentation, and Implementation of Reorganization Plans folder, Series [39.32], Bureau of Budget file, Office of Management and Budget.

52. Atkinson, "Lessons from 1945–46 Experience on Reorganization Plans," 1 August 1946, ibid.

53. Truman, *Public Papers, 1946,* pp. 261–65. The message and plan are also contained in U.S., President, 1945–1953 (Truman), *Message from the President of the United States Transmitting Reorganization Plan No. 3 of 1946,* pp. 1–13. Plan three carried out the following additional reorganizations: transferred the Hydrographic Office and the Naval Observatory from the Bureau of Naval Personnel to the Office of the Chief of Naval Operations; consolidated the Paymaster's Department and the Quartermaster's Department of the U.S. Marine Corps into a single supply unit; vested in the National Park Service responsibility for "housekeeping" functions at the Franklin D. Roosevelt Library at Hyde Park; abolished the National Labor Relations Board function of conducting strike ballots; transferred responsibility for the Canal Zone Biological Area to the Smithsonian Institution; transferred to the Department of Interior jurisdiction over mineral deposits on land held by the Department of Agriculture; and transferred the functions of two divisions of the National Bureau of Standards (Division of Simplified Trade Practices and the Division of Commercial Standards) to the secretary of commerce; transferred to the secretary of agriculture the functions and duties of the Agricultural Adjustment Administration and Surplus Marketing Administration and the administration of the programs of the Federal Crop Insurance Corporation and the Commodity Credit Corporation; transferred legal responsibility for the patients of St. Elizabeth's Hospital to the navy and clarified the legal relationship between the hospital and the Veterans' Administration and Coast Guard; transferred to the U.S. Employment Service functions of the Selective Service System relating to job placement of ex-servicemen.

54. For studies of the economic and political conflicts that led to this reorganization see Phillip O. Foss, *Politics and Grass: The Administration of Grazing on the Public Domain,* pp. 171–86; Marion Clawson, *The Bureau of Land Management,* pp. 28–38.

55. Truman, *Public Papers, 1946,* p. 260.

56. Smith to Truman, 8 February 1946, Reorganization Program for 1946 folder, Series [39.32], Bureau of Budget file, Office of Management and Budget.

57. Smith Diary, 16 May 1946.

58. E. Drexel Godfrey, *The Transfer of the Children's Bureau* (pamphlet), p. 18; Herbert Emmerich, *Essays on Federal Reorganization,* pp. 43–44.

59. Godfrey, *Transfer of the Children's Bureau,* pp. 19–20; Atkinson, "Post–War Reconstruction of the Department of Labor," [April 1945]; D. H. Stowe to Martin, 1 May 1945; Atkinson, "Suggested Division of Children's Bureau Functions Between Labor and Federal Security Agency," 6 June 1945, Organization-Labor Department-Manpower Organization folder, David H. Stowe papers.

60. Monte Poen, "The Truman Administration and National Health Insurance" (Ph.D. diss.), pp. 85–86, 89–93; L. B. Schwellenbach to Truman, [15 March 1946], with attached memorandum of Schwellenbach and Watson Miller to Truman, 15 March 1946, Bills-National Health Act folder, Department of Labor papers, RG (Record Group) 174, National Archives.

61. John W. Gibson to Oscar A. Ehrhardt, 24 September 1945, Labor: General Correspondence folder, John W. Gibson papers; Schwellenbach to Truman, 20 May 1946, OF 285A, Truman papers.

62. Lenroot to Schwellenbach, 21 May 1946, OF 285A, Truman papers.

63. Godfrey, *Transfer of the Children's Bureau*, pp. 22–23.

64. Avery Leiserson, "Political Limitations on Executive Reorganization," p. 73; Godfrey, *Transfer of the Children's Bureau*, p. 18.

65. Godfrey, *Transfer of the Children's Bureau*, p. 23.

66. See LaFell Dickinson to Truman, 13 June 1946, unsigned, undated memorandum [this is probably a memorandum Mrs. Dickinson brought with her in her visit to Truman], OF 285A, Truman papers; M. J. C. [Matthew J. Connelly] to Edwin Locke, 18 June 1946, Mary Norton to Truman, 22 May 1946, Truman to Locke, 28 May 1946, Locke to Truman, 29 May 1946, Special Assistant to the President folder, Edwin A. Locke papers. Hundreds of individuals and representatives of organizations urged Truman to amend the plan to protect the Children's Bureau. These included Sen. Robert M. La Follette (a Progressive from Wisconsin), Dr. Edwin E. Witte, respected social welfare economist at the University of Wisconsin, and representatives of the National Consumers League, National Women's Trade Union, National Congress of Parents and Teachers, American Legion, Child Welfare League of America, Association of Colored Women, and American Association of University Women. Robert M. La Follette to Truman, 24 May 1946, OF 7, William D. Hassett to H. D. Smith, 5 June 1946, Hassett to Smith, 6 June 1946, John Stelle to Truman, 14 June 1946, OF 285A, Elizabeth Christman to Truman, 21 May 1946, Ms. William A. Hastings to Truman, 22 May 1946, OF 15E, Truman papers; Reorganization Plan Letters folder, Federal Security Agency Papers, RG 235, National Archives.

67. Godfrey, *Transfer of the Children's Bureau*, pp. 23–24.

68. Truman to Katharine Lenroot, 10 June 1946, Special Assistant to the President folder, Locke papers; Geoffrey May to Locke, 7 June 1946, OF 15E, Truman papers; Godfrey, *Transfer of the Children's Bureau*, p. 24.

69. Locke to Truman, 10 June 1946, Special Assistant to the President folder, Locke papers; Godfrey, *Transfer of the Children's Bureau*, p. 24.

70. Godfrey, *Transfer of the Children's Bureau*, p. 24. Lenroot was not satisfied with the Children's Bureau status and location within FSA, but her earlier campaign against the president's plan weakened her position so much that she had to accept the dictates of FSA officials. Godfrey, *Transfer of the Children's Bureau*, pp. 24–29.

71. Stauffacher to Stone, 30 July 1946, Budget Bureau Procedure for Formulation, Presentation, and Implementation of Reorganization Plans folder, Series [39.32], Bureau of the Budget file, Office of Management and Budget.

72. "Memorandum Concerning Recent Reorganization Plans," 17 July 1946, ibid.; Peter Page Schauffler, "A Study of the Legislative Veto" (Ph.D. diss.), pp. 287, 287 (note 561).

73. Richard F. Fenno, *The Power of the Purse: Appropriations Politics in Congress*, p. 10.

74. Atkinson, "Lessons from 1945–46 Experience on Reorganization Plans," 1 August 1946, Budget Bureau Procedure for Formulation, Presentation, and Implementation of Reorganization Plans folder, Series [39.32], Bureau of Budget file, Office of Management and Budget; Watson B. Miller to Truman, 15 June 1946, OF 419B, Truman papers; U.S., House, Committee on Expenditures in the Executive Departments, *Hearings, Reorganization Plans 1, 2, and 3 of 1946*, 79th Cong., 2d sess., pp. 58–59.

75. Truman to William Green, 21 May 1946, Green to Truman, 17 May 1946, OF 63, Truman papers.

76. Morton Bodfish to Johnson, 3 October 1946, quoted in U.S., Congress, House, Select Committee on Lobbying Activities, *United States Savings and Loan League*, H. Rept. No. 3139, 81st Cong., 2d sess., (1950), p. 283.

77. Davies, *Housing Reform During the Truman Administration*, p. 15; Leonard Freedman,

"Group Opposition to Public Housing" (Ph.D. diss.), pp. 75–76.

78. House, Select Committee on Lobbying Activities, H. Rept. No. 3139, pp. 35–36.

79. Davies, *Housing Reform During the Truman Administration*, pp. 15–18; also see Harry C. Bredemeier, "The Federal Public Housing Movement: A Case Study of Social Change" (Ph.D. diss.), Columbia University, 1955, pp. 127–48.

80. House, Committee on Expenditures in the Executive Departments, *Reorganization Plans 1, 2, and 3 of 1946*, Hearing, pp. 107–17, 123–29, 131–56. The following groups opposed the plan: Commerce and Industry Association of New York, Associated General Contractors of America, Inc., American Bankers Association, Mortgage Bankers Association, National Association of Home Builders, and National Retail Lumber Dealers Association. Supporters included top officials of the National Housing Agency, League of Women Voters, National Conference of Catholic Charities, American Federation of Labor, National Public Housing Conference. House, Committee on Expenditures in the Executive Department, *Reorganization Plans 1, 2, and 3 of 1946*, Hearing, pp. 118–21, 173–94, 210, 238–47, 249–51, 254–55, 299–302, 331–32, 340–41.

81. Ibid., pp. 203–9, 232–33, 235–38, 251–55, 289–93, 309–12.

82. By-line article by Joseph A. Loftus, the *New York Times*, 21 June 1946, p. 24; CR 79:2, 1946, vol. 92, pt. 6, p. 7894. For the committee reports see U.S., Congress, House, Committee on Expenditures in the Executive Departments, *Reorganization Plan No. 1 of 1946*, H. Rept. No. 2326, *Reorganization Plan No. 2 of 1946*, H. Rept. No. 2327, *Reorganization Plan No. 3 of 1946*, H. Rept. No. 2328, 79th Cong., 2d sess., (1946).

83. Atkinson, "Lessons from 1945–46 Experience on Reorganization Plans," 1 August 1946, Budget Bureau Procedure for Formulation, Presentation, and Implementation of Reorganization Plans folder, Series [39.32], Bureau of Budget file, Office of Management and Budget. Also see Locke to William Langer, 3 July 1946, Chronological file folder, Locke papers; Appleby to Truman, 27 June 1946, Budget Bureau Procedure for Formulation, Presentation, and Implementation of Reorganization Plans folder, Series [39.32], Bureau of Budget file, Office of Management and Budget.

84. *CR*, vol. 92, pt. 5, p. 5882.

85. McCarran to Wheeler, 5 July 1946, S. Con Res 66 Doc. 276 folder, Senate Judiciary Committee papers, RG 46, National Archives.

86. McCarran to McFarland, 5 July 1946, ibid.

87. McCarran to Avery Stitser, 26 June 1946, S. Con Res 65 Doc. 275 folder, ibid.

88. U.S. Congress, Senate, Committee on the Judiciary, *Hearings, President's Plan for Reorganization of Executive Departments* [Reorganization plans 1, 2, 3, 1946], 79th Cong., 2d sess.

89. *CR*, vol. 92, pt. 7, pp. 8887–88.

90. U.S., Congress, Senate, Committee on the Judiciary, *Reorganization Plan No. 1*, S. Rept. No. 1670, 79th Cong., 2d sess., (1946), pp. 1–3. Also see U.S., Congress, Senate, Committee on the Judiciary, *Reorganization Plan No. 2*, S. Rept. No. 1671, 79th Cong., 2d sess., (1946); U.S., Congress, Senate, Committee on the Judiciary, *Reorganization Plan No. 3*, S. Rept. No. 1672, 79th Cong., 2d sess., (1946).

91. The *Washington Post*, 28 June 1946, p. 18.

92. Appleby to Truman, 27 June 1946, OF 285A, Truman papers.

93. *CR*, vol. 92, pt. 6, pp. 7888–93, 7902–3.

94. Ibid., pp. 7902–3.

95. Ibid., pt. 6, pp. 7897–900, 7909, pt. 11, p. A3415, pt. 12, p. A3793.

96. Ibid., pt. 6, p. 7911.

97. Ibid., pp. 8901–3.

98. Ibid., pp. 8898–99.

99. Ibid., p. 8898.

100. Ibid., p. 8906; *Congressional Quarterly*, vol. 2, (1946), p. 561.

101. V. O. Key, *Southern Politics in State and Nation*, pp. 361–62; C. Dwight Dorough, *Mr.*

Sam, p. 377.

102. McNaughton Reports folder, 14 September 1945, McNaughton papers.

103. *CR,* vol. 92, pt. 7, pp. 8976–77.

104. Ibid., pp. 8968–70.

105. Ibid., pp. 8972–73.

106. Ibid., p. 8981; *Congressional Quarterly,* vol. 2, (1946), p. 561.

107. Davies, *Housing Reform During the Truman Administration,* p. 34.

108. *CR,* vol. 92, pt. 7, pp. 8986–87.

109. U.S., President, *Message from the President of the United States Transmitting Reorganization Plan No. 1 of 1946,* p. 11.

110. William L. Wheaton, "The Evolution of Federal Housing Programs" (Ph.D. diss.), pp. 248–52.

111. *CR,* vol. 92, pt. 7, p. 8994; *Congressional Quarterly,* vol. 2, (1946), p. 561.

112. See Robert L. Pritchard, "Southern Politics and the Truman Administration: Georgia as a Test Case" (Ph.D. diss.), p. 19.

113. Appleby to Truman, 27 June 1946, OF 285A, Truman papers.

114. By-line article by Jerry Kluttz, *Washington Post,* 3 June 1946, p. 1B.

115. Harold Zink, "Government Reform in the U.S.A.," pp. 72–73.

116. Note by Truman on memorandum of Smith to Truman, 8 February 1946, Reorganization Program for 1946 folder, Series [39.32], Bureau of Budget file, Office of Management and Budget.

117. Statement by Lawton, oral history interview conducted by Charles T. Morrissey.

118. Smith Diary, 2 May 1946.

119. U.S., Congress, House, Subcommittee of Committee on Government Operations, *Extending Authority for Executive Reorganization,* Hearing, 90th Cong., 2d sess., p. 13.

120. Rowland Egger, "Painless Economy and the Mythology of Administrative Reorganization," in Ronald B. Welch, ed., *Proceeding of the Forty-Second Annual Conference on Taxation,* pp. 488–94.

121. Seidman, *Politics, Position, and Power,* p. 12.

122. Rufus E. Miles, Jr., "Considerations for a President Bent on Reorganization," p. 162.

123. Statement by Frank Pace, Jr., oral history interview.

124. Seidman, *Politics, Position, and Power,* pp. 3–4.

125. David S. Brown, " 'Reforming' the Bureaucracy: Some Suggestions for the New President," pp. 166.

126. Francis E. Rourke, "The Politics of Administrative Organization: A Case History," pp. 476–77.

127. Harvey C. Mansfield, "Federal Executive Reorganization: Thirty Years of Experience," p. 334; Seidman, *Politics, Position, and Power,* pp. 9–10.

128. Frederick C. Mosher, "Introduction: ICP Case and Administrative Research," in Frederick C. Mosher, ed., *Governmental Reorganizations: Cases and Commentary,* p. xvi.

129. Ibid.

130. Herbert Emmerich, *Federal Organization and Administrative Management,* p. 159.

131. Stauffacher to Donald C. Stone, 30 July 1946, Budget Bureau Procedure for Formulation, Presentation and Implementation of Reorganization Plans folder, Series [39.32], Bureau of Budget file, Office of Management and Budget.

132. Atkinson, "Lessons from 1945–46 Experience in Reorganization Plans," 1 August 1946, ibid.

133. U.S., Congress, Senate, Committee on Expenditures in the Executive Departments, *Reestablishing Registers of Land Offices,* Hearing, 80th Cong., 1st sess., p. 21.

134. Emmerich, *Essays on Federal Reorganization,* p. 44; Godfrey, *Transfer of the Children's Bureau,* pp. 24–29.

135. Elmo R. Richardson, *Dams, Parks and Politics: Resource Development and Preservation in*

the Truman-Eisenhower Era, pp. 39–40; Aaron Wildavsky, *The Politics of the Budgetary Process,* p. 172.

136. Godfrey, *Transfer of the Children's Bureau,* pp. 24–29.

137. Arthur J. Altmeyer, *The Formative Years of Social Security,* pp. 159, 168.

Chapter 6

1. Harry S. Truman, *Public Papers of the Presidents of the United States: Harry S. Truman, 1947,* p. 2.

2. Susan M. Hartmann, *Truman and the 80th Congress,* p. 27.

3. Ibid., pp. 71–72.

4. Ibid., p. 10; Joe Martin, as told to Robert J. Donovan, *My First Fifty Years in Politics,* p. 190.

5. James Rowe, Jr., "Cooperation or Conflict?—The President's Relationships With an Opposition Congress," pp. 1–4.

6. John W. Ramsey, "The Director of the Bureau of the Budget as a Presidential Aide, 1921–1952, With Emphasis on the Truman Years" (Ph.D. diss.), pp. 142, 145–49, 168–69.

7. R. C. Atkinson, "Outline of Reorganization Program for 1947," Reorganization Program for 1947 folder, Series 39.32, Bureau of Budget file, Office of Management and Budget.

8. Charles B. Stauffacher to Arnold Miles, 14 October 1946, ibid.

9. Stauffacher, memorandum for the files, 16 October 1946, F2–Misc. 1941–1958 folder, ibid.

10. Plan one transferred the activities of the alien property custodian to the attorney general, ended the provision of a 1937 act requiring presidential approval of marketing orders issued by the secretary of agriculture, placed war-related contract settlement activities in the secretary of treasury, shifted certain duties of the National Prohibition Act from the Department of Justice to the Bureau of Internal Revenue, allowed surplus disposal functions to be administered by a single person, transferred the programs consolidated into the Agricultural Research Administration to the secretary of agriculture, and permanently moved the administration of federal responsibilities with respect to credit unions from the Farm Credit Administration to the Federal Deposit Insurance Corporation. Truman, *Public Papers, 1947,* pp. 222–26. This publication contains only the message to Congress. For the plan and message see U.S., President, 1945–1953 (Truman), *Message from the President of the United States Transmitting Reorganization Plan No. 1 of 1947,* pp. 1–8.

11. Truman, *Public Papers, 1947,* pp. 227–29. For the plan and message see U.S., President, 1945–1953 (Truman), *Message from the President of the United States Transmitting Reorganization Plan No. 2 of 1947,* pp. 1–4. The plan also transferred to the secretary of labor the functions of the administrator of the wage and hour division of the Department of Labor, and it gave the secretary authority to coordinate and regulate the enforcement of laws regulating wages and hours of workers employed on federal public works contracts.

12. Francis E. Rourke, "Reorganization of the Labor Department" (Ph.D. diss.), p. 180.

13. Gladys R. Friedman, "Reorganization Plan No. 1 of 1948: Legislative History and Background," pp. 15–17; Leonard P. Adams, *The Public Employment Service in Transition, 1933–1968: Evolution of a Placement Service into a Manpower Agency,* pp. 23–33; William Haber and Merrill G. Murray, *Unemployment Insurance in the American Economy: An Historical Review and Analysis,* pp. 418–37.

14. Franklin D. Roosevelt, *War—and Neutrality, 1939,* vol. 8 of *The Public Papers and Addresses of Franklin D. Roosevelt,* pp. 252–53.

15. Friedman, "Reorganization Plan No. 1 of 1948," pp. 15–17.

16. [Frances Perkins] to Smith, 14 October 1944, with attachment entitled "Creation of New Organizational Units in the Department of Labor by Transfer from Other Agencies of Government," Organization-Labor Department Manpower Organization folder, David H.

Stowe papers.

17. Stowe to Martin, 1 May 1945, Stowe and others to Martin, 12 May 1945, ibid.

18. Raymond C. Atkinson, "Post-War Reconstruction of the Department of Labor," [probably April 1945], ibid.

19. Daily record, 31 May 1945, Harold D. Smith Diary, Harold D. Smith papers.

20. Smith Diary, 5 June 1945.

21. William F. McCandless to Stowe, 17 July 1945, Organization-Labor Department Manpower Organization folder, Stowe papers.

22. Schwellenbach to Truman, 13 August 1945, Smith to Truman, 18 August 1945, OF (Official File) 285A, Harry S. Truman papers; Smith Diary, 18 August 1945.

23. Richard L. Neuberger, "Nobody Hates the Umpire—Yet," p. 30; "Truman Plans Consolidation of Independent Agencies With Cabinet Members Responsible for Administration," NAM News, pp. 1–2; Ed Lockett to Don Bermingham, 25 May 1945, Ed Lockett Reports folder, Frank McNaughton papers; Stowe to Stone, 12 July 1945, Organization-Labor Department Manpower Organization folder, Stowe papers.

24. Harry S. Truman, Year of Decisions, vol. 1 of Memoirs by Harry S. Truman, pp. 95, 106, 325. Also see Smith Diary, 26 April 1945.

25. Harry [Roberts] to John W. Gibson, 6 November 1948, Name File R folder, John W. Gibson papers.

26. Schwellenbach to Carl Moran, 14 June 1945, Reorganization–General–1945 folder, Department of Labor papers, RG 174, National Archives; Schwellenbach to William Green, Alvanley Johnston, A. F. Whitney, and John L. Lewis, 22 June 1945, S–Z folder, Schwellenbach papers; Neuberger, "Nobody Hates the Umpire—Yet," p. 30. Schwellenbach found it difficult to achieve his goals because he quickly lost favor with organized labor, with his department, with Congress, and with the president. Edgar L. Shor, "The Role of the Secretary of Labor" (Ph.D. diss.), pp. 50–56.

27. Schwellenbach to Smith, 16 April 1946, OF 285A, Truman papers.

28. David E. Lilienthal, The Atomic Energy Years, 1945–1950, vol. 2 of The Journals of David E. Lilienthal, p. 3.

29. "Conversation Between Sec. Schwellenbach and Director Smith," daily record, 28 May 1946, Smith Diary.

30. Schwellenbach to Truman, 20 May 1946, OF 285A, Truman papers.

31. U.S., Congress, House, Committee on Expenditures in the Executive Departments, Hearings, Reorganization Plans Nos. 1 and 2 of 1947, 80th Cong., 1st sess., pp. 109–15, 156–73.

32. Truman, Public Papers, 1947, p. 31.

33. Webb to Truman (this is the third draft of a memorandum written by Stauffacher for Webb), 21 November 1946, Reorganization Program for 1947 folder, Series [39.32], Bureau of Budget file, Office of Management and Budget; also see undersecretary of labor to Schwellenbach, [February 1947], Reorganization (working file) folder, RG 174, National Archives.

34. Stone to Webb, 1 April 1947, Reorganization Plan 1 of 1946 folder, Series 39.32, Bureau of Budget file, Office of Management and Budget; U.S., Congress, Senate, Committee on Labor and Public Welfare, Subcommittee on Labor, Hearings, The President's Reorganization Plan No. 2 of 1947, 80th Cong., 1st sess., pp. 13–16.

35. Clare Hoffman to "Colleague," 20 May 1947, House Document No. 230, Reorganization Plan No. 1 of 1947 folder, House of Representatives papers, RG 233, National Archives; statement by Herbert Roback, personal interview.

36. Roback, personal interview.

37. Rourke, "Reorganization of the Labor Department," pp. 252–53.

38. R. Alton Lee, Truman and Taft-Hartley: A Question of Mandate, pp. 8–18, 50–52; Arthur F. McClure, The Truman Administration and the Problems of Postwar Labor, 1945–1948, pp. 162–63; Harry A. Millis and Emily Clark Brown, From the Wagner Act to Taft-Hartley, pp. 311–15.

39. Francis E. Rourke, Bureaucracy, Politics, and Public Policy, p. 20; Rourke, "Reorganization

of the Labor Department," pp. 66–67, 123.

40. Rourke, "Reorganization of the Labor Department," pp. 59–60.

41. Ibid., pp. 67–68.

42. David W. MacEachron, "The Role of the United States Department of Labor" (Ph.D. diss.), p. 123; Rourke, "Reorganization of the Labor Department," p. 76. In some cases, organized labor opposed Department of Labor expansion. Union leaders had been ambivalent about placing unemployment compensation functions in the department because they feared acquisition of a mass clientele would reduce labor's influence within the department. Shor, "The Role of the Secretary of Labor," p. 246.

43. House, Committee on Expenditures in the Executive Departments, *Reorganization Plans Nos. 1 and 2 of 1947*, Hearing, p. 31.

44. Ibid., pp. 97–98, 102–9, 120–21, 124.

45. Ibid., pp. 181–83.

46. Charles S. Hyneman, *Bureaucracy in a Democracy*, pp. 109–10.

47. Many state governors opposed plan two and so informed their senators. A Labor Department official said senators, especially those up for reelection, would not want to oppose the governors' emphatic stand. May Thompson Evans to undersecretary of labor, 27 June 1947, Reorganization (plans one and two) folder, RG 174, National Archives.

48. U.S., Congress, House, Committee on Expenditures in the Executive Departments, *Reorganization Plan No. 2 of 1947*, H. Rept. No. 499, 80th Cong., 1st sess., (1947), pp. 1–4.

49. *CR (Congressional Record)* 80:1, 1947, vol. 93, pt. 5, p. 6740.

50. Senate, Committee on Labor and Public Welfare, *President's Reorganization Plan No. 2 of 1947*, Hearing, pp. 1–3.

51. Schauffler, "A Study of the Legislative Veto" (Ph.D. diss.), pp. 311–12; Senate, Committee on Labor and Public Welfare, *President's Reorganization Plan No. 2 of 1947*, Hearing, pp. 4–5.

52. Schauffler, "Study of the Legislative Veto," pp. 312–13.

53. U.S., Congress, Senate, Committee on Labor and Public Welfare, *Reorganization Plan No. 2 of 1947*, S. Rept. No. 320, 80th Cong., 1st sess., (1947), pp. 1–3.

54. Gibson to James Patton, 8 July 1947, Labor-Chronological file 1947 folder, Gibson papers.

55. *CR*, vol. 93, pt. 6, pp. 7862–66, 7868–70.

56. Ibid., pp. 7857–61, 7872.

57. Ibid., pp. 7871–72.

58. Ibid., p. 7874; *Congressional Quarterly*, vol. 3, (1947), p. 308.

59. Truman, *Public Papers, 1947*, pp. 257–58. For plan and message see U.S., President, 1945–1953 (Truman), *Message from the President of the United States Transmitting Reorganization Plan No. 3 of 1947*, pp. 1–7.

60. For example see Philip W. Klutznick to Truman, 5 December 1946, Joseph E. Loftus to William Remington, 17 December 1946, OF 63, Truman papers.

61. Truman, *Public Papers, 1947*, pp. 258–59.

62. U.S., Congress, House, Committee on Expenditures in the Executive Departments, *Reorganization Plan No. 3 of 1947*, Hearing, 80th Cong., 1st sess., pp. 50–52, 58–60, 62–63.

63. Ibid., pp. 63–64; Raymond P. Harold to Raymond M. Foley, 19 August 1947, Personal Correspondence folder, Raymond M. Foley papers; Harold to Truman, 29 May 1947, OF 285A, Truman papers; Harold to Earl Michener, 28 May 1947, House Document No. 270, Reorganization Plan No. 3 of 1947 folder, RG 233, National Archives.

64. U.S., Congress, House, Committee on Expenditures in the Executive Departments, *Reorganization Plan No. 3 of 1947*, H. Rept. No. 580, 80th Cong., 1st sess., (1947), pp. 1–2.

65. Schauffler, "Study of the Legislative Veto," p. 308; *CR*, vol. 93, pt. 6, p. 7252.

66. U.S., Congress, Senate, Committee on Banking and Currency, *Hearings, Reorganization Plan No. 3 of 1947*, 80th Cong., 1st sess., pp. 6–8, 8–10.

67. U.S., Congress, Senate, Committee on Banking and Currency, *Reorganization Plan No. 3 of 1947*, S. Rept. No. 400, 80th Cong., 1st sess., (1947), pp. 1–5.

68. Schauffler, "Study of the Legislative Veto," p. 315.

69. Bernstein, "Reluctance and Resistance: Wilson Wyatt and Veterans' Housing in the Truman Administration," p. 54.

70. Richard O. Davies, *Housing Reform During the Truman Administration*, p. 45.

71. Ibid., p. 57.

72. Ibid., pp. 59–60.

73. Ibid., pp. 62–63.

74. Ibid., pp. 60–62, 72, 129.

75. John M. Dickerman to E. Clarke King, 30 June 1947, U.S., Congress, House, Select Committee on Lobbying Activities, *Housing Lobby*, Hearing, part 2, 81st Cong., 2d sess., p. 381.

76. Davies, *Housing Reform During the Truman Administration*, p. 34.

77. Ibid., pp. 33–34; also see James T. Patterson, *Mr. Republican: A Biography of Robert A. Taft*, pp. 316–20.

78. Truman, *Public Papers, 1947*, p. 317.

79. C. J. Burns to "Association Manager," 26 June 1947, U.S., Congress, House, Select Committee on Lobbying Activities, *United States Saving and Loan League*, H. Rept. No. 3139, 81st Cong., 2d sess., (1950), pp. 321–22.

80. [Neill Davis] to Morton Bodfish, 2 July 1947, ibid., pp. 333–34.

81. [Horace] Russell to Bodfish, 15 July 1947, ibid., pp. 60–61.

82. A. Harold MacNeil to Bodfish, 18 July 1947, ibid., p. 349.

83. [Henry A. Burr] to E. Louise Johnson, 23 July 1947, ibid., p. 352.

84. Republican National Committee, Research Division, *Reorganization Plan No. 3 of 1947: Memorandum on the Pros and Cons* (pamphlet), pp. 1–11.

85. Bill [last name illegible] to Ray [Foley], 2 July [1947], Personal Correspondence folder, Foley papers.

86. Davies, *Housing Reform During the Truman Administration*, pp. 34–36; Leonard Freedman, "Group Opposition to Public Housing" (Ph.D. diss.), p. 154.

87. *CR*, vol. 93, pt. 8, pp. 9657–58, 9666–67.

88. Ibid., p. 9669; *Congressional Quarterly*, vol. 3, (1947), p. 446.

89. Davies, *Housing Reform During the Truman Administration*, p. 64.

90. [John W. Gibson] to "Roy," 10 July 1947, S folder, Gibson papers.

91. "Jim" [Albert Abrahamson] to John [Gibson], 17 September 1947, A folder, ibid.

92. Truman, *Public Papers, 1947*, p. 341.

93. Harry S. Truman, *Public Papers of the Presidents of the United States: Harry S. Truman, 1948*, pp. 102–3. For plan and message see U.S., President, 1945–1953 (Truman), *Message from the President of the United States Transmitting Reorganization Plan No. 1 of 1948*, pp. 1–4.

94. Hartmann, *Truman and the 80th Congress*, p. 128.

95. For an early example of this see Truman, *Public Papers, 1947*, p. 382.

96. Hartmann, *Truman and the 80th Congress*, pp. 152–53.

97. Gibson to Adolph Germer, 10 March 1948, G folder, Gibson papers. Also see DAM [David Morse] to Judge [Schwellenbach], 5 February [1948], Administrative-Morse folder, RG 174, National Archives.

98. U.S., Congress, House, Committee on Expenditures in the Executive Departments, *Hearings, Reorganization Plan No. 1 of 1948*, 80th Cong., 2d sess., pp. 200–202.

99. Rourke, "The Politics of Administrative Organization," p. 469.

100. House, Committee on Expenditures in the Executive Departments, *Reorganization Plan No. 1 of 1948*, Hearing, pp. 49–52, 139–49; Joseph M. Becker, *Experience Rating in Unemployment Insurance: An Experiment in Competitive Socialism*, pp. 1–2.

101. U.S., Congress, House, Committee on Expenditures in the Executive Departments,

Reorganization Plan No. 1 of 1948, H. Rept. No. 1368, 80th Cong., 2d sess., (1948), pp. 3–7.

102. *CR* 80:2, 1948, vol. 94, pt. 2, p. 1721.

103. U.S., Congress, Senate, Committee on Labor and Public Welfare, *Hearings, Reorganization Plan No. 1 of 1948*, 80th Cong., 2d sess., pp. 19–20, 31–32.

104. U.S., Congress, Senate, Committee on Labor and Public Welfare, *Reorganization Plan No. 1 of January 19, 1948*, S. Rept. No. 967, 80th Cong., 2d sess., (1948), pp. 3–5.

105. *CR*, vol. 94, pt. 3, pp. 2906–7.

106. Ibid., pp. 2913–14.

107. Ibid., p. 2921; *Congressional Quarterly*, vol. 4, (1948), p. 234.

108. Unsigned, undated memorandum entitled "Senate Vote (June 30, 1947) on the President's Reorganization Plan No. 2 of 1947. . . ," OF 285A, Truman papers.

Chapter 7

1. Clarence J. Brown to DeWitt Wallace, 21 June 1949, unsigned, undated memorandum entitled "Commission on the Organization of the Executive Branch of the Government," 1st Hoover Commission folder, Brown to Elliott V. Bell, 15 October 1953, Brown to Granville Barrere, 29 August 1953, both in Miscellaneous B folder, Brown to Herbert C. Hoover, 27 August 1953, Herbert C. Hoover Personal folder, Clarence Brown papers; Clarence Brown, Jr., to William E. Pemberton, 16 April 1975, in author's possession.

2. Brown to Hoover, 4 February 1947, Brown, Clarence, Correspondence folder, Post-Presidential papers, Individual file, Hoover papers.

3. U.S., *Statutes at Large*, vol. 61, pt. 1, pp. 246, 248.

4. Ibid., p. 246.

5. Statement by James Webb, personal interview.

6. Peter Page Schauffler, "A Study of the Legislative Veto" (Ph.D. diss.), p. 327.

7. By-line article by Ernest Lindley entitled "Toward Efficiency," name of newspaper not given, undated [about 1 July 1947], Hoover Commission on Reorganization folder, George Elsey papers.

8. Webb, personal interview.

9. Webb to George Aiken, 28 February 1947, printed in U.S., Congress, Senate, Committee on Expenditures in the Executive Departments, *Hearings on S. 164, Commission on Organization of the Executive Branch of the Government*, 80th Cong., 1st sess., p. 3.

10. U.S., Congress, House, Committee on Expenditures in the Executive Departments, *Hearings on H.R.775 for the Establishment of the Commission on Organization of the Executive Branch of the Government*, 80th Cong., 1st sess., pp. 12, 14–15.

11. Ibid., pp. 11–12, 15–17.

12. U.S., Congress, House, Committee on Expenditures in the Executive Departments, *Establish a Commission on the Organization of the Executive Branch of the Government*, H. Rept. No. 704, 80th Cong., 1st sess., (1947), pp. 1–2.

13. U.S., Congress, Senate, Committee on Expenditures in the Executive Departments, *Commission on Organization of the Executive Branch of the Government*, S. Rept. No. 344, 80th Cong., 1st sess., (1947), p. 4.

14. *CR (Congressional Record)* 80:1, 1947, vol. 93, pt. 6, pp. 7755, 7757, 7803–4; Edward H. Hobbs, *Executive Reorganization in the National Government*, pp. 43–44. For the legislative history of the bill see Ferrel Heady, "A New Approach to Federal Executive Reorganization," pp. 1118–26.

15. Dean Acheson, *Present at the Creation: My Years in the State Department*, p. 235.

16. Frank McNaughton to David Hulburd, 4 June 1947, McNaughton Reports folder, Frank McNaughton papers.

17. Statement by James Rowe, personal interview.

18. Statement by James E. Westbrook, personal interview.

19. Jules Abels, *Out of the Jaws of Victory*, p. 14.

20. Westbrook, personal interview.

21. *Who's Who in America*, vol. 26, p. 2189; statement by Ferrel Heady, personal interview; unsigned memorandum entitled "James K. Pollock," [July 1947], Organization and Staffing [of Hoover Commission] folder, Series 39.32, Bureau of Budget file, Office of Management and Budget.

22. Pollock to Ray Tucker, 30 March 1951, secretary of state, Alphabetical folder, Dean Acheson papers.

23. Heady, personal interview.

24. Unsigned, undated statement entitled "Individual Attendance at Meetings of the Commission. . . ," 1949 Feb.-Mar., Mainly Press releases folder, Brown papers.

25. Statement by James A. Fayne, oral history interview; statement by Rose Kennedy, oral history interview.

26. Hoover to Kennedy, 7 January 1949, Kennedy to Hoover, 11 January 1949, Joseph P. Kennedy folder, Commission on Organization of the Executive Branch of the Government papers, Herbert C. Hoover Presidential Library; also see David E. Koskoff, *Joseph P. Kennedy: A Life and Times*, pp. 340–46, 366.

27. Rowe to Kennedy, 23 February 1949, Hoover Commission folder, James Landis papers.

28. *Who's Who in America*, vol. 26, p. 337; Transcript of Meeting of Commission on Organization of the Executive Branch of the Government, 29 November 1948, p. 48, Commission on Organization of the Executive Branch of the Government papers, RG 264, National Archives; Walter Millis (ed.), with collaboration of E. S. Duffield, *The Forrestal Diaries*, p. 244.

29. Jack Bell, *The Splendid Misery: The Story of the Presidency and Power Politics at Close Range*, p. 213; Klein to Hoover, 2 June 1947, Klein, Julius Correspondence folder, Post-Presidential papers, Individual file, Hoover papers.

30. William S. White, *Home Place: The Story of the U.S. House of Representatives*, p. 116.

31. *Who's Who in America*, vol. 26, p. 1727; also see Stephen K. Bailey, *Congress Makes a Law: The Story Behind the Employment Act of 1946*, pp. 200–201.

32. U.S., Congress, House, Committee on Expenditures in the Executive Departments, *Reorganization Plan No. 1 of 1948*, Hearings, 80th Cong., 2d sess., p. 182.

33. [Hoover] to Brown, 1 February 1947, Brown, Clarence Correspondence folder, Post-Presidential papers, Individual file, Hoover papers.

34. Hoover to Lodge, 24 July 1947, Henry Cabot Lodge folder, Commission on Organization of the Executive Branch papers, Hoover Library.

35. Joe Martin as told to Robert J. Donovan, *My First Fifty Years in Politics*, p. 191.

36. Bernice Miller to Klein, 18 July 1947, Klein to Hoover, 18 July 1947, Klein to Hoover, 24 July 1947, Federal Field Offices folder, Commission on Organization of the Executive Branch papers, Hoover Library; unsigned memorandum, evidently on Hoover's remarks before a radio discussion panel, entitled "Hoover Remarks, April 18, 1949," Estimates of Savings Resulting from Adoption of the Recommendations of the Hoover Commission folder, Series 39.32, Bureau of Budget papers, Office of Management and Budget; also see Charles Aikin, "The Story of the Hoover Commission," p. 26.

37. *Who's Who in America*, vol. 26, p. 2368; Patrick Anderson, *The Presidents' Men: White House Assistants of Franklin D. Roosevelt, Harry S. Truman, Dwight D. Eisenhower, John F. Kennedy and Lyndon B. Johnson*, p. 65.

38. Rowe, personal interview.

39. John W. Ramsey, "The Director of the Bureau of the Budget as a Presidential Aide, 1921–1952: With Emphasis on the Truman Years" (Ph.D. diss.), p. 94; unsigned memorandum entitled "James Henry Rowe, Jr.," [July, 1947], Organization and Staffing [of the Hoover

Commission] folder, Bureau of Budget papers, Office of Management and Budget; Rowe, personal interview.

40. Rowe to Stone, 27 January 1940, [F-Miscellaneous] folder, Series 39.32, Bureau of Budget papers, Office of Management and Budget.

41. Theodore H. White, *The Making of the President, 1964*, pp. 272, 351–52.

42. Anderson, *Presidents' Men*, p. 119.

43. Series of unsigned memoranda probably by George Elsey, 7, 8 July 1947, Hoover Commission Reorganization folder, Elsey papers; statement by Frederick Lawton, personal interview.

44. Hoover to Joel T. Boone, 31 May 1949, Boone, Joel T. Correspondence folder, Post-Presidential papers, Individual file, Hoover papers.

45. Francis Brassor to Pollock, 23 May 1949, Brassor, Francis P. folder, James K. Pollock papers.

46. Jonathan Daniels, *Frontier on the Potomac*, p. 112; Paul R. Van Riper, *History of the United States Civil Service*, p. 405; Joseph P. Harris, *Congressional Control of Administration*, p. 172.

47. Statement by Joseph Miller, personal interview.

48. Lawton, personal interview.

49. Herbert Emmerich, *Essays on Federal Reorganization*, pp. 96–97. For a study of Hoover's administrative ideas, techniques, and practices see John L. Westrate, "The Administrative Theories and Practices of Herbert Hoover" (Ph.D. diss.).

50. Emmerich, *Essays on Federal Reorganization*, p. 97; Heady, personal interview.

51. Rowe, personal interview; statement by Carter Manasco, personal interview; Ferrel Heady, "The Operation of a Mixed Commission," pp. 947–48.

52. Emmerich, *Essays on Federal Reorganization*, p. 98; Heady, "Operation of a Mixed Commission," p. 945; Rowe, personal interview; memorandum by Pollock entitled "Reflections on the Organization and Work of the Commission on Organization of the Executive Branch of the Government," 5 May 1949, untitled folder in topical files 1947–1951; memorandum entitled "First Hoover Commission–Pollock File: Re: Mixed Commissions questionnaire—paraphrased answers transcribed by L. A. Hester from Professor James K. Pollock," undated, Miscellaneous folder, Pollock papers; Charles Aikin, "Task Force: Methodology," p. 242.

53. Heady, "Operation of a Mixed Commission," p. 950.

54. Acheson, *Present at the Creation*, p. 242; Rowe, personal interview.

55. Memorandum entitled "First Hoover Commission-Pollock File: Re: Mixed Commission questionnaire," undated, Miscellaneous folder, Pollock papers. Also see Rowe to secretary of state [Dean Acheson], 1 February 1949, Memoranda and Reports re Personnel Management Report folder, Rowe to Acheson, 16 April 1948, Memoranda to Dean Acheson from Charles Aikin and James Rowe folder, Acheson papers.

56. Rowe, personal interview; Miller, personal interview; Rowe to Sidney Mitchell, 3 March 1948, Administration Projects: General folder, Pollock to Hoover, 30 September 1948, Pollock, Dr. James K. folder, RG 264, National Archives; Pollock to Hoover, 24 November 1948, Procedures, Task Force Report folder, Pollock papers; Rowe to Acheson, 22 January 1948, Memoranda to Dean Acheson from Charles Aikin and James Rowe folder, Acheson papers.

57. Aikin, "Task Force," p. 249; Paul H. Appleby, "The Significance of the Hoover Commission Report," p. 20; Aikin, "Story of the Hoover Commission," p. 26.

58. For example see Hoover to Henry Stimson, 30 November 1948, Henry Stimson papers; Hoover to J. Reuben Clark, Jr., 3 October 1948, Clark, J. Reuben Correspondence folder, Hoover to Mrs. Francis W. Hirst, 4 March 1949, Hirst, Mr. and Mrs. Francis Correspondence folder, Post-Presidential papers, Individual file, Hoover papers; Sidney Shalett, "The Return of Herbert Hoover," p. 140.

59. Hoover to Walter Hope, 18 August 1947, H folder, Commission on Organization of the Executive Branch papers, Hoover Library.

60. [Hoover] to Rowe, 14 May 1948, National Defense folder, RG 264, National Archives.

61. Frank Gervasi, *Big Government: The Meaning and Purpose of the Hoover Commission Report*, p. ix.

62. Transcript of meeting of Commission on Organization of the Executive Branch of the Government, 12 January 1948, p. 18, RG 264, National Archives.

63. Charles Aikin and Louis W. Koenig, "Introduction," in "The Hoover Commission: A Symposium," p. 935.

64. Gervasi, *Big Government*, p. 8. Also see Laurin L. Henry, *Presidential Transitions*, p. 469; Herbert Emmerich, *Federal Organization and Administrative Management*, pp. 82–83.

65. James T. Patterson, *Mr. Republican: A Biography of Robert A. Taft*, p. 400.

66. Klein to Hoover, 18 July 1947, Federal Field Offices folder, Commission on Organization of the Executive Branch papers, Hoover Library.

67. Martin, *My First Fifty Years in Politics*, p. 191.

68. Ibid.

69. *New York Times*, 6 August 1947, p. 14.

70. McGeorge Bundy to Stimson, 26 April 1948, Stimson papers.

71. Senate Republican Conference, "Pick up the Challenge: II," *Senate Majority News*, 22 October 1948, Corr. Sub–R–8 Senate, Majority News temporary folder, James P. Kem papers.

72. Aikin, "Task Force," p. 242.

73. "Policy Statement Adopted at Commission Meeting on October 20, 1947," Miscellaneous folder, Frederick A. Middlebush papers.

74. [Hoover] to Robert Heller and others, 12 July 1948, Chronological folder, Executive Director's Office, RG 264, National Archives. Also see remarks by Hoover before the National Press Club, 14 September 1948, Press Release by Commission on Organization of Executive Branch folder, Department of Labor papers, RG 174, National Archives.

75. Howard Kline to staff members of medical service task force, 21 July 1948, Scope of Project folder, task force on Federal Medical Services file, RG 264, National Archives.

76. Transcript of meeting of Commission on Organization of the Executive Branch of the Government, 16 February 1948, pp. 19–22, 1 December 1947, pp. 23–24, RG 264, National Archives.

77. Jack R. Ewalt to Howard Kline, 14 August 1948, Ewalt, Jack R. folder, task force on Federal Medical Services file, RG 264, National Archives.

78. Hoover to Arthur H. Carter, 6 December 1947, Revolving Fund and Business Enterprises folder, Commission on Organization of the Executive Branch papers, Hoover Library.

79. [Sidney Mitchell] to Robert Bowie, 16 January 1948, Administration Projects: General folder, Research and Library Section, RG 264, National Archives.

80. Memorandum by Russell A. Heddleston, entitled "Notes of Meeting with Mr. Theodore Herz. . . ," 2 July 1948, Business Enterprises folder, Brown papers.

81. T. J. Coolidge to Committee on Federal-State Relations, 20 January 1948, Federal-State Relationships folder, Commission on Organization of the Executive Branch papers, Hoover Library.

82. Aikin and Koenig, "Introduction," p. 934.

83. Gene Duffield to Mitchell, 5 November 1948, Information—II folder, Executive Director's Office, RG 264, National Archives.

84. Included in McCormick to George Smith, 27 February 1952, Minority Policy Committee (Senate) folder, CCHR (Citizens Committee for the Hoover Report) papers.

85. Smith to McCormick, 10 March 1952, Minority Policy Committee (Senate) folder, CCHR papers.

86. Rowe, personal interview. Also see Acheson's Princeton Seminar, Reading Copy I, 2 July 1953, Acheson papers.

87. Rowe to Pemberton, 16 January 1975, in author's possession.

88. Aikin, "Story of the Hoover Commission," p. 82. Also see Heady, "The Reports of the Hoover Commission," pp. 376–77; Miller, personal interview; Heady, personal interview;

Aikin, "Story of the Hoover Commission," pp. 26–27, 82.

89. Aikin and Koenig, "Introduction," pp. 934–35.

90. See for example, transcript of meeting of Commission on Organization of the Executive Branch of the Government, 29 November 1948, pp. 113–30, 13 December 1948, pp. 104, 107–8, RG 264, National Archives; memorandum by [Pollock] entitled "Comments of Com. Pollock 12[15] February 23," Agenda, Notes, Papers folder, Pollock to Hoover, 23 February 1949, Hoover to Pollock, 24 February 1949, Hoover, Herbert folder, Rowe to Pollock, 25 February 1949, Rowe, James Jr. folder, Pollock papers; Rowe to Hoover, 24 February 1949, Rowe, James Jr. folder, Hoover to Aiken, 12 March 1949, George D. Aiken folder, Commission on Organization of the Executive Branch papers, Hoover Library.

91. Heady, "Operation of a Mixed Commission," p. 942 (note 5); McCormick to Franklin Hardings, Jr., 1 September 1949, McCormick to D. G. Redmond, 26 October 1949, CCHR Chrono file, Robert L. McCormick papers; Aikin and Koenig, "Introduction," p. 935; Emmerich, Essays on Federal Reorganization, pp. 113–15.

92. Rowe, personal interview.

93. Acheson, Present at the Creation, p. 249; Elsey to Clifford, 22 September 1947, Hoover Commission on Reorganization folder, Elsey papers; Aikin, "Story of the Hoover Commission," p. 26; Acheson's Princeton Seminar, Reading Copy I, 2 July 1953, Acheson papers.

94. Rowe to Acheson, 16 April 1948, Memoranda to Dean Acheson from Charles Aikin and James Rowe folder, Acheson papers.

95. Stauffacher to budget director, 19 January 1949, Organization and Staffing [of Hoover Commission] folder, Series 39.32, Bureau of Budget papers, Office of Management and Budget.

96. Rowe to Acheson, 3 February 1949, Memoranda Reports re: Personnel Management folder, Notes on Conference with Mr. Dean, 19 February 1949, Alan Dean to Acheson, 17 February 1949, General Correspondence folder, Acheson papers.

97. Rowe to Pollock, 8 February 1949, Rowe, James Jr. folder, Pollock papers.

98. Pollock to Edward A. Cottrell, 26 December 1947, A–B–C folder, ibid.

99. Pollock to Acheson, 23 February 1949, Acheson, Dean folder, ibid.

100. David E. Lilienthal, The Atomic Energy Years, 1945–1950, vol. 2 of The Journals of David E. Lilienthal, p. 257.

101. Unsigned, untitled memorandum on Truman-Hoover meeting, 28 May 1945, Truman, Harry S. Correspondence folder, Post-Presidential papers, Individual file, Hoover papers.

102. Unsigned, untitled, undated memorandum listing excerpts of Truman's compliments regarding Hoover, ibid.

103. Statement by Joseph C. Green, oral history interview.

104. Lilienthal, The Atomic Energy Years, p. 564.

105. Irwin Ross, The Loneliest Campaign: The Truman Victory of 1948, p. 219.

106. Statement by James A. Farley, oral history interview; statement by Edgar E. Robinson, oral history interview; statement by John K. Stewart, oral history interview.

107. Miller, personal interview.

108. [Hoover] to Truman, 19 December 1962, Truman, Harry S. Correspondence folder, Post-Presidential papers, Individual file, Hoover papers.

109. Emmerich, Essays on Federal Reorganization, p. 94; Miller, personal interview; U.S., Congress, Senate, Committee on Government Operations, Establish a Commission on the Organization and Management of the Executive Branch, Hearing, 90th Cong., 2d sess., p. 29.

110. Rowe to Hoover, 23 December 1947, James Rowe folder, RG 264, National Archives.

111. Unsigned memorandum entitled "Reports as to the Status of Authorized Projects," 19 April 1948, Progress Reports folder, ibid.

112. Unsigned memorandum entitled "Task Force Liaison," 26 January 1948, Liaison Offices folder, ibid.

113. David P. Findling to Ellison D. Smith, Jr., 30 August 1948, Robert Denham to Robert

Bowie, 20 September 1948, National Labor Relations Board Organization folder, Robert Denham papers; [Paul Herzog] to Jim [Reynolds], 15 September 1948, Personal-R folder, Paul Herzog papers.

114. Miller to Mitchell, 11 February 1948, Fiscal, Budgeting and Accounting, and Treasury folder, RG 264, National Archives.

115. Haas to John W. Snyder, [September 1948], Federal Reserve Banks, general folder No. 2, Snyder to Bowie, 16 September 1948, [Snyder] to Hoover, with attached memorandum, 15 December 1948, Hoover Commission folder, John W. Snyder papers.

116. Statement by Seidman, oral history interview.

117. Memorandum by Mitchell, 29 January 1948, Webb to Hoover, 25 February 1948, Agriculture folder, Russell Forbes to Francis Brassor, 12 February 1948, Personnel folder, Federal Supply Task Force, RG 264, National Archives; Hoover to Webb, 14 January 1948, Organization and Staffing [of Hoover Commission] folder, Series 39.32, Bureau of Budget papers, Office of Management and Budget; statement by Doane, oral history interview, pp. 239–40; Emmerich, *Federal Organization and Administrative Management*, p. 171.

118. Neustadt to Simpson, Donnelly and Dubois, 17 October 1947, Stauffacher to Bowie, 7 September 1948, F-Miscellaneous folder, memorandum by Arnold Miles, 22 October 1947, Hoover Commission Miscellaneous folder, memorandum by [Miles], 4 December 1947, Organization and Staffing [of Hoover Commission] folder, Series 39.32, Bureau of Budget papers, Office of Management and Budget; Stuart A. Rice to Pollock, 27 February 1948, Pollock, James K. folder, Pearson Winslow to John Meck, 8 March 1948, B folder, unsigned memorandum entitled "Reports as to the Status of Authorized Projects," 22 March 1948, Progress Reports folder, RG 264, National Archives.

119. Seidman, oral history interview.

120. Transcript of meeting of Commission on Organization of the Executive Branch of the Government, 6 December 1948, p. 34, RG 264, National Archives.

121. [Webb] to Truman, undated, Organization of the Executive Branch of the Government, Commission folder, James E. Webb papers; unsigned memorandum probably by Miles, 6 October 1947, memorandum by AM [Arnold Miles], 17 November 1947, Hoover Commission Miscellaneous folder, Bureau of Budget papers, Office of Management and Budget.

122. Stauffacher and Miles to Lawton, 4 October 1948, unsigned memorandum entitled "Items of Current Status and Development in the Commission on Organization of the Executive Branch, 11 October, 1948," 12 October 1948, Program of the Hoover Commission folder, Stone to Miles, 12 April 1948, F-Miscellaneous folder, Miles to Seidman and Scott Moore, 3 February 1949, Federal Business Enterprises folder, Series 39.32, Bureau of Budget papers, Office of Management and Budget.

123. Irving Fox and McCormick to Mitchell, 2 February 1948, Stone to Mitchell, 24 February 1948, Departmental Management folder, Webb to Hoover, 24 September 1948, Bureau of Budget: Legislative Clearance Function folder, Mitchell to Webb, 30 September 1948, Chronological Correspondence folder, RG 264, National Archives; Stone to Webb, 24 February 1948, F-Miscellaneous folder, Stone to Webb, 7 April 1948, Analysis of the Causes of Deficiencies in Departmental Administration. . .Prepared for Presentation to Hoover Commission folder, Series 39.32, Bureau of Budget papers, Office of Management and Budget; Harriet Adkinson to Laurence Ritchie, 19 March 1948, Organization of the Executive Branch of the Government, Commission folder, Webb papers.

124. Pace to Mitchell, 27 October 1948, Departmental Management in Federal Administration folder, Stauffacher to Pace, 23 March 1949, President Truman (Meetings-Truman-Pace) folder, Director's Office (Accession No. 5308–10), Stauffacher to Aikin, 30 March 1949, F-Miscellaneous folder, Stauffacher to Judge Collet, 18 April 1949, Reorganization Program for 1949 under Reorganization Act of 1949 folder, Bureau of Budget papers, Office of Management and Budget; [Pace] to Truman, 14 February 1949, OF 285E, Truman papers.

125. Heady, "Reports of the Hoover Commission," p. 377.

126. For some criticisms of the reports on policy matters see Lauren Soth, "Mr. Hoover's Department of Agriculture," pp. 201–12; Aikin, "Task Force," p. 250 (note 27); Lester B. Orfield, "The Hoover Commission and Federal Executive Reorganization," pp. 204–8; Public Affairs Institute, *The Hoover Report: Half a Loaf*, pp. 7, 35; Heady, "Reports of the Hoover Commission," p. 375; Seidman, *Politics, Position, and Power*, pp. 15–16; Emmerich, *Federal Organization and Administrative Management*, p. 93.

127. See Heady, "Reports of the Hoover Commission," p. 357; George A. Graham, "The Presidency and the Executive Office of the President," pp. 606–8; Public Affairs Institute, *Hoover Report*, p. 10; Dimock, "Objectives of Governmental Reorganization," pp. 233–41; G. Homer Durham, "An Appraisal of the Hoover Commission Approach to Administrative Reorganization in the National Government," pp. 615–23; Herman Finer, "The Hoover Commission Reports: Part I," pp, 407, 409–11; E. S. Redford, "The Value of the Hoover Commission Reports to the Educator," pp. 291–94; Emmerich, *Federal Organization and Administrative Management*, p. 90; Harvey C. Mansfield, "Federal Executive Reorganization: Thirty Years of Experience," p. 483; Don K. Price, "The Presidency," in A. S. Mike Monroney and others, *The Strengthening of American Political Institutions*, pp. 97–111.

128. Peri E. Arnold, "The First Hoover Commission and the Managerial Presidency," pp. 47–48.

129. Ibid., pp. 56, 60–62, 64.

130. Ibid., pp. 64–65.

131. Statement by Price, oral history interview.

132. Arnold, "First Hoover Commission and the Managerial Presidency," pp. 49–50.

133. Rowe to Hoover, 2 March 1949, James Rowe folder, Commission on Organization of the Executive Branch papers, Hoover Library. Even Forrestal despaired: "I am afraid that we will come up with a rather minimal accomplishment. That's what is disturbing me after a year of labor." "Conversation between Dean Acheson and Secretary Forrestal, 21 September 1948," Phone conversation folder, Forrestal papers.

134. Heady, personal interview.

135. Richard E. Neustadt, "Congress and the Fair Deal: A Legislative Balance Sheet," p. 359.

136. Ibid., p. 379.

Chapter 8

1. January 1949, McNaughton Reports folder, Frank McNaughton papers.

2. The Truman administration carefully cultivated Hoover, and in April 1948 Hoover and Truman both requested Congress to renew the president's reorganization authority. However, everyone, including the administration, seemed to decide that it would be better to wait until 1949 for renewal of the legislation. Unaddressed, unsigned memorandum (probably by Miles), 6 October 1947, unaddressed memorandum by A. M. [Miles], 17 November 1947, both in Hoover Commission Miscellaneous folder, Miles to Stone, 5 January 1948, Stone to Webb, 25 February 1948, both in untitled folder, Series 39.32, Bureau of Budget file, Office of Management and Budget; Truman to Arthur H. Vandenberg and Joseph W. Martin, 1 April 1948, Harry S. Truman, *Public Papers of the Presidents of the United States: Harry S. Truman, 1948*, pp. 199–200; Hoover to Aiken, 20 April 1948, Chronological folder, executive director's office, Commission on Organization of the Executive Branch of the Government papers, RG 264, National Archives; Peter Page Schauffler, "A Study of the Legislative Veto" (Ph.D. diss.), pp. 340–41.

3. Hoover to Sam Rayburn and Kenneth McKellar, 13 January 1949, printed in U.S., Congress, House, Committee on Expenditures in the Executive Departments, *Reorganization Act of 1949*, H. Rept. 23, 81st Cong., 1st sess., (1949), pp. 3–5; special message to Congress requesting permanent reorganization authority, 17 January 1949, Harry S. Truman, *Public Papers of the*

Presidents of the United States: Harry S. Truman, 1949, pp. 102–4.

4. Lawton to McClellan, with attached draft of bill and a memorandum, 14 January 1949, S. 526–81st, H.R. 2361, P.L. 109, E11–1/49.2 folder, Bureau of Budget papers, RG 51, National Archives; U.S., Congress, House, Committee on Expenditures in the Executive Departments, *Hearings on H.R. 1569, Reorganization of Government Agencies* [*Reorganization Act of 1949*], 81st Cong., 1st sess., p. 74; *CR (Congressional Record)* 81:1, 1949, vol. 95, pt. 1, pp. 301–2, 432. For copies of H.R. 1569 and S.526 as introduced by Dawson and McClellan see House, *Reorganization of Government Agencies*, Hearing, pp. 1–5; U.S., Congress, Senate, Committee on Expenditures in the Executive Departments, *Hearings on S. 526, Reorganization Act of 1949*, 81st Cong., 1st sess., pp. 1–5.

5. Stone to Webb, with attached memorandum, 25 February 1948, untitled folder, unsigned, undated memorandum entitled "Suggested Amendments to Reorganization Act, May, 1948," tab 9, Atkinson to Stauffacher, 12 November 1948, tab 15, unsigned, memorandum entitled "Reorganization Legislation," [November 1948], tab 6, bill drafted by Fred Levi, 4 January 1949, with Atkinson's comments, tab 19, Reorganization Act of 1949 (1948–1949), F2–11/48.1 folder, Series 39.32, Bureau of Budget file, Office of Management and Budget.

6. Pace to Truman, 11 January 1949, President Truman (Meetings-Truman-Pace) folder, Director's Office (Accession No. 5308–10), draft of bill, 11 January 1949, tab 23, final draft of bill, 11 January 1949, tab 24, Reorganization Act of 1949 (1948–1949), F2–11/48.1 folder, ibid.

7. One scholar ranked congressional committees on a liberal-conservative scale from the Eightieth to the Ninetieth Congress. He ranked the House Committee on Government Operations (Committee on Expenditures in the Executive Branch) the fourth most liberal and McClellan's Senate Committee or Government Operations the fifth most conservative. George Goodwin, Jr., *The Little Legislatures: Committees of Congress*, pp. 112–13, table 6:4.

8. Truman, *Public Papers, 1949*, p. 9; Dean Acheson, *Present at the Creation: My Years in the State Department*, p. 250.

9. John W. Ramsey, "The Director of the Bureau of the Budget as a Presidential Aide, 1921–1952: With Emphasis on the Truman Years" (Ph.D. diss.), p. 180; Frank Pace, Jr., to "Big Pops," 15 January 1949, Correspondence-Frank Pace, Sr., folder, Frank Pace, Jr., papers.

10. Ramsey, "The Director of the Bureau of the Budget," p. 198.

11. Ibid., pp. 182–83, 188, 190.

12. House, Committee on Expenditures in the Executive Departments, *Reorganization of Government Agencies*, Hearing, pp. 9–11, 12–14.

13. Ibid., pp. 64–67.

14. Ibid., p. 93.

15. Ibid., pp. 67–71.

16. Ibid., pp. 76–77.

17. Ibid., pp. 158–61. Vinson's support was important because he totally dominated his committee, and his shrewdness and power were legendary. Brooks Hays, *A Hotbed of Tranquility: My Life in Five Worlds*, p. 84; Alfred Steinberg, *Sam Johnson's Boy: A Close-up of the President from Texas*, p. 137.

18. House, Committee on Expenditures in the Executive Departments, H. Rept. No. 23, pp. 5–11.

19. *CR*, vol. 95, pt. 1, pp. 890–905.

20. Ibid., pp. 914–18.

21. Ibid., pp. 921–22.

22. Ibid., p. 923.

23. Harold Ickes, foreword in Arthur Maass, *Muddy Waters: The Army Engineers and the Nation's Rivers*, p. ix; also see John A. Ferejohn, *Pork Barrel Politics: Rivers and Harbors Legislation, 1947–1968*.

24. Maass, *Muddy Waters*, p. 40.

25. Ibid., pp. 61–118.

26. The *Times-Herald* [Washington], 13 November 1948, sec. 1, p. 2.

27. By-line article by Tris Coffin, ibid., 5 January 1949, sec. 1, pp. 10, 11.

28. James Rowe to Hoover, 11 February 1949, James Rowe folder, Commission on Organization of the Executive Branch papers, Herbert C. Hoover Presidential Library.

29. Rowe to Hoover, 19 January 1949, ibid.

30. Rowe to Hoover, 11 February 1949, ibid.

31. Task Force on Natural Resources, *Organization and Policy in the Field of Natural Resources: A Report With Recommendations Prepared for the Commission on Organization of the Executive Branch of the Government*, pp. 6–7, 23–24, 29, 66–67, 106–82.

32. Commission on Organization of the Executive Branch of the Government, *Reorganization of the Department of the Interior: A Report to the Congress by the Commission on Organization of the Executive Branch of the Government*, pp. 1–10, 17–35, 82–85.

33. Schauffler, "Study of the Legislative Veto," p. 417.

34. Statement by Lawton, personal interview; statement by Westbrook, personal interview.

35. Westbrook, personal interview.

36. Maass, *Muddy Waters*, pp. 68–69, 112–13.

37. Westbrook, personal interview.

38. Statement by Heady, personal interview.

39. Jules Abels, *Out of the Jaws of Victory*, p. 14.

40. David B. Truman, *The Congressional Party: A Case Study*, p. 111, table 17.

41. William C. Berman, *The Politics of Civil Rights in the Truman Administration*, pp. 140–41.

42. Ibid., pp. 146–56.

43. Senate, Committee on Expenditures in the Executive Departments, *Reorganization Act of 1949*, Hearing, pp. 118, 122.

44. Ibid., pp. 121–29.

45. Ibid., pp. 216–18.

46. U.S., Congress, Senate, Committee on Expenditures in the Executive Departments, *Reorganization Act of 1949*, S. Rept. 232, 81st Cong., 1st sess., (1949), pp. 14–15.

47. Stauffacher to Pace, 21 February 1949, tab 64, Reorganization Act of 1949 (1948–1949), vol. 2, F2–11/48.1 folder, Bureau of Budget file, Office of Management and Budget.

48. Ferrel Heady, "The Reorganization Act of 1949," p. 167.

49. Schauffler, "Study of the Legislative Veto," p. 453.

50. Pollock to Hoover, 3 March 1949, Hoover, Herbert C. folder, James K. Pollock papers.

51. Rowe to Hoover, 14 March 1949, James Rowe folder, Commission on Organization of the Executive Branch papers, Hoover Library.

52. Ronald J. Caridi, *The Korean War and American Politics: The Republican Party as a Case Study*, pp. 17–18.

53. Hoover to Rowe, 15 March 1949, James Rowe folder, Commission on Organization of the Executive Branch papers, Hoover Library. Also see Vandenberg to Hoover, 26 February 1949 and [Hoover] to Vandenberg, 3 March 1949, V folder, Commission on Organization of Executive Branch papers, Hoover Library.

54. Rowe to Clark Clifford and others, 16 March 1949, R General folder, Pace papers.

55. Rowe to Hoover, 29 March 1949, James Rowe folder, Commission on Organization of Executive Branch papers, Hoover Library.

56. Stauffacher to Pace and Lawton, 16 March 1949, tab 65, Reorganization Act of 1949 (1948–1949), vol. 2, F2–11/48.1 folder, Bureau of Budget file, Office of Management and Budget.

57. Ibid.

58. Vandenberg to Pollock, 25 March 1949, Vandenberg folder, Pollock papers.

59. Hoover to George H. Mead, 15 March 1949, George H. Mead folder, Arthur S. Flemming to Hoover, 15 March 1949, Arthur S. Flemming folder, Commission on Organization of the Executive Branch papers, Hoover Library

60. *CR*, vol. 95, pt. 5, p. 6227.

61. Hoover to Charles B. Coates, copy of telegram, 31 March 1949, Charles B. Coates folder, Commission on Organization of the Executive Branch papers, Hoover Library.

62. Memorandum entitled "The Situation to Date," by Coates, 1 April 1949, ibid.; *CR*, vol. 95, pt. 5, p. 6227.

63. Coates to George E. Doying, 7 July 1949, D folder, Citizen's Committee for the Hoover Report papers.

64. McCormick to Coates, 4 April 1949, Correspondence (Reorganization Plans) folder, ibid.; Senate, Committee on Expenditures in the Executive Departments, S. Rept. No. 232, pp. 12–13.

65. *CR*, vol. 95, pt. 5, pp. 6223–27.

66. Ibid., p. 6227.

67. Ibid., pp. 6228–29.

68. Ibid.

69. Ibid., p. 6230.

70. Ibid., p. 6231.

71. Atkinson to Stauffacher, 7 April 1949, tab 68, Reorganization Act of 1949 (1948–1949), vol. 2, F2–11/48.1 folder, Bureau of Budget file, Office of Management and Budget.

72. Julius Klein to Hoover, 19 May 1949, Federal Field Offices, Julius Klein folder, Commission on Organization of the Executive Branch papers, Hoover Library.

73. Rowe to Pace, 17 May 1949, tab 75, unsigned memorandum entitled "The Acceptability of the One-House Veto of Reorganization Plans," [18 May 1949], tab 76, memorandum entitled "Veto Message," 20 May 1949, tab 78, Reorganization Act of 1949 (1948–1949), vol. 2, F2–11/48.1 folder, Series 39.32, Bureau of Budget file, Office of Management and Budget.

74. Memorandum of telephone conversation between Rowe and Hoover, attached to Rowe to Hoover, 23 May 1949, James Rowe folder, Hoover to Ives, 23 May 1949, I folder, Commission on Organization of the Executive Branch papers, Hoover Library; Rowe to Pollock, 23 May 1949, James Rowe folder, Pollock papers.

75. Transcript of meeting between the president and the Hoover Commission, 26 May 1949, President Truman (Meetings—Truman—Pace) folder, Director's Office (Accession No. 5308–10), Bureau of Budget file, Office of Management and Budget.

76. Statement by the president upon receiving final report of the Hoover Commission, 26 May 1949, Truman, *Public Papers, 1949*, p. 265.

77. *CR*, vol. 95, pt. 6, pp. 7444, 7599–600; Truman, *Public Papers, 1949*, p. 295; by–line article by Anthony Leviero, *New York Times*, 14 June 1949, p. 9.

78. U.S., Congress, House, Committee of Conference, *Reorganization Act of 1949*, H. Rept. No. 843, 81st Cong., 1st sess., (1949), pp. 7–8.

79. *CR*, vol. 95, pt. 6, pp. 7831–33, 7835–36, 7785–86.

80. Truman, *Public Papers, 1949*, pp. 307–9. The act can be found at U.S., *Statutes at Large*, Public Law 109, vol. 63, part 1, 81st Cong., 1st sess., pp. 203–7.

81. Truman, *Public Papers, 1949*, p. 295.

82. Stauffacher to Webb, 3 December 1948, Hoover Commission Miscellaneous folder, Series 39.32, Bureau of Budget file, Office of Management and Budget.

Chapter 9

1. U.S., Congress, House, subcommittee of the Committee on Appropriations, *Second Supplemental Appropriation Bill for 1948, Part 2. . .Commission on Organization of Executive Branch*, Hearing, 80th Cong., 2d sess., p. 163; Herbert Emmerich, *Essays on Federal Reorganization*, p. 98.

2. Transcript of meeting of Commission on Organization of the Executive Branch of the

Government, 16 February 1948, pp. 37–39, S.A. Mitchell to Hoover, 28 April 1948, Chronological folder, Executive Director's Office, A. G. Newmeyer to Mitchell, 5 May 1948, Information-I folder, Newmeyer to Mitchell, 22 December 1948, Information-II folder, Gene Duffield to Mitchell, 21 May 1948, Mitchell to Duffield, 26 May 1948, D folder, Commission on Organization of the Executive Branch of the Government papers, RG 264, National Archives.

3. Statement by James A. Farley, oral history interview; Arthur Krock, *Memoirs: Sixty Years on the Firing Line,* p. 128; Richard E. Berlin to Hoover, 12 December 1949, Berlin, Richard E. Correspondence folder, Post-Presidential papers, Individual file, Herbert C. Hoover papers.

4. For example see N. R. Howard to Pollock, 31 December 1947, [Hoover] to Arthur Henning and others, 7 February 1948, Information-I folder, Bert Andrews to Hoover, 20 April 1948, [A] folder, RG 264, National Archives. For a study of Hoover's ability in public relations see Craig Lloyd, *Aggressive Introvert: A Study of Herbert Hoover and Public Relations Management, 1912–1932.*

5. Transcript of meeting of Commission on Organization of the Executive Branch of the Government, 6 December 1948, pp. 2–8, 20–22, 29–30, Lawrence E. Laybourne to Mitchell, 15 April 1948, Information-I folder, Mitchell to Beers, 16 November 1948, File and Distribution of Reports: General Correspondence folder, RG 264, National Archives.

6. Memorandum entitled "First Hoover Commission—Pollock File: Re: Mixed Commission questionnaire—paraphrased answers transcribed by L. A. Hester from Professor James K. Pollock," undated, Miscellaneous folder, James K. Pollock papers.

7. Coates to Charles C. Teague, 2 May 1949, General Correspondence folder, Commission on Organization of Executive Branch papers, Herbert C. Hoover Presidential Library.

8. CCHR State Chairman's Conference, 12 October 1949, State Chairman's Conference folder, CCHR papers.

9. Robert L. L. McCormick to Coates, 25 July 1949, CCHR Chronological file, Robert L. L. McCormick papers.

10. McCormick to Harold Stein, 17 November 1949, McCormick to Coates, 21 November 1949, ibid.

11. McCormick to Coates, 3 January 1950, ibid.

12. See for example *Committee Reporter,* August 1949, p. 3.

13. Ibid., pp. 1, 4.

14. Ibid., March-April 1951, pp. 1, 5; Coates to Chairmen and Executive Directors of State, Regional, and Local Committees, *Round Robin No. 9,* 9 October 1950, Publication Committee, Round Robin folder, CCHR papers.

15. *Committee Reporter,* November 1949, p. 4.

16. Ibid., October 1949, p. 1.

17. Coates to Hoover, 8 September 1950, Charles B. Coates folder, Commission on Organization of the Executive Branch papers, Hoover Library.

18. Charles Aikin and Louis W. Koenig, "Introduction," p. 933.

19. *CR (Congressional Record)* 81:1, 1949, vol. 95, pt. 6, p. 8039.

20. Ibid., p. 7445, pt. 9, p. 11557; Chronological File, Hoover Commission 1949–53 folder, Theodore Francis Green papers; G. L. Clark to File Room, 21 September 1950, OF (Official File) 285E, Harry S. Truman papers.

21. Marshall E. Dimock, "The Objectives of Governmental Reorganization," p. 233. Also see editorial in *Detroit Free Press,* 9 February 1949, p. 6.

22. Mrs. Clarence Lough to Hoover, 12 May 1949, L folder, Commission on Organization of the Executive Branch papers, Hoover Library.

23. Pollock to Clarence J. Brown, 2 May 1949, Brown, Clarence J. folder, Pollock papers.

24. J. Richard Jones to Rayburn, 9 June 1949, Hoover Commission folder, Sam Rayburn papers.

25. Address by Dr. F. L. McCluer, [7 March 1952], clipping from unnamed newspaper, folder 368, Clarence Cannon papers.

26. Emmerich, *Essays on Federal Reorganization*, pp. vii–viii.

27. Editorial, *Detroit Free Press*, 23 February 1949, p. 6.

28. Paul H. Appleby, "The Significance of the Hoover Commission Report," pp. 5–7; Rowland Egger, "Painless Economy and the Mythology of Administrative Reorganization," pp. 488–94.

29. Aikin and Koenig, "Introduction," p. 938.

30. By-line article by Clayton Knowles, *New York Times*, 22 May 1949, p. 7; *CR*, vol. 95, pt. 14, p. A2999.

31. Editorial, *Philadelphia Inquirer*, 13 April 1949, in *CR*, vol. 95, pt. 13, p. A2262.

32. *CR*, vol. 95, pt. 13, pp. A1509–10.

33. The *New York Times*, 31 May 1949, p. 15.

34. McCormick to Roger Wunderlich, 7 November 1949, CCHR Chrono file, McCormick papers.

35. Raymond Dickson to Rayburn, 6 May 1949, Bills, Reorganization Plan folder, Rayburn papers.

36. Martin Merson, *The Private Diary of a Public Servant*, p. 2; McCormick to John Stuart, 14 December 1951, McCormick to Lewis L. Strauss, 29 May 1952, CCHR Chrono file, McCormick papers.

37. Unsigned memorandum entitled "Meeting of Women's groups at U.S. Chamber of Commerce, March 29, 1950," undated, ibid.

38. Hoover to George H. Mead, 15 March 1949, George H. Mead folder, Commission on Organization of the Executive Branch papers, Hoover Library.

39. Hoover to Arthur Krock, 11 December 1949, Krock, Arthur folder, Post-Presidential papers, Individual file, Hoover papers.

40. Edward H. Hobbs, *Executive Reorganization in the National Government*, pp. 48–49.

41. Statement by Lawton, personal interview.

42. The final drafting process can be traced in the following: Stauffacher to Pace and Lawton, 16 June 1949, President Truman (Meetings-Truman-Pace) folder, Pace to Truman, 17 June 1949, Reorganization Program for 1949 folder, Series 39.32, Bureau of Budget file, Office of Management and Budget; Pace to Truman, undated, OF 285A, Truman papers. For his general message on all seven plans see U.S., President, 1945–1953 (Truman), *Message from the President of the United States Transmitting Recommendations of an Initial Program of Reorganization of the Executive Branch of the Government*, 81st Cong., 1st sess., House, Document No. 221.

43. Harry S. Truman, *Public Papers of the Presidents of the United States: Harry S. Truman, 1949*, p. 310.

44. Ibid., p. 37.

45. Harry S. Truman, *Public Papers of the Presidents of the United States: Harry S. Truman, 1948*, pp. 354–55.

46. U.S., Commission on Organization of the Executive Branch of the Government, *Department of Labor: A Report to the Congress by the Commission on Organization of the Executive Branch of the Government*, pp. 9–19.

47. Truman, *Public Papers, 1949*, pp. 312–13; U.S., President, 1945–1953 (Truman), *Message from the President of the United States Transmitting Reorganization Plan No. 2 of 1949*, pp. 4–5.

48. U.S., Commission on Organization of the Executive Branch of the Government, *General Management of the Executive Branch: A Report to the Congress by the Commission on Organization of the Executive Branch of the Government*, p. 34.

49. Truman, *Public Papers, 1949*, pp. 314–15; U.S. President, 1945–1953 (Truman), *Message from the President of the United States Transmitting Reorganization Plan No. 3 of 1949*, pp. 3–4.

50. Truman, *Public Papers, 1949*, pp. 316–17; U.S., President, 1945–1953 (Truman), *Message from the President of the United States Transmitting Reorganization Plan No. 4 of 1949*, p. 2.

51. U.S., Commission on Organization of the Executive Branch of the Government, *Personnel Management: A Report to the Congress by the Commission on Organization of the Executive Branch

of the Government, pp. 3–6.

52. Stauffacher to Pace, 17 March 1949, Reorganization Plan 5 of 1949 folder, Bureau of Budget file, Office of Management and Budget.

53. Unsigned memorandum entitled "A Memorandum on the Reorganization of the Civil Service Commission," undated, attached to Pace to Truman, [probably March or April 1949], OF 285A, Truman papers.

54. Truman, *Public Papers, 1949,* pp. 317–18; U.S., President, 1945–1953 (Truman), *Message from the President of the United States Transmitting Reorganization Plan No. 5 of 1949,* pp. 4–5. This plan, which went into effect without opposition, would have been regarded as important and controversial before the Hoover Commission reports. One scholar wrote: "This change was more dramatic than may have appeared on the surface. It enabled many operating decisions to be made without suffering the time–consuming process of obtaining a vote of three commissioners. It also established one point of contact for both the White House and the agency heads. The reorganization was perhaps the single most significant step in a long struggle toward the central personnel agency that had been so long sought." Donald R. Harvey, *The Civil Service Commission,* p. 22.

55. Unsigned memorandum entitled "Memorandum on the Reorganization of the Civil Service Commission," undated, attached to Pace to Truman, [probably March or April 1949], OF 285A, Truman papers.

56. Stauffacher to Pace and Lawton, 16 June 1949, President Truman (Meetings-Truman-Pace) folder, Bureau of Budget file, Office of Management and Budget; Truman to Perkins, 20 June 1949, OF 285A, Truman papers; Harry Mitchell to John McClellan, 19 July 1949, printed in *CR,* vol. 95, pt. 8, p. 10147.

57. Samuel A. Lawrence, *United States Merchant Shipping Policies and Politics,* p. 263.

58. Memorandum by Atkinson entitled "Inventory of Possible Reorganization Actions," 3 February 1949, Reorganization Program for 1949 folder, Series [39.32], Bureau of Budget file, Office of Management and Budget; *Truman, Public Papers, 1949,* pp. 319–20; U.S., President, 1945–1953 (Truman), *Message from the President of the United States Transmitting Reorganization Plan No. 6 of 1949,* p. 3.

59. Memorandum by Atkinson entitled "Inventory of Possible Reorganization Actions," 3 February 1949, Reorganization Program for 1949 folder, Series [39.32], Bureau of Budget file, Office of Management and Budget; U.S., Commission on Organization of the Executive Branch of the Government, *Department of Commerce: A Report to the Congress by the Commission on Organization of the Executive Branch of the Government,* pp. 11–21; Truman, *Public Papers, 1949,* pp. 321–23; U.S., President, 1945–1953 (Truman), *Message from the President of the United States Transmitting Reorganization Plan No. 7 of 1949,* p. 3. On 18 July 1949, Truman submitted plan eight to reorganize the National Military Establishment. He designed this plan to force Congress to act on legislation to carry further the unification of the military forces begun in 1947. Congress either had to act on legislation or let the president initiate change with this plan. Congress did pass the merger legislation and then it set plan eight aside, after having accomplished the plan's purposes by direct legislation.

Carroll F. Miles, "The Office of the Secretary of Defense, 1947–1953: A Study in Administrative Theory" (Ph.D. diss.), pp. 1–2, 142–44; Peter Page Schauffler, "A Study of the Legislative Veto" (Ph.D. diss.), p. 493; McNaughton to Bermingham, 16 July 1949, McNaughton Reports folder, McNaughton papers; MJC [Matthew J. Connelly] to Truman, 15 July 1949, OF 285A, Truman papers. For Truman's message and plan see Truman, *Public Papers, 1949,* pp. 382–85; U.S., President, 1945–1953 (Truman), *Message from the President of the United States Transmitting Reorganization Plan No. 8 of 1949,* pp. 4–7; Stephen Early to Clark Clifford, 20 June 1949, Unification: Amendment of National Security Act of 1949 folder, Clark Clifford papers; Richard F. Haynes, *The Awesome Power: Harry S. Truman as Commander in Chief,* pp. 111–13.

60. [Pace] to "Big Pops," 21 June 1949, Correspondence-Frank Pace, Sr. folder, Frank Pace, Jr. papers.

61. Schauffler, "Study of the Legislative Veto," pp. 531–32.

62. McCormick to Coates, 20 June 1949, CCHR Chrono file, McCormick papers.

63. U.S., Congress, Senate, Committee on Expenditures in the Executive Departments, *Reorganization Plans of 1949* [Plans 1–7], Hearing, 81st Cong., 1st sess., p. 19.

64. McCormick to Coates, 25 July 1949, CCHR Chrono file, McCormick papers.

65. McCormick to Hoover, 1 August 1949, McCormick folder, Commission on Organization of the Executive Branch papers, Hoover Library.

66. Johnson to Truman, 12 August 1949, F2-Miscellaneous 1941–1958 folder, Series 39.32, Bureau of Budget file, Office of Management and Budget.

67. Monte Poen, "The Truman Administration and National Health Insurance" (Ph.D. diss.), pp. 54–59.

68. Ibid., pp. 59–63.

69. Ibid., pp. 64–69.

70. Ibid., p. 168.

71. Frank R. Kennedy, "The American Medical Association: Power, Purpose, and Politics in Organized Medicine," pp. 1011–15; Stanley Kelley, Jr., *Professional Public Relations and Political Power*, pp. 67–106; Richard Harris, *A Sacred Trust*, chapters 7–11.

72. Richard Carter, *The Doctor Business*, p. 209; also see Theodore R. Marmor, *The Politics of Medicare*, pp. 12–13.

73. Transcript of meeting of Commission on Organization of the Executive Branch of the Government, 12 January 1949, p. 108, RG 264, National Archives.

74. U.S., Commission on Organization of the Executive Branch of the Government, *Reorganization of Federal Medical Activities: A Report to the Congress by the Commission on Organization of the Executive Branch of the Government*, p. 2.

75. U.S., Commission on Organization of the Executive Branch of the Government, *Social Security and Education, Indian Affairs: A Report to the Congress by the Commission on Organization of the Executive Branch of the Government*, pp. 5–6.

76. Unsigned memorandum entitled "Agency Comments on the Reports of the Hoover Commission," undated, Analysis and Agency Comments on Hoover Commission Report on Regulatory Agencies folder, Bureau of Budget file, Office of Management and Budget.

77. Schauffler, "Study of the Legislative Veto," p. 506 (note 934).

78. Truman, *Public Papers, 1949*, p. 311.

79. James G. Burrow, *AMA: Voice of American Medicine*, pp. 380–81.

80. U.S., President, 1945–1953 (Truman), *Message from the President of the United States Transmitting Reorganization Plan No. 1 of 1949*, pp. 3–4.

81. Arthur J. Altmeyer, *The Formative Years of Social Security*, pp. 175–76; Alonzo L. Hamby, *Beyond the New Deal: Harry S. Truman and American Liberalism*, pp. 296–97.

82. *CR*, vol. 95, pt. 6, p. 74'.

83. H. Alexander and J. R. Slevin, "Mr. Welfare State Himself," p. 13.

84. By-line article by Daniel McKidney, *Washington Daily News*, undated, quoted in *CR*, vol. 95, pt. 9, p. 11370.

85. Ibid.; by-line article by Tris Coffin, *Times-Herald* [Washington], 22 November 1948, p. 7.

86. U.S., Congress, Senate, Committee on Expenditures in the Executive Departments, *Reorganization Plans No. 1 and 2 of 1949*, Hearing, 81st Cong., 1st sess., pp. 33–35.

87. Ibid., pp. 98–100.

88. *CR*, vol. 95, pt. 9, pp. 11527–32.

89. Senate, Committee on Expenditures in the Executive Departments, *Reorganization Plans No. 1 and 2 of 1949*, Hearing, pp. 75–78, 106–9.

90. U.S., Congress, Senate, Committee on Expenditures in the Executive Departments, *Reorganization Plan No. 1 of 1949*, S. Rept. No. 851, 81st Cong., 1st sess., (1949), p. 8.

91. "Rough Going for Harry," *Newsweek*, p. 14.

92. *CR*, vol. 95, pt. 9, pp. 11360–61.

93. Ibid., pp. 11441–43.

94. Ibid., pp. 11442, 11542–46.

95. Ibid., pp. 11523–27, 11532–33.

96. Ibid., pp. 11547–48, 11556–58.

97. Ibid., pp. 11537–38.

98. Ibid., p. 11560.

99. *Congressional Quarterly Almanac*, vol. 5, (1949), p. 672.

100. U.S., Congress, House, Committee on Expenditures in the Executive Departments, *Reorganization Plan No. 2 of 1949*, Hearing, 81st Cong., 1st sess.; U.S., Congress, House, Committee on Expenditures in the Executive Departments, *Reorganization Plan No. 2 of 1949*, H. Rept. No. 1204, 81st Cong., 1st sess., (1949), pp. 1–9, 11–13.

101. *CR*, vol. 95, pt. 8, p. 11314.

102. U.S., Congress, Senate, Committee on Expenditures in the Executive Departments, *Reorganization Plan No. 2 of 1949*, S. Rept. 852, 81st Cong., 1st sess., (1949).

103. *CR*, vol. 95, pt. 9, p. 11616.

104. Ibid., pp. 11598–600.

105. Ibid., pp. 11602–3, 11620, 11622–24.

106. Ibid., pp. 11625–26.

107. Francis E. Rourke, "Reorganization of the Labor Department" (Ph.D. diss.), p. 283.

108. [Robert A. Taft] to Walter J. Mackey, 6 August 1949, [Taft] to W. G. Vollmer, 9 August 1949, Reorganization Plan folder, Robert A. Taft papers; Edgar L. Shor, "The Role of the Secretary of Labor" (Ph.D. diss.), p. 261 (note 1).

109. Shor, ibid.

110. *Congressional Quarterly Almanac*, vol. 5, (1949), p. 672.

111. Francis E. Rourke, "The Politics of Administrative Organization: A Case History," p. 477.

112. Stanley R. Ruttenberg and Jocelyn Gutchess, *Manpower Challenge of the 1970's: Institutions and Social Change*, p. 75.

113. Leonard P. Adams, *The Public Employment Service in Transition, 1933–1968: Evolution of a Placement Service into a Manpower Agency*, p. 99.

114. William Haber and Daniel H. Kruger, *The Role of the United States Employment Service in a Changing Economy*, pp. 70–74.

115. Adams, *Public Employment Service in Transition*, pp. 65–68, 71, 75.

116. Ibid., p. 47.

117. See Ruttenberg and Gutchess, *Manpower Challenge of the 1970's.*

118. Schauffler, "Study of the Legislative Veto," pp. 532, 534–45. Also see *CR*, vol. 95, pt. 9, pp. 11407–8, 11565–66.

119. Truman, *Public Papers, 1949*, pp. 321–23.

120. Ibid.

121. *CR*, vol. 95, pt. 9, p. 11626.

122. U.S., Congress, Senate, Committee on Expenditures in the Executive Departments, *Reorganization Plan No. 7 of 1949*, S. Rept. No. 927, 81st Cong., 1st sess., (1949), pp. 1–2.

123. Alfred Steinberg, *Sam Johnson's Boy: A Close-up of the President from Texas*, p. 290.

124. *CR*, vol. 95, pt. 9, pp. 11626–29.

125. Ibid., p. 11631.

126. Schauffler, "Study of the Legislative Veto," p. 545; *Congressional Quarterly Almanac*, vol. 5, (1949), p. 672.

Chapter 10

1. Harry S. Truman, *Public Papers of the Presidents of the United States: Harry S. Truman, 1950,* p. 237.

2. John W. Ramsey, "The Director of the Bureau of the Budget as a Presidential Aide, 1921–1952: With Emphasis on the Truman Years" (Ph.D. diss.), p. 202; statement by Frederick Lawton, oral history interview.

3. Ramsey, "Director of the Bureau of the Budget," p. 205.

4. Ibid., pp. 210, 212–14.

5. Truman, *Public Papers, 1950,* pp. 195–96.

6. Ibid., pp. 200–201.

7. Ibid., pp. 203–6. *Public Papers* contains the messages to Congress; for the plans see: U.S., President, 1945–1953 (Truman), *Message from the President of the United States Trans-|mitting Reorganization Plan No. 1 of 1950, Plan No. 2 of 1950, Plan No. 3 of 1950, Plan No. 4 of 1950, Plan No. 5 of 1950, Plan No. 6 of 1950.|*

8. Truman, *Public Papers, 1950,* pp. 201–2.

9. Ibid., pp. 207–9. For the plans see: U.S., President, 1945–1953 (Truman), *Plan No. 7 of 1950, Plan No. 8 of 1950, Plan No. 9 of 1950, Plan No. 10 of 1950, Plan No. 11 of 1950, Plan No. 12 of 1950, Plan No. 13 of 1950.*

10. Truman, *Public Papers, 1950,* pp. 210–11; U.S., President, 1945–1953 (Truman), *Plan No. 14 of 1950.*

11. Truman, *Public Papers, 1950,* pp. 211, 215–17; U.S., President, 1945–1953 (Truman), *Plan No. 15 of 1950, Plan No. 16 of 1950, Plan No. 17 of 1950.*

12. Truman, *Public Papers, 1950,* pp. 217–18; U.S., President, 1945–1953 (Truman), *Plan No. 18 of 1950.*

13. Truman, *Public Papers, 1950,* pp. 219–22; U.S., President, 1945–1953 (Truman), *Plan No. 19 of 1950.*

14. Truman, *Public Papers, 1950,* pp. 221–22; U.S., President, 1945–1953 (Truman), *Plan No. 20 of 1950.*

15. Truman, *Public Papers, 1950,* pp. 223–26; U.S., President, 1945–1953 (Truman), *Plan No. 21 of 1950.*

16. Truman, *Public Papers, 1950,* pp. 315–16; U.S., President, 1945–1953 (Truman), *Plan No. 22 of 1950.*

17. Truman, *Public Papers, 1950,* pp. 316–18; U.S., President, 1945–1953 (Truman), *Plan No. 23 of 1950.*

18. Truman, *Public Papers, 1950,* pp. 318–19; U.S., President, 1945–1953 (Truman), *Plan No. 24 of 1950.*

19. Truman, *Public Papers, 1950,* pp. 320–21; U.S., President, 1945–1953 (Truman), *Plan No. 25 of 1950.*

20. Truman, *Public Papers, 1950,* pp. 442–43; U.S., President, 1945–1953 (Truman), *Plan No. 26 of 1950.*

21. Truman, *Public Papers, 1950,* pp. 443–45; U.S., President, 1945–1953 (Truman), *Plan No. 27 of 1950.*

22. Fred A. Hartley, *Our New National Labor Policy: The Taft-Hartley Act and the Next Steps,* p. 140.

23. Seymour Scher, "The Politics of Agency Organization," pp. 328–30; R. Alton Lee, *Truman and Taft-Hartley: A Question of Mandate,* pp. 184–86; Schauffler, "A Study of the Legislative Veto" (Ph.D. diss.), pp. 606–8, 607 (note 1100). One lawyer who specialized in labor affairs for management and who opposed the plan wrote: "It was apparent to some observers that in addition to the power struggle there was an underlying feeling that the Board and its personnel were not kindly disposed toward or sympathetic with Taft-Hartley whereas the General Counsel was. Our experience caused us to share that view. We were

convinced that the Congressional intent evidenced by and expressed in Taft-Hartley would not be effectuated as it should be were the Board to prevail." Karl H. Mueller to author, 24 February 1970, in author's possession.

24. SJS [Stephan J. Spingarn] to [Clark] Clifford, 17 November 1949, Chronological file folder, Stephan J. Spingarn papers; also see Lee, *Truman and Taft-Hartley*, pp. 186–87.

25. The *CIO News*, 14 February 1949, p. 7; R. N. Denham to Alexander Campbell, 9 December 1949, 792 folder, Robert Denham papers; *Times-Herald* [Washington], 30 April 1950, sec. 1, p. 2.

26. Lee, *Truman and Taft-Hartley*, pp. 187–89; Robert Denham, as told to Stacy V. Jones, "And So I Was Purged," p. 23.

27. Denham to Parker Arnold, 3 August 1950, 769 folder, Denham papers.

28. Lee, *Truman and Taft-Hartley*, p. 186.

29. Schauffler, "Study of the Legislative Veto," pp. 608–9; also see Bill Davidson, "Labor's Biggest Boss," p. 87; Guy Farmer, "Problems of Organization and Administration of the National Labor Relations Board," pp. 353–67; Frank W. McCulloch and Tim Bernstein, *The National Labor Relations Board*, pp. 58–60; Denham, "And So I Was Purged," pp. 22–23, 73–74.

30. Lee, *Truman and Taft-Hartley*, pp. 168–69, 194–95.

31. SJS [Spingarn] to Clifford, 24 October 1949, Legislation—Relating to Labor Presidential Assistant file, Spingarn papers.

32. SJS [Spingarn] to Clifford, 17 November 1949, Chronological file folder, ibid.; see copies of Denham's Speeches of 12 January 1950, 30 January 1950, 30 March 1950 in National Labor Relation Board folder, Charles Murphy file, Truman papers; by-line article by James Marlow, [*Duluth Herald*], 21 April 1950.

33. Truman, *Public Papers, 1950*, pp. 202–3.

34. McCormick to Hoover, 10 March 1950, Citizens Committee for the Hoover Report Chronological file, McCormick papers; Citizens Committee for the Hoover Report, *Circular Letter No. 2*, 10 April 1950, United States-Executive-Departments-Reorganization folder, Bureau of Budget file, Office of Management and Budget.

35. Benjamin Vander Poel to McCormick, 5 April 1950, CCHR Chrono file, McCormick papers.

36. Paul [St. Sure] to Herzog, 3 May 1950, Personal Sa to Sp folder, Paul Herzog papers.

37. *NAM News*, 25 March 1950, p. 3.

38. Charles S. Dudley to Membership of Associated Industries of Georgia, 24 March 1950, Clarence Miles to U.S. Chamber of Commerce officials, 27 March 1950, 972 folder, Benjamin R. Miller to American Trucking Association Officials, 14 April 1950, 888 folder, Denham papers.

39. W. M. Caldwell to [Denham], 24 April 1950, 791 folder, Associated Industries of Maryland, "Reorganization Plan No. 12," newsletters of 12, 21 April 1950, 826 folder, Ohio Newspaper Association, *Bulletin No. 7*, 4 April 1950, *Confidential Bulletin of the Georgia Press Association*, 7 April 1950, Denham papers. For information on lobbying see "Reorganization Plans," *Congressional Quarterly Almanac*, vol. 6, (1950), pp. 369–70.

40. U.S., Congress, House, Committee on Expenditures in the Executive Departments, *Reorganization Plan No. 12 of 1950*, Hearing, 81st Cong., 2d sess., p. 3; U.S., Congress, House, Committee on Expenditures in the Executive Departments, *Reorganization Plan No. 12 of 1950*, H. Rept. No. 1852, 81st Cong., 2d sess., (1950), pp. 1, 18–30.

41. Lee, *Truman and Taft-Hartley*, p. 197.

42. Taft to Denham, 18 May 1950, 956 folder, Denham papers.

43. U.S., Congress, Senate, Committee on Expenditures in the Executive Departments, *Reorganization Plan No. 12 of 1950*, Hearing, 81st Cong., 2d sess., pp. 13–15.

44. Ibid., pp. 26–35, 43.

45. U.S., Congress, Senate, Committee on Expenditures in the Executive Departments, *Reorganization Plan No. 12 of 1950*, S. Rept. No. 1516, 81st Cong., 2d sess., (1950), pp. 1–2, 17.

46. Phileo Nash to Spingarn, 3 May 1950, Reorganization Plan No. 12-White House Desk Manual 6 folder, Spingarn papers.

47. Unsigned memorandum entitled "Reorganization Plan No. 12," 8 May 1950, ibid; SJS [Spingarn] to Murphy, 8 May 1950.

48. Spingarn to W. Stuart Symington, 10 May 1950, General Government-Reorganization Plan No. 12, Presidential Assistant folder, ibid.

49. Truman, *Public Papers, 1950*, pp. 363–64.

50. *CR*, 81:2, 1950, vol. 96, pt. 5, p. 6874.

51. Ibid., pp. 6880–84.

52. Ibid., p. 6886.

53. *Congressional Quarterly Almanac*, vol. 6, (1950), p. 540.

54. In September 1950, White House officials asked Denham to resign, which he did. Denham, "And So I Was Purged," p. 22.

55. Atkinson to Miles, 8 November 1949, Transfer of Functions from Subordinate Officials and Units to the Heads of Departments folder, Series [39.32], Bureau of Budget file, Office of Management and Budget.

56. From an unidentified CCHR official to Francis J. Chesterman, undated, B folder, CCHR papers.

57. McCormick to Tom Ridgway, 29 September 1949, CCHR Chrono file, McCormick papers.

58. Atkinson to Miles, 8 November 1949, Transfer of Functions from Subordinate Officials and Units to the Heads of Departments folder, Series [39.32], Bureau of Budget file, Office of Management and Budget.

59. Lawton, Oral history interview.

60. Davies, *Housing Reform During the Truman Administration*, p. 42.

61. John W. Snyder to Mitchell, 14 June 1950, Administrative-General-1946-1952 Folder #2 Alphabetical file folder, John W. Snyder papers.

62. Snyder to Pace, with attachment, 17 February 1950, Administrative-General-1946-1952 Folder #3 Alphabetical file folder, ibid.

63. Atkinson to Miles, 8 November 1949, Transfer of Functions from Subordinate Officials and Units to the Heads of Departments folder, Series [39.32], Bureau of Budget file, Office of Management and Budget.

64. U.S., Congress, Senate, Committee on Expenditures in the Executive Departments, *Reorganization Plan No. 1 of 1950*, Hearing, 81st Cong., 2d sess., pp. 4–5.

65. Ibid., pp. 6–7, 8–9, 11–13, 16–17.

66. Ibid., pp. 3–4.

67. Ibid., pp. 35–36.

68. U.S., Congress, Senate, Committee on Expenditures in the Executive Departments, *Reorganization Plan No. 1 of 1950*, S. Rept. No. 1518, 81st Cong., 2d sess., (1950), pp. 1–2.

69. McCormick to Hoover, 5 May 1950, Robert L. L. McCormick folder, Commission on Organization of the Executive Branch of the Government papers, Herbert C. Hoover Presidential Library.

70. *CR*, vol. 96, pt. 5, p. 6898.

71. Robert L. Johnson to CCHR State Chairman, 15 May 1950, Johnson folder, CCHR papers.

72. Marver H. Bernstein, *Regulating Business by Independent Commission*, pp. 5, 54–58, 67–70, 164–65.

73. Herbert Emmerich, *Essays on Federal Reorganization*, pp. 36–37. According to some experts, Truman's plans affected the commissions adversely by causing them to become politicized and more easily captured by the regulated industries. Joe L. Evins, *Understanding Congress*, pp. 223–49; Louis M. Kohlmeier, Jr., *The Regulators: Watchdog Agencies and the Public Interest*, pp. 46–52; Bernard Schwartz, *The Professor and the Commissions*, pp. 209–14.

74. Olney quoted in Louis L. Jaffe, "The Effective Limits of the Administrative Process," in Alan A. Altshuler, *The Politics of the Federal Bureaucracy*, p. 327 (note 2).

75. Bernstein, *Regulating Business by Independent Commission*, p. 90.

76. Statement by Lawton, personal interview.

77. Bernstein, *Regulating Business by Independent Commission*, pp. 4–5; Atkinson, "Nature and Extent of the President's Powers Under the Reorganization Act," 6 September 1946, Reorganization Act of 1945: Legal Opinions and Interpretation folder, Series 39.32, Bureau of Budget file, Office of Management and Budget.

78. Erwin G. Krasnow and Lawrence D. Longley, *The Politics of Broadcast Regulation*, pp. 54–55.

79. Bernstein, *Regulating Business by Independent Commission*, p. 152. For study of relationships between the commissions and Congress see Kohlmeier, *The Regulators*, pp. 53–68.

80. Paul H. Douglas, *In the Fullness of Time: The Memoirs of Paul H. Douglas*, pp. 185–86.

81. Theodore H. White, *Citadel: The Story of the U.S. Senate*, pp. 129–30.

82. Truman, *Public Papers, 1950*, p. 517.

83. Richard L. Riedel, *Halls of the Mighty: My 47 Years at the Senate*, pp. 241–42.

84. Schauffler, "Study of the Legislative Veto," p. 589.

85. U.S., Congress, House, Committee on Expenditures in the Executive Departments, *Reorganization Plan No. 7 of 1950*, Hearing, 81st Cong., 2d sess., pp. 3–5; U.S., Congress, House, Committee on Expenditures in the Executive Departments, *Reorganization Plan No. 7 of 1950*, H. Rept. No. 1971, 81st Cong., 2d sess., (1950), pp. 1–26.

86. U.S., Congress, Senate, Committee on Expenditures in the Executive Departments, *Reorganization Plans Nos. 7, 8, 9, and 11 of 1950*, Hearing, 81st Cong., 2d sess., pp. 13–15.

87. Frank Pace, "Memorandum for the Record," 20 January 1950, Truman, meetings with the president, Agendas and Memorandums folder, Lawton papers; Pace to J. R. Steelman, 5 July [1949], Truman to Charles Sawyer, 30 August 1949, OF 173, Truman papers.

88. Senate, Committee on Expenditures in the Executive Departments, *Reorganization Plans Nos. 7, 8, 9, and 11 of 1950*, Hearing, pp. 161–63.

89. Samuel P. Huntington, "The Marasmus of the ICC: The Commission, the Railroads, and the Public Interest," p. 475 (note 35).

90. Senate, Committee on Expenditures in the Executive Departments, *Reorganization Plans Nos. 7, 8, 9, and 11 of 1950*, Hearing, pp. 29–32.

91. Ibid., pp. 42–45, 216–17.

92. Ibid., pp. 121–24, 128, 133.

93. U.S., Congress, Senate, Committee on Expenditures in the Executive Departments, *Reorganization Plan No. 7 of 1950*, S. Rept. No. 1567, 81st Cong., 2d sess., (1950), p. 1.

94. *CR*, vol. 96, pt. 6, pp. 7155–58.

95. Ibid., pp. 7167–68.

96. Ibid., pp. 7160–67.

97. Ibid., p. 7173.

98. Bernstein, *Regulating Business by Independent Commission*, pp. 134–37.

99. Senate, Committee on Expenditures in the Executive Departments, *Reorganization Plans Nos. 7, 8, 9, and 11 of 1950*, Hearing, pp. 115, 139–42, 149, 189–93.

100. U.S., Congress, Senate, Committee on Expenditures in the Executive Departments, *Reorganization Plan No. 11 of 1950*, S. Rept. No. 1564, 81st Cong., 2d sess., (1950), p. 1.

101. *CR*, vol. 96, pt. 6, p. 7177.

102. [CCHR Official] to Francis J. Chesterman, undated, B folder, CCHR papers.

103. *Congressional Quarterly Almanac*, vol. 6, (1950), p. 540.

104. Grant McConnell, *The Decline of Agrarian Democracy*, p. 127; also see Charles M. Hardin, *The Politics of Agriculture: Soil Conservation and the Struggle for Power in Rural America*, p. 223.

105. Lawton, personal interview.

106. Ibid.

107. Roback, personal interview.

108. McCormick to John Stuart, 17 September 1951, CCHR Chrono file, McCormick papers; Schauffler, "Study of the Legislative Veto," pp. 567–68. CCHR officials met with leaders of the major farm organizations to discuss plan four. The dominant theme that emerged was the real fear these leaders had of Brannan. Benjamin Vander Poel to McCormick, 5 April 1950, CCHR Chrono file, McCormick papers.

109. U.S., Congress, Senate, Committee on Government Operations, *Reorganization Plan No. 2 of 1953*, Hearing, 83d Cong., 1st sess., pp. 126–28.

110. Ibid., p. 132.

111. Ibid., p. 194.

112. See Lauren Soth, "Mr. Hoover's Department of Agriculture," pp. 208–12, 210 (note 8), 211 (note 10), 212 (note 12).

113. Hardin, *Politics of Agriculture*, p. 224.

114. U.S., Congress, Senate, Committee on Expenditures in the Executive Departments, *Reorganization Plan No. 4 of 1950*, Hearing, 81st Cong., 2d sess.; U.S., Congress, Senate, Committee on Expenditures in the Executive Departments, *Reorganization Plan No. 4 of 1950*, S. Rept. No. 1566, 81st Cong., 2d sess., (1950), pp. 1, 9–20; *Congressional Quarterly Almanac*, vol. 6, (1950), p. 365.

115. Stauffacher to Pace, 22 May 1950, Reorganization Program for 1950 folder, Series 39.32, Bureau of Budget file, Office of Management and Budget.

116. *CR*, vol. 96, pt. 6, p. 7226.

117. Ibid., pp. 7228–32, 7235; *Congressional Quarterly Almanac*, vol. 6, (1950), p. 365.

118. *Congressional Quarterly Almanac*, ibid.

Chapter 11

1. U.S., Congress, House, Committee on Expenditures in the Executive Departments, *Reorganization Plan No. 6 of 1950*, Hearing, 81st Cong., 2d sess., pp. 37–40.

2. Peter Page Schauffler, "A Study of the Legislative Veto" (Ph.D. diss.), pp. 585–86.

3. U.S., Congress, House, Committee on Expenditures in the Executive Departments, *Reorganization Plan No. 6 of 1950*, H. Rept. No. 1907, 81st Cong., 2d sess., (1950), pp. 1, 14–21.

4. *CR*, 81:2, 1950, vol. 96, pt. 6, p. 7266.

5. U.S., Congress, Senate, Committee on Expenditures in the Executive Departments, *Reorganization Plan No. 6 of 1950*, S. Rept. No. 1684, 81st Cong., 2d sess., (1950), pp. 1–6.

6. Francis E. Rourke, "Reorganization of the Labor Department" (Ph.D. diss.), pp. 286–91, 298–300.

7. R. W. Stokley to Pace, 19 October 1949, President Truman (Meetings-Truman-Pace) folder, Director's Office (Accession No. 5308–10), Bureau of Budget file, Office of Management and Budget.

8. Lindsay Warren to Sam Rayburn, 6 February 1950, OF (Official File) 126, Truman papers.

9. U.S., Commission on Organization of the Executive Branch of the Government, *The Independent Regulatory Commissions: A Report to the Congress by the Commission on Organization of the Executive Branch of the Government*, p. 12; U.S., President's Advisory Committee on the Merchant Marine, *Report of the President's Advisory Committee on the Merchant Marine*, pp. iv, 8.

10. Pace to Truman, stamped 7 March 1950, OF 285A, Truman papers.

11. Robert L. L. McCormick to Hoover, 10 March 1950, Citizens Committee for the Hoover Report Chronological file, Robert L. L. McCormick papers.

12. U.S., Congress, Senate, Committee on Expenditures in the Executive Departments, *Reorganization Plan No. 21 of 1950*, Hearing, 81st Cong., 2d sess., pp. 16–18.

13. Ibid., pp. 20–21.

14. Harry S. Truman, *Public Papers of the Presidents of the United States: Harry S. Truman, 1950*, p. 197.

15. Senate, Committee on Expenditures in the Executive Departments, *Reorganization Plan No. 21 of 1950*, Hearing, pp. 99–101.

16. Ibid., pp. 101–2.

17. Ibid., pp. 102–4.

18. Samuel A. Lawrence, *United States Merchant Shipping Policies and Politics*, p. 320 (note 24); Senate, Committee on Expenditures in the Executive Departments, *Reorganization Plan No. 21 of 1950*, Hearing, pp. 73, 75, 78–82, 94, 111–14, 123–24, 128–31, 133–37, 140–41, 146, 155–57.

19. McCormick to Hoover, 16 February 1950, Dr. Robert L. Johnson folder, Commission on Organization of the Executive Branch of the Government papers, Herbert C. Hoover Presidential Library.

20. Senate, Committee on Expenditures in the Executive Departments, *Reorganization Plan No. 21 of 1950*, Hearing, pp. 85–86.

21. U.S., Congress, Senate, Committee on Expenditures in the Executive Departments, *Reorganization Plan No. 21 of 1950*, S. Rept. No. 1674, 81st Cong., 2d sess., (1950), p. 1.

22. George W. Malone to Guy Gabrielson, 19 May 1950, M folder, Commission on Organization of the Executive Branch papers, Hoover Library.

23. *CR*, vol. 96, pt. 6, p. 7321; statistical material on this and other votes comes from *Congressional Quarterly Almanac*, vol. 6, (1950), p. 540.

24. U.S., Congress, Senate, Committee on Expenditures in the Executive Departments, *Reorganization Plan No. 8 of 1950*, S. Rept. No. 1562, *Reorganization Plan No. 9 of 1950*, S. Rept. No. 1563, 81st Cong., 2d sess., (1950); *CR*, vol. 96, pt. 6, pp. 7382–83.

25. [Samuel Shaffer], "Reorganization: Bill Benton Blitz," *Newsweek*, p. 21.

26. William Benton to Robert L. Johnson, 24 March 1952, B folder, CCHR papers; Sidney Hyman, *The Lives of William Benton*, p. 300; [Shaffer], "Reorganization: Bill Benton Blitz," p. 21.

27. Benton to "Dear Friend," 14 August 1950, OF 285A, Truman papers; Benton to Hoover, 16 May 1950, B folder, Commission on Organization of the Executive Branch papers, Hoover Library.

28. Hyman, *Lives of William Benton*, p. 430.

29. Benton to Frederick J. Lawton, 28 April 1950, Benton to Connelly, 28 April 1950, Correspondence-Congressional folder, Frederick J. Lawton papers; Benton to Hoover, 16 May 1950, B folder, Commission on Organization of the Executive Branch papers, Hoover Library.

30. *CR*, vol. 96, pt. 6, pp. 7363–66.

31. Ibid., p. 7369.

32. Ibid., p. 7375. For a discussion of FTC's administrative problems and frequent reorganizations since 1949 see Susan Wagner, *The Federal Trade Commission*, pp. 39–44, 220–29.

33. *CR*, vol. 96, pt. 6, pp. 7380–82.

34. Ibid., p. 7383.

35. [Shaffer], "Reorganization: Bill Benton Blitz," p. 22.

36. [McCormick] to Charles Coates, 23 May 1950, CCHR Chrono file, McCormick papers.

37. McCormick to Hoover, ibid. One CCHR supporter reported that several Republicans shifted to support the plans after Hoover intervened directly to Taft. Leopold Lippman to Raymond B. Allen, 7 June 1950, L folder, CCHR papers. Also see McCormick to Hoover, 22 May 1950, Robert L. L. McCormick folder, Commission on Organization of the Executive Branch papers, Hoover Library.

38. [McCormick] to Coates, 23 May 1950, CCHR Chrono file, McCormick papers.

39. [Shaffer], "Reorganization: Bill Benton Blitz," p. 22. For McClellan's angry attack on this article see *CR*, vol. 96, pt. 6, pp. 8045–46.

40. Edward Strait to Miles, 24 May 1950, Reorganization Plans-General Congressional Votes, White House Desk Manual 75 folder, Stephan J. Spingarn papers.

41. Atkinson to Miles, 8 November 1949, Transfer of Functions from Subordinate Officials and Units to the Heads of Departments folder, Series [39.32], Bureau of Budget file, Office of Management and Budget.

42. Stacy V. Jones, *The Patent Office,* pp. 169–73.

43. Charles Sawyer, *Concerns of a Conservative Democrat,* pp. 175–76, 186–88.

44. Bernard Gladieux to Ralph J. Burton, 22 December 1949, VI–2/50.1 folder, Series 47.1, Bureau of Budget papers, RG 51, National Archives; Burton memorandum for the record, 23 December 1949, Transfer of Functions from Subordinate Officials and Units to the Heads of Departments folder, Series [39.32], Bureau of Budget file, Office of Management and Budget.

45. U.S., Congress, House, Committee on Expenditures in the Executive Departments, *Reorganization Plan No. 5 of 1950,* Hearing, 81st Cong., 2d sess.; U.S., Congress, House, Committee on Expenditures in the Executive Departments, *Reorganization Plan No. 5 of 1950,* H. Rept. No. 1976, 81st Cong., 2d sess., (1950), pp. 1, 21–25.

46. *CR,* vol. 96, pt. 6, pp. 7266–70, 7272–74.

47. U.S., Congress, Senate, Committee on Expenditures in the Executive Departments, *Reorganization Plan No. 5 of 1950,* Hearing, 81st Cong., 2d sess., pp. 6–8.

48. U.S., Congress, Senate, Committee on Expenditures in the Executive Departments, *Reorganization Plan No. 5 of 1950,* S. Rept. No. 1561, 81st Cong., 2d sess., (1950), pp. 1–5.

49. *CR,* vol. 96, pt. 6, pp. 7383–87.

50. Ibid., p. 7479.

51. U.S., Congress, Senate, Committee on Expenditures in the Executive Departments, *Reorganization Plans Nos. 17 and 18 of 1950,* Hearing, 81st Cong., 2d sess., pp. 9–11, 15–16, 18–19.

52. U.S., Congress, Senate, Committee on Expenditures in the Executive Departments, *Reorganization Plan No. 17 of 1950,* S. Rept. No. 1676, 81st Cong., 2d sess., (1950), p. 1.

53. *CR,* vol. 96, pt. 6, pp. 7480–82.

54. Ibid., p. 7486.

55. The Hoover Commission recommended such a reorganization. U.S., Commission on Organization of the Executive Branch of the Government, *Office of General Services: A Report to the Congress by the Commission on Organization of the Executive Branch of the Government,* p. 10.

56. William L. Dawson, press release, 27 March 1950, R–8 (A-G) Reorganization Plan temporary folder, James P. Kem papers.

57. U.S., Congress, House, Committee on Expenditures in the Executive Departments, *Reorganization Plan No. 18 of 1950,* H. Rept. No. 1947, 81st Cong., 2d sess., (1950), p. 1; Schauffler, "Study of the Legislative Veto," p. 643.

58. Senate, Committee on Expenditures in the Executive Departments, *Reorganization Plans Nos. 17 and 18 of 1950,* Hearing, pp. 66–67, 72–75, 92–94, 96–100, 116–17, 121–25, 127.

59. Ibid., pp. 67–72, 78–83, 87–89, 118–20, 125–26.

60. Radio program transcript, "America United Program," 4 June 1950, Speeches folder, CCHR papers.

61. U.S., Congress, Senate, Committee on Expenditures in the Executive Departments, *Reorganization Plan No. 18 of 1950,* S. Rept. No. 1675, 81st Cong., 2d sess., (1950), pp. 1–5; Schauffler, "Study of the Legislative Veto," p. 643.

62. *CR,* vol. 96, pt. 6, pp. 7486–87.

63. Ibid., p. 7489.

64. Truman, *Public Papers, 1950,* p. 7.

65. Charles Sawyer to Truman, 14 February 1950, Small Business Program, White House Desk Manual folder, Spingarn papers.

66. Truman to Sawyer, 18 February 1950, Small Business Program, White House Desk Manual folder, Spingarn to Pace, 27 February 1950, Chronological File folder, Spingarn papers.

67. U.S., Commission on Organization of the Executive Branch of the Government, *Treasury Department: A Report to the Congress by the Commission on Organization of the Executive Branch of the Government*, pp. 10–11.

68. Stauffacher to Pace, 3 March 1950, Small Business: President's Program in 81st Congress, Volume 1 folder, tab 18, Spingarn file, Truman papers.

69. Truman, *Public Papers, 1950*, pp. 288–93.

70. U.S., Congress, House, Committee on Expenditures in the Executive Departments, *Reorganization Plan No. 24 of 1950*, Hearing, 81st Cong., 2d sess.; U.S., Congress, House, Committee on Expenditures in the Executive Departments, *Reorganization Plan No. 24 of 1950*, H. Rept. No. 2321, 81st Cong., 2d sess., (1950), p. 1.

71. *CR*, vol. 96, pt. 7, p. 9617.

72. Schauffler, "Study of the Legislative Veto," p. 657 (note 1203).

73. Ibid.

74. U.S., Congress, Senate, Committee on Expenditures in the Executive Departments, *Reorganization Plan No. 24 of 1950*, Hearing, 81st Cong., 2d sess., pp. 3–6.

75. U.S., Congress, Senate, Committee on Expenditures in the Executive Departments, *Reorganization Plan No. 24 of 1950*, S. Rept. No. 1868, 81st Cong., 2d sess., (1950), pp. 1, 3–4, 12; *CR*, vol. 96, pt. 7, pp. 9693–94.

76. *CR*, vol. 96, pt. 7, pp. 9684–87.

77. Ibid., pp. 9680–82, 9692–93.

78. REN [Neustadt] to Spingarn, 3 July 1950, Small Business file #3 folder, Spingarn file, Truman papers.

79. *CR*, vol. 96, pt. 7, pp. 9689–91.

80. Ibid., p. 9694.

81. The Hoover Commission also recommended this. U.S., Commission on Organization of the Executive Branch, *Reorganization of Federal Business Enterprises: A Report to the Congress on Organization of the Executive Branch of the Government*, p. 32.

82. Stauffacher to Pace, 3 March 1950, Small Business: President's Program in the 81st Congress, Volume I folder, tab 18, Neustadt to Spingarn, [about 1 May 1950], Small Business: President's Program in the 81st Congress, Volume II folder, Spingarn file, Truman papers; Elmer Staats, memorandum for the record, 8 May 1950, Truman, meetings with the president, Agendas and Memorandums folders, Lawton papers.

83. Johnson to CCHR State Chairmen, 29 June 1950, Correspondence (Reorganization Plans) folder, CCHR papers.

84. Davies, *Housing Reform During the Truman Administration*, p. 63.

85. U.S., Congress, Senate, Committee on Expenditures in the Executive Departments, *Reorganization Plan No. 22 of 1950*, Hearing, 81st Cong., 2d sess., pp. 4–9.

86. Ibid., pp. 11–27.

87. Ibid., pp. 31–36, 40–44.

88. U.S., Congress, Senate, Committee on Expenditures in the Executive Departments, *Reorganization Plan No. 22 of 1950*, S. Rept. No. 1936, 81st Cong., 2d sess., (1950), p. 1.

89. *CR*, vol. 96, pt. 7, pp. 9694–95, 9701–3.

90. Ibid., p. 9704.

91. Statement by Lawton, personal interview.

92. Lawton, memorandum for the record, 23 May 1950, Truman, meetings with the president, Agendas and Memorandums folder, Lawton papers.

93. McCormick to Coates, 6 September 1949, CCHR Chrono file, McCormick papers.

94. Stauffacher to Pace, 16 February 1950, President Truman (Meetings-Pace-Truman) folder, Director's Office (Accession No. 5308–10), Bureau of Budget file, Office of Management and Budget.

95. David Bell to Murphy, 24 May 1950, OF 285A, Truman papers.

96. McCormick to Hoover, 8 May 1950, McCormick folder, Commission on Organization of

the Executive Branch papers, Hoover Library; Lawton to Truman, 23 May 1950, Truman, meetings with the president, Agendas and Memorandums folder, Lawton papers.

97. Miles to Lawton, draft of memorandum, 13 June 1950, Reorganization Plans 1–27 of 1950 (consideration by Congress in general) folder, Series 39.32, Bureau of Budget file, Office of Management and Budget.

98. Richard Harris, *A Sacred Trust*, p. 53.

99. U.S., Congress, House, Committee on Expenditures in the Executive Departments, *Reorganization Plan No. 27 of 1950*, Hearing, 81st Cong., 2d sess., pp. 27–32.

100. U.S., Congress, House, Committee on Expenditures in the Executive Departments, *Reorganization Plan No. 27 of 1950*, H. Rept. No. 2320, 81st Cong., 2d sess., (1950), pp. 1, 11–15.

101. Lawton, memorandum for the record, 23 May 1950, Truman, meetings with the president, Agendas and Memorandums folder, Lawton papers; House, Select Committee on Lobbying Activities, *Legislative Activities of Executive Agencies*, Hearing, part 10, p. 436; Spingarn to Truman, 30 June 1950, Small Business File #3 folder, Spingarn file, Truman papers. For Senate hearings and report see U.S., Congress, Senate, Committee on Expenditures in the Executive Departments, *Reorganization Plan No. 27 of 1950*, Hearing, 81st Cong., 2d sess.; U.S., Congress, Senate, Committee on Expenditures in the Executive Departments, *Reorganization Plan No. 27 of 1950*, S. Rept. No. 1943, 81st Cong., 2d sess., (1950).

102. Unsigned, untitled memorandum [probably from Spingarn to Truman], 10 July 1950, Suggested Items for Discussion with Congressional Leaders, White House Desk Manual 18 folder, Spingarn papers.

103. U.S., Congress, House, Select Committee on Lobbying Activities, *Legislative Activities of Executive Agencies*, Hearing, part 10, 81st Cong., 2d sess., p. 435.

104. *CR*, vol. 96, pt. 7, pp. 9843–45.

105. Ibid., pp. 9861–62.

106. Ibid., p. 9858.

107. Ibid., pp. 9852–56.

108. Ibid., pp. 9845, 9850–52, 9856–60.

109. Ibid., pp. 9862–63.

110. Ibid., p. 9864.

111. James G. Burrow, *AMA: Voice of American Medicine*, pp. 380–81 (note 72).

112. Charles Murphy to Truman, 20 May 1950, Memos to and from the President folder, Charles Murphy papers.

113. U.S., Congress, Senate, Committee on Expenditures in the Executive Departments, *Reorganization Plan No. 4 of 1950*, Hearing, 81st Cong., 2d sess., pp. 63–65.

114. James M. Landis, "Report on Regulatory Agencies to the President-Elect," pp. 60–61.

115. Harold Seidman, *Politics, Position, and Power: The Dynamics of Federal Organization*, p. 90.

116. Norton E. Long, "Reflections on Presidential Power," pp. 442–50.

117. Seidman, *Politics, Position, and Power*, p. 277.

118. Stanley R. Ruttenberg and Jocelyn Gutchess, *Manpower Challenge of the 1970's: Institutions and Social Change*, p. 92.

119. Roger G. Noll, *Reforming Regulation: An Evaluation of the Ash Council Proposals, A Staff Paper*, pp. 31, 33–46.

120. Marver H. Bernstein, *Regulating Business by Independent Commission*, pp. 172–73.

121. Landis, "Report on Regulatory Agencies," pp. 12–13.

122. Ibid.; Noll, *Reforming Regulation*, pp. 36–37.

123. Louis M. Kohlmeier, *The Regulators: Watchdog Agencies and the Public Interest*, pp. 47–48.

124. Lawrence, *United States Merchant Shipping Policies and Politics*, p. 264.

125. Ibid., pp. 128–29.

126. Ibid., pp. 243, 257–59, 300.

Chapter 12

1. Harry S. Truman, *Public Papers of the Presidents of the United States: Harry S. Truman, 1950,* p. 581.

2. Truman to Alben Barkley and Sam Rayburn, 18 December 1950, Truman, *Public Papers, 1950,* pp. 749–50.

3. Herbert Roback to author, 6 November 1969, letter in author's possession.

4. "Outline of Remarks by Mr. Lawton, PACMI," 18 September [1950], Speeches, Mtg. and Public Appearances folder, Frederick J. Lawton papers.

5. Cabell Phillips, *The Truman Presidency: The History of a Triumphant Succession,* pp. 402–6.

6. Paul I. Wellman, *Stuart Symington: Portrait of a Man With a Mission,* pp. 140–47.

7. Jules Abels, *The Truman Scandals,* pp. 70–76.

8. Ibid., pp. 5–6; Haynes Johnson and Bernard M. Gwertzman, *Fulbright: The Dissenter,* p. 120; Paul H. Douglas, *In The Fullness of Time: The Memoirs of Paul H. Douglas,* pp. 187–88.

9. Abels, *The Truman Scandals,* pp. 6–8; Johnson and Gwertzman, *Fulbright,* pp. 121–23; Alfred Steinberg, *The Man from Missouri: The Life and Times of Harry S. Truman,* pp. 404–6; also see the statement by George Meader, oral history interview.

10. U.S., Congress, Senate, Committee on Banking and Currency, *Study of Reconstruction Finance Corporation: Favoritism and Influence,* S. Rept. No. 76, 82d Cong., 1st sess., (1951), pp. 1–3.

11. Harry S. Truman, *Public Papers of the Presidents of the United States: Harry S. Truman, 1951,* pp. 144–46.

12. Charles S. Murphy to Burnet R. Maybank, 17 February 1951, Murphy to Miles, 17 February 1951, Reconstruction Finance Corporation folder, Charles S. Murphy file, Harry S. Truman papers.

13. Truman, *Public Papers, 1951,* pp. 158–60; U.S., President, 1945–1953 (Truman), *Message from the President of the United States Transmitting Reorganization Plan No. 1 of 1951.*

14. Press release by Joseph Short, 23 February 1951, Reconstruction Finance Corporation folder, Charles S. Murphy file, Truman papers.

15. Abels, *The Truman Scandals,* pp. 8–10.

16. U.S., Congress, House, Committee on Expenditures in the Executive Departments, *Reorganization Plan No. 1 of 1951,* Hearing, 82d Cong., 1st sess., pp. 21–31.

17. U.S., Congress, House, Committee on Expenditures in the Executive Departments, *Reorganization Plan No. 1 of 1951,* H. Rept. No. 188, 82d Cong., 1st sess., (1951).

18. *CR (Congressional Record)* 82:1, 1951, vol. 97, pt. 2, pp. 2336–43, 2347–50, 2410–12.

19. Ibid., pp. 2346, 2409–10, 2412.

20. Ibid., pp. 2341–42, 2348–49, 2413–17.

21. Ibid., pp. 2344–45.

22. Ibid., p. 2418.

23. Peter Page Schauffler, "A Study of the Legislative Veto" (Ph.D. diss.), p. 713.

24. U.S., Congress, Senate, Committee on Expenditures in the Executive Departments, *Reorganization Plan No. 1 of 1951,* Hearing, 82d Cong., 1st sess., pp. 23–36.

25. Ibid., pp. 134–41, 149–58.

26. Ibid., pp. 121–33.

27. Ibid., pp. 16–21, 100–113, 115–17, 121–33; also see radio address by John W. Bricker, 27 February 1952, Radio Reports from Washington folder, John W. Bricker papers.

28. U.S., Congress, Senate, Committee on Expenditures in the Executive Departments, *Reorganization Plan No. 1 of 1951, Providing for the Reorganization of the Reconstruction Finance Corporation,* S. Rept. No. 213, 82d Cong., 1st sess., (1951), pp. 1–7, 10–16.

29. Schauffler, "Study of the Legislative Veto," pp. 712–13.

30. *CR,* vol. 97, pt. 3, pp. 3726–29, 3731, 3735, 3740–43, 3814–19, 3826–27, 3836–39, 3845, 3847–53.

31. Ibid., pp. 3715–16. According to a White House official, Senator Tobey was strongly opposed to the plan but changed on condition that he could name the deputy administrator of the new agency. Statement by Joseph G. Feeney, oral history interview.

32. *CR*, vol. 97, pt. 3, p. 3855.

33. Addison W. Parris, *The Small Business Administration*, pp. 8–25.

34. See memoranda in Reorganization Program for 1952 folder, Bureau of Budget file, Office of Management and Budget.

35. Joseph B. Gorman, *Kefauver: A Political Biography*, p. 121.

36. Joseph P. Harris, *The Advice and Consent of the Senate: A Study of the Confirmation of Appointments by the United States Senate*, p. 240.

37. William Hillman, *Mr. President: The First Publication from the Personal Diaries, Private Letters, Papers and Revealing Interviews of Harry S. Truman*, p. 62.

38. James H. Shelton, "The Tax Scandals of the 1950's" (Ph.D. diss.), pp. 315–17.

39. Ibid., pp. 17–18; John W. Snyder, "The Reorganization of the Bureau of Internal Revenue," pp. 221–23; Clara Penniman, "Reorganization and the Internal Revenue Service," pp. 122–25; John C. Chommie, *The Internal Revenue Service*, pp. 30–31; Lillian Doris (ed.), *The American Way in Taxation: Internal Revenue, 1862–1963*, pp. 38–41.

40. Shelton, "Tax Scandals of the 1950's," p. 7; Royal D. Sloan, Jr., "The Extension of Civil Service in the Bureau of Internal Revenue: 1952" (Master's thesis), pp. 6–7.

41. Penniman, "Reorganization and the Internal Revenue Service," p. 124; Shelton, "Tax Scandals of the 1950's," pp. 7–8.

42. Sloan, "Extension of Civil Service in the Bureau of Internal Revenue," pp. 7–8.

43. Shelton, "Tax Scandals of the 1950's," pp. 22–27.

44. Ibid., pp. 27–30.

45. Ibid., pp. 41–45, 49–52.

46. Abels, *Truman Scandals*, pp. 11–19; Shelton, "Tax Scandals of the 1950's," pp. 229–73; Penniman, "Reorganization and the Internal Revenue Service," p. 123; Steinberg, *Man from Missouri*, p. 406; Sloan, "Extension of Civil Service in the Bureau of Internal Revenue," pp. 11–16.

47. Shelton, "Tax Scandals of the 1950's," pp. 276–87.

48. Truman, *Public Papers, 1951*, pp. 544–45, 567.

49. Gorman, *Kefauver*, pp. 114–22; Shelton, "Tax Scandals of the 1950's," pp. 289–92; Michael Marsh, "Ethics in Government," pp. 831–32.

50. Truman, *Public Papers, 1951*, p. 641 (note 2).

51. Statement by Donald Hansen, oral history interview.

52. Harry S. Truman, *Public Papers of the Presidents of the United States: Harry S. Truman, 1952–53*, pp. 1–2.

53. Commissioner Dunlap's Press Conference, 2 January 1952, History of the Internal Revenue Reorganization Plan folder, John W. Snyder papers; Truman, *Public Papers, 1952–53*, p. 6.

54. Truman, *Public Papers, 1952–53*, pp. 27–31; U.S., President, 1945–1953 (Truman), *Message from the President of the United States Transmitting Plan No. 1 of 1952*.

55. U.S., Congress, House, Committee on Expenditures in the Executive Departments, *Reorganization Plan No. 1 of 1952*, Hearing, 82d Cong., 2d sess., pp. 7–22, 28–32, 39–44, 58, 67–69, 80–90, 95–114, 202–11; U.S., Congress, House, Committee on Expenditures in the Executive Departments, *Reorganization Plan No. 1 of 1952 (Bureau of Internal Revenue)*, H. Rept. No. 1271, 82d Cong., 2d sess., (1952), pp. 1–9.

56. *CR*, 82:2, 1952, vol. 98, pt. 1, pp. 644–68, 671.

57. Hoover to Cecil King, 18 January 1952, K folder, Commission on Organization of the Executive Branch papers, Herbert C. Hoover Presidential Library.

58. McCormick to John Stuart, 1 April 1952, CCHR Chronological file, Robert L. L. McCormick papers.

59. Hoover to Curtis McGraw, 24 January 1952, Mc folder, Commission on Organization of the Executive Branch papers, Hoover Library.

60. George Bender to Samuel Burk, 25 January 1952, Personnel Management folder, No. 2, CCHR papers.

61. George Malone to Robert L. Johnson, 18 March 1952, Reorganization Plan No. 1 of 1952 General folder, ibid.

62. Richard A. Ware to McCormick, 20 March 1952, ibid.

63. McCormick to Gilbert Darlington, 12 March 1952, D folder, ibid.

64. Statement by Roback, personal interview; Penniman, "Reorganization and the Internal Revenue Service," p. 125; McCormick to Gerald Morgan, 5 November 1951, CCHR Chrono file, McCormick papers; Sen. B. B. Hickenlooper to D. I. Iversen, 17 April 1952, I folder, Sen. Irving M. Ives to Robert Johnson, 5 March 1952, Reorganization Plan No. 1 of 1952, General folder, CCHR papers.

65. John W. Sundstrom to James P. Mitchell, 14 February 1952, Personnel Management folder No. 2, CCHR papers; Donald Hansen to [Charles] Murphy, 3 March 1952, Bureau of Internal Revenue folder, OF (Official File) 21, Truman papers.

66. McCormick to Hoover, 17 January 1952, K folder, Commission on Organization of the Executive Branch papers, Hoover Library.

67. Statement by Lawton, personal interview.

68. Westbrook, personal interview.

69. "Only the First Steps Are Being Taken," Good Government, pp. 1–6.

70. U.S., Congress, Senate, Committee on Government Operations, Reorganization Plan No. 1 of 1952, Hearing, 82d Cong., 2d sess., pp. 25–34, 143–54.

71. Ibid., pp. 35–57, 98–140, 232–43, 245, 250, 260, 283–306.

72. Shelton, "Tax Scandals of the 1950's," p. 299.

73. Senate, Committee on Government Operations, Reorganization Plan No. 1 of 1952, Hearing, pp. 183–90, 199–212.

74. Hansen to Murphy, 27 February 1952, Hansen, Donald folder, Charles Murphy papers.

75. McCormick to Marx Leva, 27 February 1952, Marx Leva folder, CCHR papers.

76. U.S., Congress, Senate, Committee on Government Operations, Reorganization Plan No. 1 of 1952, Providing for Reorganizations in the Bureau of Internal Revenue, S. Rept. No. 1259, 82d Cong., 2d sess., (1952), part 1, pp. 1–12, part 2, pp. 2–36.

77. Hansen to Murphy, 27 February 1952, Hansen, Donald folder, Murphy papers.

78. CCHR, Reorganization News, April 1952, Reorganization News folder, McCormick papers.

79. Shelton, "Tax Scandals of the 1950's," p. 303.

80. Lawton, personal interview. For example see John W. Snyder to members of Senate and House, 7 January 1952, Snyder to Rayburn et al., 15 January 1952, Snyder to John W. Byrnes, 16 January 1952, History of the Internal Revenue Reorganization Plan folder, Dunlap to Collectors of Internal Revenue, 26 March 1952, Internal Revenue Service 1952 folder, Snyder papers.

81. Truman, Public Papers, 1952–53, pp. 197–98.

82. Schauffler, "Study of the Legislative Veto," pp. 764–65, 764 (note 1416).

83. CR, vol. 98, pt. 2, pp. 2163–68.

84. Ibid.

85. The Washington Post, 8 March 1952, pp. 1, 4, quoted in Shelton, "Tax Scandals of the 1950's," pp. 301–2.

86. CR, vol. 98, pt. 2, pp. 2153–54, 2170–72, 2176, 2179, 2239–40.

87. Ibid., p. 2272.

88. For CCHR activity see McCormick to M. H. Harris et al., 13 March 1952, Reorganization Plan No. 1 of 1952 folder, CCHR papers.

89. Lawton, personal interview; Schauffler, "Study of the Legislative Veto," pp. 763–64

(note 1415). For studies of the plan's implementation see Shelton, "Tax Scandals of the 1950's," pp. 306–14; "Has Tax Reorganization Worked?" *Good Government*, pp. 31–34; Penniman, "Reorganization and the Internal Revenue Service," pp. 126–29; Snyder, "Reorganization of the Bureau of Internal Revenue," pp. 223–30; Hugh C. Bickford, *Bureau of Internal Revenue Reorganization: Successful Tax Practice*, pp. 3–28; Chommie, *Internal Revenue Service*, pp. 32–33, 37.

90. Dawson to Truman, 7 January 1952, Reorganization Plan—Dept. of Treasury 1952 (Internal Revenue and Customs) folder, Martin L. Friedman file, Truman papers.

91. Murphy to Truman, 23 January 1952, Chrono file folder, Murphy papers; David D. Lloyd to Murphy, 5 February 1952, chrono file folder, David D. Lloyd papers; William Finan to Lawton, 6 February 1952, Reorganization Program for 1952 folder, Series 39.32, Bureau of Budget file, Office of Management and Budget.

92. Truman, *Public Papers, 1952–53*, pp. 251–54.

93. Ibid., pp. 254–57; U.S., President, 1945–1953 (Truman), *Message from the President of the United States Transmitting Reorganization Plan No. 2 of 1952, Plan No. 3 of 1952, Plan No. 4 of 1952.*

94. Truman, *Public Papers, 1952–53*, pp. 310–15.

95. John Sundstrom to McCormick, 16 April 1952, Reorganization Plan No. 2 of 1952, General folder, CCHR papers; CCHR, *Washington Watchdog No. 34*, 28 April 1952, Reorganization Plan 2 of 1952 folder, Series 39.32, Bureau of Budget file, Office of Management and Budget.

96. "Reorganization Plans 2, 3, and 4," *Newsletter*, May 1952, No. 27, Illinois Citizens for the Hoover Report, B folder, CCHR papers.

97. CCHR, *Action Sheet: For Immediate Action* (pamphlet); CCHR, Research Department, Washington, "Memorandum to the Press," 11 June 1952; Charles Coates, "Special Bulletin," 11 June 1952, R–7 Reorganization Plan folder, James P. Kem papers.

98. Gerald Cullinan, *The Post Office Department*, pp. 220–22; Harris, *Advice and Consent of the Senate*, p. 351.

99. Lloyd to Murphy, 14 February 1952, Chrono file folder, Lloyd papers.

100. Cullinan, *Post Office Department*, p. 221.

101. Ibid., p. 222.

102. Harris, *Advice and Consent of the Senate*, p. 353.

103. Milton D. Stewart to Finan and Miles, 18 April 1952, Reorganization Plan 2 of 1952 (Action by Congress) folder, Series 39.32, Bureau of the Budget file, Office of Management and Budget.

104. The *Washington Post*, 20 June 1952, p. 22.

105. Ibid., 11 April 1952, p. 1.

106. John M. Butler to Howard MacCarthy, 20 June 1952, D folder, CCHR papers.

107. Edward Strait, memorandum for the file, 8 August 1952, Reorganization Plan 2 of 1952 (Action by Congress) folder, Series 39.32, Bureau of the Budget file, Office of Management and Budget.

108. Moody to Pollock, 26 June 1952, Reorganization Plan No. 2 of 1952, General folder, CCHR papers.

109. U.S., Congress, Senate, Committee on Government Operations, *Reorganization Plans Nos. 2, 3, and 4 of 1952*, Hearing, 82d Cong., 2d sess., pp. 38–46, 68–74, 87–91, 99–100, 166–82, 213–18.

110. William Benton to William J. Pape, 1 July 1952, Reorganization Plan No. 2 of 1952, General folder, CCHR papers.

111. Harris, *Advice and Consent of the Senate*, p. 353.

112. Paul R. Van Riper, *History of the United States Civil Service*, p. 445.

113. Cullinan, *Post Office Department*, pp. 159–63.

114. Senate, Committee on Government Operations, *Reorganization Plans Nos. 2, 3, and 4 of 1952*, Hearing, pp. 36–38, 118–21, 137–39, 145–46, 152.

115. U.S., Congress, Senate, Committee on Government Operations, *Reorganization Plan No. 2 of 1952, Providing for Reorganizations in the Post Office Department*, S. Rept. No. 1747, part 1 and 2, *Reorganization Plan No. 3 of 1952, Providing for Reorganizations in Bureau of Customs of the Department of Treasury*, S. Rept. No. 1748, part 1 and 2, *Reorganization Plan No. 4 of 1952, Providing for Reorganizations in the Department of Justice*, S. Rept. No. 1749, part 1 and 2, 82d Cong., 2d sess., (1952).

116. By-line article by John Cramer, *Washington Daily News*, 17 May 1952, Reorganization Plan 2 of 1952 (publicity) folder, Series 39.32, Bureau of Budget file, Office of Management and Budget.

117. McCormick to Walter Fuller, 5 June 1952, Post Office General folder, CCHR papers.

118. McCormick to Arthur Flemming, 6 June 1952, CCHR Chrono file, McCormick papers.

119. Coates and James P. Mitchell to Truman, 12 June 1952, Reorganization Plan 2 of 1952 (support and publicity of CCHR) folder, Bureau of Budget file, Office of Management and Budget; unsigned, undated memorandum entitled "Items for Discussion With Congressional Leaders, 16 June 1952," Chrono file folder, Murphy papers; McCormick to Humphrey, 13 June 1952, McCormick to Merlo Pusey, 17 June 1952, CCHR Chrono file, McCormick papers.

120. *CR*, vol. 98, pt. 6, pp. 7468–74.

121. Ibid., pp. 7480, 7482–85, 7493.

122. Ibid., pp. 7474–77, 7481, 7487–90.

123. Ibid., p. 7495.

124. Schauffler, "Study of the Legislative Veto," pp. 792–93.

125. Lawton, personal interview.

126. McCormick to Fuller, 1 July 1952, Post Office General folder, Coates to State and Local Committees, 20 June 1952, "Special Memoranda Round Robin Number 16," Round Robin folder, CCHR papers; McCormick to Hoover, 20 June 1952, CCHR Chrono file, McCormick papers.

127. The *Washington Post*, 20 June 1952, p. 22.

128. Margaret Chase Smith to Jean Weidensall, 19 June 1952, Reorganization Plan 2 of 1952 (Action by Congress) folder, Bureau of Budget file, Office of Management and Budget.

129. *CR*, vol. 98, pt. 6, pp. 7496–7502, 7512–13.

130. Harry S. Truman, *Year of Decisions*, vol. 1 of *Memoirs by Harry S. Truman*, p. 148.

131. Murphy to Hopkins, 4 December 1951, Re Proposals for the Reorganization of the Government of the District of Columbia folder, OF 51, Truman papers.

132. Lawton to Truman, memorandum stamped 5 April 1951 but probably should be 1952, F. Joseph Donohue to Truman, 7 April 1952, ibid.

133. Atkinson to Finan, 17 April 1952, ibid.

134. John L. McMillan to Truman, 22 April 1952, ibid.

135. Statement by Lawton, oral history interview.

136. Truman, *Public Papers*, 1952–53, pp. 303–5; U.S., President, 1945–1953 (Truman), *Message from the President of the United States Transmitting Reorganization Plan No. 5 of 1952*.

137. U.S., Congress, Senate, Committee on Government Operations, *Reorganization Plan No. 5 of 1952*, Hearing, 82d Cong., 2d sess., pp. 12–24, 28–57, 59–67, 76–97.

138. U.S., Congress, Senate, Committee on Government Operations, *Reorganization Plan No. 5 of 1952—Reorganization of the Government of the District of Columbia*, S. Rept. No. 1735, 82d Cong., 2d sess., (1952), pp. 1–9.

139. Chommie, *The Internal Revenue Service*, p. 185.

Conclusion

1. Truman to Winston Churchill, 23 November 1948, President's Secretary's file, Harry S. Truman papers.

2. Robert Wood, "When Government Works," p. 45.

3. Statement by James Webb, personal interview.

4. Laurin L. Henry, *Presidential Transitions*, p. 640.

Bibliography

A. Manuscript Collections

Acheson, Dean, papers. Harry S. Truman Library, Independence, Mo.

Assistants, Aides and Counsels to the President Files. Harry S. Truman Library, Independence, Mo.

Bennett, Marion T., papers. Western Historical Manuscripts Collection, University of Missouri Library, Columbia, Mo.

Bricker, John W., papers. Ohio Historical Society, Columbus, Ohio.

Brown, Clarence, papers. Ohio Historical Society, Columbus, Ohio.

Bureau of the Budget Files. Record Group 51, National Archives, Washington, D.C.

Bureau of the Budget Files. Office of Management and Budget, Executive Office of the President, Washington, D.C.

Cannon, Clarence, papers. Western Historical Manuscripts Collection, University of Missouri Library, Columbia, Mo.

Citizens Committee for the Hoover Report Files. Herbert Hoover Institute, Stanford University, Stanford, Calif.

Clifford, Clark, papers. Harry S. Truman Library, Independence, Mo.

Commission on Organization of the Executive Branch of the Government Files. Herbert Hoover Presidential Library, West Branch, Iowa.

Commission on Organization of the Executive Branch of the Government Files. Record Group 264, National Archives, Washington, D.C.

Committee on the Judiciary Files, Senate. Record Group 46, National Archives, Washington, D.C.

Democratic National Committee Clipping File. Harry S. Truman Library, Independence, Mo.

Denham, Robert N., papers. Western Historical Manuscripts Collection, University of Missouri Library, Columbia, Mo.

Department of Labor Files. Record Group 174, National Archives, Washington, D.C.

Elsey, George, papers. Harry S. Truman Library, Independence, Mo.

Federal Security Agency Files. Record Group 235, National Archives, Washington, D.C.

Foley, Raymond M., papers. Harry S. Truman Library, Independence, Mo.

Forrestal, James, papers. Princeton University Library, Princeton, N.J.

Gibson, John W., papers. Harry S. Truman Library, Independence, Mo.

Green, Theodore F., papers. Library of Congress, Washington, D.C.

Herzog, Paul, papers. Harry S. Truman Library, Independence, Mo.

Hoover, Herbert C., papers. Post-Presidential, Individual File. Herbert C. Hoover Presidential Library, West Branch, Iowa.

House of Representative Files. Record Group 233, National Archives, Washington, D.C.

229

Ickes, Harold, papers. Library of Congress, Washington, D.C.

Kem, James P., papers. Western Historical Manuscripts Collection, University of Missouri Library, Columbia, Mo.

Landis, James, papers. Library of Congress, Washington, D.C.

Lawton, Frederick J., papers. Harry S. Truman Library, Independence, Mo.

Lloyd, David D., papers. Harry S. Truman Library, Independence, Mo.

Locke, Edwin A., papers. Harry S. Truman Library, Independence, Mo.

McCormick, Robert L. L., papers. Yale University Library, New Haven, Conn.

McNaughton, Frank, papers. Harry S. Truman Library, Independence, Mo.

Middlebush, Frederick A., papers. Western Historical Manuscripts Collection, University of Missouri Library, Columbia, Mo.

Murphy, Charles, papers. Harry S. Truman Library, Independence, Mo.

Pace, Frank, Jr., papers. Harry S. Truman Library, Independence, Mo.

Pollock, James K., papers. Michigan Historical Collections, University of Michigan, Ann Arbor, Mich.

Rayburn, Sam, papers. Sam Rayburn Library, Bonham, Texas.

Schwellenbach, Lewis B., papers. Library of Congress, Washington, D.C.

Smith, Harold D., papers. Franklin D. Roosevelt Library, Hyde Park, N.Y. Xerox copies at Harry S. Truman Library, Independence, Mo.

Snyder, John W., papers. Harry S. Truman Library, Independence, Mo.

Spingarn, Stephen J., papers. Harry S. Truman Library, Independence, Mo.

Stimson, Henry, papers. Yale University Library, New Haven, Conn.

Stowe, David H., papers. Harry S. Truman Library, Independence, Mo.

Taft, Robert A., papers. Library of Congress, Washington, D.C.

Truman, Harry S., Official Files. Harry S. Truman Library, Independence, Mo.

Truman, Harry S., President's Secretary's Files. Harry S. Truman Library, Independence, Mo.

United States Employment Service: Missouri Files. Record Group 183, National Archives. Xerox copies at Harry S. Truman Library, Independence, Mo.

Vorys, John, papers. Ohio Historical Society, Columbus, Ohio.

Webb, James E., papers. Harry S. Truman Library, Independence, Mo.

White House Bill File. Harry S. Truman Library, Independence, Mo.

B. *Interviews*

Doane, D. H. Oral history interview. Western Historical Manuscript Collection, University of Missouri Library, Columbia, Mo.

Farley, James A. Oral history interview by Raymond Henle, 7 December 1966. Herbert Hoover Presidential Library, West Branch, Iowa.

Fayne, James A. Oral history interview by Raymond Henle, 8 August 1968. Herbert Hoover Presidential Library, West Branch, Iowa.

Feeney, Joseph G. Oral history interview by Jerry N. Hess, 20 September 1966. Harry S. Truman Library, Independence, Mo.

Green, Joseph C. Oral history interview by Raymond Henle, 22 November 1967. Herbert Hoover Presidential Library, West Branch, Iowa.

Hansen, Donald. Oral history interview by Charles T. Morrissey, 5 April 1963. Harry S. Truman Library, Independence, Mo.

Heady, Ferrel. Personal interview, November 1969.

Hinde, Edgar G. Oral history interview by J. R. Fuchs, March 1962. Harry S. Truman Library, Independence, Mo.

Jones, Roger W. Oral history interview by Jerry N. Hess, August 1969. Harry S. Truman Library, Independence, Mo.

Kennedy, Rose. Oral history interview by Raymond Henle, 1 February 1968. Herbert Hoover Presidential Library, West Branch, Iowa.

Lawton, Frederick. Oral history interview by Charles T. Morrissey, June/July 1963. Harry S. Truman Library, Independence, Mo.

———. Personal interview, August 1969.

Manasco, Carter. Personal interview, April 1975.

Marks, Ted. Oral history interview by J. R. Fuchs, September 1962. Harry S. Truman Library, Independence, Mo.

Matscheck, Walter. Oral history interview by J. R. Fuchs, April 1963. Harry S. Truman Library, Independence, Mo.

———. Personal interview by Lyle Dorsett, April 1963.

Meader, George. Oral history interview, June 1963. Harry S. Truman Library, Independence, Mo.

Miller, Joseph. Personal interview, August 1969.

Pace, Frank, Jr. Oral history interview by Jerry N. Hess, January, February, June 1972. Harry S. Truman Library, Independence, Mo.

Price, Don K. Oral history interview by Raymond Henle, July 1970. Herbert Hoover Presidential Library, West Branch, Iowa.

Roback, Herbert. Personal interview, August 1969.

Robinson, Edgar E. Oral history interview by Raymond Henle, 13 September 1967. Herbert Hoover Presidential Library, West Branch, Iowa.

Rowe, James. Personal interview, August 1969.

Seidman, Harold. Oral history interview by Jerry N. Hess, July 1970. Harry S. Truman Library, Independence, Mo.

Stewart, John K. Oral history interview by Raymond Henle, 2 October 1967. Herbert Hoover Presidential Library, West Branch, Iowa.

Veatch, Nathan T. Oral history interview by J. R. Fuchs, November 1961. Harry S. Truman Library, Independence, Mo.

Webb, James. Personal interview, April 1975.

Westbrook, James E. Personal interview, December 1969.

C. Letters in Author's Possession

Brown, Clarence, Jr., to author, 16 April 1975.
Mueller, Karl H., to author, 24 February 1970.
Roback, Herbert, to author, 6 November 1969.
Rowe, James, to author, 16 January 1975.
Webb, James, to author, 21 April 1975.

D. Books

Abels, Jules. *The Truman Scandals*. Chicago: Henry Regnery Co., 1956.

———. *Out of the Jaws of Victory*. New York: Henry Holt & Co., 1959.

Acheson, Dean. *Present at the Creation: My Years in the State Department*. New York: W. W. Norton and Co., Inc., 1969.

Adams, Leonard P. *The Public Employment Service in Transition, 1933–1968: Evolution of a Placement Service into a Manpower Agency.* Ithaca, N.Y.: New York State School of Industrial and Labor Relations, Cornell University, 1969.

Allen, Robert S., and William V. Shannon. *The Truman Merry-Go-Round.* New York: Vanguard Press, Inc., 1950.

Altmeyer, Arthur J. *The Formative Years of Social Security.* Madison: University of Wisconsin Press, 1966.

Altshuler, Alan A. *The Politics of the Federal Bureaucracy.* New York: Dodd, Mead & Company, 1968.

Anderson, Jack, and Ronald W. May. *McCarthy: The Man, the Senator, the "Ism."* Boston: Beacon Press, 1952.

Anderson, Patrick. *The Presidents' Men: White House Assistants of Franklin D. Roosevelt, Harry S. Truman, Dwight D. Eisenhower, John F. Kennedy and Lyndon B. Johnson.* Garden City, N.Y.: Doubleday & Co., Inc., 1968.

Bailey, Stephen K. *Congress Makes a Law: The Story Behind the Employment Act of 1946.* New York: Columbia University Press, 1950.

Barber, James D. *The Presidential Character: Predicting Performance in the White House.* Englewood Cliffs, N.J.: Prentice-Hall, Inc., 1972.

Becker, Joseph M. *Experience Rating in Unemployment Insurance: An Experiment in Competitive Socialism.* Baltimore: Johns Hopkins University Press, 1972.

Bell, Jack. *The Splendid Misery: The Story of the Presidency and Power Politics at Close Range.* Garden City, N.Y.: Doubleday & Co., Inc., 1960.

Berman, William C. *The Politics of Civil Rights in the Truman Administration.* Columbus: Ohio State University Press, 1970.

Bernstein, Marver H. *Regulating Business by Independent Commission.* Princeton, N.J.: Princeton University Press, 1955.

Bickford, Hugh C. *Bureau of Internal Revenue Reorganization: Successful Tax Practice.* New York: Prentice-Hall, Inc., 1952.

Binkley, Wilfred E. *President and Congress.* New York: Alfred A. Knopf, Inc., 1947.

Blaisdell, Donald C. *American Democracy Under Pressure.* New York: Ronald Press Co., 1957.

Bolling, Richard. *House out of Order.* New York: E. P. Dutton & Co., Inc., 1965.

Brownlow, Louis. *A Passion for Anonymity: The Autobiography of Louis Brownlow.* Chicago: University of Chicago Press, 1958.

Bundschu, Henry A. *Harry S. Truman: The Missourian.* Reprinted from the *Kansas City Star,* 26 December 1948.

Burns, James M. *Roosevelt: The Lion and the Fox.* New York: Harcourt, Brace & Co., 1956.

———. *The Deadlock of Democracy: Four-Party Politics in America.* Englewood Cliffs, N.J.: Prentice-Hall, Inc., 1963.

Burrow, James G. *AMA: Voice of American Medicine.* Baltimore: Johns Hopkins University Press, 1963.

Byrnes, James F. *Speaking Frankly.* New York: Harper & Brothers, 1947.

Caraley, Demetrios. *The Politics of Military Unification: A Study of Conflict and the Policy Process.* New York: Columbia University Press, 1966.

Caridi, Ronald J. *The Korean War and American Politics: The Republican Party as a Case Study.* Philadelphia: University of Pennsylvania Press, 1968.

Carter, Richard. *The Doctor Business*. New York: Doubleday & Co., Inc., 1958.

Chommie, John C. *The Internal Revenue Service*. New York: Praeger Publishers, Inc., 1970.

Clawson, Marion. *The Bureau of Land Management*. New York: Praeger Publishers, Inc., 1971.

Cleveland, Harlan. *The Future Executive: A Guide for Tomorrow's Managers*. New York: Harper & Row, Publishers, Inc., 1972.

Cochran, Bert. *Harry Truman and the Crisis Presidency*. New York: Funk & Wagnalls, Inc., 1973.

Coffin, Tris. *Missouri Compromise*. Boston: Little, Brown & Company, 1947.

Cullinan, Gerald. *The Post Office Department*. New York: Frederick A. Praeger, Inc., 1968.

Daniels, Jonathan. *Frontier on the Potomac*. New York: Macmillan Co., 1946.

———. *The Man of Independence*. Philadelphia: J. B. Lippincott Company, 1950.

Davies, Richard O. *Housing Reform During the Truman Administration*. Columbia: University of Missouri Press, 1966.

Davis, James W., and Delbert Ringquist. *The President and Congress: Toward a New Power Balance*. Woodbury, N.Y.: Barron's Educational Series, Inc., 1975.

Destler, I. M. *Presidents, Bureaucrats and Foreign Policy: The Politics of Organizational Reform*. Princeton, N.J.: Princeton University Press, 1972.

Donovan, Robert J. *Conflict and Crisis: The Presidency of Harry S. Truman, 1945–1948*. New York: W. W. Norton & Co., Inc., 1977.

Doris, Lillian, ed. *The American Way in Taxation: Internal Revenue, 1862–1963*. Englewood Cliffs, N.J.: Prentice-Hall, Inc., 1963.

Dorough, C. Dwight. *Mr. Sam*. New York: Random House, Inc., 1962.

Dorsett, Lyle W. *The Pendergast Machine*. New York: Oxford University Press, 1968.

Douglas, Paul H. *In the Fullness of Time: The Memoirs of Paul H. Douglas*. New York: Harcourt Brace Jovanovich, Inc., 1972.

Downs, Anthony. *Inside Bureaucracy*. Boston: Little, Brown & Company, 1967.

Eccles, Marriner S. *Beckoning Frontiers: Public and Personal Recollections*. New York: Alfred A. Knopf, Inc., 1966.

Edelman, Murray. *The Symbolic Uses of Politics*. Urbana: University of Illinois Press, 1964.

Emmerich, Herbert. *Essays on Federal Reorganization*. University, Ala.: University of Alabama Press, 1950.

———. *Federal Organization and Administrative Management*. University, Ala.: University of Alabama Press, 1971.

Evins, Joe L. *Understanding Congress*. New York: Clarkson N. Potter, Inc., 1963.

Fenno, Richard F. *The President's Cabinet: An Analysis in the Period from Wilson to Eisenhower*. Cambridge, Mass.: Harvard University Press, 1959.

———. *The Power of the Purse: Appropriations Politics in Congress*. Boston: Little, Brown & Company, 1966.

Ferejohn, John A. *Pork Barrel Politics: Rivers and Harbors Legislation, 1947–1968*. Stanford, Calif.: Stanford University Press, 1974.

Foss, Phillip O. *Politics and Grass: The Administration of Grazing on the Public Domain*. New York: Greenwood Press, Inc., 1960.

Freeman, J. Leiper. *The Political Process: Executive Bureau-Legislative Committee*

Relations. Rev. ed. New York: Random House, Inc., 1965.

Galloway, George. *Congress at the Crossroads*. New York: Thomas Y. Crowell, Co., Inc., 1946.

Garson, Robert A. *The Democratic Party and the Politics of Sectionalism, 1941–1948*. Baton Rouge: Louisiana State University Press, 1974.

Gervasi, Frank. *Big Government: The Meaning and Purpose of the Hoover Commission Report*. New York: McGraw-Hill Book Co., 1949.

Goodwin, George, Jr. *The Little Legislatures: Committees of Congress*. N.P.: University of Massachusetts Press, 1970.

Gorman, Joseph B. *Kefauver: A Political Biography*. New York: Oxford University Press, 1971.

Graham, Otis L., Jr. *Toward a Planned Society: From Roosevelt to Nixon*. New York: Oxford University Press, 1976.

Graves, W. Brooke. *Reorganization of the Executive Branch of the Government of the United States: A Compilation of Basic Information and Significant Documents, 1912–1948*. Public Affairs Bulletin No. 66. Washington, D.C.: Library of Congress, Legislative Reference Service, 1949.

Greater Kansas City Regional Planning Association. *Results of County Planning: Jackson County, Missouri*. Kansas City, Mo.: Greater Kansas City Regional Planning Association, 1932.

Griffith, Ernest S. *Congress: Its Contemporary Role*. 3d ed. New York: New York University Press, 1961.

Grossman, Jonathan. *The Department of Labor*. New York: Praeger Publishers, Inc., 1973.

Haber, William, and Daniel H. Kruger. *The Role of the United States Employment Service in a Changing Economy*. Kalamazoo, Mich.: W. E. Upjohn Institute for Employment Research, 1964.

Haber, William, and Merrill G. Murray. *Unemployment Insurance in the American Economy: An Historical Review and Analysis*. Homewood, Ill.: Richard D. Irwin, Inc., 1966.

Hamby, Alonzo L. *Beyond the New Deal: Harry S. Truman and American Liberalism*. New York: Columbia University Press, 1973.

Hamilton, Alexander, James Madison, and John Jay. *The Federalist*. Edited by Benjamin Fletcher Wright. Cambridge, Mass.: Belknap Press, 1961.

Hammond, Paul Y. *Organizing for Defense: The American Military Establishment in the Twentieth Century*. Princeton, N.J.: Princeton University Press, 1961.

Hardin, Charles M. *The Politics of Agriculture: Soil Conservation and the Struggle for Power in Rural America*. Glencoe, Ill.: Free Press, 1952.

Hargrove, Erwin C. *The Power of the Modern Presidency*. Philadelphia: Temple University Press, 1974.

Harris, Joseph P. *The Advice and Consent of the Senate: A Study of the Confirmation of Appointments by the United States Senate*. Berkeley: University of California Press, 1953.

——. *Congressional Control of Administration*. Washington, D.C.: Brookings Institution, 1964.

Harris, Richard. *A Sacred Trust*. New York: The New American Library Inc., 1966.

Hartley, Fred A. *Our New National Labor Policy: The Taft-Hartley Act and the Next Steps*. New York: Funk & Wagnalls, Inc., 1948.

Hartmann, Susan M. *Truman and the 80th Congress.* Columbia: University of Missouri Press, 1971.

Harvey, Donald R. *The Civil Service Commission.* New York: Praeger Publishers, Inc., 1970.

Hatch, Alden. *The Byrds of Virginia.* New York: Holt, Rinehart & Winston, 1969.

Haynes, Richard F. *The Awesome Power: Harry S. Truman as Commander in Chief.* Baton Rouge: Louisiana State University Press, 1973.

Hays, Brooks. *A Hotbed of Tranquility: My Life in Five Worlds.* New York: Macmillan Co., 1968.

Henry, Laurin L. *Presidential Transitions.* Washington, D.C.: Brookings Institution, 1960.

Hess, Stephen. *Organizing the Presidency.* Washington, D.C.: Brookings Institution, 1976.

Hillman, William. *Mr. President: The First Publication from the Personal Diaries, Private Letters, Papers and Revealing Interviews of Harry S. Truman.* New York: Farrar, Straus & Young, 1952.

Hobbs, Edward H. *Executive Reorganization in the National Government.* University, Miss.: University of Mississippi Press, 1953.

Horn, Stephen. *The Cabinet and Congress.* New York: Columbia University Press, 1960.

Hyman, Sidney. *The Lives of William Benton.* Chicago: University of Chicago Press, 1969.

Hyneman, Charles. *Bureaucracy in a Democracy.* New York: Harper & Brothers, 1950.

Jacob, Charles E. *Policy and Bureaucracy.* Princeton, N.J.: D. Van Nostrand Company, 1966.

Johnson, Haynes, and Bernard M. Gwertzman. *Fulbright: The Dissenter.* Garden City, N.Y.: Doubleday & Co., Inc., 1968.

Johnson, Lady Bird. *A White House Diary.* New York: Holt, Rinehart & Winston, 1970.

Johnson, Richard T. *Managing the White House: An Intimate Study of the Presidency.* New York: Harper & Row, Publishers, Inc., 1974.

Jones, Stacy V. *The Patent Office.* New York: Praeger Publishers, Inc., 1971.

Kansas City Chamber of Commerce. *Where These Rocky Bluffs Meet, Including the Story of the Kansas City Ten-Year Plan.* Kansas City, Mo.: Smith-Grieves Co., 1938.

Karl, Barry D. *Executive Reorganization and Reform in the New Deal: The Genesis of Administrative Management, 1900–1939.* Cambridge, Mass.: Harvard University Press, 1963.

Kelley, Stanley. *Professional Public Relations and Political Power.* Baltimore: Johns Hopkins University Press, 1956.

Key, V. O. *Southern Politics in State and Nation.* New York: Vintage Books, 1949.

Kofmehl, Kenneth. *Professional Staffs of Congress.* Lafayette, Ind.: Purdue University Press, 1962.

Kohlmeier, Louis M. *The Regulators: Watchdog Agencies and the Public Interest.* New York: Harper & Row, Publishers, Inc., 1969.

Koskoff, David E. *Joseph P. Kennedy: A Life and Times.* Englewood Cliffs, N.J.: Prentice-Hall, Inc., 1974.

Kraines, Oscar. *Congress and the Challenge of Big Government.* New York: Bookman Associates, 1958.

Krasnow, Erwin G., and Lawrence D. Longley. *The Politics of Broadcast Regulation.* New York: St. Martin's Press, Inc., 1973.

Krock, Arthur. *Memoirs: Sixty Years on the Firing Line.* New York: Funk & Wagnalls, 1968.

Lawrence, Samuel A. *United States Merchant Shipping Policies and Politics.* Washington, D.C.: Brookings Institution, 1966.

Lee, Jay M. *The Artilleryman: The Experiences and Impressions of an American Artillery Regiment in the World War.* Kansas City, Mo.: Spencer Printing Co., 1920.

Lee, R. Alton. *Truman and Taft-Hartley: A Question of Mandate.* Lexington: University of Kentucky Press, 1966.

Lilienthal, David E. *The Atomic Energy Years, 1945–1950.* Vol. 2 of *The Journals of David E. Lilienthal.* New York: Harper and Row, 1964.

———. *Venturesome Years, 1950–1955.* Vol. 3 of *The Journals of David E. Lilienthal.* New York: Harper and Row, 1966.

Lloyd, Craig. *Aggressive Introvert: A Study of Herbert Hoover and Public Relations Management, 1912–1932.* Columbus: Ohio State University Press, 1972.

Lubell, Samuel. *The Future of American Politics.* New York: Harper & Brothers, 1952.

Maass, Arthur. *Muddy Waters: The Army Engineers and the Nation's Rivers.* Cambridge, Mass.: Harvard University Press, 1951.

McClure, Arthur F. *The Truman Administration and the Problems of Postwar Labor, 1945–1948.* Rutherford, N.J.: Fairleigh Dickinson University Press, 1969.

McConnell, Grant. *The Decline of Agrarian Democracy.* Berkeley: University of California Press, 1959.

McCulloch, Frank W., and Tim Bernstein. *The National Labor Relations Board.* New York: Praeger Publishers, Inc., 1974.

Marmor, Theodore R. *The Politics of Medicare.* Chicago: Aldine Publishing Company, 1973.

Martin, Joe, and Robert J. Donovan. *My First Fifty Years in Politics.* New York: McGraw-Hill Book Co., 1960.

Mauldin, Bill. *Back Home.* New York: William Sloane Associates, 1947.

Meriam, Lewis, and Laurence F. Schmeckebier. *Reorganization of the National Government: What Does it Involve?* Washington, D.C.: Brookings Institution, 1939.

Merson, Martin. *The Private Diary of a Public Servant.* New York: Macmillan Co., 1955.

Miles, Arnold, and Alan L. Dean. *Issues and Problems in the Administrative Organization of National Governments.* Brussels: International Institute of Administrative Sciences, 1950, printed in this form in 1954, rpt., 1959.

Milligan, Maurice. *The Inside Story of the Pendergast Machine by the Man Who Smashed It.* New York: Charles Scribner's Sons, 1948.

Millis, Harry A., and Emily Clark Brown. *From the Wagner Act to Taft-Hartley.* Chicago: University of Chicago Press, 1950.

Millis, Walter, ed., with collaboration of E. S. Duffield. *The Forrestal Diaries.* New York: The Viking Press, 1951.

Missouri State Planning Board. *A Preliminary Report on a State Plan for Missouri.* 1934.

Morrow, William L. *Congressional Committees.* New York: Charles Scribner's Sons, 1969.

Murphy, John F. *The Pinnacle: The Contemporary American Presidency.* Philadelphia: J. B. Lippincott Company, 1974.

Neustadt, Richard E. *Presidential Power: The Politics of Leadership*. New York: John Wiley & Sons Inc., 1960.

Noll, Roger G. *Reforming Regulation: An Evaluation of the Ash Council Proposals, A Staff Paper*. Washington: Brookings Institution, 1971.

Ostrom, Vincent. *The Intellectual Crisis in American Public Administration*. University, Ala.: University of Alabama Press, 1974.

Parris, Addison W. *The Small Business Administration*. New York: Praeger Publishers, Inc., 1968.

Patterson, Caleb Perry. *Presidential Government in the United States: The Unwritten Constitution*. Chapel Hill: University of North Carolina Press, 1947.

Patterson, James T. *Congressional Conservatism and the New Deal: The Growth of the Conservative Coalition in Congress, 1933–1939*. Lexington: University of Kentucky Press, 1967.

———. *Mr. Republican: A Biography of Robert A. Taft*. Boston: Houghton Mifflin Company, 1972.

Phillips, Cabell. *The Truman Presidency: The History of a Triumphant Succession*. New York: Macmillan Co., 1966.

Polenberg, Richard. *Reorganizing Roosevelt's Government: The Controversy Over Executive Reorganization, 1936–1939*. Cambridge, Mass.: Harvard University Press, 1966.

Public Affairs Institute. *The Hoover Report: Half a Loaf*. Washington, D.C.: Public Affairs Institute, 1949.

Reddig, William M. *Tom's Town*. New York: J. B. Lippincott Co., 1947.

Richardson, Elmo R. *Dams, Parks and Politics: Resource Development and Preservation in the Truman-Eisenhower Era*. Lexington: University of Kentucky Press, 1973.

Riddle, Donald H. *The Truman Committee*. New Brunswick, N.J.: Rutgers University Press, 1964.

Riedel, Richard L. *Halls of the Mighty: My 47 Years at the Senate*. Washington, D.C.: Robert B. Luce, Inc., 1969.

Roosevelt, Franklin D. *Looking Forward*. New York: John Day Co., 1933.

———. *The Continuing Struggle for Liberalism, 1938*. Vol. 7 of *The Public Papers and Addresses of Franklin D. Roosevelt*. Edited by Samuel I. Rosenman. New York: Macmillan Co., 1941. Reissued 1969 by Russell and Russell.

———. *War—And Neutrality, 1939*. Vol. 8 of *The Public Papers and Addresses of Franklin D. Roosevelt*. Edited by Samuel I. Rosenman. New York: Macmillan Co., 1941. Reissued 1969 by Russell and Russell.

Roper, Elmo. *You and Your Leaders: Their Actions and Your Reactions, 1936–1956*. New York: William Morrow & Co., 1957.

Ross, Irwin. *The Loneliest Campaign: The Truman Victory of 1948*. New York: New American Library, Inc., 1968.

Rourke, Francis E. *Bureaucracy, Politics, and Public Policy*. Boston: Little, Brown & Company, 1967.

Ruttenberg, Stanley R., and Jocelyn Gutchess. *Manpower Challenge of the 1970's: Institutions and Social Change*. Baltimore: Johns Hopkins University Press, 1970.

Sawyer, Charles. *Concerns of a Conservative Democrat*. Carbondale: Southern Illinois University Press, 1968.

Schwartz, Bernard. *The Professor and the Commissions*. New York: Alfred A. Knopf, Inc., 1959.

Seckler-Hudson, Catheryn. *Processes of Organization and Management*. Washington, D.C.: Public Affairs Press, 1948.

Seidman, Harold. *Politics, Position, and Power: The Dynamics of Federal Organization*. New York: Oxford University Press, 1970.

Sherwood, Robert E. *Roosevelt and Hopkins: An Intimate History*. Rev. ed. New York: Universal Library, Grosset & Dunlap, Inc., 1950.

Smith, Frank E. *Congressman from Mississippi*. New York: Pantheon Books, Inc., 1964.

Smith, Harold D. *The Management of Your Government*. New York: McGraw-Hill Book Co., Inc., 1945.

Somers, Herman M. *Presidential Agency: OWMR, the Office of War Mobilization and Reconversion*. Cambridge, Mass.: Harvard University Press, 1950.

Steinberg, Alfred. *The Man from Missouri: The Life and Times of Harry S. Truman*. New York: G. P. Putnam's Sons, 1962.

———. *Sam Johnson's Boy: A Close-up of the President from Texas*. New York: Macmillan Co., 1968.

Toulmin, Harry A., Jr. *Diary of Democracy*. New York: Richard R. Smith Co., Inc., 1947.

Truman, David B. *The Congressional Party: A Case Study*. New York: John Wiley & Sons, Inc., 1959.

Truman, Harry S. *Year of Decisions*. Vol. 1 of *Memoirs by Harry S. Truman*. Garden City, N.Y.: Doubleday and Co., Inc., 1955.

———. *Years of Trial and Hope*. Vol. 2 of *Memoirs by Harry S. Truman*. Garden City, N.Y.: Doubleday and Co., Inc., 1956.

———. *Mr. Citizen*. New York: Bernard Geis Associates, 1960.

———. *Public Papers of the Presidents of the United States: Harry S. Truman, 1945–1953*. Washington: Government Printing Office, 1961–1966.

Van Riper, Paul R. *History of the United States Civil Service*. Evanston, Ill.: Row, Peterson & Co., 1958.

Voorhis, Jerry. *Confessions of a Congressman*. Garden City, N.Y.: Doubleday and Co., Inc., 1947.

Wagner, Susan. *The Federal Trade Commission*. New York: Praeger Publishers, Inc., 1971.

Waldo, Dwight. *Perspectives on Administration*. University, Ala.: University of Alabama Press, 1956.

Wann, Andrew J. *The President as Chief Administrator*. Washington: Public Affairs Press, 1968.

Weber, Gustavus A. *Organized Efforts for the Improvement of Methods of Administration in the United States*. New York: D. Appleton and Co., 1919.

Wellman, Paul I. *Stuart Symington: Portrait of a Man with a Mission*. Garden City, N.Y.: Doubleday and Co., Inc., 1960.

White, Theodore H. *The Making of the President 1964*. New York: Atheneum Publishers, 1965.

———. *Citadel: The Story of the U.S. Senate*. New York: Harper and Brothers, 1957.

———. *Home Place: The Story of the U.S. House of Representatives*. Boston: Houghton Mifflin Co., 1965.

Who's Who in America. Vol. 26. Chicago: Marquis Who's Who, Inc., 1950.

Wicker, Tom. *JFK and LBJ: The Influence of Personality upon Politics*. New York: William Morrow & Co., Inc., 1968.

Wildavsky, Aaron. *The Politics of the Budgetary Process*. Boston: Little, Brown & Co., 1964.

Woll, Peter. *American Bureaucracy*. New York: W. W. Norton & Co., Inc., 1963.

Wright, Jim. *You and Your Congressman*. New York: Coward-McCann, Inc., 1965.

Young, Roland. *Congressional Politics in the Second World War*. New York: Columbia University Press, 1956.

E. *Articles*

Aikin, Charles, and Louis W. Koenig. Introduction to "The Hoover Commission: A Symposium." *The American Political Science Review*, edited by Louis W. Koenig, 43, 5 (October 1949):933–40.

Aikin, Charles. "The Story of the Hoover Commission." *California Monthly*, June 1949, pp. 26–27, 82.

———. "Task Force: Methodology." *Public Administration Review* 9, 4 (Autumn 1949):241–51.

Alexander, H., and J. R. Slevin. "Mr. Welfare State Himself." *Collier's* 135 (4 February 1950):13–15.

Appleby, Paul H. "Harold D. Smith—Public Administrator." *Public Administration Review* 7, 2 (Spring 1947):77–81.

———. "Organizing Around the Head of a Large Federal Department." In *Processes of Organization and Management*, by Catheryn Seckler-Hudson, pp. 220–30. Washington: Public Affairs Press, 1948.

———. "The Significance of the Hoover Commission Report." *The Yale Review* 39, 1 (September 1949):1–22.

Arnold, Peri E. "Reorganization and Politics: A Reflection on the Adequacy of Administrative Theory." *Public Administration Review* 34, 3 (May–June 1974):205–11.

———. "The First Hoover Commission and the Managerial Presidency." *The Journal of Politics* 38, 1 (February 1976):46–70.

Bernstein, Barton. "Reluctance and Resistance: Wilson Wyatt and Veterans' Housing in the Truman Administration." *The Register of the Kentucky Historical Society* 65, 1 (January 1967):47–66.

Brant, Irving. "Harry S. Truman." *The New Republic* 112, 18 (30 April 1945):577–79; 19 (7 May 1945):635–38.

Brown, David S. " 'Reforming' the Bureaucracy: Some Suggestions for the New President." *Public Administration Review* 37, 2 (March/April 1977):163–70.

Brownlow, Louis. "Reconversion of the Federal Administrative Machinery from War to Peace." *Public Administration Review* 4, 4 (Autumn 1944):309–26.

Byrnes, James F. "Why We Must Give the President a Clear Road." *American Magazine* 140 (August 1945):20–21, 101–2.

Cleveland, Harlan. "Survival in the Bureaucratic Jungle." In *The Politics of the Federal Bureaucracy*, by Alan A. Altshuler, pp. 121–26. New York: Dodd, Mead and Co., 1968.

Coker, F. W. "Dogmas of Administrative Reform, as Exemplified in the Recent Reorganization in Ohio." *The American Political Science Review* 16, 3 (August

1922):399–411.

Cole, Kenneth R., Jr. "Should Cabinet Departments and Agencies Be More Independent?" In *Has the President Too Much Power? The Proceedings of a Conference for Journalists Sponsored by the Washington Journalism Center,* edited by Charles Roberts, pp. 125–38. New York: Harper's Magazine Press, 1974.

Congressional Quarterly 1 (1945), 2 (1946), 3 (1947), 4 (1948), 5 (1949), 6 (1950).

Cornwell, Elmer E., Jr. "The Truman Presidency." In *The Truman Period as a Research Field,* by Richard S. Kirkendall, pp. 213–55. Columbia: University of Missouri Press, 1967.

Coy, Wayne. "Basic Problems " In "Federal Executive Reorganization Re-Examined: A Symposium, I." *The American Political Science Review,* planned and arranged by Fritz Morstein Marx, 40, 6 (December 1946):1124–37.

Cronin, Thomas E. " 'Everybody Believes in Democracy Until He Gets to the White House. . .': An Examination of White House—Departmental Relations." *Law and Contemporary Problems* 35, 3 (Summer 1970):573–625.

Davidson, Bill. "Labor's Biggest Boss." *Collier's* 120, 18 (1 November 1947):12–13, 84–87.

Denham, Robert, as told to Stacy V. Jones. "And So I Was Purged." *The Saturday Evening Post* 223, 27 (30 December 1950):22–23, 73–74.

Dimock, Marshall E. "The Objectives of Governmental Reorganization." *Public Administration Review* 11, 4 (Autumn 1951):233–41.

———. "Bureaucracy Self-Examined." In *Reader in Bureaucracy,* by Robert K. Merton and others, pp. 397–406. Glencoe, Ill.: The Free Press, 1952.

———. "Expanding Jurisdictions: A Case Study in Bureaucratic Conflict." In *Reader in Bureaucracy,* by Robert K. Merton and others, pp. 282–91. Glencoe, Ill.: The Free Press, 1952.

Durham, G. Homer. "An Appraisal of the Hoover Commission Approach to Administrative Reorganization in the National Government." *The Western Political Quarterly* 2, 4 (December 1949):615–23.

Eckart, Dennis R., and John C. Ries. "The American Presidency." In *People vs. Government: The Responsiveness of American Institutions,* by Leroy N. Rieselbach, pp. 15–65. Bloomington: Indiana University Press, 1975.

Edwards, William H. "The State Reorganization Movement." *Dakota Law Review,* part 1, 1, 1 (January 1927):13–30; part 2, 1, 2 (April 1927):15–41; part 3, 2 (February 1928):17–67; part 4, 2, 2 (May 1928):103–37.

———. "The Public Efficiency Experts." *Political and Social Science Quarterly* 10, 3 (December 1929):301–12.

Egger, Rowland. "Painless Economy and the Mythology of Administrative Reorganization." In *Proceeding of the Forty-Second Annual Conference on Taxation,* edited by Ronald B. Welch, pp. 488–94. Sacramento, Calif.: National Tax Association, 1950.

Farmer, Guy. "Problems of Organization and Administration of the National Labor Relations Board." *The George Washington Law Review* 29 (1960):353–67.

Fesler, James W. "Administrative Literature and the Second Hoover Commission Reports." *The American Political Science Review* 51, 1 (March 1957):135–57.

Finer, Herman. "The Hoover Commission Reports: Part I." *Political Science Quarterly* 64, 3 (September 1949):405–19.

Fischer, John. "Mr. Truman Reorganizes." *Harper's Magazine* 192, 1148 (January 1946):26–35.

Freeman, J. Leiper. "The Bureaucracy in Pressure Politics." *The Annals of the American Academy of Political and Social Science* 319 (September 1958):10–19.

Friedman, Gladys R. "Reorganization Plan No. 1 of 1948: Legislative History and Background." *Social Security Bulletin* 11, 5 (May 1948):15–21.

Fuller, Helen. "Manasco, One-Man Bottleneck." *The New Republic* 113, 24 (10 December 1945):795–96.

Gilpin, Dewitt. "Truman of Battery D." *Salute,* August 1946, pp. 9–10.

Golembiewski, Robert T. "Organization Development in Public Agencies: Perspectives on Theory and Practice." *Public Administration Review* 29, 4 (July/August 1969):367–77.

Graham, George A. "The Presidency and the Executive Office of the President." *The Journal of Politics* 12, 4 (November 1950):599–621.

Gunther, John. "The Man from Missouri." *The Reader's Digest* 46, 278 (June 1945):32–36.

"Has Tax Reorganization Worked?" *Good Government* 70, 4 (July/August 1953):31–34.

Heady, Ferrel. "A New Approach to Federal Executive Reorganization." *The American Political Science Review* 41, 6 (December 1947):1118–26.

———. "The Reorganization Act of 1949." *Public Administration Review* 9, 3 (Summer 1949):165–74.

———. "The Reports of the Hoover Commission." *The Review of Politics* 11, 3 (July 1949):355–78.

———. "The Operation of a Mixed Commission." *The American Political Science Review* 43, 5 (October 1949):940–52.

Herring, E. Pendleton. "Social Forces and the Reorganization of the Federal Bureaucracy." *The Southwestern Social Science Quarterly* 15, 3 (December 1934):185–200.

Herter, Christian. "Our Most Dangerous Lobby." *The Reader's Digest* 51, 305 (September 1947):5–10.

Holden, Matthew, Jr. " 'Imperialism' in Bureaucracy." *The American Political Science Review* 60, 4 (December 1966):943–51.

Huntington, Samuel P. "The Marasmus of the ICC: The Commission, the Railroads, and the Public Interest." *The Yale Law Journal* 51, 4 (April 1952):467–509.

Hyneman, Charles S. "Administrative Reorganization." *The Journal of Politics* 1, 1 (February 1939):62–75.

Jaffe, Louis L. "The Effective Limits of the Administrative Process." In *The Politics of the Federal Bureaucracy,* by Alan A. Altshuler, pp. 324–40. New York: Dodd, Mead and Co., 1968.

Kennedy, Frank R. "The American Medical Association: Power, Purpose, and Politics in Organized Medicine." *The Yale Law Journal* 63, 7 (May 1954):938–1022.

Kirkendall, Richard S. "Truman's Path to Power." *Social Science* 43, 2 (April 1968):67–73.

———. "Harry S Truman: A Missouri Farmer in the Golden Age." *Agricultural History* 48, 4 (October 1974):467–83.

Kraines, Oscar. "The President Versus Congress: The Keep Commission, 1905–1909, First Comprehensive Presidential Inquiry Into Administration." *The Western Political Quarterly* 23, 1 (March 1970):5–54.

Landau, Martin. "Redundancy, Rationality, and the Problem of Duplication and Overlap." *Public Administration Review* 29, 4 (July/August 1969):346–58.

Lawton, Frederick J. "Legislative-Executive Relationships in Budgeting as Viewed by the Executive." In *Legislative-Executive Relationships in the Government of the United States*, edited by O. B. Conaway, pp. 38–49. Washington, D.C.: Graduate School, United States Department of Agriculture, 1954.

Leiserson, Avery. "Political Limitations on Executive Reorganization." In "Federal Executive Reorganization Re-Examined: A Symposium, II," *The American Political Science Review*, planned and arranged by Fritz Morstein Marx, 41, 1 (February 1947):68–84.

Long, Norton E. "Power and Administration." In *Bureaucratic Power in National Politics*, by Francis E. Rourke, pp. 14–23. Boston: Little, Brown and Co., 1965.

———. "Reflections on Presidential Power." *Public Administration Review* 29, 5 (September/October 1969):442–50.

McCormick, Anne O'Hare. "Roosevelt's View of the Big Job." *The New York Times Magazine*, 11 September 1932, pp. 1–2, 16.

McCune, Wesley, and John R. Beal. "The Job That Made Truman President." *Harper's Magazine* 190, 1141 (June 1945):616–21.

Mansfield, Harvey C. "Federal Executive Reorganization: Thirty Years of Experience." *Public Administration Review* 29, 4 (July/August 1969):332–45.

Marsh, Michael. "Ethics in Government." *Editorial Research Reports* 2 (5 December 1951).

Masters, Nicholas A. "Committee Assignments." In *New Perspectives on the House of Representatives*, by Robert L. Peabody and Nelson W. Polsby, pp. 33–58. Chicago: Rand McNally and Co., 1963.

Miles, Rufus E., Jr. "Considerations for a President Bent on Reorganization." *Public Administration Review* 37, 2 (March/April 1977):155–62.

"Modernizing the Government." *The New Republic* 113, 18 (29 October 1945):557–58.

Moore, John R. "The Conservative Coalition in the United States Senate, 1942–1945." *The Journal of Southern History* 33, 3 (August 1967):368–76.

Mosher, Frederick. "Some Notes on Reorganizations in Public Agencies." In *Public Administration and Democracy: Essays in Honor of Paul H. Appleby*, edited by Roscoe C. Martin, pp. 129–50. Syracuse, New York: Syracuse University Press, 1965.

———. "Introduction: The ICP Case and Administrative Research." In *Governmental Reorganizations: Cases and Commentary*, edited by Frederick Mosher, pp. ix–xx. Indianapolis: Bobbs-Merrill, 1967.

"Mr. Smith Stays in Town." *Newsweek* 26, 7 (13 August 1945):29.

Musicus, Milton. "Reappraising Reorganization." *Public Administration Review* 24, 2 (June 1964):107–12.

Neuberger, Richard L. "Nobody Hates the Umpire—Yet." *Collier's* 116, 18 (3 November 1945):11, 26–30.

Neustadt, Richard E. "Congress and the Fair Deal: A Legislative Balance Sheet." *Public Policy* 5 (1954):351–81.

"Only the First Steps Are Being Taken." *Good Government* 69, 6 (January/February 1952):1–6.

Orfield, Lester B. "The Hoover Commission and Federal Executive Reorganization." *Temple Law Quarterly* 24, 2 (October 1950):162–217.

"Payroll Ax Handed to Truman." *Business Week*, 22 December 1945, pp. 17–19.

Penniman, Clara. "Reorganization and the Internal Revenue Service." *Public Administration Review* 21, 3 (Summer 1961):121–30.

Pinkett, Harold T. "The Keep Commission, 1905–1909: A Rooseveltian Effort for Administrative Reform." *The Journal of American History* 52, 2 (September 1965):297–312.

Polenberg, Richard. "Historians and the Liberal Presidency: Recent Appraisals of Roosevelt and Truman." *The South Atlantic Quarterly* 75, 1 (Winter 1976):20–35.

Price, Don K. "The Presidency." In *The Strengthening of American Political Institutions,* by A.S. Mike Monroney and others. Port Washington, N.Y.: Kennikat Press, 1949. Rpt. 1972.

Propeller Club of the United States. "Exemption of the United States Maritime Commission from Reorganization of Agencies." *American Merchant Marine Conference: Resolutions, Nineteenth Annual Meeting* 2 (1945):322.

Public Utilities Fortnightly 36 (11 October 1945):6, 8.

Redford, E. S. "The Value of the Hoover Commission Reports to the Educator." *The American Political Science Review* 44, 2 (June 1950):283–98.

Rhodes, Richard. "Harry's Last Hurrah." *Harper's Magazine* 240, 1436 (January 1970):48–58.

Roback, Herbert. "Do We Need a Department of Science and Technology." *Science* 165 (4 July 1969):36–43.

Rogers, Lindsay. "Reorganization: Post Mortem Notes." *Political Science Quarterly* 53, 2 (June 1938):161-72.

"Rough Going for Harry." *Newsweek* 34, 9 (29 August 1949):14.

Rourke, Francis E. "The Politics of Administrative Organization: A Case History." *The Journal of Politics* 19, 3 (August 1957):461–78.

Rowe, James, Jr. "Cooperation or Conflict?—The President's Relationships with an Opposition Congress." *The Georgetown Law Journal* 36, 1 (November 1947):1–15.

Scher, Seymour. "The Politics of Agency Organization." *Western Political Quarterly* 15, 2 (June 1962):328–44.

Schaffer, Samuel. "Reorganization: Bill Benton Blitz." *Newsweek* 35, 23 (5 June 1950):21.

Shalett, Sidney. "The Return of Herbert Hoover." *The American Magazine* 144, 3 (September 1947):30–31.

Simon, Herbert A. "The Proverbs of Administration." *Public Administration Review* 6, 1 (Winter 1946):53–67.

"Smith, Harold Dewey." *Current Biography: Who's News and Why, 1943,* pp. 710–13. New York: H. W. Wilson Co., 1944.

Snyder, John W. "The Reorganization of the Bureau of Internal Revenue." *Public Administration Review* 12, 4 (Autumn 1952):221–33.

Soth, Lauren. "Mr. Hoover's Department of Agriculture." *Journal of Farm Economics* 31, 2 (May 1949):201–12.

Steinberg, Alfred. "Watchdog on Washington Waste." *The Reader's Digest* 61 (August 1952):121–24.

Strout, Richard L. "Harry S. Truman Sets His Course." *Tomorrow,* August 1945, pp. 17–20.

Theoharis, Athan. "The Truman Presidency: Trial and Error." *Wisconsin Magazine of History* 55, 1 (Autumn 1971):49–58.

"Truman Plans Consolidation of Independent Agencies with Cabinet Members

Responsible for Administration." *NAM News* 12, 23 (26 May 1945):1–2.

Twohey Analysis of Newspaper Opinion 7 (1945), 10 (1948), 11 (1949), 12 (1950).

Waldo, Dwight. "Scope of the Theory of Public Administration." In *Theory and Practice of Public Administration: Scope, Objectives, and Methods,* by James C. Charlesworth, pp. 1–26. Philadelphia: American Academy of Political and Social Science, 1968.

Walker, Harvey. "Theory and Practice in State Administrative Organization." *National Municipal Review* 19 (April 1930):249–54.

"Warren, Lindsay Carter." *Current Biography: Who's News and Why, 1949,* pp. 624–26. New York: The H. W. Wilson Co., 1950.

Watson, Goodwin. "Bureaucracy as Citizens See It." *The Journal of Social Issues* 1, 4 (1945):4–13.

Wood, Robert. "When Government Works." *The Public Interest* 18 (Winter 1970): 39–51.

Zink, Harold. "Government Reform in the U.S.A." *The Political Quarterly* 21, 1 (January–March 1950): 69–79.

F. Pamphlets and Newsletters

American Farm Bureau Federation. *Official News Letter* (1945).

"Can the County Government Be Efficient." *Kansas City's Public Affairs* 30 (29 March 1923).

Citizens Committee for the Hoover Report. *Circular Letter No. 2* (10 April 1950).

———. *Round Robin No. 9* (9 October 1950).

———. *Washington Watchdog No. 34* (28 April 1952).

———. *Reorganization News* (April 1952).

———. *Action Sheet: For Immediate Action* (28 April 1952).

"A County Budget?" *Kansas City's Public Affairs* 17 (28 December 1922).

Godfrey, E. Drexel, Jr. *The Transfer of the Children's Bureau.* The Inter-University Case Program, CPAC no. 21. Indianapolis: Bobbs-Merrill Co., 1952.

Illinois Citizens for the Hoover Report. "Reorganization Plans #2, 3 and 4." *Newsletter* (May 1952).

"Modernize County Government." *Kansas City's Public Affairs* 98 (17 July 1924).

Republican National Committee, Research Division. *Reorganization of the Executive Branch: The Problem Before Congress in 1945.* Washington: 28 September 1945.

———. *Reorganization Plan No. 3 of 1947: Memorandum on the Pros and Cons.* Washington: 10 June 1947.

G. Dissertations and Manuscripts

Biederman, Dan. "Harold Smith and the Growth of the Bureau of the Budget, 1939–1946." Senior thesis presented to the faculty of the Department of Politics and the Woodrow Wilson School of Public and International Affairs, Princeton University, April 1975.

Edwards, Nancy Ann. "Congress and Administrative Reorganization." Ph.D. dissertation, Columbia University, 1955.

Freedman, Leonard. "Group Opposition to Public Housing." Ph.D. dissertation, University of California, 1959.

Hinchey, Mary H. "The Frustration of the New Deal Revival, 1944–46." Ph.D. dissertation, University of Missouri, 1965.

Landis, James M. "Report on Regulatory Agencies to the President-Elect." December 1960.

MacEachron, David W. "The Role of the United States Department of Labor." Ph.D. dissertation, Harvard University, 1953.

Miles, Carroll F. "The Office of the Secretary of Defense, 1947–1953: A Study in Administrative Theory." Ph.D. dissertation, Harvard University, 1956.

Pak, Chong Mo. "The Dynamics of Governmental Reorganization." Ph.D. dissertation, University of Southern California, 1962.

Parker, Daniel P. "Neither Left Nor Right: The Political Philosophy of Harry S. Truman." Manuscript in the possession of the Harry S. Truman Library.

Poen, Monte. "The Truman Administration and National Health Insurance." Ph.D. dissertation, University of Missouri, 1967.

Pow, Alexander S. "The Comptroller General and the General Accounting Office of the U.S." Ph.D. dissertation, New York University, 1960.

Pritchard, Robert L. "Southern Politics and the Truman Administration: Georgia as a Test Case." Ph.D. dissertation, University of California, Los Angeles, 1970.

Ramsey, John W. "The Director of the Bureau of the Budget as a Presidential Aide, 1921–1952: With Emphasis on the Truman Years." Ph.D. dissertation, University of Missouri, 1967.

Rourke, Francis E. "Reorganization of the Labor Department." Ph.D. dissertation, University of Minnesota, 1951.

Rudoni, Dorothy. "Harry S. Truman: A Study in Presidential Perspective." Ph.D. dissertation, Southern Illinois University, 1968.

Schauffler, Peter P. "A Study of the Legislative Veto." Ph.D. dissertation, Harvard University, 1956.

Shelton, James H. "The Tax Scandals of the 1950's." Ph.D. dissertation, American University, 1971.

Shor, Edgar L. "The Role of the Secretary of Labor." Ph.D. dissertation, University of Chicago, 1954.

Sloan, Royal D., Jr. "The Extension of Civil Service in the Bureau of Internal Revenue: 1952." Master's thesis, University of Chicago, 1955.

Street, Kenneth W. "Harry S. Truman: His Role as Legislative Leader, 1945–1948." Ph.D. dissertation, University of Texas, 1963.

Trotter, Samuel E. "A Study of Public Housing in the United States." Ph.D. dissertation, University of Alabama, 1956.

Westrate, John L. "The Administrative Theories and Practices of Herbert Hoover." Ph.D. dissertation, University of Chicago, 1963.

Wheaton, William L. "The Evolution of Federal Housing Programs." Ph.D. dissertation, University of Chicago, 1953.

H. Speeches

Arnold, Peri. "Executive Reorganization and Administrative Theory: The Origin of the Managerial Presidency." Paper delivered at the American Political Science Association Convention, 2–5 September 1976.

Cronin, Thomas E. "The Textbook Presidency and Political Science." Paper delivered at the American Political Science Association Convention, 7–12 September 1970. Printed in U.S., *Congressional Record*, vol. 116, pt. 26 (1972):34915–28.

Fesler, James. Speech at Air War College, 12 October 1967. Printed in U.S., Congress, Senate, Committee on Government Operations, *Establish a Commission on the Organization and Management of the Executive Branch*. Hearing, 90th Cong., 2d sess., 22–24, 31 January, 1 February, 4 April, 15 May 1968. Washington: Government Printing Office, 1968.

I. Newspapers

The Sun (Baltimore)
Boonville Daily News (Missouri)
The CIO News
Committee Reporter (Citizens Committee for the Hoover Report)
Detroit Free Press
The Examiner (Independence, Mo.)
The Kansas City Star
The Kansas City Times
Lee's Summit Journal (Missouri)
New York Herald-Tribune
The New York Times
Senate Majority News (Republican party)
The Times-Herald (Washington)
The Washington Daily News
The Washington Post

J. Government Documents

1. Presidential messages and plans

U.S., President, 1945–1953 (Truman). *Message from the President of the United States Transmitting Reorganization Plan No. 1 of 1946*. 79th Cong., 2d sess., House, Document No. 594. Washington: Government Printing Office, 1946.
———. *Plan No. 2 of 1946*. Document No. 595.
———. *Plan No. 3 of 1946*. Document No. 596.
———. *Plan No. 1 of 1947*. 80th Cong., 1st sess., House, Document No. 230. 1947.
———. *Plan No. 2 of 1947*. Document No. 231.
———. *Plan No. 3 of 1947*. Document No. 270.
———. *Plan No. 1 of 1948*. 80th Cong., 2d sess., House, Document No. 499. 1948.
———. *Message from the President of the United States Transmitting Recommendations of an Initial Program of Reorganization of the Executive Branch of the Government*. 81st Cong., 1st sess., House, Document No. 221. Washington: Government Printing Office, 1949.
———. *Plan No. 1 of 1949*. 81st Cong., 1st sess., House, Document No. 222. 1949.
———. *Plan No. 2 of 1949*. Document No. 223.
———. *Plan No. 3 of 1949*. Document No. 224.
———. *Plan No. 4 of 1949*. Document No. 225.
———. *Plan No. 5 of 1949*. Document No. 226.
———. *Plan No. 6 of 1949*. Document No. 227.

———. *Plan No. 7 of 1949.* Document No. 228.
———. *Plan No. 8 of 1949.* Document No. 262.
———. *Plan No. 1 of 1950.* 81st Cong., 2d sess., House, Document No. 505. 1950.
———. *Plan No. 2 of 1950.* Document No. 506.
———. *Plan No. 3 of 1950.* Document No. 507.
———. *Plan No. 4 of 1950.* Document No. 508.
———. *Plan No. 5 of 1950.* Document No. 509.
———. *Plan No. 6 of 1950.* Document No. 510.
———. *Plan No. 7 of 1950.* Document No. 511.
———. *Plan No. 8 of 1950.* Document No. 512.
———. *Plan No. 9 of 1950.* Document No. 513.
———. *Plan No. 10 of 1950.* Document No. 514.
———. *Plan No. 11 of 1950.* Document No. 515.
———. *Plan No. 12 of 1950.* Document No. 516.
———. *Plan No. 13 of 1950.* Document No. 517.
———. *Plan No. 14 of 1950.* Document No. 518.
———. *Plan No. 15 of 1950.* Document No. 520.
———. *Plan No. 16 of 1950.* Document No. 521.
———. *Plan No. 17 of 1950.* Document No. 522.
———. *Plan No. 18 of 1950.* Document No. 523.
———. *Plan No. 19 of 1950.* Document No. 524.
———. *Plan No. 20 of 1950.* Document No. 525.
———. *Plan No. 21 of 1950.* Document No. 526.
———. *Plan No. 22 of 1950.* Document No. 587.
———. *Plan No. 23 of 1950.* Document No. 588.
———. *Plan No. 24 of 1950.* Document No. 589.
———. *Plan No. 25 of 1950.* Document No. 590.
———. *Plan No. 26 of 1950.* Document No. 609.
———. *Plan No. 27 of 1950.* Document No. 610.
———. *Plan No. 1 of 1951.* 82d Cong., 1st sess., House, Document No. 60. 1951.
———. *Plan No. 1 of 1952.* 82d Cong., 2d sess., House, Document No. 327. 1952.
———. *Plan No. 2 of 1952.* Document No. 425.
———. *Plan No. 3 of 1952.* Document No. 426.
———. *Plan No. 4 of 1952.* Document No. 427.
———. *Plan No. 5 of 1952.* Document No. 447.

2. *Congressional hearings*

U.S., Congress. House. Committee on Expenditures in the Executive Departments. *President's Message* [of 9 December 1932] *on Consolidation of Government Agencies.* 72d Cong., 2d sess., 14, 20, 22, 23 December 1932. Washington: Government Printing Office, 1932.

———. House. Committee on Expenditures in the Executive Departments. *To Provide for Reorganizing Agencies of the Government* [Reorganization Act of 1945]. 79th Cong., 1st sess., 4–5 September 1945. Washington: Government Printing Office, 1945.

———. Senate. Subcommittee of Committee on the Judiciary. *Reorganization of the Executive Departments.* 79th Cong., 1st sess., 6–18 September 1945. Washington:

Government Printing Office, 1945.

—————. House. Committee on Expenditures in the Executive Departments. *Reorganization Plans 1, 2, and 3 of 1946*. 79th Cong., 2d sess., 4–13 June 1946. Washington: Government Printing Office, 1946.

—————. Senate. Committee on the Judiciary. *President's Plan for Reorganization of Executive Departments* [Plans 1, 2, and 3, 1946]. 79th Cong., 2d sess., 14–27 June 1946. Washington: Government Printing Office, 1946.

—————. House. Committee on Expenditures in the Executive Departments. *Reorganization Plans Nos. 1 and 2 of 1947*. 80th Cong., 1st sess., 21–27 May 1947. Washington: Government Printing Office, 1947.

—————. House. *Reorganization Plan No. 3 of 1947*. 80th Cong., 1st sess., 9–10 June 1947. Washington: Government Printing Office, 1947.

—————. House. Committee on Expenditures in the Executive Departments. *Hearings, on H.R. 775 for the Establishment of the Commission on Organization of the Executive Branch of the Government*. 80th Cong., 1st sess., 25 June 1947. Washington: Government Printing Office, 1947.

—————. Senate. Committee on Expenditures in the Executive Departments. *Reestablishing Registers of Land Offices*. 80th Cong., 1st sess., 10 March 1947. Washington: Government Printing Office, 1947.

—————. Senate. Committee on Labor and Public Welfare, Subcommittee on Labor. *The President's Reorganization Plan No. 2 of 1947*. 80th Cong., 1st sess., 16–17 June 1947. Washington: Government Printing Office, 1947.

—————. Senate. Committee on Banking and Currency. *Reorganization Plan No. 3 of 1947*. 80th Cong., 1st sess., 18, 19 June 1947. Washington: Government Printing Office, 1947.

—————. Senate. Committee on Expenditures in the Executive Departments. *Hearing, on S.164 Commission on Organization of the Executive Branch of the Government*. 80th Cong., 1st sess., 13 March 1947. Washington: Government Printing Office, 1947.

—————. House. Committee on Expenditures in the Executive Departments. *Reorganization Plan No. 1 of 1948*. 80th Cong., 2d sess., 5–7 February 1948. Washington: Government Printing Office, 1948.

—————. House. Subcommittee of Committee on Appropriations. *Second Supplemental Appropriation Bill for 1948, Part 2 . . . Commission on Organization of the Executive Branch*. 80th Cong., 2d sess., Washington: Government Printing Office, 1948.

—————. Senate. Subcommittee of Committee on Labor and Public Welfare. *Reorganization Plan No. 1 of 1948*. 80th Cong., 2d sess., 27–28 February 1948. Washington: Government Printing Office, 1948.

—————. House. Committee on Expenditures in the Executive Departments. *Reorganization of Government Agencies* [Reorganization Act of 1949]. 81st Cong., 1st sess., 24–31 January 1949. Washington: Government Printing Office, 1949.

—————. House. Committee on Expenditures in the Executive Departments. *Reorganization Plan No. 2 of 1949*. 81st Cong., 1st sess., 2–4 August 1949. Washington: Government Printing Office, 1949.

—————. Senate. Committee on Expenditures in the Executive Departments. *Reorganization Act of 1949*. 81st Cong., 1st sess., 2–15 February 1949. Washington: Government Printing Office, 1949.

—————. Senate. Committee on Expenditures in the Executive Departments. *Reorga-*

nization Plans of 1949. 81st Cong., 1st sess., 30 June 1949. Washington: Government Printing Office, 1949.

———. Senate. Committee on Expenditures in the Executive Departments. *Reorganization Plans No. 1 and No. 2 of 1949.* 81st Cong., 1st sess., 21, 22, 25–29 July, 3 August 1949. Washington: Government Printing Office, 1949.

———. House. Committee on Expenditures in the Executive Departments. *Reorganization Plan No. 5 of 1950.* 81st Cong., 2d sess., 26, 27 April 1950. Washington: Government Printing Office, 1950.

———. House. Committee on Expenditures in the Executive Departments. *Reorganization Plan No. 6 of 1950.* 81st Cong., 2d sess., 30–31 March, 3 April 1950. Washington: Government Printing Office, 1950.

———. House. Committee on Expenditures in the Executive Departments. *Reorganization Plan No. 7 of 1950.* 81st Cong., 2d sess., 24–25 April 1950. Washington: Government Printing Office, 1950.

———. House. Committee on Expenditures in the Executive Departments. *Reorganization Plan No. 12 of 1950.* 81st Cong., 2d sess., 21–23 March 1950. Washington: Government Printing Office, 1950.

———. House. Committee on Expenditures in the Executive Departments. *Reorganization Plan No. 24 of 1950.* 81st Cong., 2d sess., 15–20 June 1950. Washington: Government Printing Office, 1950.

———. House. Committee on Expenditures in the Executive Departments. *Reorganization Plan No. 27 of 1950.* 81st Cong., 2d sess., 15, 19–20 June 1950. Washington: Government Printing Office, 1950.

———. House. Select Committee on Lobbying Activities. *Housing Lobby.* Part 2. 81st Cong., 2d sess., 19–21, 25–28 April, 3, 5, 17 May 1950. Washington: Government Printing Office, 1950.

———. House. Select Committee on Lobbying Activities. *Legislative Activities of Executive Agencies.* Part 10. 30 March, 5 May, 26, 28 July 1950. Washington: Government Printing Office, 1950.

———. Senate. Committee on Expenditures in the Executive Departments. *Reorganization Plan No. 1 of 1950.* 81st Cong., 2d sess., 11, 12 April 1950. Washington: Government Printing Office, 1950.

———. Senate. Committee on Expenditures in the Executive Departments. *Reorganization Plan No. 4 of 1950.* 81st Cong., 2d sess., 2, 3 May 1950. Washington: Government Printing Office, 1950.

———. Senate. Committee on Expenditures in the Executive Departments. *Reorganization Plan No. 5 of 1950.* 81st Cong., 2d sess., 27 April 1950. Washington: Government Printing Office, 1950.

———. Senate. Committee on Expenditures in the Executive Departments. *Reorganization Plans Nos. 7, 8, 9, and 11 of 1950.* 81st Cong., 2d sess., 24–26 April 1950.

———. Senate. Committee on Expenditures in the Executive Departments. *Reorganization Plan No. 12 of 1950.* 81st Cong., 2d sess., 4–6 April 1950. Washington: Government Printing Office, 1950.

———. Senate. Committee on Expenditures in the Executive Departments. *Reorganization Plans Nos. 17 and 18 of 1950.* 81st Cong., 2d sess., 16 May 1950. Washington: Government Printing Office, 1950.

———. Senate. Committee on Expenditures in the Executive Departments. *Reorga-*

nization Plan No. 21 of 1950. 81st Cong., 2d sess., 8–9 May 1950. Washington: Government Printing Office, 1950.

———. Senate. Committee on Expenditures in the Executive Departments. *Reorganization Plan No. 22 of 1950.* 81st Cong., 2d sess., 28–29 June 1950. Washington: Government Printing Office, 1950.

———. Senate. Committee on Expenditures in the Executive Departments. *Reorganization Plan No. 24 of 1950.* 81st Cong., 2d sess., 14–15 June 1950. Washington: Government Printing Office, 1950.

———. Senate. Committee on Expenditures in the Executive Departments. *Reorganization Plan No. 27 of 1950.* 81st Cong., 2d sess., 6–7 July 1950. Washington: Government Printing Office, 1950.

———. House. Committee on Expenditures in the Executive Departments. *Hearings, Reorganization Plan No. 1 of 1951.* 82d Cong., 1st sess., 2, 5 March 1951. Washington: Government Printing Office, 1951.

———. Senate. Committee on Expenditures in the Executive Departments. *Hearings, Reorganization Plan No. 1 of 1951.* 82d Cong., 1st sess., 21, 22 March, 3 April 1951. Washington: Government Printing Office, 1951.

———. House. Committee on Expenditures in the Executive Departments. *Hearings, Reorganization Plan No. 1 of 1952.* 82d Cong., 2d sess., 18–23 January 1952. Washington: Government Printing Office, 1952.

———. Senate. Committee on Government Operations. *Hearings, Reorganization Plan No. 1 of 1952.* 82d Cong., 2d sess., 30 January–4 March 1952. Washington: Government Printing Office, 1952.

———. Senate. Committee on Government Operations. *Hearings, Reorganization Plans Nos. 2, 3, and 4 of 1952.* 82d Cong., 2d sess., 14 May–4 June 1952. Washington: Government Printing Office, 1952.

———. Senate. Committee on Government Operations. *Hearings, Reorganization Plan No. 5 of 1952.* 82d Cong., 2d sess., 15, 20 May 1952. Washington: Government Printing Office, 1952.

———. House. Committee on Government Operations. *To Amend the Reorganization Act of 1949.* 83d Cong., 1st sess., 27 January 1953. Washington: Government Printing Office, 1953.

———. Senate. Committee on Government Operations, Subcommittee on Reorganization. *Reorganization Plan No. 2 of 1953.* 83d Cong., 1st sess., 12–13, 18 May 1953. Washington: Government Printing Office, 1953.

———. House. Committee on Government Operations. *Extending Authority for Executive Reorganization.* 90th Cong., 2d sess., 13 March 1968. Washington: Government Printing Office, 1968.

———. Senate. Committee on Government Operations, Subcommittee on Executive Reorganization. *Modernizing the Federal Government.* 90th Cong., 2d sess., 22–24, 31 January, 1 February, 4 April, 15 May 1968. Washington: Government Printing Office, 1968.

3. *Committee reports*

U.S., Congress. Senate. Special Committee Investigating the National Defense Program. *Investigation of the National Defense Program.* 77th Cong., 2d sess., 1942, Report No. 480. Washington: Government Printing Office, 1942.

———. Senate. Special Committee Investigating the National Defense Program.

Investigation of the National Defense Program. 78th Cong., 1st sess., 1943, Report No. 10. Washington: Government Printing Office, 1943.

————. House. Committee on Expenditures in the Executive Departments. *Reorganizations in Executive Branch* [Reorganization Act of 1945]. 79th Cong., 1st sess., 1945, Report No. 971. Washington: Government Printing Office, 1945.

————. House. Committee of Conference. *Reorganizations in Executive Branch* [Conference Report on Reorganization Act of 1945]. 79th Cong., 1st sess., 1945, Report No. 1378. Washington: Government Printing Office, 1945.

————. Senate. Committee on the Judiciary. *Reorganization of Government Agencies* [Reorganization Act of 1945]. 79th Cong., 1st sess., 1945, Report No. 638. Washington: Government Printing Office, 1945.

————. House. Committee on Expenditures in the Executive Departments. *Reorganization Plan No. 1 of 1946*. 79th Cong., 2d sess., 1946, Report No. 2326. Washington: Government Printing Office, 1946.

————. House. Committee on Expenditures in the Executive Departments. *Reorganization Plan No. 2 of 1946*. 79th Cong., 2d sess, 1946, Report No. 2327. Washington: Government Printing Office, 1946.

————. House. Committee on Expenditures in the Executive Departments. *Reorganization Plan No. 3 of 1946*. 79th Cong., 2d sess., 1946, Report No. 2328. Washington: Government Printing Office, 1946.

————. Senate. Committee on the Judiciary. *Reorganization Plan No. 1* [1946]. 79th Cong., 2d sess., 1946, Report No. 1670. Washington: Government Printing Office, 1946.

————. Senate. Committee on the Judiciary. *Reorganization Plan No. 2* [1946]. 79th Cong., 2d sess., 1946, Report No. 1671. Washington: Government Printing Office, 1946.

————. Senate. Committee on the Judiciary. *Reorganization Plan No. 3* [1946]. 79th Cong., 2d sess., 1946, Report No. 1672. Washington: Government Printing Office, 1946.

————. House. Committee on Expenditures in the Executive Departments. *Reorganization Plan No. 2 of 1947*. 80th Cong., 1st sess., 1947, Report No. 499. Washington: Government Printing Office, 1947.

————. House. Committee on Expenditures in the Executive Departments. *Reorganization Plan No. 3 of 1947*. 80th Cong., 1st sess., 1947, Report No. 580. Washington: Government Printing Office, 1947.

————. House. Committee on Expenditures in the Executive Departments. *Establish a Commission on the Organization of the Executive Branch of the Government*. 80th Cong., 1st sess., 1947, Report No. 704. Washington: Government Printing Office, 1947.

————. Senate. Committee on Labor and Public Welfare. *Reorganization Plan No. 2 of 1947*. 80th Cong., 1st sess., 1947, Report No. 320. Washington: Government Printing Office, 1947.

————. Senate. Committee on Banking and Currency. *Reorganization Plan No. 3 of 1947*. 80th Cong., 1st sess., 1947, Report No. 400. Washington: Government Printing Office, 1947.

————. Senate. Committee on Expenditures in the Executive Departments. *Commission on Organization of the Executive Branch of the Government*. 80th Cong., 1st sess., 1947, Report No. 344. Washington: Government Printing Office, 1947.

————. House. Committee on Expenditures in the Executive Departments. *Reorganization Plan No. 1 of 1948.* 80th Cong., 2d sess., 1948, Report No. 1368. Washington: Government Printing Office, 1948.

————. Senate. Committee on Labor and Public Welfare. *Reorganization Plan No. 1 of January 19, 1948.* 80th Cong., 2d sess., 1948, Report No. 967. Washington: Government Printing Office, 1948.

————. House. Committee on Expenditures in the Executive Departments. *Reorganization Act of 1949.* 81st Cong., 1st sess., 1949, Report No. 23. Washington: Government Printing Office, 1949.

————. House. Committee of Conference. *Reorganization Act of 1949.* 81st Cong., 1st sess., 1949, Report No. 843. Washington: Government Printing Office, 1949.

————. House. Committee on Expenditures in the Executive Departments. *Reorganization Plan No. 2 of 1949.* 81st Cong., 1st sess., 1949, Report No. 1204. Washington: Government Printing Office, 1949.

————. Senate. Committee on Expenditures in the Executive Departments. *Reorganization Act of 1949.* 81st Cong., 1st sess., 1949, Report No. 232. Washington: Government Printing Office, 1949.

————. Senate. Committee on Expenditures in the Executive Departments. *Reorganization Plan No. 1 of 1949.* 81st Cong., 1st sess., 1949, Report No. 851. Washington: Government Printing Office, 1949.

————. Senate. Committee on Expenditures in the Executive Departments. *Reorganization Plan No. 2 of 1949.* 81st Cong., 1st sess., 1949, Report No. 852. Washington: Government Printing Office, 1949.

————. Senate. Committee on Expenditures in the Executive Departments. *Reorganization Plan No. 7 of 1949.* 81st Cong., 1st sess., 1949, Report No. 927. Washington: Government Printing Office, 1949.

————. House. Committee on Expenditures in the Executive Departments. *Reorganization Plan No. 5 of 1950.* 81st Cong., 2d sess., 1950, Report No. 1976. Washington: Government Printing Office, 1950.

————. House. Committee on Expenditures in the Executive Departments. *Reorganization Plan No. 6 of 1950.* 81st Cong., 2d sess., 1950, Report No. 1907. Washington: Government Printing Office, 1950.

————. House. Committee on Expenditures in the Executive Departments. *Reorganization Plan No. 7 of 1950.* 81st Cong., 2d sess., 1950, Report No. 1971. Washington: Government Printing Office, 1950.

————. House. Committee on Expenditures in the Executive Departments. *Reorganization Plan No. 12 of 1950.* 81st Cong., 2d sess., 1950, Report No. 1852. Washington: Government Printing Office, 1950.

————. House. Committee on Expenditures in the Executive Departments. *Reorganization Plan No. 18 of 1950.* 81st Cong., 2d sess., 1950, Report No. 1947. Washington: Government Printing Office, 1950.

————. House. Committee on Expenditures in the Executive Departments. *Reorganization Plan No. 24 of 1950.* 81st Cong., 2d sess., 1950, Report No. 2321. Washington: Government Printing Office, 1950.

————. House. Committee on Expenditures in the Executive Departments. *Reorganization Plan No. 27 of 1950.* 81st Cong., 2d sess., 1950, Report No. 2320. Washington: Government Printing Office, 1950.

————. House. Select Committee on Lobbying Activities. *United States Savings and*

Loan League. 81st Cong., 2d sess., 1950, Report No. 3139. Washington: Government Printing Office, 1950.

————. Senate. Committee on Expenditures in the Executive Departments. *Reorganization Plan No. 1 of 1950.* 81st Cong., 2d sess., 1950, Report No. 1518. Washington: Government Printing Office, 1950.

————. Senate. Committee on Expenditures in the Executive Departments. *Reorganization Plan No. 4 of 1950.* 81st Cong., 2d sess., 1950, Report No. 1566. Washington: Government Printing Office, 1950.

————. Senate. Committee on Expenditures in the Executive Departments. *Reorganization Plan No. 5 of 1950.* 81st Cong., 2d sess., 1950, Report No. 1561. Washington: Government Printing Office, 1950.

————. Senate. Committee on Expenditures in the Executive Departments. *Reorganization Plan No. 6 of 1950.* 81st Cong., 2d sess., 1950, Report No. 1684. Washington: Government Printing Office, 1950.

————. Senate. Committee on Expenditures in the Executive Departments. *Reorganization Plan No. 7 of 1950.* 81st Cong., 2d sess., 1950, Report No. 1567. Washington: Government Printing Office, 1950.

————. Senate. Committee on Expenditures in the Executive Departments. *Reorganization Plan No. 8 of 1950.* 81st Cong., 2d sess., 1950, Report No. 1562. Washington: Government Printing Office, 1950.

————. Senate. Committee on Expenditures in the Executive Departments. *Reorganization Plan No. 9 of 1950.* 81st Cong., 2d sess., 1950, Report No. 1563. Washington: Government Printing Office, 1950.

————. Senate. Committee on Expenditures in the Executive Departments. *Reorganization Plan No. 11 of 1950.* 81st Cong., 2d sess., 1950, Report No. 1564. Washington: Government Printing Office, 1950.

————. Senate. Committee on Expenditures in the Executive Departments. *Reorganization Plan No. 12 of 1950.* 81st Cong., 2d sess., 1950, Report No. 1516. Washington: Government Printing Office, 1950.

————. Senate. Committee on Expenditures in the Executive Departments. *Reorganization Plan No. 17 of 1950.* 81st Cong., 2d sess., 1950, Report No. 1676. Washington: Government Printing Office, 1950.

————. Senate. Committee on Expenditures in the Executive Departments. *Reorganization Plan No. 18 of 1950.* 81st Cong., 2d sess., 1950, Report No. 1675. Washington: Government Printing Office, 1950.

————. Senate. Committee on Expenditures in the Executive Departments. *Reorganization Plan No. 21 of 1950.* 81st Cong., 2d sess., 1950, Report No. 1674. Washington: Government Printing Office, 1950.

————. Senate. Committee on Expenditures in the Executive Departments. *Reorganization Plan No. 22 of 1950.* 81st Cong., 2d sess., 1950, Report No. 1936. Washington: Government Printing Office, 1950.

————. Senate. Committee on Expenditures in the Executive Departments. *Reorganization Plan No. 24 of 1950.* 81st Cong., 2d sess., 1950, Report No. 1868. Washington: Government Printing Office, 1950.

————. Senate. Committee on Expenditures in the Executive Departments. *Reorganization Plan No. 27 of 1950.* 81st Cong., 2d sess., 1950, Report No. 1943. Washington: Government Printing Office, 1950.

————. House. Committee on Expenditures in the Executive Departments. *Reorga-*

nization Plan No. 1 of 1951. 82d Cong., 1st sess., 1951, Report No. 188. Washington: Government Printing Office, 1951.

———. Senate. Committee on Banking and Currency. *Study of Reconstruction Finance Corporation: Favoritism and Influence.* 82d Cong., 1st sess., 1951, Report No. 76. Washington: Government Printing Office, 1951.

———. Senate. Committee on Expenditures in the Executive Departments. *Reorganization Plan No. 1 of 1951, Providing for the Reorganization of the Reconstruction Finance Corporation.* 82d Cong., 1st sess., 1951, Report No. 213. Washington: Government Printing Office, 1951.

———. House. Committee on Expenditures in the Executive Departments. *Reorganization Plan No. 1 of 1952 (Bureau of Internal Revenue).* 82d Cong., 2d sess., 1952, Report No. 1271. Washington: Government Printing Office, 1952.

———. Senate. Committee on Government Operations. *Reorganization Plan No. 1 of 1952, Providing for Reorganizations in the Bureau of Internal Revenue.* 82d Cong., 2d sess., 1952, Report No. 1259. Washington: Government Printing Office, 1952.

———. Senate. Committee on Government Operations. *Reorganization Plan No. 2 of 1952, Providing for Reorganization in the Post Office Department.* 82d Cong., 2d sess., 1952, Report No. 1747. Washington: Government Printing Office, 1952.

———. Senate. Committee on Government Operations. *Reorganization Plan No. 3 of 1952, Providing for Reorganizations in Bureau of Customs of the Department of the Treasury.* 82d Cong., 2d sess., 1952, Report No. 1748. Washington: Government Printing Office, 1952.

———. Senate. Committee on Government Operations. *Reorganization Plan No. 4 of 1952, Providing for Reorganization in the Department of Justice.* 82d Cong., 2d sess., 1952, Report No. 1749. Washington: Government Printing Office, 1952.

———. Senate. Committee on Government Operations. *Reorganization Plan No. 5 of 1952—Reorganization of the Government of the District of Columbia.* 82d Cong., 2d sess., 1952, Report No. 1735. Washington: Government Printing Office, 1952.

4. Statutes

U.S., *Statutes at Large.* 79th Cong., 1st sess., 1945, vol. 59, part 1, Public Law 263 [Reorganization Act of 1945], pp. 613–19.

———. *Statutes at Large.* 80th Cong., 1st sess., 1947, vol. 61, part 1, Public Law 162 [Commission on Organization of the Executive Branch of the Government], pp. 246–48.

———. *Statutes at Large.* 81st Cong., 1st sess., 1949, vol. 63, part 1, Public Law 109 [Reorganization Act of 1949], pp. 203–7.

5. Congressional record

U.S., *Congressional Record,* vols. 84 (1939), 87 (1941), 89 (1943), 91 (1945), 92 (1946), 93 (1947), 94 (1948), 95 (1949), 96 (1950), 97 (1951), 98 (1952).

6. Miscellaneous

U.S., President's Advisory Committee on the Merchant Marine. *Report of the President's Advisory Committee on the Merchant Marine.* Washington: Government Printing Office, 1947.

7. Commission reports

U.S., Commission on Organization of the Executive Branch of the Government,

Task Force on Natural Resources. *Organization and Policy in the Field of Natural Resources: A Report with Recommendations Prepared for the Commission on Organization of the Executive Branch of the Government.* Washington: Government Printing Office, 1949.

———. Commission on Organization of the Executive Branch of the Government. *Reorganization of the Department of the Interior: A Report to the Congress by the Commission on Organization of the Executive Branch of the Government.* Washington: Government Printing Office, 1949.

———. Commission on Organization of the Executive Branch of the Government. *Department of Commerce: A Report to the Congress by the Commission on Organization of the Executive Branch of the Government.* Washington: Government Printing Office, 1949.

———. Commission on Organization of the Executive Branch of the Government. *Reorganization of Federal Medical Activities: A Report to the Congress by the Commission on Organization of the Executive Branch of the Government.* Washington: Government Printing Office, 1949.

———. Commission on Organization of the Executive Branch of the Government. *Social Security and Education, Indian Affairs: A Report to the Congress by the Commission on Organization of the Executive Branch of the Government.* Washington: Government Printing Office, 1949.

———. Commission on Organization of the Executive Branch of the Government. *Department of Labor: A Report to the Congress by the Commission on Organization of the Executive Branch of the Government.* Washington: Government Printing Office, 1949.

———. Commission on Organization of the Executive Branch of the Government. *Personnel Management: A Report to the Congress by the Commission on Organization of the Executive Branch of the Government.* Washington: Government Printing Office, 1949.

———. Commission on Organization of the Executive Branch of the Government. *The Independent Regulatory Commissions: A Report to the Congress by the Commission on Organization of the Executive Branch of the Government.* Washington: Government Printing Office, 1949.

———. Commission on Organization of the Executive Branch of the Government. *Reorganization of Federal Business Enterprises: A Report to the Congress by the Commission on Organization of the Executive Branch of the Government.* Washington: Government Printing Office, 1949.

———. Commission on Organization of the Executive Branch of the Government. *Office of General Services: A Report to the Congress by the Commission on Organization of the Executive Branch of the Government.* Washington: Government Printing Office, 1949.

———. Commission on Organization of the Executive Branch of the Government. *Treasury Department: A Report to the Congress by the Commission on Organization of the Executive Branch of the Government.* Washington: Government Printing Office, 1949.

———. Commission on Organization of the Executive Branch of the Government. *General Management of the Executive Branch: A Report to the Congress by the Commission on Organization of the Executive Branch of the Government.* Washington: Government Printing Office, 1949.

Index

Acheson, Dean G.: Hoover Commission, 85, 91, 94; quoted, 91, 92; evaluated Hoover Commission reports, 95–96

Aiken, George: reorganization plan two, 1947, 71; reorganization plan one, 1948, 77–78; Hoover Commission, 81–82; reorganization plan one, 1949, 120; reorganization plan seventeen, 1950, 147

American Federation of Labor, 68–69, 148, 171, 194*n*

American Medical Association: opposed reorganization plan one, 1949, 117–20; opposed reorganization plan twenty-seven, 1950, 151, 152

Appleby, Paul: on relationship between policy and reorganization, 14; quoted, 48; and reorganization program of 1946, 58; on savings and reorganization, 181*n*

Ball, Joseph, 70–71, 77

Barkley, Alben: Reorganization Act of 1945, 34, 37, 41; reorganization program of 1946, 59; reorganization plans two and three, 1946, 59–60; reorganization plan one, 1949, 119; mentioned, 167

Benton, William: reorganization plan seven, 1950, 136; reorganization plan four, 1950, 139; quoted, 144; gave important support to Truman's reorganization program, 144–45; reorganization plan one, 1952, 168; reorganization plan two, 1952, 171

Bernstein, Marver: quoted, 134, 136–37; evaluation of regulatory commission reorganizations, 154

Brown, Clarence: author of bill to create Hoover Commission, 79–80; Hoover Commission, 83, 85, 87; reorganization plan twenty-seven, 1950, 152; mentioned, 14. *See also* Brown-Lodge Act

Brown-Lodge Act: provisions of, 79–80; Congress passes, 80–81; Truman administration reluctantly supports, 80; Hoover's views on, 83–84; policy of, 88

Budget, Bureau of: Reorganization Act of 1945, 41; rivalry with Office of War Mobilization and Reconversion, 48–50, 64; reorganization program of 1946, 55; reorganization program of 1946, 56, 57, 58, 63; reorganization program of 1947, 64–65; reorganization plan two, 1947, 67, 68; attitude toward creation of Hoover Commission, 80;

relationship with James Rowe, 84; relationship with Hoover Commission, 93, 94, 95; Reorganization Act of 1949, 104; reorganization plan five, 1949, 115; reorganization plan one, 1950, 132; reorganization plan twenty-one, 1950, 140–41, 143; reorganization plan five, 1950, 146; reorganization plan eighteen, 1950, 147; reorganization plan twenty-four, 1950, 148; reorganization plan twenty-seven, 1950, 150; reorganization program of 1951–1952, 157–58; reorganization program of 1952, 162; reorganization plan five, 1952, 172–73; mentioned *passim*

Bureaucracy: public reaction toward, 29–30, 79, 111, 174

Byrd, Harry: Reorganization Act of 1945, 38, 39, 44, 45; relationship with Franklin D. Roosevelt, 42; relationship with Truman, 42; quoted, 42–43; Reorganization Act of 1939, 42–43; Truman's 1946 reorganization program, 61; reorganization plan two, 1947, 71

Byrnes, James F., 29, 37, 49, 58

Capehart, Homer, 132–33, 145, 160

Children's Bureau: reorganization plan two, 1946, 63, 193*n*; suggested reorganization of, 67; mentioned, 65. *See also* Reorganization plans: plan two, 1946

Citizens Committee for the Hoover Report: and Reorganization Act of 1949, 105; creation of, 109–13; reasons for support by the public, 111–12; Republican domination of, 113; relationship with the Truman administration, 113, 116; reaction to Truman's 1949 reorganization program, 116; reorganization plan twelve, 1950, 128–29; quoted, 131, 169; reaction to defeat of reorganization plan one, 1950, 133; reorganization plan seven, 1950, 136; reorganization plan twenty-one, 1950, 141, 142–43; and 1950 reorganization program, 144, 145; reorganization plan one, 1952, 165–66; reorganization plans two, three, and four, 1952, 169; reorganization plan two, 1952, 172; mentioned *passim*

Civil rights program: affect on reorganization plan one, 1948, 76, 77, 78; Reorganization Act of 1949, 103, 107; reorganization plan one, 1949, 118; and reorganization program of 1950, 144, 145; reorganization plan twenty-seven, 1950, 152

Civil Service Commission: Reorganization Act of 1945, 35, 36, 40; difficulty of reorganization, 62; Arthur Flemming's service on, 85; reorganization plan five, 1949, 114–15; Hoover Commission recommendations on, 114–15; and Truman's 1949 reorganization program, 123; reorganization plan eighteen, 1950, 147; 1949 reorganization of, 154

Clifford, Clark, 84, 91, 104

Coast Guard, 54, 57, 192n

Coates, Charles, 110, 113; quoted, 105

Cochran, John J., 34–35, 39, 45

Cold War: and Hoover Commission, 81; spurs public support for reorganization, 111–12

Columbia, District of: Truman's interest in reorganizing, 24, 172–73; reorganization plan five, 1952, 172–73, 175. See also Reorganization plans: plan five, 1952

Commerce, Department of: reorganization plan three, 1946, 54, 57, 59; reorganization plan seven, 1949, 115, 122, 123; reorganization plans seven and twenty-two, 1950, 135, 150; mentioned, 162. See also Reorganization plans: plan five, 1950, plan twenty-one, 1950, plan twenty-four, 1950

Conservative coalition: Reorganization Act of 1945, 44–45; and reorganization, 51; reorganization plan one, 1948, 78; and 1951–1952 reorganization program, 157; mentioned, 38, 39

Currency, Comptroller of. See Reorganization plans: plan one, 1950, plan twenty-six, 1950

Davies, Richard O.: quoted, 73, 75, 150

Dawson, William: Reorganization Act of 1949, 97, 99, 100, 106; role in Truman's reorganization program, 98; reorganization plan two, 1949, 120; reorganization plans five, six, twenty-four, and twenty-seven, 1950, 140, 146, 148, 151, 152; reorganization plan one, 1951, 159, 160

Defense, Department of, 2, 125, 153

Democrats: and reorganization, 14; Truman wishes to use reorganization to unite, 30–31, 51; Reorganization Act of 1945, 37–39, 41, 43, 44, 45; and reorganization, 1945–1946, 61; reorganization plan two, 1947, 68; reorganization plan one, 1948, 76, 77, 78; reorganization plan one, 1951, 160, 161, 162. See also Reorganization plans

Denham, Robert, 128–30, 153

Donnell, Forrest C., 42, 59, 60

Douglas, Paul: quoted, 135; and Reconstruction Finance Corporation, 158, 159, 160

Eastland, James, 45, 106, 172

Eightieth Congress: and Truman's reorganization program, 64, 65, 78; weakened Department of Labor, 65, 75; reorganization plan three, 1947, 73; and Truman, 76; created Hoover Commission, 79

Eisenhower, Dwight D., 2, 14, 153

Election of 1948: reorganization plan one, 1948, 76; and Hoover Commission, 79, 89–90; John McClellan predicts Truman's defeat, 82, 102; James Rowe's role in, 84; Truman and Hoover during, 92; and Truman's reorganization program, 97

Emmerich, Herbert, quoted, 16, 63, 111–12

Engineers, Army Corps of: conflicts with Bureau of Reclamation, 1, 31, 101–2; Truman's inability to reorganize, 28, 124–25; Reorganization Act of 1945, 35, 44, 45, 188–89n; Reorganization Act of 1949, 99–103, 104, 106–7; political power of, 100–101; and Hoover Commission, 101–2, 103

Ewing, Oscar: reorganization plan one, 1949, 118, 119, 120; relationship with Truman, 118, 150–51; reorganization plan two, 1949, 121; reorganization plan twenty-seven, 1950, 150, 151, 152

Executive Office of the President: Truman initiates study of, 1; established, 11; reorganization plan four, 1949, 114; and reorganization program of 1949, 123; Truman strengthens, 175

Experience rating, 77, 120, 121

Fair Employment Practices Commission: controversy over affects reorganization plan one, 1948, 76; controversy over affects reorganization plan twelve, 1950, 131; and 1950 reorganization program, 137, 144, 145; mentioned, 41. See also Civil rights program

Farm Credit Administration, 138–39, 191n, 196n

Federal Communications Commission, 35, 40. See also Reorganization plans: plan eleven, 1950

Federal Deposit Insurance Corporation: Reorganization Act of 1945, 40; Reorganization Act of 1949, 106; reorganization plan one, 1950, 133; reorganization plan one, 1946, 191n; reorganization plan one, 1947, 196n

Federal Housing Administration, 53, 57, 72

Federal Security Agency: Truman desires to elevate to department level, 1, 13, 50–51, 123, 175. See also Reorganization plans: plan two, 1946, plan one, 1949, plan twenty-seven, 1950; conflicts with Department of

Labor over reorganization, 50–51, 66–67; reorganization plan two, 1946, 55, 56, 192*n*; reorganization plan two, 1947, 69. *See also* Reorganization plans: plan two, 1947, plan one, 1948, plan two, 1949, plan sixteen, 1950, plan nineteen, 1950

Federal Trade Commission, 35, 45, 106. *See also* Reorganization plans: plan eight, 1950

First War Powers Act, 53, 65, 66, 71, 157

Foley, Raymond, 53, 71, 73–74, 150

Fulbright, J. William: reorganization plan one, 1949, 119, 120; reorganization plan twenty-four, 1950, 149; investigated Reconstruction Finance Corporation, 158–59; and Truman, 158–59; quoted, 161

General Counsel of National Labor Relations Board, Office of. *See* Reorganization plans: plan twelve, 1950; Denham, Robert

General Services Administration, 122, 175. *See also* Reorganization plans: plan fifteen, 1950, plan sixteen, 1950, plan seventeen, 1950, plan eighteen, 1950, plan twenty, 1950

George, Walter: Reorganization Act of 1945, 38, 39, 43–44; Reorganization Act of 1939, 43–44; Truman's 1946 reorganization program, 61; reorganization plan twenty-two, 1950, 150; reorganization plan one, 1952, 166, 167, 168; and Truman, 167–68; reorganization plan two, 1952, 172

Gibson, John W.: quoted, 71, 75, 76

Halleck, Charles, 39, 40, 152

Harding, Warren G., 10, 113–14

Hoffman, Clare: Reorganization Act of 1945, 40–41; reorganization plans two and three, 1947, 68–69, 72; reorganization plan one, 1948, 76, 77; Reorganization Act of 1949, 106; quoted, 118; reorganization plans five and twenty-seven, 1950, 146, 151, 152; reorganization plan one, 1951, 159

Holifield, Chet, 98, 106, 120, 152

Hoover, Herbert C.: reorganization program during presidency, 10; alliance with Truman, 78, 79, 92–93, 116, 124, 145, 165; appointed to Hoover Commission, 83–84; quoted, 84–87, 89, 90, 92, 93, 105, 108, 113, 116, 165; relationship with Roosevelt, 92, 93; and the presidency, 95; and Truman's reorganization program, 97, 145; Reorganization Act of 1949, 97, 104, 105, 206*n*2; creation of Citizens Committee for the Hoover Report, 109–10; and Citizens Committee for the Hoover Report, 113; and Truman's 1949 reorganization program, 116, 119; reorganization plan twelve, 1950,
129; reorganization plan one, 1952, 165; mentioned, 13, 43, 141. *See also* Hoover Commission; Citizens Committee for the Hoover Report

Hoover Commission: and Truman administration, 2, 79; spurs Truman's reorganization program, 52, 64, 97, 100, 116, 121, 175–76; used against reorganization plan one, 1948, 76, 77; reasons for establishing, 79; as anti-New Deal instrument, 80–81, 86–91; and Cold War, 81; Hoover's domination of, 85–89; conservative orientation of, 86–91; 1947 policy statement of, 88–89, 90; conflict over policy versus structure, 88–91; impact of 1948 election on, 89–90; shifts away from its anti-New Deal stance, 89–96; relationship between Hoover and Truman, 92–93; intertwining of Truman administration with, 93–95; evaluation of reports, 94–96; comparison with President's Committee on Administrative Management, 94–95, 109; and the presidency, 95; and Reorganization Act of 1949, 97, 106–7; and Army Corps of Engineers, 99, 101–2, 103; task force on natural resources, 101; public support of, 109–13, 124; as safety valve to reduce fear of "big government," 112; Truman's attitude toward its recommendations, 113; recommends creation of department of welfare, 114; reorganization plan two, three, and four, 1949, 114; reorganization plan five, 1949, 114–15; reorganization plan seven, 1949, 115, 127; used as weapon against reorganization plans, 116; reorganization plan one, 1949, 116, 117, 118, 119, 120; Republican support of, 121; and Truman's 1950 reorganization program, 125, 145; reorganization plan twelve, 1950, 128–29, 130; and banking interest groups, 131; reorganization plans one and seven, 1950, 133, 136; and Department of Labor, 140; reorganization plan twenty-one, 1950, 141, 143; and William Benton, 144; treatment of by Congress, 144, 145; reorganization plans seventeen, twenty-two, and twenty-four, 1950, 147, 148, 150, 152; reorganization plan one, 1951, 160; as instrument to protect New Deal, 174; mentioned, *passim. See also* Citizens Committee for the Hoover Report; Brown-Lodge Act; Hoover, Herbert C.

Housing, federal activities: Truman's desire to reorganize, 1, 25, 29; opposition to reorganization of, 13. *See also* Reorganization plans: plan one, 1946, plan three, 1947, plan seventeen, 1950, plan twenty-two, 1950, plan twenty-three, 1950; Housing and

Home Finance Agency
Housing and Home Finance Agency, 71–72, 74–75. *See also* Reorganization plans: plan one, 1946, plan three, 1947, plan seventeen, 1950, plan twenty-two, 1950, plan twenty-three, 1950
Housing and Urban Development, Department of, 2, 75, 175
Humphrey, Hubert: 104, 120, 121, 136, 139, 149, 168

Interest groups: opposition to reorganization, 19–20, 62; reorganization plan one, 1946, 56–57; reorganization plan three, 1947, 72–73, 74; reorganization plan one, 1948, 77; and Hoover Commission, 87; reorganization plans one and two, 1949, 117–18, 121; reorganization plan twelve, 1950, 129–30; reorganization plans one through six, 1950, 131; reorganization plan seven, 1950, 135–36; and reorganization program of 1950, 137, 144; reorganization plans four, five, twenty-one, and twenty-two, 1950, 137–39, 141, 142, 146, 150; reorganization plan twenty-seven, 1950, 151, 152; and department organization, 154; and regulatory commissions, 154–55; reorganization plan two, 1952, 171
Interior, Department of, 100–101, 103, 123, 192*n*. *See also* Reorganization plans: plan three, 1950, plan fifteen, 1950
Internal Revenue, Bureau of, 162–64, 196*n*. *See also* Reorganization plans: plan one, 1952; Internal Revenue Service
Internal Revenue Service, 175. *See also* Internal Revenue, Bureau of; Reorganization plans: plan one, 1952
Interstate Commerce Commission: Reorganization Act of 1945, 35, 36, 45; Reorganization Act of 1949, 99, 106; reorganization plan twenty-one, 1950, 142; mentioned, 134. *See also* Reorganization plans: plan seven, 1950
Ives, Irving, 106, 120–21

Johnson, Edwin C.: opposes reorganization of regulatory commissions, 135–37; reorganization plans seven, eight, nine, and eleven, 1950, 136, 137, 143, 145
Johnson, Robert: Reorganization Act of 1949, 105; heads Citizens Committee for the Hoover Report, 109–10, 113; quoted, 116; reorganization plan twenty-two, 1950, 150
Johnston, Olin, 147, 148, 170, 172
Justice, Department of, 196*n*. *See also* Reorganization plans: plan two, 1950

Kefauver, Estes, 120, 164, 167

Labor, Department of: Truman desires to reorganize, 1, 25, 27, 29, 50–51; Truman rebuilds, 2, 123, 155, 175; difficulty of reorganizing, 13; Reorganization Act of 1945, 37; conflict with Federal Security Agency over reorganization, 50–51, 66–67; reorganization plan two, 1946, 55–56; evaluation of Truman's plans on, 140; reorganization plan two, 1947, 196*n*; reorganization of, 198*n*. *See also* Reorganization plans: plan two, 1946, plan two, 1947, plan one, 1948, plan two, 1949, plan six, 1950, plan fourteen, 1950, plan nineteen, 1950; United States Employment Service
Lawton, Frederick: quoted, 17, 134, 151, 173; Reorganization Act of 1949, 98; as budget director, 124; reorganization plans seven, eight, and nine, 1950, 136, 143; reorganization plans one through four, 1952, 167, 170
Legislative veto: Reorganization Act of 1939, 11–12; features of, 12, 178*n*; importance of to reorganization, 12; congressional criticism of, 13; Reorganization Act of 1945, 32, 36, 40, 41, 42, 43, 44, 45, 46; modified by Reorganization Act of 1949, 97, 107; and John McClellan, 102, 103; limitations of, 176. *See also* Reorganization Act of 1939; Reorganization Act of 1945; Reorganization Act of 1949
Lenroot, Katharine, 55–56, 63, 193*n*
Lucas, Scott, 74, 105–6, 120, 144

McCarran, Pat: Reorganization Act of 1945, 33, 41, 45, 58; relationship with Truman, 36; and reorganization program of 1946, 57–58, 59; reorganization plan three, 1946, 63; mentioned, 35–37
McClellan, John L.: supported Army Corps of Engineers, 44, 101, 102; and Hoover Commission, 82; Reorganization Act of 1949, 97, 102–7; and legislative veto, 102; relationship with Truman, 102, 145; reorganization plans one, two, and seven, 1949, 119, 120, 123; reorganization plans one, five through nine, eleven, twelve, seventeen, eighteen, twenty-two, twenty-four, and twenty-seven, 1950, 129, 132, 136, 137, 140, 141, 143, 144, 145, 146, 147, 148, 149; reorganization plan one, 1951, 160; reorganization plan one, 1952, 166, 167; reorganization plans two through four, 1952, 170, 171, 172; reorganization plan five, 1952, 173
McCormack, John, 98, 106, 120
McCormick, Robert L. L.: quoted, 20, 116,

131, 138, 145, 165, 166–67, 171; Citizens Committee for the Hoover Report, 110, 113
McNaughton, Frank: quoted, 34, 38, 39, 41, 45, 59, 82, 188–89n
Malone, George, 143; quoted, 165–66
Manasco, Carter: Reorganization Act of 1945, 33, 34, 39, 40, 45; and Army Corps of Engineers, 44, 102; reorganization program of 1946, 56, 58; reorganization plan three, 1947, 72; Hoover Commission, 83; and Department of Welfare, 117; mentioned, 36, 37
Marine Inspection and Navigation, Bureau of, 54, 57, 59
Martin, Joseph, 39, 83, 84, 87, 97
Maybank, Burnet, 121, 132, 159
Merchant Marine, 25. See also United States Maritime Commission; Reorganization plans: plan six, 1949; plan twenty-four, 1950
Merit rating. See Experience rating.
Military Services, 29, 48, 40. See Reorganization plans: plan eight, 1949
Miller, Watson, 55, 63, 70
Morse, Wayne, 59, 71, 121
Murdock, Abe, 41, 43, 44, 45

National Archives and Records Service. See Reorganization plans: plan twenty, 1950
National Association of Home Builders, 57, 72, 194n
National health insurance: obstacle to creation of department of welfare, 13; Hoover Commission, 89; reorganization plan one, 1949, 117–20; reorganization plan twenty-seven, 1950, 151, 152
National Housing Agency, 53, 60, 71–72, 194n. See also Reorganization plans: plan one, 1946, plan three, 1947
National Labor Relations Board, 37, 65, 67, 93, 192n. See also Reorganization plans: plan twelve, 1950
National Rivers and Harbors Congress, 44, 99, 102
National Security Council, 2, 114, 123, 175
National Security Resources Board, 114, 123, 175. See also Reorganization plans: plan twenty-five, 1950
Neustadt, Richard: on Truman's self-image, 26; on Truman as administrator, 28; quoted, 30, 96, 149; mentioned, 26, 27

Pace, Frank, Jr., 62, 98, 124
Pollock, James K.: quoted, 55, 91, 109, 111; and Hoover Commission, 82, 91, 95–96; Reorganization Act of 1949, 104; reorganization plan seven, 1950, 136; mentioned, 105

Post Office, Department of: 123, 125, 147, 153. See also Reorganization plans: plan three, 1949, plan two, 1952
President's Committee on Administrative Management, 3–4, 11, 94–95, 109, 113–14
Public Roads Administration, 115, 122, 123. See Reorganization plans: plan seven, 1949

Railroad labor agencies, 40, 45, 106
Rayburn, Sam: Reorganization Act of 1945, 37–38, 39, 41; quoted, 134–35; mentioned, 111, 112
Reclamation, Bureau of, 1, 31, 101–2
Reconstruction Finance Corporation, 158–62, 175. See also Reorganization plans: plan twenty-two, 1950, plan twenty-three, 1950, plan twenty-four, 1950, plan one, 1951
Regulatory commissions, 133–35, 175, 182n, 212n73
Reorganization: evaluation of Truman's program, 2–3, 7–8, 174–77; and creation of strong presidency, 3–6; administrative theory of, 3–8, 62–63, 176–77; critics of, 3–8, 62–63; limitations of, 6–8, 152–56, 175–77; history of in nineteenth century, 9–10; and Theodore Roosevelt, 10; and William Howard Taft, Warren Harding, Woodrow Wilson, and Herbert C. Hoover, 10; and Franklin D. Roosevelt, 10–12; difficulty of achieving, 12, 20, 134–35, 176–77; and savings to be achieved, 15, 62, 112, 116; and Congress, 17–19; and Democrats, 61; and House of Representatives, 98; as safety valve for public hostility to "big government," 112; as shield for New Deal, 174. See also Triangle of power; Legislative veto
Reorganization Act of 1939, 11–12, 32, 42, 43, 44, 45
Reorganization Act of 1945: Truman requests legislation, 1, 32–33; comparison with other reorganization acts, 32, 34, 46, 98; as product of Truman's political skills, 32, 35, 52; administration's draft of, 33; and House of Representatives, 33, 34–35, 39–41; Truman's legislative strategy, 34, 37–39, 42, 43, 44, 45; and Senate, 36, 41–45; Republicans, 36–37, 39, 41, 42, 43, 44; Southern Democrats, 38–39, 40, 41, 42, 43, 44, 45; Democrats, 43, 44, 45; conference committee, 45–46; provisions of, 45–46, 178n; mentioned, 2, 97
Reorganization Act of 1949: administration draft, 97–98; House of Representatives, 97, 98–100, 106–7; Hoover supports, 97; comparison with 1945 act, 98; Senate, 100, 103–7; Army Corps of Engineers, 104, 106–7; conference committee, 106–7; provi-

sions of, 107, 178n; evaluation of, 109; mentioned, 157

Reorganization plans: plan one, 1946, 52–53, 56–61; plan two, 1946, 53–60; plan three, 1946, 54, 56–59; plan one, 1947, 65; plan two, 1947, 65–71, 78; plan three, 1947, 71–75; plan one, 1948, 75–78; plan one, 1949, 113–14, 117–20; plan two, 1949, 114, 120–22, 140; plan three, 1949, 114, 115–16; plan four, 1949, 114, 115–16; plan five, 1949, 114–15, 116; plan six, 1949, 115–16; plan seven, 1949, 115, 122, 123, 155; plan eight, 1949, 212n59; plans one through six, 1950, 131; plans seven through thirteen, 1950, 133–35; plan one, 1950, 125, 132–33, 139, 152, 153; plans two and three, 1950, 125, 127, 153; plan four, 1950, 125, 137–39, 152; plan five, 1950, 125, 146, 153; plan six, 1950, 125, 140, 153; plan seven, 1950, 125, 133, 135–37, 139, 153; plan eight, 1950, 125, 135–36, 143, 144–45, 154; plan nine, 1950, 125, 135–36, 143, 144, 145, 154; plan ten, 1950, 125, 127, 154; plan eleven, 1950, 125, 133, 135–36, 137, 139, 153; plan twelve, 1950, 125, 127, 129–31, 139, 153; plans thirteen and fourteen, 1950, 125, 127, 154, 155; plans fifteen and sixteen, 1950, 125–26, 127, 155; plans seventeen and eighteen, 1950, 125–26, 147–48, 155; plans nineteen and twenty, 1950, 126, 127, 155; plan twenty-one, 1950, 126, 141–43, 155, 156; plan twenty-two, 1950, 126, 140–50, 155; plan twenty-three, 1950, 126–27, 150, 155; plan twenty-four, 1950, 127, 148–49, 153, 155, 162; plan twenty-five, 1950, 127, 155; plan twenty-six, 1950, 127, 153; plan twenty-seven, 1950, 127, 151, 152, 153; plan one, 1951, 158–59, 160, 161, 162, 173; plan one, 1952, 162–68, 173; plans two, 1952, 162, 168–72; plans three and four, 1952, 162, 168–72; plan five, 1952, 173

Reorganization program: of 1946, 52, 54, 61–63; of 1947, 64–65; of 1949, 115–16, 127; of 1950, 109, 139, 143, 144, 145, 152–56; of 1951–1952, 158, 162, 168–69, 173

Republicans: and reorganization, 14; Reorganization Act of 1945, 36–37, 39, 41, 42, 43, 44; reorganization plan two, 1947, 68, 70; reorganization plan three, 1947, 74; reorganization plan one, 1948, 76, 77–78; Hoover Commission, 79, 86–91, 121; Reorganization Act of 1949, 100, 104–5; Citizens Committee for the Hoover Report, 113; reorganization plan twelve, 1950, 127–31; reorganization plans one through six, 1950, 131; 1950 reorganization plans, 137; reorganization plan one, 1951, 160, 161, 162; and

Truman scandals, 162, 164; reorganization plan one, 1952, 165–66. See also Eightieth Congress; Reorganization plans

Robertson, A. Willis, 132–33, 161

Roosevelt, Franklin D.: and President's Committee on Administrative Management, 3; and strong presidency, 3–4; reorganization program of, 10–12, 49; quoted, 11, 15, 18; attitude toward reorganization, 15; creates National Housing Agency, 53; creates Federal Security Agency, 54; reorganizes United States Employment Service, 66, 70, 76; relationship with Hoover, 92, 93; Army Corps of Engineers, 100–101; advocates a department of welfare, 153; administrative preparation for World War II, 157; mentioned, 1, 2, 8, 21, 35, 60, 83, 84, 85, 109, 163

Rowe, James: quoted, 84, 90, 91, 104; Hoover Commission, 84, 91, 95–96; and Bureau of Budget, 94; Reorganization Act of 1949, 101, 104; reorganization plan seven, 1950, 136

Sawyer, Charles, 141, 146, 148

Scandals, and the 1951–1952 reorganization program, 158, 162, 168

Schwellenbach, Lewis, 51, 55, 67–68, 70, 197n

Securities and Exchange Commission, 35, 45, 99–100, 106. See also Reorganization plans: plan ten, 1950

Smith, Harold D.: quoted, 1, 36, 45, 49; Reorganization Act of 1945, 32, 33, 34, 37, 41, 45; reorganization program of 1946, 47, 48, 53, 54; rivalry for control of reorganization program, 48–50; relationship with Truman, 64; on United States Employment Service location, 67; mentioned, 27, 29

Smith, Margaret Chase, 120, 170, 172

Snyder, John W.: rivalry for control of reorganization program, 49–50; delays submission of 1946 plans, 53; Hoover Commission, 93; quoted, 132; response to scandals in Bureau of Internal Revenue, 162–63; reorganization plans one and two, 1952, 167, 172

Social Security Board, 54, 63, 66

Southern Democrats: Reorganization Act of 1945, 38–39, 40, 41, 42, 43, 44, 45; and Truman's reorganization program, 51; reorganization program of 1946, 61; reorganization plan three, 1947, 74, 75; reorganization plan three, 1948, 76, 78; reorganization plan one, 1949, 118; reorganization plan two, 1949, 121; reorganization plan two, 1952, 172

State, Department of, 85, 125, 153. See also Reorganization plans: plan twenty, 1950

Stauffacher, Charles: quoted, 56, 63, 65

Taft, Robert: Reorganization Act of 1945, 42; reorganization plan one, 1946, 59, 60; reorganization plan two, 1946, 60; reorganization plan three, 1947, 73–75; reorganization plan one, 1949, 119, 120; reorganization plan twelve, 1950, 129–30; and Truman's reorganization program for 1950, 144; mentioned, 90
Taft-Hartley Act, 68, 127–31, 139
Tobey, Charles, 72, 74, 158, 159, 225n31
Transportation, Department of: Truman prepares way for, 2, 123, 135, 141, 142, 155, 175
Transportation: reorganization of federal activities, 24, 65, 155, 156
Treasury, Department of, 54, 93–94, 148. See also Reorganization plans: plan one, 1950, plan twenty-six, 1950
Triangle of power, 6–7, 16–20, 50
Truman, Harry S.: quoted, 1, 2, 3, 13, 15, 19, 21, 23, 24, 25, 26, 27, 28, 29, 30, 37, 46, 48, 49, 50, 51, 54, 56, 74, 75, 92, 107, 135, 162, 167, 174; initiates reorganization program, 1–2; uses reorganization to protect New Deal, 2, 96, 174; and strong presidency, 2, 3, 4; and Hoover Commission, 2, 80, 84, 85, 113; twenty-one point address, 2, 30, 37, 52–53; evaluation of reorganization program, 2–3, 174–77; administrative theory of, 3, 21, 22, 23, 24–25, 50–52, 55, 134, 153–54, 175; part of movement for administrative reform, 9; attitude toward reorganization, 13, 15; influence of early career on reorganization program, 21–25; comparisons with Franklin D. Roosevelt, 21, 26, 28, 30, 31, 32, 34, 38, 43, 52, 177; interest in planning, 22–23; reasons for initiating reorganization program, 25–31, 51; conception of presidency, 26–28; as decisionmaker, 28; relationship with Harry Byrd, 42; changing attitude toward reorganization, 46, 47–52, 61, 107–8, 157, 175–77; desire to delegate authority, 50; and Southern Democrats, 61; desire to rebuild Department of Labor, 67, 140, 155, 175. See also Reorganization plans: plan two, 1947, plan one, 1948, plan two, 1949, plan fourteen, 1950, plan nineteen, 1950; attacks real-estate lobby, 74; and Army Corps of Engineers, 100–101; and reorganization plan one, 1949, 119; small business program, 148, 149. See also Reorganization plans: plan one, 1949, plan twenty-seven, 1950; request for emergency reorganization authority in Korean War, 157; affect of loss of popularity on reorganization, 157; and Reconstruction Finance

Corporation scandal, 158–59; and Bureau of Internal Revenue, 163; and reorganization plan one, 1952, 167; and Walter George, 167–68; mentioned passim. See also Reorganization Act of 1945; Reorganization Act of 1949
Tydings, Millard, 38, 43, 61

Unemployment compensation, 77, 198n; for relationship with employment service, see Reorganization plans: plan two, 1947, plan one, 1948, plan two, 1949
United States Chamber of Commerce, 57, 72, 129
United States Employment Service, 23–24, 66–69, 192n. See also Reorganization plans: plan two, 1947, plan one, 1948, plan two, 1949
United States Maritime Commission: difficulty of reorganizing, 18; Reorganization Act of 1945, 36, 40, 44, 45, 188–89n; Reorganization Act of 1949, 106; reorganization plan six, 1949, 115; reorganization programs of 1949, 123; reorganization of, 154. See also Reorganization plans: plan six, 1949, plan twenty-one, 1950
United States Tariff Commission, 35, 40, 106

Vandenberg, Arthur, 81, 82, 104, 105–6
Veterans' Administration, 20, 35, 117, 149, 150, 188–89n, 192n

Wagner-Ellender-Taft housing bill, 53, 56, 57, 60
Wallace, Henry, 45, 48, 146
War Mobilization and Reconversion, Office of, 48–50, 64
Warren, Lindsay: Reorganization Act of 1945, 34–35, 36, 37, 46; Hoover Commission, 93
Washington Post, 33, 168, 170
Webb, James: becomes budget director, 64; and reorganization program of 1947, 65; reorganization plan two, 1947, 68, 69, 70; quoted, 69; reorganization plan one, 1948, 77; Brown-Lodge Act, 80; Hoover Commission, 93; grooms Frank Pace as replacement, 98
Welfare, proposed department of: Truman desires to create, 1, 29, 50–51, 123, 153, 175. See also Reorganization plans: plan two, 1946, plan one, 1949, plan twenty-seven, 1950
Whittington, William: Reorganization Act of 1945, 38, 39–40, 44, 45; Reorganization Act of 1949, 98–99, 100